BRITISH UNEMPLOYMENT
PROGRAMS, 1920-1938

CONSTITUENT ORGANIZATIONS OF THE SOCIAL SCIENCE RESEARCH COUNCIL

The Social Science Research Council was organized in 1923 and formally incorporated in 1924, composed of representatives chosen from the seven constituent societies and from time to time from related disciplines such as law, geography, psychiatry, medicine, and others. It is the purpose of the Council to plan, foster, promote, and develop research in the social field.

AMERICAN ANTHROPOLOGICAL ASSOCIATION
AMERICAN ECONOMIC ASSOCIATION
AMERICAN HISTORICAL ASSOCIATION
AMERICAN POLITICAL SCIENCE ASSOCIATION
AMERICAN PSYCHOLOGICAL ASSOCIATION
AMERICAN SOCIOLOGICAL SOCIETY
AMERICAN STATISTICAL ASSOCIATION

BRITISH UNEMPLOYMENT PROGRAMS, 1920-1938

By EVELINE M. BURNS

A
REPORT PREPARED FOR THE
COMMITTEE ON SOCIAL SECURITY

Washington
Committee on Social Security
Social Science Research Council
1941

MANUFACTURED IN THE
UNITED STATES OF AMERICA

FOREWORD

AFTER THE WORLD WAR OF 1914-18 Great Britain's attempt to restore the normal functioning of her industrial and social life was beset by many difficulties. The greatly expanded industrial framework developed for war production purposes was unable under post-war conditions to provide jobs for all available workers. The unemployment insurance system as it had developed since 1911 and the pre-war social services were seriously over-taxed by the unprecedented and urgent emergency that confronted them. Many experimental programs to alleviate distress due to unemployment were adopted and later discarded as failures or only partial successes. An attempt to expand the unemployment insurance system to provide benefits for both short and long periods of unemployment was, after many make-shift compromises, abandoned in 1931. The years that followed witnessed two other experiments which attempted to find for the long-term unemployed half-way stages between a strictly conceived unemployment insurance system and local provision of poor relief.

The latest of these experiments in Great Britain's search between 1920 and 1938 for satisfactory means of meeting the problems growing out of long-continued mass unemployment, an uncertain industrial outlook, and changing attitudes on the part of both the public and the government toward the responsibility of each for the economic and social welfare of the more insecure members of society, was begun in 1934 and continues to operate, with some modifications, today. This program consists of a national system of unemployment insurance which in the main compensates short-term unemployment, and a supplementary needs test assistance system for normally employed workers which is centrally administered and financed. The locally administered public assistance system, whose clientele is the residual group of needy persons, provides only to an insignificant degree for the unemployed. This comprehensive social insurance and assistance system serves Great Britain currently as the means of ameliorating the effects of war-time dislocations and will presumably constitute her primary defense against the effects of unemployment when the time comes to demobilize the present war economy.

v

The techniques for handling large-scale unemployment that had been in operation in other industrial countries for many years were not adopted in the United States until the depression of the 1930's. Thus, while the unemployment compensation system established since 1935 has begun to pay benefits, it has not so far been subjected to the test of prolonged and heavy unemployment. Its first severe test is likely to come when the present defense boom is over.

In view of the long experience of Great Britain with the problems of mass unemployment, a critical study of the British schemes adopted between the end of the last war and the beginning of the present war (when the character of the problem was entirely changed by the impetus to employment given by rearmament and by the tremendous demands upon the assistance and welfare authorities for civilian relief) is of especial significance to the United States in pointing out the hazards of ill-advised and hasty lines of action and the need of well-considered planning of the unemployment programs to be used in the post-demobilization period in this country.

The investigation from which this volume resulted was undertaken for the Committee on Social Security by Dr. Eveline M. Burns, Lecturer in Economics at Columbia University. Dr. Burns was formerly an officer in the British Ministry of Labour and a member of the faculty of the London School of Economics. In 1933 she returned to England, in connection with a grant from the Columbia University Council for Research in the Social Sciences, and observed the operation of the various programs at the depth of the depression. She again visited Great Britain in 1937, under the auspices of the Committee on Social Security, to examine the then recently inaugurated comprehensive assistance system. Her findings are based upon extensive interviews with government and lay officials and with private citizens, upon documentary materials collected during both visits, and upon additional data which she has from time to time obtained from correspondents in Great Britain.

During her field work in Great Britain the author was greatly assisted by the helpful cooperation of public officials of both the central and local governments, trade union leaders, members of local advisory committees and students of unemployment problems. She especially records her appreciation of the assistance given by two officials of the Unemployment Assistance Board. Sir Wilfred Eady, when Secretary of the Board, not only placed every facility at her disposal but also gave generously of his own time in discussing the broader policy issues. Mr. G. T. Reid, his successor, despite the heavy demands of the war read and helpfully criticized those sections of the manuscript relating to the operation of the Assistance Board. Harry Malisoff assisted in the preparation of statistical and legislative materials and carried a large share of the responsibility for the statistical appendix. The completed manuscript was checked back to the original sources by Franz Huber. The author is also gratefully aware of the improvement in the manuscript which has resulted from the careful and precise editorial work of Mary Charles Cole, of the Committee's staff, who prepared the volume for publication.

While Dr. Burns' study has been sponsored by the Committee on Social Security, it has not been submitted to the Committee or to the Social Science Research Council for formal review or approval. The Committee regards it as its responsibility to make certain that the studies which it sponsors are based upon ample investigation so that the investigator will acquire full knowledge of all relevant data and factors, and to satisfy itself that the author of a report has considered carefully all aspects of any controversial questions with which the report may deal. The author is, however, responsible for all statements and conclusions and these do not therefore purport to express opinions or attitudes on the part of the Committee or of the Social Science Research Council.

PAUL WEBBINK, *Director*
Committee on Social Security
Social Science Research Council

May 29, 1941

CONTENTS

TABLES

APPENDICES

APPENDIX TABLES

INTRODUCTION

AMONG THE PROBLEMS that have confronted industrial nations during the last 20 years, none has proved more challenging and baffling than that created by mass unemployment. The enforced idleness of literally millions of would-be workers has compelled the governments of all important industrial countries to take action in the interests of the stability of society itself. For as the blight of unemployment affected an ever larger proportion of the citizens it became evident that the welfare of the unemployed and the economic repercussions of positive or negative policies adopted in regard to them were of much more than individual or local interest.

It is not surprising therefore that these same years have witnessed a tremendous expansion of governmental measures for dealing with unemployment. These have ranged all the way from utilizing the basic poor law or general relief systems to the organization and operation by government of elaborate work projects. At the same time increasing attention has been paid to the development of measures having as their objective the more speedy reabsorption of the unemployed into private employment. Publicly provided placement and guidance services have become widespread. To these have been added training and rehabilitation programs and controlled and assisted transference schemes.

Of all the various governmental measures taken to meet the many-sided problem of unemployment, none has been more generally adopted or received more widespread approval than unemployment insurance. The reasons for the popularity of this method of providing against loss of income attributable to unemployment are not far to seek.

To the worker the right to insurance benefits of an amount calculated by a legally set formula represented a highly preferable alternative to assistance secured through the poor law. It obviated the necessity not merely for undergoing a test of need with its resultant loss of privacy, but also for having any contact with a poor law system which in the public mind had come to be associated with a high degree of odium. At the same time the knowledge that an assured income, however small, could be counted on when earnings were interrupted made individual saving worth while. For it removed the fear that the individual would be compelled to reach the level of destitution before public aid was available.

For government also unemployment insurance had many evident advantages. It was administratively a relatively simple method of providing income to large numbers of the unemployed, and one which reduced the exercise of administrative discretion to a minimum. Moreover the linking of benefits with specific payments made it possible to tap new sources of revenue for financing an increasingly heavy item of expenditure and in particular to lay taxes on low income receivers. Above all, unemployment insurance was a method of introducing some degree of permanence into the public unemployment policies. For once the system was instituted, tax collections continued through good years as well as bad and when an emergency arose government was to some degree prepared with both funds and an administrative mechanism.

Yet unemployment insurance is not, nor have its exponents ever claimed that it could be, a complete answer to all of the problems presented by unemployment. Perhaps the most important of its limitations is due to its essentially limited objective. For it aims to do no more than provide income to offset losses in earnings attributable to unemployment. As the wider social consequences of unemployment have become more generally appreciated, there has been a growing recognition of the need for more constructive programs. This broader conception of the social problem of unemployment has involved some change of emphasis. It has led to no depreciation of the inherent values of unemployment insurance. But it has meant that the institution must increasingly be regarded as one of several methods of providing for the unemployed, and that its precise rôle must be determined by the relatively greater or lesser appropriateness of other available measures.

In addition to these considerations, certain characteristic features of the insurance laws limit the extent to which at any time the needs of unemployed workers can be met by the payment of insurance benefits. Not all workers are covered or can satisfy the conditions for benefits; benefits are not payable immediately a man becomes unemployed and are limited in duration; the amount of benefit is not adequate in all cases to meet needs created by loss of wage income.

There are numerous reasons for these limitations to the rôle played by unemployment insurance in maintaining workers whose normal source of income has temporarily disappeared. In part they arise out of the attachment of the word insurance to this type of social provision against loss of income. To many people social insurance is still conceived of in terms of private insurance. Inasmuch as rights to benefits are in the nature of a private contract, they must, it is held, be limited to persons who have themselves made payments, or on whose behalf payments have been made. Unemployment insurance laws define the groups of workers within their scope and normally require, as a condition for benefit, membership in the scheme for a specified period. Great emphasis has also been placed upon the solvency of the funds, to preserve which it is necessary to restrict the claims that can be made by individual unemployed persons.[1] The limitations on the amount and duration of benefit are largely thus explained.

Somewhat similar in its restrictive effects upon the significance of unemployment insurance schemes is the widely held conviction that this type of aid for the unemployed should be financed exclusively out of certain taxes, and specifically, wage and payroll taxes. The political and economic difficulties inherent in the imposition of these taxes imply a definite upper limit to the sum of money that can be regarded as available for the insurance system. Hence it becomes necessary to adjust benefit rights in such a way that they can be financed out of this limited fund. Emphasis upon these taxes as the peculiarly appropriate, if not exclusive, source of income for unemployment insurance restricts its scope in yet another way. The technical difficulty of collecting these taxes, particularly when the basis selected involves treating each covered individual as a separate case, has led in many countries to the restriction of the system to those groups presenting fewer difficulties from the point of view of the tax collector.

[1] For the influence of these ideas on American legislation, see Harry Malisoff, "The Emergence of Unemployment Compensation," *Political Science Quarterly*, June, September and December 1939.

There have also been a number of considerations which, quite apart from financial factors, have tended to restrict the scope of unemployment insurance plans. One of the most important of these is the judgment that it is socially and economically dangerous to grant unemployed workers a definite, and more or less unconditional, right to a stated money benefit. The desire to avoid weakening the incentive to work has generally led to the adoption of benefit formulas which make certain that insurance benefits shall fall substantially below the earnings of employed workers. Fears concerning the effect of unlimited payment of insurance benefits upon the rigidity of wage rates, and the judgment that it is unreasonable to expect the income-receiving members of a community to contribute indefinitely to assistance paid to unemployed workers regardless of need, have led to the limitation of the period for which insurance benefits can be drawn as a right. This limitation on the duration of the insurance type of benefit has also been viewed as a convenient method of drawing a line between workers whose needs can be met fully by the payment of a cash sum and those, usually the longer unemployed, whose needs call for more individual treatment and for measures designed to maintain and increase working capacity.

Opinions as to the extent to which unemployed workers can maintain themselves in the absence of government assistance have also played a part in limiting unemployment insurance measures. The requirement of a waiting period before becoming entitled to benefits rests largely on the assumption that the average worker has adequate resources to tide him over the first few days of unemployment.

These viewpoints find expression in the provisions of the laws which relate to coverage, eligibility, disqualifications, waiting periods, duration and amount of benefit. The limitations to the significance of unemployment insurance in the entire unemployment program resulting from these provisions are nowhere more evident than in the laws of the fifty-one jurisdictions of the United States.[2] But America is not unique in limiting the scope

[2] A summary of the relevant provisions of the laws and a more detailed discussion of their implications will be found in Eveline M. Burns, "Unemployment Compensation in the United States," *International Labour Review*, May 1938, pp. 584-617. Cf. also Harry Malisoff, *loc. cit.* For an analysis of the American state laws, see Social Security Board, *Comparison of State Unemployment Compensation Laws as of October 1, 1940* (Washington, 1940).

of its insurance systems. To a lesser degree, analogous clauses are also found in the unemployment insurance laws of other countries.

Some indication of the limited contribution which an insurance system hedged around by protective conditions makes to the problem presented by unemployment can be obtained by observing the experience of the British system. During the years 1932 to 1938, between 39 per cent and 60 per cent of the insured unemployed persons at any given time were assisted through that system, the remainder receiving aid from other sources or not at all.[3] This figure is the more significant when it is recalled that the normal duration of benefit in Great Britain is 26 weeks (in contrast to the American *maximum* of 16 to 18 weeks), that the waiting period in those years varied between 3 and 6 days (in contrast to the American 2 to 4 weeks), while the coverage of the scheme is much wider (there are in Great Britain no exclusions on account of the size of the employer's labor force). Furthermore, the eligibility requirements are more favorable to the worker (in that a worker can claim benefits so long as he can show 30 contributions in the 2 years preceding a benefit claim), the benefits, although at a uniform rate for all workers, provide additional sums for dependents (i.e., they are relatively generous to the workers in the lower wage brackets whose resources are likely to be least, whereas the American laws give the lowest benefits to the lowest paid workers), and finally the specific disqualifications are generally more favorable to the worker than is the case in the majority of the American state laws.

Under these circumstances, it is not surprising that a supplementary relief system, or systems, is found in all countries which have instituted unemployment insurance schemes. These supplementary unemployment relief programs have been of various kinds. They range from the customarily locally administered and financed general poor law systems to highly centralized schemes

---

[3] In only 7 months in the period between 1932 and 1937 has the British insurance system paid benefits to more than 50 per cent of the insured unemployed at any one date. In 1938 the corresponding percentage varied between 58.3 and 60.8 per cent in different months of that year. These figures refer to the general (industrial) scheme only, and do not include the agricultural system which commenced the payment of benefits in November 1936. Cf. *Report of the Unemployment Insurance Statutory Committee on the Financial Condition of the Unemployment Fund on the 31st December 1937*, pp. 49-51, and *1938*, pp. 28-29.

2

such as those administered by the Unemployment Assistance Board in Great Britain and the Work Projects Administration in the United States. Sometimes, as in Great Britain from 1931 to 1934 and in Germany from 1927 on, they take the form of an additional relief organization midway between insurance and local relief. Benefits in a system of this kind are paid only to previously insured workers who can pass a test of needs, but they are normally related in amount to the benefits of the insurance system, are wholly or predominantly financed by the central government, and are administered jointly by the central government and the local authorities.

It is obvious that the co-existence of two or more types of aid to the unemployed should give rise to serious problems. As the benefits are determined on different bases and subject to different conditions, it is to be expected that workers will make comparisons and prefer one type to another. And as unemployment insurance provides benefits that are limited in amount and paid only for a relatively short period, many workers will of necessity have experience with both systems. Those who claim to speak for the unemployed are likely to exert pressure to secure a more general adoption of that type of unemployment aid which appears most favorable to workers.

The existence of several unemployment systems also directly concerns the taxpayer. As the total costs of relief mount, it is inevitable that taxpayers too should compare the several available systems with a view to discovering whether or not economies could be secured by limiting the benefits payable under any of the existing schemes. The ear-marking of certain taxes for the payment of a specific type of benefit, a characteristic feature of insurance schemes, may give rise to considerable disparities in the payments received by unemployed workers who fall into the different relief categories. Unless, therefore, the system which results in relatively higher payments can be justified in broad economic or social terms, taxpayers can be expected to press for its elimination or at any rate for a diminution of its relative importance.

The co-existence of several unemployment programs is also of interest to governmental units, and particularly, may involve a conflict of interest between central and local governments. The taxes which finance unemployment insurance are characteristically collected by central governmental authorities. Residual relief equally characteristically is financed locally. Hence a relative decrease in the rôle of the insurance system will tend to throw a greater burden on local authorities whose fiscal systems may not be appropriate to their responsibilities. In both Great Britain and Germany, for example, local authorities have opposed restrictions of the scope of the insurance system in order to protect themselves from having to carry what they regarded as an undue share of the costs of unemployment relief.

Finally, the co-existence of several methods of aiding the unemployed gives rise to serious administrative problems. Long waiting periods in an insurance system mean that workers who have no other resources must be carried by a supplementary system until insurance benefits are payable. If the insurance system is so constituted that administrative delays over and above the regular waiting period are unavoidable, the residual relief system must again be utilized. If benefits prove to be inadequate and workers have no other resources of their own, they may have to seek the aid of the supplementary relief system even while drawing insurance benefits. As insurance benefits are limited in duration, workers who are still unemployed must, on exhausting benefits, be cared for wholly by the supplementary relief system or systems. These conditions give rise to a considerable movement of workers between the various programs. If this occurs on a large scale, the justification of a separate insurance scheme will be questioned. In any case, it is obvious that cooperative arrangements must be worked out between the administrators of the different programs in order to avoid duplication of investigation, delays in making payments, and waste of public money arising out of unwarranted double payments.

No country has had a longer experience of the relationships between insurance and supplementary relief systems than Great Britain, which instituted unemployment insurance in 1911. British experience is also of particular interest because, since that date, many changes have been made not only in the scope and importance of the insurance system, but also in the nature of the supplementary measures. It would seem therefore that a study of British policy in handling the many-sided problems created by mass unemployment will throw considerable light upon the effectiveness of insurance systems of varying comprehensiveness and of different types of supplementary relief systems. An investigation of these problems will be undertaken in the following pages. In general the analysis follows the three major periods during which distinctive methods of dealing with the residual unemployed were in force. These periods are respectively 1920 to 1931, 1931 to 1935, and 1935 to 1938. The sections dealing with the experience of these three periods are preceded by a more general account of the broad legislative and policy developments and of the nature of the residual poor law or public assistance system.

BRITISH UNEMPLOYMENT
PROGRAMS, 1920-1938

CHAPTER I

UNEMPLOYMENT INSURANCE AND SUPPLEMENTARY NATIONAL PROGRAMS

UNTIL 1911, WHEN THE first unemployment insurance act was passed, the only form of public provision for unemployed workers in Great Britain was poor relief. Unemployment benefits had been a feature of trade union organization for at least seventy years, but they were provided by only a few unions in the skilled and highly organized trades.[1] The desirability of providing special measures for involuntarily unemployed workers had been indicated in 1885 and 1895 when the Local Government Board (the central authority supervising poor law administration at the time) suggested that municipalities should provide work relief for unemployed men. This principle was given legislative recognition in the Unemployed Workmen Act of 1905,[2] which provided for the establishment of local "distress committees" on which the poor relief authorities were to be represented with other "persons experienced in the relief of distress." Given power to establish and assist labor exchanges (employment offices),[3] these bodies endeavored to place workers in private employment and in some cases organized municipal relief works. To a more limited extent the distress committees made use of their power to assist emigration, but their net importance was slight.

[1] In 1911 unemployment benefits were available to only about 1.5 millions out of nearly 2.5 million organized workers who, in turn, constituted a very small proportion (approximately 14 per cent) of the estimated number of all wage earners. Even in well organized trades such as textiles and coal mining, unemployment benefits were little developed, the industries relying on short-time work to meet depressions.

[2] Repealed by the Local Government Act of 1929.

[3] When the Labour Exchanges Act was passed in 1909, the functions of most of these bodies were transferred to the national system, while the remainder were closed. (W. H. Beveridge, *Unemployment: A Problem of Industry* [London: Longmans, Green and Co., 1931], p. 296)

3

The Unemployment Insurance System

The 1911 Unemployment Insurance Act, which made unemployment benefits available to $2\frac{1}{4}$ million workers, marks the first significant departure from reliance upon general poor relief as the normal form of public aid for the unemployed.[4] Amended in 1916 to cover another $1\frac{1}{2}$ million workers (mainly those in the munitions, chemical, metal, leather, and rubber industries) the Act was finally expanded to cover the great majority of wage earners in November 1920. After the institution of a special insurance scheme for agriculture in 1936, domestic service remained the only significant employment in which unemployed workers were compelled to rely solely on poor relief or public assistance.[5] All non-manual workers earning over £250 a year were, however, excluded from the insurance scheme. Moreover, until July 1934 the minimum age of entry was 16 years. Thereafter it was the age at which liability to attend school ceased (usually 14 years). After 1927, when the old-age and survivors insurance system commenced benefit payments, persons 65 and over were not entitled to insurance benefits.

Insurance benefits have from the first been confined to persons who had paid a certain number of contributions, and who could satisfy a number of other general conditions, the object of which was to limit payment of benefits to persons who were capable of

[4] The trades originally covered were building, construction of works, shipbuilding, mechanical engineering, iron founding, construction of vehicles, and sawmilling carried on in connection with any other insured trade.

[5] Certain limited groups of domestic employees were covered in 1938. Other excluded groups were: permanent civil servants, female professional nurses, members of the army, navy, and air force, teachers, commission agents if dependent mainly on some other occupation or not mainly dependent on any one employer, members of the police force covered by the Police Act of 1919, persons in specified part-time employments, share fishermen, persons employed by parents or spouse, persons receiving payment solely in kind, and relief workers on schemes organized by poor law authorities. In addition, the Minister of Labour has the power of granting under certain conditions certificates of exception to a proportion of workers employed by government departments, local authorities and public utility companies, and to certain grades of railway workers who have completed 3 years of service. Certain other persons might apply for certificates of exemption, of whom the most important were persons in receipt of independent incomes or of pensions of at least £26 a year, persons dependent for their livelihood mainly on others, persons mainly dependent on an uninsurable occupation, and persons engaged only in seasonal occupations extending over not more than 18 weeks a year. An estimate of the numbers excluded by these provisions is given in Royal Commission on Unemployment Insurance, *Final Report*, 1932, pp. 56-57 (hereafter referred to as *Final Report*).

and available for work and involuntarily unemployed.[6] Certain types of conduct disqualified workers from benefit rights, at least for a period of time. Since 1911 a worker has been disqualified if unemployment is due to a stoppage of work on account of a labor dispute at the factory or workshop where he is employed,[7] or for misconduct or voluntary quitting without just cause.[8] Furthermore, as workers could receive benefits under the 1911 and 1920 Acts only if they were capable of work but unable to obtain suitable employment, refusal of the latter automatically disbarred a man from benefit rights. Such behavior, together with refusal to carry out written instructions from the employment exchange, given with a view to assisting the worker to find suitable employment, has been a specific ground for disqualification since 1930.[9]

Under the 1911 Act the duration of benefits was for a maximum period of 15 weeks in a year. This limit was incorporated in the 1920 Act, raised to 26 weeks in 1921 and abolished in 1928.[10] Reimposed in 1931, the 26-week limit was retained in the Unemployment Act of 1934 which, however, granted additional days of benefit to workers with a long record of employment.[11] Until 1928

[6] Certain workers could be required to attend courses of instruction as a condition of receipt of benefit. Since 1931, additional conditions have to be satisfied by persons who are (a) employed at a high rate of wages for 1 or 2 days a week and claiming benefit on other days, (b) seasonal workers, (c) persons whose normal employment is for not more than 2 days in the week, and (d) married women.

[7] The definition of a trade dispute was subsequently modified so as to protect the benefit rights of workers who were not directly participating in, financing or directly interested in the dispute in question, and who were not of the same grade or class as the persons employed at the place of dispute who were so participating, financing and directly interested. Disqualification lasts for the duration of the dispute unless the worker has in the meantime secured other insurable work (covered employment).

[8] The disqualification may be up to 6 weeks from the date of loss of employment.

[9] Since 1934 workers can also be disqualified for neglecting to avail themselves of a reasonable opportunity for suitable employment. The period of disqualification can be up to 6 weeks from whatever date the adjudicating authorities may determine.

[10] In practice, the contributory requirement automatically limited continuous benefits to 74 weeks. Benefit was also unlimited in principle for a short period in 1924-25. The changes in the insurance system between 1921 and 1931, which are mentioned briefly here, are discussed in detail in Chapter III.

[11] Payable if a worker had been insured and had paid some contributions during 5 insurance years prior to the benefit year. He was allowed 3 additional days of benefit for every 5 weekly contributions paid in the 5 years, less one day for every 5 days for which benefit had been drawn in that period. Additional

these overriding maxima were qualified in varying degrees by the
operation of a ratio rule which adjusted the duration of each individual's benefit to the number of contributions paid by him in a
defined preceding period. A waiting period varying from 3 to 6
days has always been part of the insurance plan. Under the 1911
Act the benefit was a uniform 7s. a week, which was described by
the sponsors of the Act as being "very exiguous" and "narrowly
cut." Increased to 11s. in 1919, the benefit rate was differentiated
for men and women in 1920 and again increased for men to 15s.
and for women to 12s. In 1921 benefits for dependents were
introduced and thereafter benefit rates were frequently changed
in a continuously upward direction in terms of real income, except in 1931.

All payments are made from the Unemployment Fund. The
income of the fund has from the first been obtained from contributions in which employers, workers and the government have
shared in differing proportions. By April 1929 the share of the
government had gradually increased from 33 to 50 per cent of
the combined worker and employer contributions. These in turn
were at fixed rates varying only with age and sex. Until July
1921, both employers and workers had paid equal sums; thereafter until October 1931 the employer's contribution was slightly
in excess of the worker's. Since October 1931 all three parties
have paid the same contribution in consequence of the adoption
of the "equal thirds" method of financing.[12]

Between 1911 and 1920 the Unemployment Fund was permitted to borrow from the Treasury to meet deficits. This provision was omitted from the Act of 1920, but was reintroduced
in March 1921. Although the extent of borrowing has at all
times been legally limited, the maximum permitted was steadily
increased until by 1931 it was set at £115 millions.[13] Between
October 1931 and July 1934 further borrowing was made legally
impossible, and whatever deficits occurred were met by non-

---

benefits were made more liberal in 1937 by deducting one day for every 8 in
which benefit was drawn, and in 1938, one day for every 10.

[12] A table of the changing contribution rates up to 1931 for adult men appears
on page 19 of the *Final Report* of the Royal Commission on Unemployment
Insurance (1932).

[13] The 1911 Act fixed a limit of £3 millions. In 1921 this was raised to £10
millions.

which had, indeed, much wider coverage than the Unemployment Insurance Act, but still excluded some groups.[16] Secondly, until April 1, 1937 the Board took over responsibility only for those workers who would otherwise have been entitled to transitional payments, i.e., workers over 18 who had at some time been covered by the unemployment insurance system. Nevertheless, after April 1, 1937 those who were assisted under neither the insurance nor the assistance system were a negligible fraction of the total number of able-bodied unemployed.

The unemployment assistance plan also differed from both the expanded insurance system and transitional payments in that for the first time a positive attempt was made to avoid poor law supplementation. The Unemployment Assistance Board was given the function of "the assistance of persons . . . who are in need of work and the promotion of their welfare," and demonstrated need on account of unemployment was to be met in full. No person who was a client of the Board could obtain unemployment relief under the poor law, and after April 1, 1937 persons drawing insurance benefits that proved inadequate for their needs had to seek supplementary aid from the Board instead of, as formerly, from the public assistance system.

The cost of the unemployment assistance allowances has been carried to the extent of roughly 95 per cent by the national government. The local authorities' share in the cost, based upon a formula which took into account the assumed saving to them as a result of the new scheme, was originally intended to be paid directly to the central government, but, as explained more fully in Chapter VI, after 1937 their share was simply deducted from the subsidies paid by the national government (block grants) toward the cost of various locally administered social services.

MISCELLANEOUS RELIEF MEASURES

Public Works under the Unemployment Grants Committee

Expansion of public works for the purpose of providing unemployment relief has been a relatively unimportant feature of Brit-

---

[16] However, juveniles who had secured no remunerative work since attaining the age of 16 were covered if they could reasonably have expected to have been in covered employment but for the industrial circumstances of their district. For details of groups excluded, see Chapter VII.

ish unemployment policy. The public works program, inaugurated in 1920, was administered by the Unemployment Grants Committee.[17] The total value of all projects approved under this program between December 1920 and January 1932, when the formal works program was abandoned, amounted to £191 millions, of which only some £69.5 millions were actually expended—an insignificant sum compared with the total expenditures of close to £600 millions on unemployment insurance and relief. In 1931, the year in which the public works program was most fully developed, only 59,000 men were directly employed on the schemes, while in some years the numbers fell as low as 10,000. Yet the number of unemployed in this period ranged from about 900,000 to over 2,000,000.

The object of the grants was to assist local authorities in carrying out approved schemes of useful work other than work on roads and on housing projects. The central government offered inducements to local authorities in the form of non-repayable subsidies toward the cost of labor employed, and contributions toward the loan repayment charges. The terms of the grants varied greatly between 1920 and 1932, but it has been estimated that they averaged approximately 35 per cent of the total commitments. The remainder of the cost was borne by the local authorities. The projects were those characteristic of most public works programs, except that in view of the separate roads and housing programs these items occupied a relatively small place. Sewers, secondary roads and footpaths, and electricity supply accounted for nearly 58 per cent of the total expenditure.

Workers were hired through the public employment offices, although persons could be nominated by the public assistance authorities subject to clearance with the employment offices. Married men and those with dependents were given preference, while from 50 to 75 per cent of the men taken on were to be ex-service men.[18] The workers received prevailing rates of wages or those

[17] This brief summary is taken from the *Final Report of the Unemployment Grants Committee, 1933* (Cmd. 4354). A fuller discussion of this program is presented in Chapter IV.

[18] Between November 1928 and July 1930 when special financial inducements were offered for their employment, men from depressed areas accounted for 50 per cent of the numbers employed on certain schemes.

normally paid by local authorities for the work in question and overtime was strictly limited. A number of authorities rotated unemployed men on the projects to enable work opportunity to be spread more widely among the unemployed, while the men could at all times be recalled by the local employment offices for placement on private jobs.

Between 1921 and 1925, and again between 1929 and 1932, grants were made from the Treasury to various central government departments (mainly those concerned with land drainage and forestry, public buildings and royal parks) to undertake work projects. The grants, were, however, relatively small, and after 1930, insignificant.

Highways and Roads

Between 1920 and 1930, the central government adopted three major programs designed to accelerate roadbuilding in order to relieve unemployment. The 1920-25 plans encouraged local authorities to undertake work on bridges and roads by the offer of a substantial subsidy. In all, projects involving a total commitment of £57.2 millions were approved and carried out between 1921 and 1938, their major impact being felt in the years 1926-28.[19]

Under the Trunk Road program and the Five Years' program, announced in 1929, subsidies were given for the construction of roads of national importance and for certain other specified roads. Despite some delay on the part of local authorities, by the end of August 1931 the estimated cost of approved projects amounted to £45.1 millions (out of a total anticipated program of £48.5 millions). But the economy wave of 1931 caused a sharp contraction in these commitments. Local authorities were persuaded to abandon or curtail projects, with the result that the total approved program was reduced to £23.4 millions.[20] By March 1938 the greater part of this program had been completed.

[19] The central government's share of the total commitment was to be approximately £35.5 millions. All but £1,395,005 of this was to be derived from the Road Fund, which is obtained from the taxation of motor vehicles. (Ministry of Transport, *Report on the Administration of the Road Fund*, 1933-34, p. 9)
[20] The central government's share was to amount to approximately £17.6 millions. (*Ibid.*, 1932-33, p. 9)

3

Assisted Migration

Efforts were also made to alleviate the unemployment situation by the promotion of migration to the Dominions. The Empire Settlement Act of 1922 was passed as a result of a conference with the Dominions in the previous year, and provided for the assistance of emigrants to the Empire countries up to a maximum of £1.5 millions the first year and £3 millions in subsequent years. Further stimulus was given to this policy by the Imperial Economic Conferences of 1923 and 1926, by the publication of the report of the Industrial Transference Board in 1928, and by the restrictive immigration policy pursued by the United States, especially after 1924. More generous schemes were devised for promoting settlement in Australia and Canada. The program concentrated almost exclusively on the promotion of migration of agricultural workers, farmers, and domestic servants. In general the encouragement to migration took the form of assisted passages, provision of training especially within Great Britain to prepare migrants for agricultural and domestic work, and loans and advances made by the British and Dominion governments for the erection of farm buildings, and purchase of land and livestock.[21]

The onset of the world depression dampened the enthusiasm of the Dominions, and at the Imperial Conference in 1930 it was decided to regulate migration in accordance with the believed capacities of the Dominions to absorb new populations. Thereafter the net outward movement fell sharply. Assisted migration was, however, never very significant in relation to the previous unassisted movement and was unimportant in regard to the total volume of unemployment. Whereas in 1923 there was a net unassisted emigration of 86,034 to the United States alone, the total assisted migration in the peak year of the program (1929) was only 71,750, and the total assisted migrations in the 10 years from 1922 to 1932 amounted to only 404,329,[22] or less than

---

[21] A brief account of the different schemes is given in the *Report of the Overseas Settlement Committee,* 1933 (Cmd. 4391), pp. 14-17.
[22] In this period a total of 1,070,000 persons migrated. (Cf. Royal Commission on the Geographical Distribution of the Industrial Population, *Minutes of Evidence,* 1938, p. 320; *Twenty-First Abstract of Labour Statistics,* p. 202; *Twenty-Second Abstract of Labour Statistics,* p. 203)

twice the net migration to the United States alone in the 4 years 1920-24. Indeed the net migration to the Empire exceeded the 1923 net movement to the United States only in 1926, the year of the general strike. After 1929 migration both to the Empire and to other countries fell off sharply, and from 1931 there was a net movement into the United Kingdom.

Measures for the Revival of Industry

Relatively few positive measures to revive industry were taken by the British government with the direct objective of reducing unemployment. Four programs, however, deserve mention: The Trade Facilities Acts, the Export Credits Guarantee Scheme, the Public Utility Grants, and the Special Areas legislation. The Trade Facilities Acts operated between 1921 and 1926 for the purpose of promoting employment in the United Kingdom by facilitating the raising of new capital. The national treasury was authorized to guarantee the payment of interest and/or principal of loans for capital construction work which might otherwise be delayed or not undertaken at all. The limit of the guarantees, originally set at £25 millions, was finally raised to £75 millions.[23]

Between 1919 and 1921 the government attempted to stimulate exports by guaranteeing payment to private British exporters. Little use was made of the facilities, only £1,752,000 out of £26,000,000 permitted being actually advanced. More than a million pounds of the sum advanced involved a dead loss to the Treasury. In July 1921 a modified Exports Credits Scheme was introduced.[24] Here too the achievement was modest. Exports guaranteed amounted to only £19 millions, although provision was made for a total guarantee of £30 millions. In July 1926 an Export Credits Guarantee Scheme provided a method of insuring bills as a general stimulus to export. This third measure proved more successful. By May 1937 guarantees had been given for exports amounting in all to £123 millions, and it was proposed to raise the limits of the then outstanding guarantees from

[23] By March 1927 when the scheme was abandoned, actual commitments amounted to £74.25 millions. By March 1932 the total cost to the Treasury in fulfillment of the guarantees was £1.29 millions (A.C.C. Hill and I. Lubin, *The British Attack on Unemployment* [Washington: The Brookings Institution, 1934], p. 80)

[24] For a description of the revised scheme, see *Ibid.*, pp. 80-81.

£26 millions to £50 millions and to make the arrangements permanent.[25]

In 1929 a system of grants from the Treasury toward the development, reconstruction, and re-equipment of public utility companies was inaugurated. Part I of the Development (Loan Guarantees and Grants) Act permitted the Treasury to guarantee loans up to £25 millions, or to pay all or part of the interest on loans up to an unstated maximum for not more than 15 years. The projects subsidized had to be self-liquidating, useful and unlikely to have been undertaken without government aid. Workers were to be drawn from the employment exchanges and the works were to be undertaken as speedily as possible. In 1932 the Development (Loan Guarantees and Grants) Act was allowed to lapse, after grants amounting to more than £12 millions toward schemes costing some £39 millions had been made.[26]

The heavy and prolonged unemployment in certain areas, which was characteristic of the employment situation after 1920, led in 1934 to the adoption by the national government of special measures for the benefit of these areas. In December 1934 the Special Areas (Development and Improvement) Act provided for the appointment of two commissioners,[27] one for England and Wales, and one for Scotland, to administer the initial grant of £2 millions for "the initiation, organization, prosecution, and assistance of measures designed to facilitate the economic development and social improvement" of certain specified depressed areas. The funds granted (which by September 1938 had amounted to £16 millions)[28] were used to promote industrial development, to acquire and develop property (trading estates) for industrial purposes, to improve local health services and housing, to encourage land settlement and allotment schemes (garden plots), to provide occupational and welfare centers, and to assist

[25] *Export Guarantees*: *Memorandum Explaining Financial Resolution*, May 1937 (Cmd. 5467). Use of the scheme increased greatly after 1935 and the premiums received have exceeded the claims paid and administrative expenses.

[26] Most of the assistance took the form of grants rather than guarantees. (Hill and Lubin, *op. cit.*, pp. 76-78)

[27] The commissioners were in a semi-independent position, but had to account for their expenditures to the Minister of Labour and the Secretary of State for Scotland respectively.

[28] *Report of the Commissioner for the Special Areas* (*England and Wales*), September 1938 (Cmd. 5896), p. 91.

public works which met local needs and were not merely for the purpose of creating employment.

In 1937 an amending act extended the operation of the original law, and enabled further measures to be taken to promote the location of new industries and establishments in the special areas. Under the new law the commissioners were empowered to rent factories, to make contributions towards payment of rent, of rates (local property taxes), and of the national income taxes of employers willing to establish new factories, and to subsidize road and drainage expenses in the depressed areas. The act also initiated a program of loans from the Treasury to prospective employers in these areas.[29]

Résumé

Thus, since 1913, when insurance benefits were first paid, the residual relief system in Great Britain has taken five major forms. From 1913 to 1918 the poor law was the only supplementary relief system for all workers except a relatively small number of men discharged from the armed forces. From the end of 1918 to 1921, unemployment resulting from demobilization and the immediate post-war adjustments was provided for through the Out-of-Work Donation system. From 1921 to 1931 the major unemployment relief load was carried by the expanded insurance system, with the poor law playing a secondary but not unimportant rôle. From November 1931 to early January 1935 there were two residual relief systems: transitional payments and public assistance (the successor of the poor law). Finally, from 1935 the central Unemployment Assistance Board has carried almost the entire responsibility for residual relief, with public assistance still part of the picture, but playing an insignificant rôle.

Only the last three of these methods of handling the residual relief problem will be analyzed in the following chapters. Little is to be learned regarding the wisdom of exclusive reliance upon the poor relief system from the experience of a period in which the need for residual relief was by modern standards negligible.

[29] In addition, the Finance Act of 1937 permitted the Treasury to remit all or part of the National Defense Contribution in certain cases where new firms were established in the depressed areas.

The period from 1913 to 1919 was abnormal. For the greater part of that time the war was in progress and there was a shortage of men rather than jobs. Even 1913 was a year of good employment, and during 1919 the percentage of unemployment among trade unionists was only 2.4.

Nor does the experience of the Out-of-Work Donation scheme repay detailed investigation. Brought into being to meet an emergency, it could hardly have hoped to survive the conditions responsible for its birth. With the return to normalcy, it was inevitable that the relatively lax administration of this system should have been tightened, and that some more specific test of eligibility than the claim to be unemployed as a result of the war should have been required. The relatively high benefits payable under easy conditions could command public support only so long as the country was still under the influence of the war psychology and anxious to conciliate labor by making the country, to use the then current phrase, "a land fit for heroes to live in." The rapid return to normal conditions and the industrial disturbances of 1919-21 soon dispelled these dreams of a new order.

CHAPTER II

POOR RELIEF AND PUBLIC ASSISTANCE

BEFORE TURNING TO a detailed consideration of the three methods of handling residual unemployment relief in effect after 1920, it is necessary to obtain a clearer picture of the nature of the general poor law or public assistance system which throughout the period covered by this study, has been the general residual relief service in Great Britain. Even after the creation of the Unemployment Assistance Board in 1934, it remained the ultimate resort of the relatively few unemployed workers who could claim neither unemployment insurance nor unemployment assistance. The nature of poor relief in England and Wales on the one hand, and in Scotland on the other, is sufficiently different to call for separate treatment.

LOCAL RELIEF IN ENGLAND AND WALES

The basic general relief system was known as poor relief until 1930. Thereafter, as a result of the changes initiated by the Local Government Act of 1929, it has been called public assistance. It is essentially a local service both administratively and financially, although the local bodies are subject to the general supervision of a central department. Until 1919 this central body was the Local Government Board. In that year the poor law functions of the Board were transferred to the newly created Ministry of Health.

Administrative Organization

Prior to 1930 the local units of administration were some 600 boards of guardians, who were unpaid representatives, administering relief for an area that consisted of a large parish, or more usually, a group or union of parishes. These bodies were abolished by the Local Government Act of 1929 which transferred their poor law functions to the councils of 62 administrative counties and 83 county boroughs.[1] All poor law functions,

---

[1] The county is the largest local administrative unit and roughly corresponds to the American county. County boroughs are urban areas, originally within one

except the power to impose a property tax or borrow money, are now exercised by the public assistance committee of a council, which may and usually does add to the membership by cooption.[2] Under the Public Assistance Order of 1930 each council had to designate a special officer, the public assistance officer, who was responsible for carrying out the administration of the poor law. In all except a few small counties, sub-committees of the public assistance committee—known as guardians committees [3] —have been appointed to consider applications for relief and determine the nature and amount of assistance to be given, and to visit, inspect or manage any of the poor law institutions in their areas, subject to the public assistance committee's guidance as to general principles. In the county boroughs the public assistance committees have wider discretion in the appointment of sub-committees and the allocation of functions to them.

Both before and after the changes brought about by the 1929 Act, the day-to-day contact with and the investigation of relief clients have been carried out by relieving officers. Normally this officer reports the circumstances of the case to his local committee and issues relief upon its instructions. He is, however, required to give immediate relief (in kind or through admission to an institution) in cases of sudden and urgent need, and there is considerable variation in the extent to which the local committees have concerned themselves with the details of individual cases. In the smaller urban areas and among those guardians committees where the volume of work is not large, the members of the assistance committees are likely to possess personal knowledge, if not of the applicant, at least of his circumstances. This was generally the case before 1930, when the areas administered by the boards of guardians were small. But in the large urban areas, where the relief claims are many or where it proves difficult to obtain adequate representation through cooption on the local committees, this is less likely to be the case, and the committees may sat-

---

or more counties, which are so large that many of the functions of counties have been transferred to them.

[2] The councils can appoint special committees or designate some existing committee to act as the public assistance committee. The majority have adopted the former course.

[3] Consisting of county councillors, district councillors, and up to one-third, of coopted members.

isfy themselves by laying down general principles, ruling directly on only a proportion of the individual cases and relying very largely upon the discretion of the relieving officers. Indeed, in 1935, the London County Council, by far the largest local relief authority, delegated to a so-called adjudicating officer certain duties hitherto carried out by its assistance sub-committees. Under this arrangement, which by 1939 had been adopted by 8 of the 145 authorities, the adjudicating officers are responsible for determining the amount and nature of relief and for issuing orders accordingly, after taking into consideration the reports of the relieving officers. They must report their actions to the assistance sub-committees, and refer to them certain specified cases and all those in which the applicant asks for reconsideration, together with other cases where the special circumstances appear to call for action by the sub-committees.

The supervisory powers of the Ministry of Health are, at least in law, considerable. It has power to order local councils to appoint the necessary administrative officers and can fix their salaries and define their duties and conditions of tenure. In default of action by the local authority, the Minister may appoint officers directly. He may also regulate the service performed by these local bodies by ordering the enlargement or alteration of poor law institutions (workhouses), the provision of casual wards, and may make rules regulating to what extent and for what period outdoor relief (home relief) may be provided for able-bodied persons and their families, and whether or not relief shall be granted in the form of a loan. He has, however, no power to consider complaints from individuals regarding the inadequacy or unsuitability of the relief offered.

To enforce its policy the Ministry possesses certain financial and other controls. The Minister can appoint general inspectors to supervise and report on the operations of the local authorities. These officers have power to inspect institutions and to take part in the proceedings of the local assistance committees, but not to vote. Control over the action of the local bodies is exercised in two ways. First, the expenditures of the public assistance officers are subject to the control of the district auditor's staff which is a unit of the Ministry of Health. The auditors have power to dis-

allow and surcharge for any expenditure which in their judgment
is illegal, i.e., which is more than is required for the relief of
destitution.[4] Second, if a public assistance authority wished to
anticipate revenue by means of an overdraft, it was necessary
until 1933 to obtain the sanction of the Minister, and this was
liable to be refused if the local authority had been pursuing what
was regarded as an extravagant or unduly generous policy.
Under an act of 1926 (repealed by the Poor Law Act of 1930),
the Minister of Health was given power himself to appoint guardians where it appeared to him that a board of guardians either
had ceased to act, or was acting in such a manner as to render
them unable to carry out their duties.[5] This power was, however,
exercised on only three occasions.

In general the central authority has refrained from making
very drastic use of its supervisory controls.[6] It has issued mandatory relief regulation orders indicating the types of relief to be
made available to different classes of persons and has paid particular attention to the conditions under which outdoor relief may
be granted. It has recommended the more general adoption of
work and training schemes, and especially between 1927 and 1928
endeavored to bring about more stringent administration of relief
to the able-bodied. The Ministry of Health has "most strongly
deprecated" other practices, such as ignoring the needs of an able-
bodied man when determining the amount of relief to be granted
to the family, and has called attention to defects in the administration of relief to the indigent casuals. But as a rule the central
authority has exercised guidance rather than "control." [7] In the

[4] Appeals against surcharges involving over £500 go to the High Court, and
either the Minister or the High Court considers cases involving less than £500.
Rate (local tax) payers may also apply to the Court for an injunction against
expenditures by the public assistance authorities which they regard as illegal.

[5] In such circumstances the Minister appointed 3 special commissioners who
were legally a board of guardians in all respects and carried out all the functions
of the superseded board.

[6] For an evaluation of the control exercised by the Ministry, see S. and B.
Webb, *English Poor Law History* (London: Longmans, Green and Co., 1929),
Part II, Vol. II, pp. 907-43.

[7] This is evident from the tone of the circular letters. The letter of March
1910, elaborating the basic relief principles, closes with the words, "The [Local
Government] Board trust [sic], therefore, that the Guardians will earnestly
endeavor to make the administration of public relief within their [poor law]
union conform to the principles to which their attention has now been drawn."
In the circular of January 3, 1930, the Minister "desires to offer observations

main it has confined itself to issuing regulations governing the general type of assistance to be provided and the classes of persons for whom certain types of assistance are appropriate.[8] It has never indicated specifically the content that should be given to the word "destitution," [9] nor committed itself to the definition of an adequate relief scale. Some attempt has been made through the inspectorate to offer suggestions and advice to local authorities whose standards of relief and administration differed widely from the general average or whose expenditure appeared unduly high.[10] More recently the Ministry has encouraged the authorities to adopt a wider view of their functions. Thus Circular 1622 of November 22, 1937, while stressing the necessity of economical administration of the grant of relief in kind and institutional care in certain difficult cases, also suggested the desirability of increasing staff, setting up central machinery for revision of the decisions of local sub-committees in order to ensure uniformity within the central committee's area, and increasing relief with rising prices. Occasionally, the Ministry has taken drastic action, but only to curb authorities who have adopted too generous a view of the functions of public assistance.[11] Direct control through the exercise of coercive pressure has, however, been rare.

for the guidance of Boards of Guardians." In the circular of November 22, 1937, the Minister "desires to invite the attention" of the councils to certain matters. (Cf. Ministry of Health, *Annual Report, 1937-38*, p. 95)

[8] "It has been the view of the Department that . . . it has not been thought right by any rigid attitude of disapproving departures from the letter of the regulations, to fetter the discretion of the Guardians in deciding in what form and subject to what conditions relief which they had determined to be necessary could most properly be administered." (*Ibid., 1921-22*, p. 84)

[9] The nearest approach to a definition was offered by the Legal Advisor to the Local Government Board in evidence before the Royal Commission on the Poor Laws, 1905-09, but this ran in general terms and gave no guidance as to what was necessary "in order to maintain life" or "to obviate, mitigate or remove causes endangering life or likely to endanger life or impair health or bodily fitness for self-support." Nor was any guidance given as to what material resources could be regarded as "directly available" and "appropriate for satisfying his physical needs." The circular letter of 1910 which embodied this definition did, however, point out that a person might be destitute with respect to some particular necessity of life (such as medical attention) without being destitute in all respects.

[10] ". . . every effort has been made to keep permanently before the Guardians the principles which should govern their actions, and to draw attention to the defects in the local machinery which might lead to unnecessary expenditure." (*Ibid.*, p. 84)

[11] The annual reports of the Ministry of Health between 1921 and 1929 contain few instances of intervention by the central authority. In 1921-22 the

Nature of the Relief Available

Broadly speaking, the nature of poor relief or public assistance has been within the control of the local authorities and has varied considerably from one area to another. Since 1930 variability has been somewhat less marked as a result of the transfer of public assistance functions to the counties and to county boroughs. But in many cases the assistance sub-committees have their own scales, and by no means all the central committees have adequate machinery for reviewing claims to ensure uniformity.[12] In general the poor law in England has been traditionally deterrent and recourse to it has carried a stigma which is recognized even today, though it is becoming steadily less prevalent. Indeed, one of the most significant consequences of the post-war depression, which brought so many thousands of previously independent workers in contact with poor relief, has been a trend away from the old deterrent and repressive poor law toward a more humane and generous treatment of all types of destitute persons. This trend has taken two forms. First, more and more forms of assistance have been given through measures other than the poor law, the Local Government Act of 1929 specifically encouraging local authorities to transfer as many as possible of the services then under the poor law to departments administering the special assistance

---

guardians of Poplar (in East London) requested permission to float further loans but the Minister, before approving, conducted an inquiry into prevailing methods of administration. This inquiry indicated that "the administration of the Guardians is far more costly than is the case in other and apparently comparable unions," a fact which was not denied by the guardians. (*Ibid.*, pp. 91-92; *1922-23*, pp. 82-83)

Similarly in 1922-23, when the City of Sheffield requested permission to increase borrowing for unemployment relief purposes, an inquiry was undertaken which revealed that the guardians had been unprepared to meet an increasing relief load, that the scales of relief had been "unnecessarily high" and that relief had been granted on terms which contravened the Ministerial circulars. (*Ibid.*, p. 83)

In 1925-26, the Treasury Committee, which considered an application for further loans from the West Ham Union, recommended that approval be conditioned upon reductions in expenditure by the guardians. These conditions were refused, and after a period of 4 weeks in which the Minister issued relief orders in kind, and threatened to take over the administration of relief in the union, the guardians accepted the proposed conditions. (*Ibid., 1925-26*, p. 113) Reference has already been made to the three occasions on which the Minister resorted to the drastic step of superseding the guardians by his own representatives.

[12] See Chapter V, pp. 140-47, and Circular 1662 of the Ministry of Health, p. 3.

acts. Second, there has been a great improvement from the applicant's point of view in the relief afforded by the poor law itself. This has taken the form of the removal of some of the penalties, such as loss of certain civic rights,[13] a more generous concept of what constitutes destitution, and changes in favor of the applicants in the form and the amount of relief afforded.

The inappropriateness of the system prevailing at the turn of the century to handle the contemporary problem of poverty was clearly demonstrated by the voluminous reports of the Royal Commission on the Poor Laws, 1905-09. It was shown that the system tended to perpetuate and even increase poverty. The Commissioners particularly criticized the lack of uniformity in the principles for the administration of outdoor relief which resulted in the grant of inadequate relief in some cases and indiscriminate and unconditional relief in others.

While no legislative changes were immediately forthcoming, the circular letter issued in 1910 by the Local Government Board, the central supervisory body at the time, was based on some of the recommendations of the Commission. This circular was followed in 1911 by a Relief Regulation Order which governed the principles on which relief was administered until 1930. Under this order the normal form of relief to the able-bodied was to be institutional. The genuineness of an applicant's need for aid was to be put to the acid test of the offer of relief in the workhouse. In exceptional cases, however, outdoor relief could be given if a man performed test work. Also, under what was known as the "modified workhouse test," an able-bodied man's dependents could be relieved in their own home while the man was relieved in an institution. Departures from these principles, if otherwise lawful, might be permitted if the board of guardians reported the special circumstances of the particular case to the Minister of Health and he did not disapprove. Outdoor relief to able-bodied persons was, indeed, negligible until 1920. But thereafter, the great increase in unemployment made the grant of institutional relief to all applicants impracticable. As a result, outdoor relief became the customary type of aid and was usually given with-

---

[13] For an account of the earlier and current civil disabilities which accompany the receipt of aid under the poor law, see S. and B. Webb, *op. cit.*, pp. 992-96.

out even the work test requirement. From 1926 onwards the Ministry of Health attempted to encourage a return to the stricter conditions of the Relief Regulation Order of 1911. The guardians were urged to devise test work schemes, at least for a proportion of the applicants, with, however, little result although the more obvious cases of lax administration were eliminated.[14] In 1930, after the reorganization initiated by the Local Government Act of 1929 had been carried through, a new Relief Regulation Order was issued. This again laid down special conditions for the grant of out-relief to the able-bodied. At least one-half of the relief was to be in kind.[15] The requirement to report to the Minister on each individual case in which outdoor relief was given to able-bodied persons was waived entirely for able-bodied women, and was required for able-bodied men only if they were given out-relief without being required to undertake work, training or instruction.

Thus, by 1930 there had been a significant change in the complexion of poor relief as it affected the unemployed.[16] The coupling of out-relief with the requirement to accept work or training was no longer regarded as a deterrent device, but, as the Circular of the Ministry of Health introducing the Relief Regulation Order of 1930 makes clear, it was to be in the interests of the welfare of the unemployed. "A primary objective," runs the Circular, "should be to maintain the employability of those able and willing to work, so that when opportunity offers, these men may have no difficulty in resuming their places in industry." [17]

The public assistance authorities were required to formulate such arrangements "as may in the circumstances of their areas be practicable" for putting to work the male recipients of out-relief, or for training and instructing them, or arranging for their attendance at suitable classes for physical training or of an educational character. Despite the urging of the Ministry, however, by

[14] See Ministry of Health, *Annual Report, 1926-27*, pp. 129-30.
[15] This requirement was rescinded in December 1931 and the matter left to the discretion of the local administrators.
[16] For a fuller account of the nature and development of this change, see Helen F. Hohman, *The Development of Social Insurance and Minimum Wage Legislation in Great Britain* (Boston: Houghton Mifflin Co., 1933), Chapter VI.
[17] Ministry of Health, *Circular 1097*. Reprinted in full, with the order, in Royal Commission on Unemployment Insurance, 1932, *Minutes of Evidence* (hereafter referred to only as *Minutes of Evidence*), pp. 283-84.

no means all the relief authorities have set up adequate schemes.[18] As a result, the normal form of relief for the unemployed not drawing assistance under the national schemes has continued to be unconditional out-relief.

The nature of the relief afforded by the poor law or public assistance system has also changed in other ways, favorably to the applicant. It is a general principle that relief is afforded only when destitution exists, and in determining destitution income and means from every source available to the household are in principle taken into account. Also, certain specified relatives have a legal liability to maintain needy persons.[19] But great latitude is left to the local administrators in the application of these principles. In practice, the legal obligation is enforced on comparatively small numbers of people.[20] With the rise of labor to political power, there has been a tendency, especially evident in urban areas and predominantly working-class districts, to apply the tests of destitution and availability of resources less rigorously, particularly by allowing earning members of a household to keep for their own use a growing proportion of their earnings, and by exempting certain forms of income.[21] The more generous treatment of able-bodied public assistance recipients became more marked and general after 1931 when the local relief authorities administered the means test to thousands of applicants for transitional payments. The belief that it was not desirable to reduce many of these persons to the level of destitution previously re-

---

[18] *Ibid.*, pp. 286-93.

[19] For example, husbands are responsible for wives; parents, for children up to 16, and over that age if the child is unable to work on account of sickness or other causes; stepfathers, for children of the wife at the time of marriage (up to the age of 16) as long as the wife is living; married women with separate estates are responsible for husbands, children under 16 and parents; single women are responsible for illegitimate children under 16; and legitimate children for their parents. Liability does not extend to brothers or sisters or grandchildren.

[20] Percy Ford, "The Family and the Social Services," *Public Administration*, April 1938, pp. 146-56.

[21] The first 5s. of Friendly Societies' or trade unions' sick pay, and the first 7s. 6d. of national health insurance benefits are disregarded. The Unemployment Insurance Act of 1920 provided for excluding the first 10s. of unemployment benefits, but this was suspended in 1921 and abolished in 1922. Under the War Pensions Administrative Provisions Act, 1918, a disablement pension cannot be regarded as a resource available for support of any person other than the recipient. In 1930 the Minister in Circular 1069 (*Minutes of Evidence*, pp. 280-81) also recommended more generous treatment of certain other types of resources.

quired of poor law applicants led many authorities, particularly those who held that transitional payments were merely another form of benefit under the expanded insurance system, to require less drastic realization of available resources, not only by transitional payment applicants but also by their other able-bodied public assistance applicants. The Transitional Payments (Determination of Need) Act of 1932 permitted the local relief authorities to make concessions with regard to home ownership and other capital resources to their able-bodied clients seeking out-relief, similar to those made mandatory by the same Act with regard to transitional payment applicants.[22] Many authorities, believing it unwise to apply different standards to two groups of people whose circumstances and characteristics were largely similar, took advantage of this new power. This provision was continued in the Poor Law Act of 1934, which also required the authorities to disregard certain additional types of resources.[23]

The amount of assistance given to individual applicants has also increased since 1921, at least in the urban areas. Here again the local authorities have been left complete discretion as to the total sum to which income from relief plus income from other sources may be brought. As a result, the level of assistance has varied with the political complexion, the social theories, and the financial status of the individual relief authorities. There has been a growing tendency for the poor law authorities to formulate scales of relief for the guidance of their public assistance committees.[24] These scales serve as standards for normal cases, but can be departed from if the circumstances of a given case so indicate, and do not in any sense represent a sum to which any individual applicant has a right. Those authorities which have adopted scales have been, to a greater or lesser degree, influenced by the levels of unemployment insurance benefits.[25]

[22] Specifically, the authorities were permitted to disregard one-half of any disability pensions and workmen's compensation; the first £25 of money and investments, while each subsequent £25 up to £300 could be treated as yielding a weekly income of one shilling; and any sum which might be obtained by an applicant by selling or mortgaging his interest in the house in which he lived.
[23] For example, maternity benefits under the health insurance acts and the first pound a week of any wounds or disability pension.
[24] Not all authorities have these scales, however. At the beginning of 1931, there were 16 county boroughs and 51 counties with no scales, as against 67 county boroughs and 11 counties issuing scales.
[25] Ibid., p. 273.

Financing Local Relief

The costs of public assistance given both to the unemployed and to all other dependent persons are defrayed mainly out of local rates (taxes) levied on real property.[26] Small sums have been derived from ownership of buildings, from repayments from relatives and the property of persons assisted, and from various payments by the central government. Up to 1930 small grants were made by the national Treasury to county and county borough councils and boards of guardians under the Agricultural Rates Acts (1896 to 1923), but, except during 1920, these have amounted to less than 10 per cent of the total poor relief expenditures. After 1929, when the Local Government Act abolished local rates on agricultural property and reduced those on property used for productive industry or freight transport, the central government granted to the local authorities a sum equal to the estimated loss of income from these sources.[27] Because this was distributed as a "block grant" which also included sums in lieu of the earlier percentage grants, of revenues ear-marked for health services, and of other income sources, as well as a further lump sum subsidy from national funds, there is no way of knowing what proportion of the cost of poor relief was met from the grant received by each county or county borough council. Finally, as will be shown in more detail in Chapter VI, between March 1935 and April 1937 the local authorities received grants from the Treasury to compensate them for the expenditures they incurred for the maintenance of certain unemployed workers who, but for the delayed operation of one provision of the 1934 Unemployment Act, would have been the responsibility of the Unemployment Assistance Board.

[26] The yield of the so-called "Poor Rate" is, however, not always exclusively used for meeting the cost of public assistance. Certain small miscellaneous expenses of the county councils, rural district councils and parish councils have been defrayed from it, as well as the education expenses of urban district councils.
[27] Known as the "derating scheme." In 1930-31 the government grant to offset losses due to reduced rates amounted to £22.6 millions out of the total block grant of £45.5 millions. (Ministry of Health, *Annual Report, 1930-31*, pp. 182-84) The relative significance of the different sources of income of the poor relief authorities both before and after the derating scheme can be seen from the table entitled "Income and Expenditures for Poor Relief in England and Wales," published by the Ministry of Health before 1934 in *Annual Local Taxation Returns (England and Wales)*, Part I, and thereafter in *Local Government Financial Statistics (England and Wales)*, Part I.

4

The financing of public assistance by borrowing is permitted under careful control. The Local Authorities (Financial Provisions) Act of 1921 permitted temporary borrowing to meet a proportion of the then abnormal expenditures, subject (until 1933) to the approval of the Ministry of Health. Where a poor law authority was unable to secure this permission because of its credit standing or for other reasons, the central government could advance funds on terms approved by a special Treasury Committee (known as the Goshen Committee).[28]

LOCAL RELIEF IN SCOTLAND

The poor relief system in Scotland, in so far as it affected the unemployed, has differed in several respects from the corresponding institution in England and Wales. Before 1921 public relief was not legally available to able-bodied persons. Because of the inability of private charity to provide for the unemployed workers in periods of depression prior to 1921, a number of local authorities evaded the letter of the law and gave relief to the able-bodied.[29] Others organized municipal work relief schemes. Although the prohibition of public aid to the unemployed had been condemned by the Poor Law Commission of 1905-09, no change was made until the heavy and unprecedented unemployment that began at the end of 1920 finally demonstrated the need for a changed policy. Accordingly, the Poor Law Emergency Provisions (Scotland) Act of 1921 authorized public relief for able-bodied persons who were "destitute and unable to obtain employment." [30] Various modifications in the law and its administration were made by a series of enactments between 1921 and 1927, most of which were embodied in the comprehensive Poor Law (Scotland) Act of 1934.

Administrative Organization

As in England, the system is locally administered, subject, however, to central supervision (by the Department of Health for

---

[28] *Ibid., 1921-22,* pp. 88-89.
[29] *Minutes of Evidence,* p. 332, Question 2468.
[30] This power was made permanent in the Poor Law (Scotland) Act of 1934. Destitute dependents of able-bodied persons out of work because of direct involvement in a labor dispute are also entitled to relief.

Scotland). Before 1930 the local administrative unit was even smaller than in England, being the single civic parish of which there were some 870. These were abolished by the Local Government (Scotland) Act of 1929, and their poor law functions were transferred to the public assistance committees of 31 county councils and 24 town councils. These bodies frequently delegate the consideration of individual cases to special sub-committees, or to the minor administrative authorities under their jurisdiction who perform the functions of the guardians committees in the English counties.[31] Since 1921 the responsible local authorities have in general issued scales of relief for the guidance of their administrative or subordinate authorities,[32] and the Poor Law (Scotland) Act of 1934 provided that within the area of a single local authority all poor persons whose circumstances were similar should, regardless of their place of settlement, receive equal treatment.

The local executive officer is the chief public assistance officer, who before 1930 was known as the inspector of poor. His functions are similar to those of the English relieving officer in that he receives all applications for relief and may grant relief provisionally until he can bring the case before his public assistance committee.[33] But his position differs from that of the corresponding English official inasmuch as he can be superseded or dismissed only by the central Department of Health. He has, therefore, a certain amount of independence in relation to his local committee.

The powers of the Department of Health for Scotland differ somewhat from those of the central authority in England and Wales. It has no power to issue poor law orders of a mandatory character. Nor can it compel an authority to appoint a sufficient number of officers or determine the salaries to be paid. From

[31] As in England, a limited number of persons who are not members of the council may be coopted to serve on the public assistance committee, or its sub-committees.

[32] The original scale was drawn up by a Conference of Inspectors of Poor and was issued by the central department with a recommendation that it should be adopted. By the end of 1932 there were still 10 counties and 2 large burghs without scales.

[33] He is also liable at law for any breach of his duties which may affect the life and health of a poor person. In heavily populated areas, the work of investigating and inspecting clients may be performed by assistant inspectors.

time to time, however, it issues circulars for the general guidance
of the local authorities.[34] It can inquire into local administration
and review the relief given or offered if appealed to by dissatisfied clients. It may invoke an order of the Court of Session to
compel a refractory or negligent authority to perform its duties.
Like its English counterpart, it has also been able to influence
local administration to a limited extent, by its control over the
issue of poor law loans.[35]

For the exercise of its supervisory powers, the Scottish central
authority utilizes three groups of persons. It appoints inspectors
who are authorized to attend meetings of the local authorities and
take part in discussion, but not to vote. It receives reports from
the accountants, who audit expenditures and who must satisfy
themselves that the expenditures incurred are lawful.[36] They
have, however, no power to surcharge. They report to the Secretary of State for Scotland who surcharges where he thinks fit.
Because there are no mandatory orders, control by audit is necessarily less effective than in England.[37] Finally, the public assistance officer is entitled to report to the central department if he
believes that his local committee is giving relief which is too generous or too niggardly. If the department holds the complaint to
be justified, it can send a recommendation to the local authority.
In the last resort, the Department of Health as such has "no
effective and final power of interference." [38]

Nature of the Relief Available

From the point of view of the applicant, poor relief in Scotland has tended to be more favorable than that available in England. Less attention has been paid to the principle of "less eligibility" (i.e., that the position of the relief recipient should be less

[34] Thus, in 1921 it recommended the adoption of certain scales of relief, and
in 1926, that existing scales should be reduced.

[35] Where an authority is not able to meet the entire expenditure out of the
current rates, it must borrow and loans require the sanction of the central
department. In 1926 the central department made the reduction of local relief
scales to the level of insurance benefits a condition for sanctioning loans.

[36] There are no special poor law district auditors in Scotland. The work is
carried out by private accountants of recognized standing, who are appointed
by the Scottish Office to audit all the accounts of local authorities.

[37] Cf. *Minutes of Evidence,* p. 333, Questions 2497 to 2501.

[38] *Ibid.,* p. 333, Question 2503.

favorable than that of self-supporting persons), with its implication that relief should be given under deterrent conditions. The standard of destitution has, in the words of the Secretary to the Department of Health, "not been carried to an extreme." [39] As in England, various types of income have been exempt from assessment in determining need, and these exemptions were greatly increased after 1931 as a result of the experience with the administration of the transitional payments system and the passage of the Transitional Payments (Determination of Need) Act of 1932. Until 1936, when the situation was clarified by a decision of the House of Lords, these exemptions had been made in determining how much relief a person, if eligible at all, was to receive. Thereafter they were taken into account also in the determination of the existence of "destitution" and therefore of eligibility for aid.[40]

The typical form of relief has been outdoor relief,[41] and payment in kind has been exceptional. The relief scales appear to have been more generous than the English. Relief in the form of loans was permitted as an emergency measure in 1927, but was prohibited after 1934. Work relief has been provided by some authorities, but they had no legal power until 1934 to put men to work as a condition for the receipt of relief, and then only for certain individual cases. Powers to provide training and instruction to persons over 18 years of age were conferred on the authorities in 1934, but attendance cannot be made a condition of relief. Nor have as many civic disabilities been attached to the receipt of relief. There is no prohibition against recipients running for public office.[42] Even the requirement that an applicant must be both destitute and unable to find employment has not prevented the Scottish authorities from relieving persons who obtain small amounts of work insufficient to provide a livelihood.[43]

[39] *Ibid.*, p. 333, Questions 2482-86.

[40] I.e., a person might have a weekly income of £1 from a wounds or disability pension and 5s. from his Friendly Society sick payment fund, and might own property worth £25, but still be regarded as destitute within the meaning of the law. (Department of Health for Scotland, *Annual Report, 1936*, p. 129)

[41] Even the attempt to test the genuineness of need by offering assistance in a workhouse only, which had been adopted by a few authorities, ceased after a protest from Glasgow labor organizations in 1929. (*Minutes of Evidence*, p. 690)

[42] There were even cases in which men on relief were members of the committees administering relief. (*Ibid.*, p. 337, Questions 2589-91)

[43] A man in employment for part of a week only "would be deemed to be out of work for the rest of the week and his allowance from the poor law would be

The Scottish recipient of poor relief is also in a more favorable position than his English counterpart in that he has the right to appeal to the Department of Health for Scotland if he is dissatisfied with the nature or the amount of relief granted.[44] But until 1934, the unemployed worker, unlike other relief clients, had no right to appeal if he were refused any relief at all.[45]

Financing of Local Relief

As in England, the major portion of the funds for public assistance are derived from rates (taxes) levied by local authorities upon the property owners. Temporary borrowing is permitted subject to the approval of the Department of Health for Scotland. Until 1930 the only money provided from central funds (over and above a small grant from the Local Taxation Account) was used for insane paupers and poor law medical relief. But these payments were relatively unimportant.[46] After the passage of the Local Government (Scotland) Act of 1929, Scottish local authorities, like the English, received grants from the central government to reimburse them for loss of income due to the enforced reduction of rates (derating scheme), to which reference has already been made, together with other block grants in lieu of certain discontinued grants-in-aid. But here, as in England, it is impossible to state how much of this new combined grant was applied by the local authorities toward the costs of poor relief. Between 1935 and 1937, the Scottish authorities participated in the grant from the national Treasury to compensate them for the postponement of the full effectiveness of the unemployment assistance system.

---

given in respect of that period," though his earnings would be taken into account in fixing the allowance. (*Ibid.*, p. 336, Question 2560)

[44] If satisfied that the complaint is well-founded, the Department may determine the amount of relief provisionally and issue to the applicant a "Minute" entitling him to take his case to the Court of Session, which has broad power to determine the amount of relief to be granted. In practice, the issue of a formal "Minute" is seldom necessary, the Department's finding usually being accepted by the local authority. Public assistance officers, on whom rests the responsibility of preventing any suffering because of lack of relief, have also power to afford interim relief pending the Department's consideration of the complaint. Considerable use is made of the right to appeal. (Department of Health for Scotland, *Annual Report, 1934*, p. 133)

[45] The right of appeal cannot in any case be exercised if the applicant is refused relief prohibited under the Unemployment Act of 1934.

[46] *Minutes of Evidence,* p. 706.

beginning of the insurance year preceding the current benefit year), the Minister of Labour was given power to waive the first of the two conditions. The object of the waiver was to avoid the large number of disqualifications which would otherwise have followed the enforcement of the new contributory requirement, but, in keeping with this purpose, the power to waive was originally limited to the period ending October 1, 1925.[6] By the Acts of 1925 and 1926, however, it was extended to December 31, 1927.

The power to waive the normal contributory requirement was freely exercised by the Minister under somewhat differing conditions: In August 1924 the requirement was waived up to October 15, 1924 for people who had claims to benefits authorized during the first benefit year, or who had at any time paid not less than 12 contributions.[7] After October 1924 automatic waiver was permitted only in the case of persons who had paid not less than 12 contributions at any time, and for others, only on recommendation of the local employment committee. In fact, up to the end of December 1924 the requirement was waived "in the great majority of cases when the question arose." [8]

In February 1925 the waiver rules were again revised. Waiver was allowed only in cases of claimants (other than certain disabled ex-service men) who had paid 8 contributions since the beginning of the 2 insurance years preceding the benefit year, or 30 contributions at any time. Claimants unable to satisfy either of these conditions were to be disqualified from both "standard" benefits (as the earlier covenanted benefits came to be called) and "extended" benefits (as the former uncovenanted benefits were called from 1924 to 1928).[9] Provided that they could show 20 contributions in the preceding insurance year, persons eligible by virtue

[6] Ministry of Labour, *Report for the Years 1923 and 1924* (Cmd. 2481), p. 132.

[7] Other cases where 30 contributions had not been paid were referred to local employment committees for a recommendation, but it was suggested that waiver was only justifiable where failure to qualify could not reasonably be attributed to the fault of the applicant (e.g., a disabled ex-service man under treatment for a prolonged period).

[8] *Ibid.,* p. 133.

[9] Between August 1, 1924 and December 8, 1924, 20,713 claims for waiver of the 30-contributions rule were heard by the local employment committees, 15,736 being granted. (*Ibid.,* p. 140) The total number of disallowances under the waiver rule from January 13, 1925 to December 28, 1925 was 15,258. (*Ibid., 1925,* p. 65)

of the waiver of the 30-contributions rule could draw standard benefits as a right up to the limits permitted by the prevailing ratio rule and the regulations governing the maximum duration of benefits.

Provisions Necessitated by the Prolonged and Heavy Unemployment

It soon became evident that the severity of the depression would greatly increase the number of workers (whether newly insurable or not) who were unable to satisfy the prevailing contributory requirement. From March 1921 to 1931, therefore, persons unable to satisfy the contributory rule could nevertheless receive benefits—successively known as uncovenanted, extended, and transitional [10]—if they could satisfy certain additional conditions. Introduced originally as an emergency measure, these modifications of the contributory requirement were continued by a series of amending acts until November 1931.

In March 1921 claimants unable to satisfy the statutory contributory conditions became entitled to receive uncovenanted benefits for a limited time if, since December 1919, they had been engaged for 20 weeks in what would have been an insurable employment had the Act been in force, and if they also satisfied certain additional conditions (see footnote 16 below). The same principle was applied by the Act of 1922, although the conditions under which the privilege was granted were changed.[11]

Between August 1924 and April 1928, otherwise qualified persons who had paid less than 20 contributions in the insurance year immediately preceding the benefit year could draw extended benefits provided they satisfied certain additional conditions, which differed slightly from those previously prevailing (see footnote 16 below).

[10] "Uncovenanted" as against "covenanted" benefits from March 1921 to July 1924; "extended" as against "standard" benefits from August 1924 to April 1928; and "transitional" as against "standard" benefits from April 1928 to November 1931.

[11] Payment of these uncovenanted benefits became subject to the Minister's discretion and the privilege was extended only to a worker who had paid not less than 20 contributions under the Act, or if "having regard to the opportunities of employment in his normal employment, he had, since 31 December 1919, been employed for a reasonable length of time" in some employment subsequently insurable. The other conditions were the same as those in the 1921 Act.

From April 1928 to November 1931, persons over 18 years of age who failed to satisfy the 30-contributions rule, which the Minister no longer had power to waive, could draw transitional benefits if they could satisfy a modest contributory requirement,[12] and two additional conditions designed to test the involuntary character of their unemployment (see footnote 16). Originally regarded as a temporary measure to avoid hardship resulting from a strict application of the 30-contributions rule and the abolition of the Minister's power to waive it, the payment of these transitional benefits was continued from year to year, ending only in November 1931.

Unlike the persons qualifying for benefits by the relaxations outlined in the preceding section, those granted benefits by virtue of the concessions just described were not entitled to draw covenanted or standard insurance benefits. The recipients of uncovenanted, extended or transitional benefits, however, received payments identical *in amount* with the covenanted or standard insurance benefits. Moreover, until 1929, their cost was entirely paid for out of the unemployment insurance fund (about half the cost of transitional benefits in 1929-30 was paid by the national Treasury, and the whole cost thereafter). But in several other respects these benefits differed from the covenanted or standard benefits.

In the first place, the benefit under the relaxed conditions prevailing from 1921 to 1931 was paid for a considerable part of the time not as a right, but subject to the Minister's discretion. From April 6, 1922 to August 1924, and again from August 1925 to April 1928, uncovenanted or extended benefits could be allowed by the Minister of Labour to persons failing to meet the contributory requirement only if he was satisfied in each individual case that it was expedient in the public interest to do so.[13] In the exercise of his discretionary power, the Minister decided that certain classes of workers were in principle not to be granted the

---

[12] Eight contributions in the 2 years preceding claim for benefits, or 30 at any time.

[13] Between August 1, 1924 and August 20, 1925, however, extended benefits were payable as a right under the No. 2 Act of 1924, which was passed by the Labour Government.

uncovenanted or extended benefits.[14] But these limitations "were never intended to be applied rigidly, and the committees acting under the Minister's directions have consistently had regard to the circumstances of each individual case in order to avoid the disallowance of benefit where definite hardship would be caused." [15] The determination of whether or not hardship would be caused normally involved the application of a rough test of means. From April 1928, however, transitional benefits were payable as a right to all persons who could satisfy the statutory conditions laid down for their receipt. There was no element of discretion.

In the second place, between 1922 and 1924 recipients of uncovenanted or extended benefits were subjected to periods in which no benefit at all could be drawn. The system of "gaps" in benefit as a concomitant of uncovenanted benefits was introduced by the Act of April 1922. After a claimant had received these benefits for 5 weeks, there had to be an interval of 5 weeks before further uncovenanted benefits could be drawn. This provision was very soon changed (by the No. 2 Act of 1922) to a gap of only one week after receipt of 5 weeks of uncovenanted benefits. The Act of 1923, which made uncovenanted benefits available for 44 weeks out of 50, provided for a gap of 2 weeks without benefit if and when 22 weekly benefits had been drawn since November 1922. From October 18, 1923 to February 21, 1924, there was a gap of 3 weeks without benefit after 12 weeks of uncovenanted benefits had been received. The system of "gaps" was ended by the Act of February 1924.

---

[14] He ruled that benefits should not in principle be available to (a) juveniles living with relatives to whom they might reasonably look for support; (b) single persons wholly or mainly maintained by relatives; (c) short-time workers except where their earnings were so low as to justify the grant of benefits; (d) persons who were unwilling to accept, on fair terms and conditions, work other than that to which they were accustomed; (e) aliens, except British-born wives or widows of aliens; (f) from July 1922, married women living at home, whose husbands were employed. The rules relating to single persons living with relatives and to aliens were somewhat modified in April 1923. In February 1924 the right to claim extended benefits was again given to all the above classes except those who refused unaccustomed work offered on fair conditions, and certain groups of aliens. In 1925, when the Minister's discretion was restored, "rules were made in terms practically identical with those of the rules in operation" from April 1923 to February 1924. (*Ibid., 1923 and 1924*, pp. 132-36; *1925*, pp. 65-66)

[15] Ministry of Labour, *Report on National Unemployment Insurance to July 1923*, p. 112.

In the third place, the claimant to unconvenanted, extended or transitional benefits had to satisfy conditions not required of claimants for covenanted or standard benefits. These provisions were designed as a substitute for the contributory requirement and in general placed on the claimant the onus of proving that his failure to satisfy it was not due to any lack of zeal in seeking work in an insurable trade, or of willingness to accept work even in other than his usual occupation. The task of determining in each individual case whether these conditions were satisfied was delegated by the Minister to the representative employment committees attached to the local employment exchanges.[16]

The imposition of these additional conditions resulted in the denial of uncovenanted and extended benefits to about 13 per

---

[16] From March 3, 1921, when uncovenanted benefits were available to persons who were unable to fulfill the statutory contributory requirement (at that time, 12 contributions under the Act), but who had been engaged for 20 weeks since December 31, 1919 in an employment which was subsequently insurable, it was necessary for claimants to prove in addition that they were normally in an employment which would make them insured workers within the meaning of the Act and also that they were genuinely seeking full-time employment but were unable to obtain it. The same conditions were applied to uncovenanted benefit claimants during 1922 and 1923.

Furthermore, from February 1922 until August 1924, uncovenanted benefits were denied to workers who were unwilling to accept, on fair terms and conditions, work other than that to which they were accustomed but which they were reasonably capable of performing.

From August 1, 1924 a claimant to extended benefits had to prove that he was (a) normally employed in an insurable employment and would normally seek to obtain his livelihood by means of insurable employment; (b) that in normal times insurable employment suited to his capacities would be likely to be available to him; (c) that he had during the 2 years prior to his benefit application been employed in insurable work to such an extent as was reasonable, having regard to all the circumstances of the case, and in particular to the opportunities for obtaining insurable employment during the period; (d) that he was making every reasonable effort to obtain work suited to his capacities and was willing to accept this employment. These conditions were retained after 1925 when extended benefits again became discretionary with the Minister.

Finally, after April 1928, when transitional benefits were payable to workers over 18 who could not satisfy the 30-contributions requirement, claimants, in addition to satisfying a modified contributory qualification (8 contributions in the last 2 years or 30 at any time), had also to show that (a) they were normally employed in insurable employment and would normally seek to obtain their livelihood in an insurable industry, and (b) that they had during the preceding 2 years been employed in insurable work to a reasonable extent, taking into account the opportunities for obtaining covered employment in the period and the circumstances of the case. This last condition was abolished by the Act of 1930.

cent of the claimants during the years 1921 to 1928.[17] The most effective were those relating to the genuineness of the applicant's search for full-time employment (48.9 per cent of all cases disqualified from October 18, 1923 to July 31, 1924), to his inability to show a reasonable period of insurable employment in the preceding 2 years (between 32 and 37 per cent of all disqualifications after August 1, 1924), and to his failure to make every reasonable effort to obtain suitable employment or to accept suitable employment (24 to 31 per cent of all disqualifications after August 1, 1924).

CHANGES IN THE RATIO OF CONTRIBUTIONS TO BENEFITS

Even though the minimum contributory requirements were made more generous, qualified individuals could have drawn benefit for very few weeks unless changes had also been made in the ratio rule.[18] Hence, during the 10 years in which an attempt was made to use the insurance system as the major unemployment relief institution, this rule was subject to considerable amendment.

The relaxation of the original rule of one week's benefit for each 6 contributions was achieved in several ways. First, during certain periods benefits drawn between preceding specified dates were disregarded, thus automatically increasing the unexhausted contributions standing to the credit of a claimant.[19] Second, addi-

---

[17] For the different periods the percentages denied benefits were:

		Per cent
Mar. 3, 1921 to Nov. 2, 1921	......	6.1
Nov. 3, 1921 to Apr. 5, 1922	......	7.7
Apr. 6, 1922 to Nov. 1, 1922	......	15.4
Nov. 2, 1922 to Oct. 17, 1923	......	15.0
Oct. 18, 1923 to July 31, 1924	......	11.5
Aug. 1, 1924 to Jan. 12, 1925	......	13.1
Jan. 13, 1925 to Jan. 11, 1926	......	13.3
Jan. 12, 1926 to Jan. 10, 1927	......	14.7
Jan. 11, 1927 to Jan. 16, 1928	......	17.0

Source: Ministry of Labour, *Report on National Unemployment Insurance to July 1923*, pp. 226-27; *Report for the Years 1923 and 1924*, p. 139; *1925*, p. 68; *1926*, pp. 45-46, *1927*, pp. 42-43.

[18] So long as the 1-to-6 rule prevailed, a man who, under the relaxed eligibility rules could qualify by working for 6 weeks, would be entitled only to one week of benefits in an insurance year.

[19] From July 2, 1922 to October 17, 1923, benefits drawn between November 8, 1920 and November 2, 1922 were disregarded. From October 18, 1923 to October 15, 1924, no account was taken of benefits drawn between November 8, 1920 and October 18, 1923.

tional contributions were credited to the workers insured as of certain dates.[20] And, third, after July 1922 the ratio rule was practically suspended by the specific grant of uncovenanted, and later extended, benefits (subject to the prevailing conditions governing the receipt and duration of these benefits) to persons who could have been barred from further benefit rights by application of the ratio rule. Finally, in April 1928 the ratio rule was entirely abolished.[21]

CHANGES IN THE MAXIMUM DURATION OF BENEFITS

Even with a modified ratio rule and a relaxation of the contributory requirements, the unemployment insurance system would have played a relatively small rôle in the face of continued depression unless changes had also been made in the statutory provisions governing the maximum duration of benefits to be drawn in any one year. The 1920 Act had provided a maximum of 15 weeks of benefit in an insurance year, but with continued unemployment the proportion of unemployed out of work for longer than this period steadily increased. This fact was recognized in a series of complicated changes made in the duration rule. In the main, these changes took two forms: the duration of normal standard benefits, payable as a right, was extended; and additional weeks of benefit were granted as an emergency provision subject to certain conditions.

[20] Thus, the Act of July 1921 provided that 25 additional contributions should be credited to workers insured on July 2, 1922. From November 2, 1922 to October 17, 1923, each contribution paid (minus 5 for each week of benefit drawn before November 8, 1920) was to be counted twice, thus in effect changing the 1-to-6 rule to a 1-to-3 rule. Also, in order to allow workers to draw uncovenanted benefits up to the maximum permissible at any time, they were treated as if they had paid the number of contributions that would have been necessary to satisfy the ratio rule. Until 1924, subsequent contributions were charged against these past benefits when the ratio rule was applied to claimants for covenanted benefits.

[21] It was revived again in 1934, but only as a device for giving certain workers the right to more than the standard 26 weeks of benefit payable to all qualified claimants. The 1-to-6 rule had not been applied directly to uncovenanted benefits. In the period November 2, 1922 to April 11, 1923, an analogous rule was applied to these benefits in excess of 12 weeks. But the limitation was removed immediately thereafter. (Ministry of Labour, *Report on National Unemployment Insurance to July 1923*, p. 101)

5

Extensions of Covenanted or Standard Benefit Duration

The March 1921 Act provided for the extension of duration from 15 to 26 weeks in an insurance year, to become effective July 3, 1922. But, because of the creation of and subsequent changes in the effective dates of four so-called "special periods," in which special and temporary maximum duration rules prevailed, this general extension did not become effective until October 18, 1923.[22]

During the operation of the "special periods," the length of time in which any prescribed number of weekly benefits was payable was less than an insurance year. Amendments were also made both to the prevailing maximum benefit duration and the length of the special periods on occasions when large numbers of workers were about to exhaust their benefit rights, as indicated in the tabular summary on the opposite page.

It is evident that the effective number of weeks in which benefit could be drawn in any 12-month period was greatly increased between 1920 and 1931. Apart from the temporary extensions which took place in the four "special periods" between March 3, 1921 and October 17, 1923, the most important extensions of the duration of standard benefits took place after April 19, 1928 as a result of the 1927 Act. Thereafter, the only limitation to the duration of standard insurance benefits was provided by the requirement that, to qualify at all, a worker should be able to show 30 contributions in the 2 years immediately before claiming benefit. In consequence a qualified claimant was entitled to an uninterrupted 74 weeks of benefit. After July 1928, the claims of workers who had drawn benefit for 78 days or 13 weeks within a period of 4 months were subject to review by the courts of referees. The procedure was, however, relatively formal and the number of claims disallowed was insignificant.[23]

[22] The four special periods, as revised, were:
(1) March 3 to November 2, 1921
(2) November 3, 1921 to April 5, 1922 (originally to July 2, 1922)
(3) April 6 to November 1, 1922
(4) November 2, 1922 to October 17, 1923 (originally to July 1, 1923)

[23] Of the 1,300,000 cases which came up for review in the 10 months ending May 1929, only 4.3 per cent were disallowed. (*Report of the Committee on Procedure and Evidence for the Determination of Claims for Unemployment Insurance Benefit, 1929*, pp. 37, 47)

was itself modified so as to provide almost unlimited benefits to persons who could show very small amounts of insurable employment.

As a result, during 1921-31, unemployment insurance came to be the major institution for providing unemployment relief. The appropriateness of this method of meeting the problems resulting from mass unemployment will be examined in the following chapter.

Chapter IV

EXPANDED INSURANCE AS THE MAJOR UNEMPLOYMENT RELIEF MEASURE

During the years 1921 to 1931, the unemployed in Great Britain received assistance in the form of either insurance benefit or poor relief or a combination of both. The major burden was, however, carried by the insurance system, and the British experience may therefore be expected to throw considerable light upon the advantages and disadvantages of this method of handling the unemployment problem. The resulting dual relief system may be studied from four angles: (1) its repercussions upon the local authorities which, being responsible for poor law relief, would otherwise have had to carry the entire residual relief burden; (2) its effect upon the insurance system considered as an isolated institution; (3) the appropriateness of the assistance provided in view of the needs of the unemployed, and in particular the social and economic justification for the division of the unemployed into two categories; and (4) the extent to which there was overlapping or lack of administrative coordination between the two major programs.

Repercussions on the Local Relief Authorities

One of the clearest consequences of the expansion of the insurance system was a reduction in the burden of unemployment relief that would otherwise have fallen upon the local authorities who were responsible for general poor relief. Between September 1922 and September 1931 the insurance system, as it was expanded, paid benefits to between 75.3 and 94.5 per cent of the total estimated number of unemployed, as shown in Table 1.

The estimated number of persons (excluding dependents) receiving local relief on account of unemployment fell from between 239,000 and 356,000 in 1922 to between 66,000 and 69,000 in the first three quarters of 1931, despite the fact that the estimated number of unemployed persons had approximately doubled in the meantime—from about 1.5 millions to 2.9 millions. Throughout

52

these years the relative numbers of unemployed receiving local relief declined as the scope and importance of the insurance system increased. Thus, during the period from August 1924 to August 1925 when extended benefits were a matter of right and

TABLE 1. NUMBER OF PERSONS[a] ASSISTED ON ACCOUNT OF UNEMPLOYMENT IN
GREAT BRITAIN, 1922-1931[b]

Date	Estimated number unemployed	Number receiving		Per cent of unemployed assisted by	
		Insurance benefits[c]	Poor relief	Central government	Local governments
		In thousands			
1922–June	1,504	690	356	45.9	23.7
Sept.	1,397	1,046	267	75.3	19.1
Dec.	1,409	1,107	239	77.4	17.0
1923–June	1,256	1,061	205	83.6	16.3
1924–Dec.	1,262	1,035	113	82.0	9.0
1925–June	1,388	992	117	71.5	8.4
Sept.	1,415	1,205	140	85.2	9.9
Dec.	1,217	971	162	79.8	13.3
1927–June	1,091	825	157	75.6	14.4
Sept.	1,163	876	147	75.3	12.6
Dec.	1,210	943	154	77.9	12.7
1928–June	1,285	1,057	120	82.3	9.3
Sept.	1,384	1,118	107	80.8	7.7
Dec.	1,355	1,092	112	80.6	8.3
1929–Mar.	1,235	952	113	77.1	9.1
June	1,193	951	95	79.7	8.0
Sept.	1,245	940	90	75.5	7.2
Dec.	1,377	1,126	94	81.8	6.8
1930–Mar.	1,710	1,534	92	89.7	5.4
June	1,913	1,706	43	89.2	2.2
Sept.	2,203	1,879	46	85.3	2.1
Dec.	2,493	2,356	59	94.5	2.4
1931–Mar.	2,679	2,338	69	87.3	2.6
June	2,720	2,377	66	87.4	2.4
Sept.	2,914	2,532	69	86.9	2.4

[a] Excluding dependents.
[b] Until 1927 the lack of comparable data, except for the dates shown, precludes the presentation of a continuous series. Data for the year 1926 have been omitted because, as explained in Appendix III, the English component of the numbers receiving poor relief is completely distorted by the inclusion of strikers assisted on account of the general strike and the long-continued mining strike in that year.
[c] Insurance and expanded insurance beneficiaries. Data shown for Sept. and Dec., 1922, June 1923 and June 1925 relate to Oct., Nov., April and May of the respective years.

Sources: Appendix Tables I, col. 8; II, cols 4, 7; VI, col. 3

not subject to ministerial discretion, the numbers in receipt of relief fell sharply despite a relatively high level of unemployment. From 1928 to 1931, when the maximum limit to the duration of insurance benefits was removed and transitional benefits took the place of the discretional extended benefits, the numbers locally maintained again showed a marked drop, while a still further decline followed the abolition of the genuinely-seeking-work clause in March 1930. In September of that year when unemployment rose above 2 millions, the local authorities were maintaining only 46,000 unemployed persons. In the following September when unemployment was almost 3 millions, their unemployment relief burden had risen to only 69,000 persons, excluding dependents.[1]

The numbers of persons obtaining assistance from one or the other system are, however, apt to be misleading unless accompanied by figures relating to expenditures. For a certain proportion of the persons assisted by the poor law authorities were receiving only supplementary assistance.[2] Expenditures per head on this type of relief were much lower than the per head expenditures of the insurance system.[3] Hence, a more revealing picture of the relative importance of the insurance and the relief systems can be obtained by a comparison of their expenditures. Table 2 indicates even more clearly that during the years 1921-31 the insurance system carried the major share of the burden of maintaining the unemployed. While in the financial year 1922-23 the local relief authorities contributed 20.9 per cent of the expenditures on unemployment relief, by the year 1930-31 their share had fallen to 2.4 per cent.

[1] For further evidence of the direct effect of changes in the insurance system on the local relief burden, see *Minutes of Evidence*, Questions 2309 and 2561, and p. 328; also Ministry of Health, *Annual Report, 1930-31*, p. 193. The Association of Municipal Corporations, however, claimed that the gains due to the 1930 changes were subsequently discounted by decisions of the courts of referees which disqualified large numbers from benefit. (*Minutes of Evidence*, p. 524)

[2] Although these people formed an extremely small proportion of the insured unemployed, they bulked large among the insured clients of the poor relief authorities. On April 17, 1926, recipients of concurrent benefits and relief in England and Wales constituted 25.3 per cent of the insured heads of families receiving relief. (Ministry of Health, *Annual Report, 1926-27*, p. 115) In the financial year 1928-29, they formed between 9.3 per cent and 12.4 per cent of all the insured persons on the relief rolls (*Minutes of Evidence*, p. 298), while by February 1931 they had increased to 41.7 per cent of all insured persons relieved on account of unemployment by local authorities. (Royal Commission on Unemployment Insurance (1932), *Appendices to the Minutes of Evidence*, Part II, pp. 76-77)

[3] During 1928-29 supplementary assistance amounted to between 21.7 and 25.5 per cent of the combined amount of benefits and poor relief drawn by recipients of concurrent relief and benefits in England and Wales (*Minutes of Evidence*, p. 298). In the sample week of February 7, 1931, the 14,155 insured persons receiving both relief and insurance benefits in Great Britain received £19,208 in benefits (27s. per head) and only £5,080 in supplementary relief (7s. per head). (*Appendices to Minutes of Evidence*, Part II, p. 102)

in the areas of relatively heavy unemployment that the fiscal resources of the local authorities were most limited.

For somewhat similar reasons, the other unemployment relief measures taken by the central government, such as grants for roads and for expanded public works, did relatively little for the most depressed areas. All these measures required local financial participation, and being relatively expensive methods of unemployment relief, were almost by definition beyond the powers and the interest of localities which could not even meet their ordinary outdoor relief bills. Had the subsidies been greater, the depressed areas might have benefited more. Even the relatively generous grants for roadbuilding as an unemployment relief measure involved significant expenditures on the part of local authorities which, as was evident from the slowness of their response to the 1929-30 programs, they were increasingly reluctant to make.[16] But the government subsidy for public works was estimated to be approximately 35 per cent of the total commitments of £191 millions which were made between December 1920 and January 1932.[17] Indeed, when in 1925 the government decided to limit the grants for accelerated public works to areas where unemployment was exceptional, the result was that "the scheme of grants might almost be said to have been in abeyance until November 1928, when an entirely fresh consideration was taken into account." [18] The failure of the existing system of grants to assist the most needy areas was finally recognized in 1930, when the government provided £500,000 to meet the full cost of works in those areas.[19]

At the very end of the period 1920-31, both the total burden falling on local authorities and its unequal distribution were ma-

[16] Under the 1920-25 road program the central government's share of total commitments amounting to approximately £57.2 millions was £35.5 millions. Under the 1929-30 program the central government's share of total commitments of £23.4 millions was approximately £17.6 millions. (Ministry of Transport, *Report on the Administration of the Road Fund,* 1932-33, p. 9, 1933-34, p. 9)

[17] *Final Report of the Unemployment Grants Committee,* 1933, pp. 22-23, 34. By March 1932, however, the central government had expended only £24.3 millions.

[18] *Ibid.,* p. 7.

[19] A further reason for the failure of the grant-aided, expanded public works system to contribute materially to the relief of distressed areas was the requirement that the works should be of relatively high economic value. Although the Grants Committee applied this condition more rigidly to the prosperous than to the depressed areas, it could not disregard the fact that in some declining areas there was little justification for adding to or improving the existing capital equipment.

terially affected by the Local Government Act of 1929, which came into effect in 1930. In the first place the Act, as already pointed out, transferred public assistance functions from the small poor law unions to the counties and county boroughs. Thus the basis of taxation for poor relief purposes was widened and local discrepancies were to some extent eliminated. But differences between counties and county boroughs still remained, and there were complaints that within some areas the "disproportion between numbers to be maintained and the resources on which rates could be collected was even enhanced." [20]

In the second place, the Local Government Act lightened the burdens on local rate (tax) payers at the expense of the national government. It abolished local rates on agricultural property and reduced by 75 per cent the rates on other taxable buildings and real property used primarily for purposes of productive industry or of freight transport, and made available to the local authorities from national funds a sum equal to their estimated loss of income. This was known as the "derating scheme."

In the third place, the Act abolished a number of assigned revenues and percentage grants ear-marked for health and other services and replaced them by an equivalent sum in the form of an annual grant. To make the changes more palatable, the central government added a further sum, together with small supplementary grants to avoid hardship in individual cases and to ensure that each county or county borough would obtain at least a slight net financial advantage as compared with the earlier arrangements.[21]

[20] In Scotland, the result in many cases was a contraction of the areas of the city units (burghs), although the burden was undoubtedly spread more widely over the counties. (*Minutes of Evidence,* p. 691) West Ham (near London) was an example of an English borough which failed to gain financially from the changes.

[21] It was estimated that for England and Wales in the years 1930 and 1931 the relative importance of each of these items was as follows (in millions):

	1930-31	1931-32
Losses on account of derating	£22.60	£22.34
Losses on account of grants	16.30	16.27
Additional money	5.00	5.00
Additional Exchequer grants	0.55	0.51
Supplementary Exchequer grants	1.10	1.03
Total	£45.55	£45.15

Toward these sums the Exchequer used annually about £5.8 millions from the Road Fund, from which grants had previously been made to local authorities

The precise extent to which the change redounded to the advantage of the more heavily burdened areas cannot as yet be determined.[22] During the first years of the scheme, the new block grant, which amounted to some £45 millions a year, was distributed on the basis of a complicated formula. Each local authority received a sum equal to 75 per cent of its losses on account of changes in rates and grants, plus a share of the remaining sum determined by its relative population as weighted by certain factors.[23] Undoubtedly the more heavily burdened areas gained greatly by the grant in lieu of rates, because it was in these districts that rates were highest and most onerous. Even so it has been claimed that, as the standard year taken for the purpose of calculating loss was 1925, the redistribution failed to take account of the marked increases in rates which had occurred since that date. The poor areas also gained to some extent by the weighting of the formula in favor of areas with a high percentage of unemployment and low assessable property values. But, although there appears to be general agreement among authorities that the change in the main achieved its purpose of giving most assistance where most was needed, in part because of the inadequate weight given to the factor of unemployment there still remained a number of areas carrying disproportionately heavy burdens even after the receipt of the Exchequer grants.[24] The statutory investigation

---

for various purposes, so that the net sum provided from national tax revenues amounted to about £39.7 millions. (Ministry of Health, *Annual Report, 1930-31,* pp. 182-84; *1931-32,* p. 180)

[22] As the authorities were free to distribute their block grants between the various services as they wished, it is impossible to state what proportion was specifically applied to the costs of poor relief.

[23] The population was based on the estimated population in the calendar year 1928 weighted according to the proportion of children under 5 years of age in the population, to the percentage of unemployment among insured men, to the rateable value per head, and, for the counties, to the number of persons per mile of road.

[24] The average of rates fell from 13.25 shillings to the pound in 1928-29 to 10.97 shillings in 1932-33, while the dispersion of rates was also reduced, the standard deviation falling from 3.43 to 2.95. (Newcomer, *op. cit.,* p. 279)

Dr. Joseph Sykes in his book, *A Study in English Local Authority Finance* (London: P. S. King and Son, 1939), p. 124, selected 18 areas as illustrations of the inadequacy of the scheme to meet acute needs on account of unemployment. Of these, Merthyr Tydfil, which had the highest total rates among the areas analyzed and in which poor relief absorbed the highest proportion of the local rates (35 per cent), received the fourth lowest Exchequer grant expressed as a percentage of its total rates (29 per cent). The two areas which received from the Exchequer an amount equal to 46 per cent of their total rates expended

6

into the operation of the scheme in 1937 led to certain changes in the weighting of unemployment and in the principles by which, in the London area, the funds were distributed among subordinate authorities. It has also been pointed out that, as a method of equalizing burdens, the new plan was unnecessarily expensive since it gave assistance to areas and types of industry where no need was apparent.[25] The 75 per cent reduction of rates applied to all industrial property regardless of the severity of the rates, while the assistance given to agriculture was a pure subsidy.[26]

Nevertheless, while the expanded insurance system from 1921 to 1931 operated only imperfectly to diminish the inequality of the relief burden, and while the effect of the Local Government Act was confined to the last two years of this period, there cannot be any doubt that the total burden on the local authorities was greatly reduced after 1927. In that year 109 authorities had found it necessary to resort to overdrafts and loans to cover poor law expenditures. By 1931-32 this number had fallen to 39, while the extent of borrowing by authorities in distressed areas had fallen from £1,227,000 in 1927-28 to £263,000. The improvement was also reflected in the tendency toward lower rates. The number of authorities levying rates of 16s. or over dropped from 275 in 1927-28 to 114 in 1931-32. Similarly, 7 authorities levied rates of 30s. or over in 1927-28, while only 3 did so in 1929-30 and none thereafter. Out of 95 authorities levying rates of 20s. or over in 1927-28, 73 were in distressed areas. By 1931-32, the total number of authorities in this category had dropped to 20, and among them 18 were in distressed areas.[27]

Finally, the solution of the residual relief problem by expanding the insurance system was far from ideal from the point of view

on poor relief only 22 and 24 per cent respectively of their total rates, and also had much lower absolute total rates than Merthyr Tydfil.

Analyses of the operation of the derating scheme may be found in Ministry of Health, *Annual Report, 1936-37,* p. 167, and the *Report* of the Committee inquiring into the operation of the scheme in 1936-37 (H.C. Paper 42); also Newcomer, *op. cit.,* p. 275. In Chapter XI, Dr. Newcomer presents some interesting examples of the effects of the new scheme in different types of communities. Cf. also Ursula Hicks, *The Finance of British Government* (Oxford: University Press, 1938), pp. 166-67.

[25] Cf. Ursula Hicks, *op. cit.,* pp. 78-81.

[26] Joseph Sykes, *British Public Expenditure, 1921-1931* (London: P. S. King and Son, 1933), pp. 269-72.

[27] Ministry of Health, *Annual Report, 1932-33,* pp. 161-62.

of the local authorities, because it was uncertain and on an emergency basis. Until 1924 the expansion was, as indicated in Chapter III, in the nature of sudden and temporary adjustments to meet situations which were regarded as emergencies. The changes in the maximum duration of uncovenanted benefits were not made until the very month when it became evident that large numbers would exhaust their benefit rights and fall back upon the poor relief system. The so-called "special periods" within which uncovenanted benefits and relaxed eligibility conditions were in operation indicate by their very name the prevailing belief that the situation was one of temporary emergency. On at least two occasions the length of these special periods was changed at the last moment in order to maintain through the insurance system the many persons who otherwise would have had to seek poor relief. Even after 1924 the waiving of the contributory requirement, which was instrumental in admitting large numbers to standard insurance or to extended benefits, continued on a year-to-year basis, while the payment of transitional benefits was also made possible only by the annual passage of acts extending for a further year the transitional period.

Thus the local authorities were at all times threatened with a sudden and great increase in their already mounting unemployment relief burdens. With the all-important question of the scope of the insurance system a matter of speculation and determined on a hand-to-mouth basis which reflected the views of the dominant political parties, the local authorities were in no position to plan ahead, or to build up any permanent and adequate administrative organization.

Various undesirable consequences flowed from the increasing, uncertain and unequal burden thrown upon the local fiscal authorities, which was alleviated, but not completely removed, by the expansion of the insurance system and the measures inaugurated by the Local Government Act of 1929. The burden contributed in a cumulative manner toward the movement of industry away from the areas of heavy unemployment toward areas, mainly in the southeast, where there was less depression and therefore lower rates. The resulting decline in the amount of assessable property increased still further the rates assessed against that which remained, and probably encouraged a transference of residence on the part of the wealthier members of the heavily rated areas. Moreover, rates are a peculiarly unsuitable source of revenue for financing rapidly increasing burdens, owing to the difficulty of adjusting valuations over short periods of time.[28]

Socially, also, the consequences were unsatisfactory because the need for increased local health and welfare measures was most evident in the areas of heavy unemployment which, owing to the loss of income resulting from declining valuations and resources, were precisely the areas compelled to curtail these services in order to supply the bare physical needs of their unemployed clientele.

THE EFFECTS UPON THE INSURANCE SYSTEM

Expansion of the insurance system permitted the country to provide maintenance for the unemployed without entirely destroying the financial stability of the local authorities. But this result was achieved at the cost of important changes in the insurance system, some of which reacted disastrously on its prestige.

Increases in the Levels of Benefits

One of the more important consequences of providing for both short and prolonged unemployment by expanding the insurance system has been the necessity of raising the benefit rates. The original plan, as introduced in 1911, had been to provide some substitute for earnings which would enable workers to support themselves during relatively short periods of unemployment without having to resort to a degrading and disliked poor law system. In keeping with this theory, the benefits in 1911 were low even for that time (7s. a week for an adult man). The duration of benefits was, however, relatively short (a maximum of 15 weeks), so that it could plausibly be argued that, together with his own savings and perhaps some help from trade union funds, a man would be able to carry himself over short periods of unemployment. Consistently also, the 1911 Act was limited to those trades where unemployment was "due not to a permanent contraction but to a temporary oscillation in their range of business." [29]

---

[28] Cf. Hicks, *op. cit.*, pp. 155, 158-165, and Sykes, *A Study in English Local Authority Finance*, pp. 217-20.

[29] Winston S. Churchill (then Home Secretary) in the course of the second reading of the Bill, said: "They are not decaying trades, they are not over-

The 1920 Act embodied the same theory of the function of insurance benefits, although coverage was widened to trades which were no longer characterized by conditions of stability. The duration of benefit was fixed at 15 weeks, and although the money value of the benefit was 15s. for an adult man, the real value was even lower than that of the 7s. provided by the 1911 Act because of the great increase in the cost of living.[30] Benefits at this low level might or might not have been justified as part of a plan providing against short-term unemployment for workers with a long record of past employment, during which they might have been expected to have accumulated private savings which could be used to supplement benefits. They were obviously inadequate, however, as soon as the system was extended to cover workers who had already been out of work for a considerable time and to pay them benefits for what ultimately became an almost indefinite period. Hence, it is not surprising that the relaxations of the insurance rules, which were discussed in Chapter III, were accompanied by increases in benefits. The changes came about in two ways: first, by increases in the normal rates for single persons, and second, by the introduction of dependents' benefits.[31]

The 15s. weekly benefit rate for an adult man remain unchanged from 1920 to August 1924 (except for 4 months in 1921 when it was 20s.), despite a considerable fall in the cost of living. In August 1924, when a deliberate attempt was made by the Labour Government to use the insurance system as the major bulwark against distress due to unemployment, the benefit was raised to 18s.[32] Reduced to 17s. in April 1928, the real value of the insurance benefit nevertheless remained relatively high, because of declines in the cost of living, until October 1931 when it was sharply cut to 15s. 3d. by the National Economy Act. Compared with the benefit rate in 1920, however, insurance benefits, even

---

stocked trades, they are not congested with a surplus or an insufficient supply of labour." (*Hansard*, May 25, 1911, col. 498)

[30] If the price level in January 1913 (when the 7s. benefit was first payable) be taken as 100, it was 276 in November 1920 when the 15s. rate came into effect. (*Final Report*, p. 20)

[31] Table XI in Appendix VI shows the rates payable to different classes of persons from 1913 to 1939.

[32] "An honest man shall not starve tho' he be unemployed, neither shall he be driven to the Guardians; . . . he shall be paid a sum of money which at any rate will keep him from starvation." (The Minister of Labour on June 18, 1924, in the committee stage of the No. 2 Act of 1924, cited in *Final Report*, p. 22)

after October 1931, were very much higher because of the payment of benefits to dependents.

These dependents' benefits were originally introduced in November 1921 as a temporary measure in response to representations to the Minister that the benefit rates were especially inadequate in the case of married men and persons with dependents.[33] At first, these payments were made to unemployed persons for their dependent wives and children, the funds being provided by a special levy on employers and workers with the addition of a government contribution. The relatively low dependents' allowances were payable only for 6 months, but in April 1922 they were made part of the permanent system. Between 1921 and 1931 the level of dependents' benefits was considerably raised, and the class of persons for whom they were payable was widened, notably by the Acts of 1924 (No. 2), 1927 and 1930. The extensions were all justified as being necessary in order to remove hardships.[34]

The net result of these increases in the real value of insurance benefits is evident from Table 3. It will be noted that by 1931 the real value of the benefit rate was higher than that in any of the preceding years. The benefit rate of 1931 represented for single men an increase of 8s. 2d., and for a married man with a wife and two children an increase of 21s. 2d., over the 15s. payable in 1920.

This continuous increase in the real value of insurance benefits by 1931 was an adjustment to the logical implications of the use of insurance to provide income for the major proportion of the unemployed. For, once benefits were paid to those with no recent period of employment, or were paid for very lengthy periods, the assumption that a worker could eke out his benefits from his own savings was no longer valid. Had benefits remained at their real 1920 level, a tremendous amount of supplementation would have been necessary. Even if supplementation had not been deemed undesirable for administrative reasons, there were two interested groups—the local poor law authorities and the organized labor movement—which united to press for the alternative course,

---

[33] Ministry of Labour, *Report on National Unemployment Insurance to July 1923*, p. 63.

[34] In 1921 dependents' benefits were limited to the normal immediate family circle consisting of the claimant's wife (or husband) and children, or a female person acting as housekeeper under certain conditions. The wide list of persons for whom allowances were payable by 1931 appears in the *Final Report*, p. 252.

namely, an increase of the benefit rate so that the needs of the majority of claimants would be more nearly covered.

It was always officially denied during this period that the standard of benefit payments was the maintenance level.[35] Yet a comparison of the insurance rates paid in 1931 with the allowances payable under the poor law relief scales (where the standard

TABLE 3. CHANGES IN THE REAL VALUE OF INSURANCE BENEFITS, 1920-1931

Date	Single man		Man, wife and 2 children	
	Money benefit rate	Excess of 1931 rate over rate in each previous year, in terms of 1931 cost of living	Money benefit rate	Excess of 1931 rate over rate in each previous year, in terms of 1931 cost of living
	s. *d.*	*s.* *d.*	*s.* *d.*	*s.* *d.*
1920	15 0	8 2	15 0	21 2
1921				
Jan. 1–Mar. 2	15 0	7 3	15 0	20 3
Mar. 3–June 29	20 0	4 0	20 0	17 0
June 30–Nov. 9	15 0	7 3	15 0	20 3
Nov. 10–Dec. 31	15 0	7 3	22 0	15 8
1922	15 0	4 11	22 0	12 4
1923	15 0	4 4	22 0	11 5
1924	15 0	4 5	22 0	11 6
1925	18 0	2 0	27 0	7 5
1926	18 0	1 7	27 0	6 11
1927	18 0	1 3	27 0	6 5
1928	17 0	1 11	28 0	5 3
1929	17 0	1 9	28 0	4 11
1930	17 0	1 2	30 0	2 1
1931	17 0	— —	30 0	— —

Source: *First Report of the Royal Commission on Unemployment Insurance* 1931 (Cmd. 3872), p. 66.

[35] In December 1923 the Inter-Departmental Committee on Public Assistance stated that benefits were designed "to supplement private effort in mitigating distress due to involuntary unemployment." (*Report,* Cmd. 2011, 1924, p. 18) The new principle, however, was specifically recognized by the Labour Government in 1924 (see footnote 32 above). This was but a temporary admission, and even the Blanesburgh Committee, which believed in a very wide insurance system, held that benefits should "certainly be so substantial that the insured contributor can feel that . . . taken in conjunction with such resources as may reasonably in the generality of cases be expected to have been built up, they will be sufficient to prevent him from being haunted while at work by the fear of what must happen to him if he is unemployed." (*Report of the Unemployment Insurance Committee,* 1927, p. 38) The Royal Commission of 1930-32 was even more emphatic: "There is no warrant for the assumption that unemployment benefit is or ever has been intended to provide full maintenance." (*First Report of the Royal Commission on Unemployment Insurance,* p. 32)

was admittedly full maintenance) suggests that an approximation to maintenance was indeed the standard. In January 1931, of 78 county or county borough public assistance authorities with published relief scales, only 12 had scales which were in all respects higher than the corresponding insurance benefits.[36]

Loss of Prestige Due to the Increasing Debt

Until April 1929 the entire cost of the expanded insurance system was borne by the Unemployment Fund. By the Act of 1930, however, the Treasury assumed responsibility for roughly half the cost of the temporary relaxation of the 30-contributions rule (i.e., transitional benefits) for the year 1929-30,[37] and the whole of the cost (including administration) thereafter. Despite increased contributions on the part of employers, workers and the government, the income of the Fund soon failed to meet expenditure. The Fund's reserve of £21,875,000 on November 8, 1920 was exhausted by July 1921. Recourse was had to borrowing, and a series of acts successively raised the maximum borrowing limit until it was finally held at £115,000,000 by the Act (No. 2) of 1931. The growth of the debt is shown in Table 4.

Since 1921 the system has never been out of debt. It is true that by August 1924 the debt, which had been as much as £16,-750,000 in March 1923, had been repaid except for £4,500,000. But after falling to this minimum it commenced again to rise, and by December 1931 had reached the high figure of £110,-320,000.[38] Some small part of the debt arose from the attempt to apply uniform definitions of employment and unemployment and uniform rates of contributions and benefits to a complex economic society.[39] But the greater part of the debt can be directly

---

[36] *Final Report*, p. 67. Another 5 authorities had scales equal to insurance benefits. It is probable that the majority of the remaining 67 authorities which did not publish scales were below insurance rates, since 51 of these were county authorities which tended to be more conservative than county boroughs, and also because in general it is the more generous authorities which openly announce scales of relief.

[37] It was to pay retroactively the entire cost of the transitional benefits paid to claimants who commenced new benefit years after March 31, 1929.

[38] *First Report of the Royal Commission on Unemployment Insurance,* 1931, p. 22; Ministry of Labour, *Report for the Year 1932,* p. 108.

[39] Involving the payment of larger amounts of benefit than had been anticipated to seasonal workers, partially employed (short-time) workers, and workers who normally work only 2 days in the week.

traced to the successive relaxation of eligibility conditions, extensions of benefit duration and increases in benefit rates which arose out of the attempt to use the insurance system to care for the residual unemployed.[40]

TABLE 4. THE BALANCE SHEET OF THE BRITISH UNEMPLOYMENT INSURANCE SYSTEM, 1920-1931

Periods	Balance of income and expenditure for the period	Status of the Unemployment Fund at end of period
Ending Nov. 7, 1920	—	£ +21,875,000
Nov. 8, 1920 to July 3, 1921	—	+ 100,000
Insurance years (July-July)		
1921-1922	£ −15,485,987	−14,959,256
1922-1923	− 1,206,958	−16,148,217
1923-1924	+ 9,038,750	− 7,093,871
1924-1925	− 1,363,411	− 8,441,690
1925-1926	− 2,426,408	−10,859,945
July 5, 1926 to March 31, 1927	−14,190,222	−25,050,167
Fiscal years (April-March)		
1927-1928	+ 422,184	−24,627,983
1928-1929	−11,384,064	−36,012,047
1929-1930	− 3,030,101	−39,042,148
1930-1931	−36,429,543	−75,471,691

Sources: *Minutes of Evidence*, pp. 157-61; Unemployment Fund Accounts, 1930, p. 5.

[40] In view of the many criticisms that have been made of the British system, it is worth noting that very little of this debt can be attributed to a lax administration of the prevailing rules. There is general agreement on the part of the various committees and investigating bodies that have studied the working of the scheme that the prevailing tests regarding inability to obtain employment have, in the main, been rigidly insisted upon, and that the alleged opportunities for unqualified persons or malingerers to obtain benefits have been exaggerated. See, for example, the conclusions of the Blanesburgh Committee, 1927: ". . . a certain number out of the 11 3/4 millions of insured persons have received relief to which they had no claim. But it is equally true that these cases are relatively few, and that result is, we think, due to the vigilance with which the Ministry, while dealing fairly with the genuine claimant, guards against abuses." (p. 20) "The Ministry is constantly on the watch for fraud, nor does it hesitate to prosecute when prosecution is called for . . . The Ministry leaves no stone unturned to bring every case to light." (p. 21) Details of the methods used by the Ministry of Labour and the results of investigations into the working life history of sample claimants will be found on pp. 9-19 of the *Minutes of Evidence* of this Committee. The *First Report* of the Royal Commission, 1930-32, offered no opinion concerning administration, but the evidence of the Principal Assistant Secretary to the Ministry of Labour indicates that ample provision exists for checking benefit claims. (See *Minutes of Evidence,* December 9, 1930, pp. 15-25, especially paragraphs 143-47 dealing with safeguards against improper payment, and the evidence of the same witness on July 9th and 10th, 1931). The *Final Report* of the Royal Commission cited the "zeal and

The precise cost of expanding the insurance system cannot, unfortunately, be ascertained. Indeed, the officials of the Ministry of Labour have repeatedly held that it was impossible to know how much of the debt was attributable to these extensions of the insurance system. Nevertheless, as is explained in Appendix VII, the cost of the majority of the extensions can be estimated from existing data, and these estimates are presented in Table 5.

TABLE 5. ESTIMATED NET COSTS[a] OF EXPANDING THE INSURANCE SYSTEM

Date	Provisions	Net Cost
July 1921– July 1924	RELAXATION OF CONTRIBUTORY REQUIRE-MENT AND PROLONGED BENEFIT DURATION Uncovenanted benefits	£28,123,000
August 1924– April 1928	Extended benefits	38,437,000
April 1928– September 1931	Benefits in excess of 156 days	22,000,000
April 1929– April 1930	Transitional benefits	3,985,000
March 1930– October 1931	ABOLITION OF GENUINELY-SEEKING-WORK CLAUSE	5,000,000
January 1926– June 1929	INCREASES IN BENEFIT RATES AND RE-DUCTIONS IN CONTRIBUTIONS	15,370,000
April 1930– September 1931	INCREASES IN BENEFIT RATES AND RE-DUCTIONS IN CONTRIBUTIONS	6,483,000
	Total	£119,398,000

[a] By net cost is meant that part of the cost of the various changes which was not met by corresponding changes in contributions (including the regular government contribution). A detailed explanation of the figures will be found in Appendix VII.

The figures in this table indicate that the cost of those items alone for which estimates can be made exceeded the total deficit of the Unemployment Fund in the fall of 1931. Thus it seems not unreasonable to conclude that, had the insurance system been restricted as originally planned, the Fund would have shown a surplus by 1931 instead of a deficit.

efficiency with which the officers of the Ministry of Labour perform the various duties falling to them in the course of the administration of the Unemployment Insurance and the Labour Exchanges Acts" as "deserving of the highest praise." (p. 306)

The existence of this debt had particularly unfortunate consequences. The difficulty of distributing responsibility for it between standard restricted insurance and the emergency extensions led to a loss of prestige for the entire insurance system. The British experience was frequently cited, especially in the United States during the early 1930's, to support the view that unemployment was not an insurable risk and even that unemployment insurance was an undesirable institution. Few of the critics of the growing debt distinguished between a restricted and an expanded system. Discussion of unemployment insurance centered around the question of how best to ensure solvency. When a Royal Commission was appointed in December 1930 to inquire into the provisions and working of the insurance scheme, its approach to the problem was very largely dominated by the desire to ensure a return to solvency.[41] Even while some of the recommendations of its *First Report* were under consideration, another committee (the Committee on National Expenditure), which was appointed to survey the entire field of government expenditures, directed special attention to the debt of the Unemployment Fund and proposed economies more drastic than those suggested by the Royal Commission.[42] The report of this Committee carried great weight, and many of its proposals in regard to unemploy-

---

[41] The Commission was authorized to make recommendations with regard to (1) its future scope, the provisions which it should contain, and *the means by which it may be made solvent and self-supporting* (author's italics), and (2) the arrangements which should be made outside the scheme for the unemployed who are capable of and available for work. Its *First Report* in June 1931 was concerned exclusively with financial adjustments, especially the increasing indebtedness of the Unemployment Fund, "matters which have been represented to us as urgent" (p. 6). But even the *Final Report* in 1932 bears the imprint of the preoccupation with the debt question, as was pointed out in the dissenting Minority Report (see especially pp. 384-88). The emphasis upon keeping the Fund solvent is evident throughout the section dealing with the future of the insurance scheme (pp. 155-62) and in the major proposal (subsequently embodied in legislation) for the appointment of a Statutory Committee charged with the duty of keeping the unemployment insurance scheme constantly under review, and of suggesting changes in the scheme which would maintain its finances upon a sound basis (pp. 163-71). The Majority Report stated specifically that "our terms of reference are directed primarily to the provisions of the Unemployment Insurance Scheme and to its future solvency." (p. 1)

[42] "We regret that we cannot regard their [the Commission's] recommendations as adequate to meet the situation. In our view a large reduction in the present Exchequer charge, as well as the practical elimination of borrowing for this service, are essential." (*Report of the Committee on National Expenditure,* July 24, 1931 [Cmd. 3920], p. 147)

ment insurance were embodied in the orders issued under the National Economy Act of September 1931. Thus, the sharp departure from the principle of indefinite extensions of insurance, brought about by the Orders in Council of October 1931, was a direct outcome of a panic-like concern over the insolvency of the Unemployment Fund, rather than of any careful analysis of the proper place of an insurance plan in the total relief system, or of the appropriate levels of insurance benefits.[43]

THE APPROPRIATENESS OF THE ASSISTANCE PROVIDED

Maintenance of the Unemployed

If the major function of an unemployment relief system, whether called insurance or by any other name, is the avoidance of suffering due to loss of wage income, there can be little doubt that the methods adopted in Great Britain between 1920 and 1931 achieved a large measure of success. An unprecedentedly high number of unemployed persons were maintained at a standard which, if not generous, at least provided a minimum of subsistence for the great majority,[44] and for some of the lower paid workers compared favorably with wages while in employment. Despite the severity of post-war unemployment, all the surveys of standards of living indicate that there has been a definite decline in the proportion of the population living at or below the

[43] For a further discussion of these orders, see Chapter V.

[44] In the study by Helen F. Hohman, *The Development of Social Insurance and Minimum Wage Legislation in Great Britain,* the rates of benefit payable to a family of five and to single women are compared with the corresponding Rowntree poverty line and the human needs standard, and it is shown that for these groups benefits fell short of both standards, although less markedly so in the later years of the period 1919-31 (pp. 262-64). It must, however, be recalled that households of these types were not numerically the most significant, and that, as is shown later in this chapter, the proportion of insurance beneficiaries who found it necessary to obtain supplementary poor law assistance was always very small, and at the end of the period was insignificant.

As a result of intensive studies among the unemployed, E. Wight Bakke in his book, *The Unemployed Man* (New York: E. P. Dutton & Co., 1934), concludes that the scheme "has alleviated the worst physical effects of unemployment. It has kept the diet from falling to unhealthful levels; it has kept workers from falling in arrears on their rent; it has made it unnecessary to dispose of home furnishings to the extent which would have been necessary without it; it has to some extent made it possible for men and women to keep up their associations with their fellows longer." (p. 251)

poverty level in comparison with the pre-war period.[45] The records reveal no cases of mass suffering attributable to the absence of any kind of assistance,[46] such as were reported to the various Senate committees of the United States Congress between 1931 and 1933. Had such cases occurred, it is fairly certain that they would have received publicity, for throughout the period from 1921 to 1931 unemployment relief was a major concern of the politically powerful Labour Party. The manifestos and the parliamentary questions of the Party did indeed constantly contain criticism of the prevailing levels of benefit and conditions for its receipt, and demands for expanding the insurance system in order to avoid recourse to the poor law. But there was no suggestion that at any time during this period the unemployed were left without any assistance whatsoever.

Training for the Insured Unemployed

Unfortunately, however, the needs of the unemployed are not limited to maintenance. Prolonged unemployment such as was characteristic of the British situation in the 1920's creates a need for social action to replace the values destroyed by loss of work opportunity.[47] Industrial skills and adaptability, the worker's self-

[45] Cf., for example, A. L. Bowley and Margaret H. Hogg, *Has Poverty Diminished?* (London: P. S. King and Son, 1925); *The New Survey of London Life and Labour* (London: P. S. King and Son, 9 vols., 1930-35); Percy Ford, *Work and Wealth in a Modern Port* (London: George Allen and Unwin, 1934); and the *Social Survey of Merseyside* (Liverpool: University Press, 1934). A summary of the results of these investigations concludes: "That the proportion unemployed can show such a phenomenal increase over what it was at the end of the last century, and that at the same time the number in poverty can show, even in the worst areas and at the worst time, such a considerable reduction, is due, of course, to the establishment of an Unemployment Insurance system. That the number in poverty varies still so greatly in accordance with the extent and duration of unemployment points to the limitations of this system." (Gertrude Williams, *The State and the Standard of Living* [London: P. S. King and Son, 1936], pp. 314-15)

[46] Even when the West Ham poor law union was completely without funds in September 1925, because of a difference of opinion between the guardians and the Ministry of Health as to the standards of relief, the unemployed did not suffer, as the Minister took the "unprecedented step" of making direct orders for payments in kind. (Ministry of Health, *Annual Report, 1925-26*, p. 113)

[47] Measures of duration of unemployment during this period are scarce. On the basis of sample studies in September 1929 and February 1931, Sir William

respect and morale, and even his physical fitness are alike endangered when unemployment lasts more than a few months.[48] Measures to counteract these undesirable consequences of unemployment might take the form of training programs to maintain or create skills, reconditioning centers to restore physical fitness and renew habits of work and discipline, or public works, work relief programs or other special schemes to provide an opportunity for employment under conditions which at least approximate those of private industry. The relative insignificance of such measures is indeed the most serious deficiency of the unemployment programs operating between 1921 and 1931.

It is true that provision was made in the insurance acts for the institution of training schemes, and certain programs were inaugurated during this period. These included Government Training Centers giving technical training to men mainly between 18 and 35 years of age; Transfer Instructional Centers providing general reconditioning and unskilled work for men over 18 years of age, training courses for women, and courses of instruction for juveniles under 18, operated mainly by local education authorities.[49]

Beveridge has estimated that the numbers and percentages out of work for different periods were as follows:

Period since last registered employment	September 1929 Benefit claimants	Per cent	February 1931 Benefit claimants	Per cent
Total (men and women)	966,800	100.0	2,350,800	100.0
Less than 3 months	758,800	78.5	1,436,000	61.1
3 months, but less than 6	102,900	10.6	431,400	18.3
6 months, but less than 9	37,250	3.8	227,200	9.7
9 months, but less than 12	22,750	2.4	138,200	5.9
12 months and over	45,100	4.7	118,000	5.0

Source: W. H. Beveridge, "An Analysis of Unemployment," *Economica*, February, 1937, p. 4.

These figures, however, under-estimate the extent of long-continued unemployment since, although short spells of employment lasting not more than 3 days have been disregarded, any period of work longer than this breaks the continuity of registration. Hence, as Sir William points out, "some of those who at any given date appear as having been out of work for less than three months may, within the last year, have had far more unemployment than employment." (p. 2) A somewhat better picture of the incidence of loss of work opportunity is afforded by the figures given in Appendix Table II, col. 3, which indicate that, on different dates between June 1930 and September 1931, there were between 323,000 and 502,000 benefit recipients who could show less than 30 contributions in the 2 years preceding their claim for benefit.

[48] For a penetrating analysis of the effects of unemployment upon workers, see Bakke, *op. cit.* See also Ronald C. Davison, *The Unemployed* (London: Longmans, Green and Co., 1929), pp. 190-200.

[49] See Appendix VIII, Table XII. In addition there were, prior to 1929, special overseas training courses for men, women and juveniles. The courses

Although the Ministry of Labour had administered training schemes for disabled ex-service men since 1915, no special courses for unemployed men were instituted until the winter of 1925-26, when two Government Training Centers were opened. These were to provide young men who had no opportunity of learning a skilled trade with certain minimum technical equipment and familiarity with workshop practices and discipline. In 1927 new centers were set up to permit the extension of the scheme to men from the depressed mining districts, and as the new centers were deliberately placed in areas of expanding activity, special allowances in addition to unemployment benefits were paid to the trainees. There was increased emphasis upon the institution of training centers as an integral part of the general program to transfer workers to areas of greater opportunity after the report of the Industrial Transference Board in July 1928 had stressed this function of training. But although the training provisions were expanded and the field of recruitment broadened, only 10 centers with accommodations for 3,770 men were in operation by January 1931, while only 24,726 men had been admitted since the centers opened. Less than 9,000 men were accepted for training during the year 1930, a negligible figure in comparison with the total number of unemployed in that year—1.7 to 2.5 millions.

There is, however, considerable evidence that, within the limits set by the duration of the courses (normally 5 to 6 months), the technical training and facilities were excellent, and the original objective—to turn out "handymen" or learners—was achieved with a considerable measure of success.[50] The proportion of workers completing the courses in any year who were subsequently placed in employment was relatively high—reaching nearly 93 per cent in the calendar year 1929.

The relatively small number of workers benefiting from these training centers was in large measure due to the belief of the

for men gave 12 weeks of training in agricultural work at certain farm centers, while those for women gave domestic training. Boys received training to fit them for farm work overseas. After 1929, the restriction of assisted migration by the Dominions led to the abandonment of the schemes. The numbers affected were never significant. In all only 10,497 men entered and 8,719 completed training, while 1,165 women and 924 boys completed training and left for employment overseas. (*Minutes of Evidence*, pp. 417-18)

[50] For a more detailed account of the operation of the training centers, see Davison, *op. cit.*, pp. 222-30.

Ministry of Labour that facilities for training should be limited
to the opportunities for placement—a view which was supported
by drawing attention to the relative costliness of training, and to
the bad psychological effect on future recruitment of the presence
of men who had undergone training but were still unable to find
employment. To some extent also the hostility and suspicion of
trade unions (by making placement of the trainees more difficult),
in view of the general attitude of the Ministry, inhibited the expansion of courses.[51] The fact that, between 1925 and 1931, the
training program was visualized as a method of implementing
geographical transfer, further limited the extent to which opportunities for training were made available to or could be utilized
by all interested workers. For, on the one hand, recruitment during the greater part of the time was confined to the depressed
areas,[52] and on the other, since the ultimate objective was geographical transference, the centers were placed in areas of expanding industrial activity which involved absence from home during
training. This created both personal and economic difficulties
which were not entirely overcome by the additional allowances
made available by the Ministry after 1929.[53]

The failure of the Government Training Centers to benefit
more than a small and very carefully selected section of the unemployed—the trainees were often referred to by Ministry
officials as the cream of the unemployed—led to the creation of a
second type of training center, the Transfer Instructional Center,
in 1929. These centers aimed to provide 8 to 12 weeks of reconditioning for workers between the ages of 18 and 35 whose record
of employment was so poor that direct transfer to even unskilled
work was scarcely feasible, and who were unsuitable for the more
elaborate courses given in the Government Training Centers.[54]

[51] Cf. *Ibid.*, p. 231.
[52] At the beginning of 1931, 90 per cent of the trainees came from the areas
scheduled as depressed and the five counties of Lanark, Northumberland, Durham, Monmouth and Glamorgan. (*Minutes of Evidence*, p. 410)
[53] Until 1929, the courses were composed almost wholly of young single men.
Although special allowances were thereafter paid to married men, their effectiveness was in part counteracted by the housing shortage which made it difficult for
the trainee to find accommodation for his family in the new area when he
obtained a job. Hence, the number of married men admitted to training was
strictly limited. (*Loc. cit.*)
[54] The greater part of the work consisted in roadbuilding, ditch digging, tree
clearance, forestry with a certain amount of indoor instruction in rough carpen-

The Transfer Instructional Centers, which were mainly residential, were placed in districts away from the men's homes in order to accustom them while in training to new surroundings. Men who showed aptitude in these courses could subsequently graduate to a Government Training Center.[55] At first the courses, as their name indicates, were conceived of as part of the transference program and their development was to a considerable extent governed by the limits of probable placement.[56] But from March 1930, when there was a growing realization of the demoralizing effects of long-continued unemployment, the program was expanded, and as is indicated later, pressure was brought to bear on workers to attend the courses, and the number of courses was increased.

Yet, although the development of the Transfer Instructional Centers was more rapid than that of the Training Centers, only 10 centers with accommodation for 1,880 men were in existence by the end of 1930, while the average number in training in the last quarter was 1,365. This figure should be compared with the 383,-000 adult benefit recipients at that time who had had less than 30 weeks of work in the preceding 2 years. The centers were not even used to full capacity, while the number who did not complete training was also great. Of 13,404 workers admitted to the courses by the end of 1930, 3,516 had been dismissed or had voluntarily left the center. Clearly the opportunities for work, training or reconditioning during the period the insurance system was expanded were sadly out of proportion to the numbers of the unemployed.

The provision for women was, if anything, even less satisfactory. Women's training had been carried on by the Ministry of Labour since 1919. In 1921 formal responsibility for training unemployed women was undertaken by the Central Committee on Women's Training and Employment, a semi-independent body

---

try, boot and shoe repairing and elementary metal work. Some ordinary educational courses were given and considerable emphasis was placed on physical exercises and games.

[55] By the end of 1930, only about 300 out of 13,404 admitted to the courses were thus transferred. (See Appendix Table XII)

[56] In view of the difficulty of finding other than heavy manual work for the ex-trainees, the number of men not physically suitable for this type of work who were admitted to training was, in the words of the Ministry, "strictly limited." (*Minutes of Evidence*, p. 412)

7

attached to the Ministry and receiving funds from it. The Committee provided Home Training Centers for training in domestic work, and an individual Vocational Training Scheme for special types of work in which women are normally employed. The former of these has been by far the most important. Training was given to women between 16 and 45 years of age, and in the main the centers were set up in the areas where unemployment was heaviest.[57] Not until 1930 was a residential center set up with the object of accustoming the women to living away from home. Specials courses for waitresses and cooks were developed in some areas, while in two cities non-vocational courses for older women between 35 and 45 were conducted. As with the men's courses, however, the numbers affected were small. By the end of 1930 not more than 50,000 women had received training since the work of the Committee began. During the year 1930, only 1,958 adults and 1,957 juveniles under 18 entered the courses, while the total number in attendance during a given week in December 1930 was only 1,225.[58]

The Individual Vocational Training Scheme, although more ambitious, was even less important numerically. For reasons of economy, the scheme was entirely suspended between June 1926 and April 1930, and during the remainder of the latter year only 200 women received grants to undertake training.[59]

Even the training for juveniles, which was provided throughout the period 1921-31, cannot be said to have made a great contribution to the problem of unemployed youth. The insurance officers, although empowered to require attendance on the part of young benefit claimants below the age of 18, could do so only where facilities for training existed. Until 1930 responsibility for setting up instruction centers for juveniles lay with the local educational authorities. Arrangements were made for financial assistance, originally from the central educational authorities and later

---

[57] In areas of especially heavy unemployment, girls between 15 and 16 were also admitted.

[58] *Ibid.*, p. 415. Courses lasted 13 weeks for adults and up to 17 weeks for juveniles. In the residential centers, more intensive training was given for from 8 to 10 weeks. The curriculum included cookery, housekeeping, laundry and needle-work.

[59] *Ibid.*, p. 416. By December 1930, only 42 women were in training. (*Final Report,* p. 333)

by a direct grant from the Treasury,[60] but these arrangements were temporary and provisional and occasionally lapsed,[61] while the initiative in any case rested with the local authorities. Hence, in many areas no courses were available.

In 1930 it became a statutory obligation of the Minister of Labour to promote the establishment of Junior Instruction Centers or Classes by making the necessary arrangements (including financial assistance) with local authorities,[62] and to require attendance on the part of the juvenile benefit claimants where these courses existed. As a result there was, after 1930, a considerable growth in the number of juveniles attending courses of instruction.[63] In the last nine months of 1930, some 74,000 juveniles attended the courses and by the end of the year the average daily attendance had risen to about 16,400. But, as the Royal Commission pointed out, these constituted only a small portion of the 60,000 boys and 50,000 girls at that time on the registers of the employment offices and bureaus.[64] The numbers attending increased somewhat during 1931. Not only was the total number of courses disproportionately small in relation to the number of unemployed juveniles, but their geographic distribution frequently varied inversely with the severity of unemployment.[65]

The significance of the juvenile instruction or training centers is, indeed, even exaggerated by the above figures, for although the total numbers enrolled in the courses in any given year may

[60] During the winter of 1922-23, the Exchequer grant was equal to 75 per cent of the cost. From April 1924 the central government paid all of the approved expenditures. From April 1926, authorities with less than 3 per cent of insured juveniles unemployed received no grant, those with between 3 and 6 per cent received a 75 per cent subsidy, and those with over 6 per cent received a 100 per cent subsidy. In the following year the maximum grant was payable only where the percentage of juvenile unemployment exceeded 7.

[61] E. g., between June and September 1923. In 1927, however, the Unemployment Insurance Act permitted the Minister of Labour to draw on the Unemployment Fund up to 50 per cent of the cost of the centers.

[62] Where courses were approved, the Ministry of Labour gave a grant equal to 75 per cent of the approved expenditure for setting up and operating them.

[63] In areas where the numbers of juveniles did not justify the formation of separate classes, existing continuation classes, normally held in the evening, were recognized as approved courses for the purposes of the Act.

[64] *Final Report*, p. 317.

[65] In 1926, when the grant-in-aid was related to the severity of unemployment among juveniles, at least 5 important cities which had been prominent among the few authorities organizing courses at that time received no grant because their percentage of unemployment was so low. (Ministry of Labour, *Report for the Year 1926*, p. 74)

appear to have been relatively large (between 1924 and 1929 they varied between 42,000 and 60,000), the turnover was extremely high. The average attendance at the classes lasted only 3 weeks, and normally the amount of instruction was but 15 hours weekly, although some authorities arranged for attendance from 20 to 30 hours a week. Because of the changing personnel of the classes, it was difficult to arrange continuous courses or to develop a curriculum that had any real educational or character-building value.[66] The Royal Commission on Unemployment Insurance, while stressing the importance of work of this kind among juveniles, criticized not only the relative inadequacy of existing facilities, but also the quality of the work and the character of the buildings in which the courses were held.[67]

It is difficult not to conclude that the inadequacy of training facilities was a major weakness of the British unemployment relief system between 1921 and 1931. Juveniles were the only group for whom any serious attempt was made to provide something more than a cash payment, but, even here, the quality of their training left much to be desired. Moreover, this group was the one least seriously affected by the demoralization of long-term unemployment.[68] More or less permanent unemployment was concentrated in a group for whom, during this period, relatively little was done.

[66] Provision was usually made for physical training and organized games, for teaching various forms of hand work and, in the case of girls, home-craft, and for "informal instruction and lectures of a useful and interesting kind." (*Ibid., 1923 and 1924*, pp. 104-5) The instruction, in other words, was occupational rather than vocational.

[67] They also commented particularly upon the problem of maintaining discipline at these courses of instruction, and urged that the coercive powers both of the Ministry and of the superintendent of the courses should be strengthened. An evaluation of the work of these courses is made every year in the *Annual Reports on the Work of Local Committees for Juvenile Employment*, published by the Ministry of Labour. Sir Ronald Davison in 1930 also drew attention to the poor equipment and accommodations, the lack of security of tenure of the teachers, the absence of coordination on the part of local education authorities, and the failure to diversify the courses in accordance with the needs of unemployed youth in different districts. (Davison, *op. cit.*, pp. 239-46)

[68] A special inquiry into the personal circumstances and industrial history of a one per cent sample of the juveniles registered for employment in July 1925 showed that "most of the boys and girls were simply young workers of the ordinary type who had been unemployed for a comparatively short period. There was no indication of a large class of boys and girls verging on the unemployable who had deteriorated markedly in consequence of long periods of unemployment. On the other hand . . . there was a residue of difficult cases which in themselves constituted a problem of the first magnitude." (Ministry of Labour, *Report for the Year 1926*, p. 73)

An analysis of the reasons for the neglect of so important an aspect of the problem of unemployment relief, namely, the need for training and reconditioning, suggests that at least part of the responsibility was due to the adoption of temporary and emergency extensions of insurance as the typical method of providing for the maintenance of the long-period unemployed. The relatively limited scope of the Government Training Centers was indeed probably due to other reasons, the most important among them being the desire to limit the number of trainees to the estimated available placement possibilities, and the relative expense of the training.[69] But the paucity of the provision of less technical courses or temporary work programs cannot be entirely thus explained.[70] Even if there had been a willingness to spend more freely, it seems probable that the arrangement under which the long-period unemployed drew a form of benefit which was identified in the popular mind with insurance inhibited any great expansion of the training program for the group in greatest need of it, namely, those who were already too demoralized by long unemployment to volunteer for training courses. For, to the average worker and to the political groups that represented the workers' interests, the insurance type of benefit was differentiated from the alternative poor law relief very largely by the fact that it was payable as a right, and not subject to the coercive pressures commonly associated with the poor law, such as the performance of test work as a condition of assistance. Pressure applied to insurance recipients appeared to undermine the very basis of insurance and was bitterly opposed by the Labour Party and organized labor.

The Act of 1920 had indeed authorized the Minister of Labour to require attendance at a course of instruction as a condition for the receipt of insurance benefits. This power was, however, exercised only to a limited extent, especially in regard to adults. In 1930 this requirement became mandatory in regard to claimants below the age of 18. Between 1920 and 1930 juveniles were normally required by the insurance officers to attend courses, but

[69] Cf. the Royal Commission's *Final Report* (p. 335): "No solution of the problem of occupation and training is possible unless the community is willing to spend a good deal of money on this service."

[70] Even here, however, until 1931 the Ministry felt it necessary to keep instruction centers below their full strength because of the prevailing employment situation. (*Minutes of Evidence,* p. 413)

the effectiveness of the compulsory pressure was limited in three ways. First, it could be applied only where training courses existed and, as already shown, by 1930 these were lacking in many districts.[71] This obstacle became less important after 1930 when the supply of centers became more adequate. Second, many juveniles preferred loss of benefits to attendance at courses, while a ruling by the Umpire limited the effectiveness of the coercive pressure.[72] Finally, coercion could be applied only to juveniles entitled to benefits. As the school-leaving age was 14, while the Insurance Act applied only to persons over 16 years (indeed, benefits could not be drawn until the claimant was $16\frac{1}{2}$), a large proportion of juveniles were outside the control of the Minister. Attempts to bring the so-called "voluntaries" within the sphere of the training system met with varying but imperfect success in different parts of the country.

Coercion of adults was limited to the Transfer Instructional Centers and was not applied until 1930.[73] Even after that date it was applied only with caution because of fear of the public reaction to this pressure, and because the administrators of the insurance system feared charges that they were using coercion "as a dodge for cutting men off benefit." [74]

Even had the principle of compulsion been applied more rigorously, it would hardly have been sufficient to meet the situation. The experience of public assistance authorities, and later of the

[71] Centers in South Wales were not opened until the end of 1926. (*Report on the Work of Advisory Committees for Juvenile Employment,* 1927, p. 32) And the number was generally inadequate in the more depressed areas. Even after 1930 "accommodation facilities necessarily limited their number in certain areas." (*Ibid.,* 1930, p. 12)

[72] The Act of 1930 permitted disqualification for failure to attend courses without good cause. But, as the Umpire ruled that juveniles permanently excluded from classes because of misconduct could be disqualified only for the day on which the misconduct took place, refractory juveniles could continue to draw benefits without attending courses of instruction. (*Final Report,* p. 321)

[73] Although the entry to Government Training Centers was on a voluntary basis, once accepted a man was under compulsion to complete the course. The same condition applied to voluntary entrants to the Instructional Centers. As women attending training courses did not receive benefits but special maintenance allowances, attendance at a training center could not be required of them as a condition for the continued payment of benefit.

[74] See answers by the Principal Assistant Secretary to the Ministry of Labour, *Minutes of Evidence,* pp. 420-26, especially Questions 3528 and 3600. The courses were confined to insured workers and were not available to those who were disqualified. Thus, those refusing suitable work, for example, could not be given training likely to improve their morale.

Unemployment Assistance Board, has indicated that the demoralization due to long-continued unemployment cannot be counteracted merely by enforced attendance for a few weeks at a training center, on pain of losing benefit rights. More personal and continuous contact with the individual is essential. And this could hardly have been supplied by an overworked insurance administration that was under constant pressure from the Labour Party and from organized labor to confine its activities strictly to discovering whether the formal statutory conditions for the receipt of benefits had been satisfied.

Training and Work Opportunity for Local Relief Recipients

Nor, during the years 1921-31, were the public assistance authorities in a position to make good the deficiencies of the insurance system. The Scottish authorities had no power to set men to work or to require them to undergo training as a condition for the receipt of assistance. A few of them did indeed make arrangements with other local bodies to offer jobs at prevailing wages to relief clients, but in general the unemployed in Scotland who were aided through the public assistance authorities drew unconditional cash relief.

In England, the Relief Regulation Order of 1911 had required that outdoor relief should be given to an able-bodied man only if he was set to work and if the Minister of Health did not disapprove. But, as has already been mentioned in Chapter II, large scale departures from this principle, necessitated by the considerable increase in unemployed applicants, were tacitly approved. Despite the efforts of the Ministry of Health to secure a stricter enforcement of the regulation, of 631 poor law unions in England and Wales 277 had no able-bodied men in receipt of outdoor relief by the end of 1929, and only 195 of the remaining 354 had some form of test work, while in 13 unions some of the men relieved were employed for wages by the local authority, which received from the guardians a sum equal to the amount which would have been paid as relief. The bulk of the unconditional relief was concentrated in a very few large unions with relatively heavy unemployment. Not all of the 195 unions having some kind of test work imposed it on all the men relieved and those that did so were mainly the smaller unions.[75] For the country as a whole, it was estimated that of 70,000 able-bodied men receiving outdoor relief at the end of 1929, a little over 41 per cent were in poor law unions in which test work was in operation, but the proportion of these men performing work as a condition for receipt of relief was just over 12 per cent.[76]

The nature of the work and the conditions under which it was performed, however, reflected the fact that test work had been imposed not in the interests of the individual worker, but as a method of implementing a deterrent relief system. Relatively few attempts were made, save in exceptional poor law unions, to adapt the test work to the requirements of the individual or to utilize it as a method of training. The employment was almost wholly unskilled, involving generally gardening and unskilled agricultural work, woodsawing and chopping, roadmaking and repairing, while 21 unions still provided a form of work traditionally associated with penal employment, namely, stone breaking.[77] The inspectors of the Ministry of Health commented on the lack of variety and absence of educational value of the work provided, and on the apparent difficulty experienced by the guardians in securing appropriate supervision, while some expressed doubts as to its value in assisting men to obtain private employment. Among the men themselves, there appeared to be little criticism of the work itself, except that stone breaking was felt to be degrading, but there was considerable objection to the fact that the performance of work was rewarded not by wages but by the ordinary relief payment.[78] Only 5 poor law unions had developed centers providing physical training, and elementary instruction in handicrafts, wood work, boot repairing, etc., and most of these had by 1929 been in operation only one or two years.

[75] *Poor Law: Report of a Special Inquiry into Various Forms of Test Work* (Cmd. 3585, 1930), pp. 5-6. The 110 unions which required it in all cases relieved only 7,633 men, while the 85 which imposed test work in some cases only, relieved 21,381 men. The test was imposed on about one man in three, excluding men given "sudden or urgent" relief.
[76] Which, as the Ministry of Health put it, meant that the number on test work in the whole country was substantially less than the number of men relieved without test work in a single union (West Derby). (*Ibid.,* p. 7)
[77] For a list of the types of work and the numbers of poor law unions in which they were found, see *Ibid.,* pp. 8 ff.
[78] Only two of the unions gave a cash allowance in addition to the normal relief grant, although the majority provided free lunches or boots and occasionally both.

The failure more adequately and suitably to provide work opportunity and training for the unemployed maintained by the poor law authorities was due to several factors. Prominent among them was the prevailing tendency to regard this function as part of a deterrent relief system, a view which inevitably affected the spirit in which test work was administered. The small size of many of the poor law unions limited the opportunities of organizing suitable projects. Finally, the severity of unemployment in certain areas, and the fact that the expanded insurance system gave the greatest relative assistance to unions in which the burden was lightest,[79] resulted in an unequal distribution of the burden among the unions. Hence, in the words of the Royal Commission on Unemployment Insurance, "in some areas the numbers of able-bodied workers to be relieved is [sic] insufficient, in the opinion of the Authority, to justify the establishment of training arrangements, while in others the numbers are so large and the financial stringency of the Authority is so acute that training facilities cannot be provided."[80]

These underlying difficulties were only in part removed by two developments in 1930: the Relief Regulation Order of the Ministry of Health, and the transference of the poor law functions of the boards of guardians to the larger county and county borough councils in March of that year. The Relief Order of 1930 laid upon the new public assistance authorities the duty of making "such arrangements as may in the circumstances of their area be practicable for setting to work male persons who are capable of work . . . and for training and instructing such men in some suitable form of useful work and for their attendance at suitable classes in physical training or of an educational character." The change of philosophy from deterrent test work to treatment likely to benefit the client, was further emphasized in the Minister's circular letter transmitting the new order.[81]

[79] See pp. 58-62 of this chapter.
[80] *Final Report*, p. 331. The Commission was referring to the situation after 1930, but the statement applied still more to the situation before 1930 when the authorities were even smaller.
[81] "They should endeavor to classify carefully the applicants with whom they have to deal and to devise measures appropriate to the various classes. A primary objective should be to maintain the employability of those able and willing to work, so that when opportunity offers these men may have no difficulty in resuming their places in industry." (Ministry of Health, *Circular 1097*, March 28, 1930)

Neither the attempt by the central authority to change the philosophy underlying the provision of test work and to emphasize the importance of training, nor the transference of public assistance functions to larger administrative units, served to overcome the fundamental difficulty to which the Royal Commission had pointed.[82] In March 1932 only some 22,000 relieved men ordinarily engaged in some regular occupation were set to work or received work or training.[83]

Public Works Programs

The deficiencies of the insurance and public assistance systems in regard to the maintenance of work habits were not offset by the special works programs initiated by the government in 1920. For here too the results were disappointing. The highest number of workers employed on projects financed by the Unemployment Grants Committee at any time was 59,000 (in March 1931 when over 1,600 projects were in operation), but for the greater part of the period from 1920 to 1932 the numbers were relatively insignificant.[84] The grants to accelerate road construction as an unemployment relief measure also led to a relatively insignificant increase in direct employment. Expenditures under the 1920-25 programs reached a maximum in the years 1926 to 1928 when a total of between £6 and £8 millions was expended annually.[85] On the basis of the estimates made by the Minister of Transport, this implied an annual direct employment of between 12,000 and 16,000 men.[86] The 1929-30 road program, which resulted in

---

[82] That the failure to make suitable provision was not entirely due to the preoccupation of the authorities with their new public assistance functions is indicated by the fact that by 1934 there were still 26 areas with no arrangements of any kind and "there remain large numbers of unemployed for whom the local authorities have not made arrangements." (Ministry of Health, *Annual Report, 1933-34*, pp. 234-35. See also Chapter V.)

[83] *Final Report,* p. 331. Subsequent inquiry indicated that a considerable part of the work was still largely of the old test work character. The London County Council was, however, a striking exception to the general rule.

[84] Between July 1927 and June 1928, only 28 schemes were in operation. In July 1929 less than 10,000 were employed, and in July 1930 some 38,000. (*Final Report of the Unemployment Grants Committee,* 1933, pp. 10, 22. Cf. also Ministry of Labour, *Report for the Year 1931,* p. 27.)

[85] Annual reports of the Road Fund, Appendix 2 or 3. The method of estimating the additional expenditures of local authorities is described in footnote 4 of this chapter.

[86] At certain periods of the year the numbers were in excess of these figures. Thus, in September of each year the numbers employed were as follows: 1924,

additional expenditures after 1930, did little more than offset the decrease in spending under the 1920-25 programs. For the financial year ending March 1931, direct employment on these road programs cannot have been in excess of 16,000.[87]

The main reason for the unimportance of public works programs in the 1920's was the lack of enthusiasm for such projects on the part of the successive governments, a lack of enthusiasm, it should be noted, which was shared by many experts.[88] After 1928 there was increasing pressure for public works projects, especially on the part of the Liberal Party.[89] The Conservative Government took the unusual step of replying in a White Paper in which the various ministries defended their existing policy and attempted to show that the proposals were impracticable, while the Treasury asserted that the financing of the program would have serious repercussions on the capital market.[90]

11,879; 1925, 19,510; 1926, 18,249; 1927, 13,094. In December, 1928, however, only 8,689 were employed. (Hill and Lubin, *op. cit.,* p. 84) "Work for 2,000 men for one year for every million pounds spent is a maximum figure for direct employment on the roads." The Minister added that secondary employment might account for from 2,000 to 2,500 men. (Ministry of Labour, *Memoranda on Certain Proposals Relating to Unemployment* [Cmd. 3331, 1929], pp. 19-20)

[87] In 1931 the total central government grant for the combined programs was £5,727,319. (*Report on the Administration of the Road Fund,* 1930-31, Appendix 3) Local payments in that year are estimated at £1,150,000 for the 1920-25 programs and at £920,000 for the 1929-30 program, making a total of slightly less than £8 millions.

[88] Cf. R. G. Hawtrey, *Trade and Credit* (London: Longmans, Green, 1929). Even Sir Ronald Davison, who has been one of the sharpest critics of the passive unemployment policy of the government, joined the ranks of the opponents of public and "relief" works. "It is difficult, if not impracticable, for the State to raise the level of employment or to stem abnormal unemployment by inventing or expediting public works for the needy unemployed." (*The Unemployed,* p. 60; also pp. 44-62) On the other hand, Sir William Beveridge regarded the difficulties as practical, limiting severely the application of a public works policy, but not insuperable (*Unemployment,* pp. 414-15) ; while Professor A. C. Pigou ("The Monetary Theory of the Trade Cycle," *Economic Journal,* June 1929), and J. M. Keynes and H. D. Henderson (*Can Lloyd George Do It?* [London: The Nation and Athenaeum, 1929]) argue the case against Hawtrey and the "Treasury view."

[89] This reached a climax in the publication in 1929 of Mr. Lloyd George's pamphlet, *We Can Conquer Unemployment,* urging specific programs. Cf. also the Liberal Party's publication, *Britain's Industrial Future* (London: Ernest Benn, Ltd., 1928).

[90] *Memoranda on Certain Proposals Relating to Unemployment* (Cmd. 3331, 1929). In general the "Treasury view," which has dominated conservative policy in regard to public works, stresses the uneconomic character of the projects and discounts the "pump priming" potentialities of this type of expenditure. (Cf. Ursula Hicks, *op. cit.,* pp. 218 ff.)

During its short period of office in 1929-31, the Labour Government made some modest efforts to encourage public works.[91]

The general lack of faith in the value of work projects resulted in the imposition of rigorous conditions for grants and narrow limitations on the total sums available. The original restriction of the unemployment grants to areas where unemployment was especially heavy, a policy intensified between 1925 and 1928, not only cut off applications from areas which failed to meet the very high requirement of a 15 per cent unemployment rate among insured men. It also tended to confine the possibility of securing a grant to the areas least likely to be able to afford the luxury of public works, and in so far as they were characterized by declining industries, least able to justify new capital improvements. In these years the scheme was indeed practically in abeyance. The attempt to encourage the transference of available workers from depressed areas by increasing the subsidies to local authorities (in some cases up to 63 per cent of the total cost) who would employ them on projects (to the extent of not less than 50 per cent of the men required), met with a response that indicated the basic importance of the amount of the subsidy. Expansion continued after the Labour Government, through the Development (Loan Guarantees and Grants) Act of 1929, in effect made these concessions available to all local authorities without the requirement to accept transferred men, and relaxed the stringency of the test of severity of unemployment.[92] Further encouragement in July 1930 (taking the form of additional grants for all areas with heavy unemployment and the voting of a £500,000 fund for works in necessitous areas) again called forth a considerable response.[93]

[91] By expanding the road program, by providing more generous subsidies under the Unemployment Grants Committee, by granting £500,000 as a 100 per cent subsidy to necessitous areas, and by passing the Public Works Facilities Act in 1930 which was intended to overcome obstacles to the acquisition of property by local authorities.

[92] It was also found necessary in 1930 to modify the conditions laid down for receipt of additional subsidies under the 1929-30 road program in order to expedite the work (see Circular No. 334 from the Ministry of Transport, July 3, 1930, reproduced in the 1930-31 Road Fund report, p. 127).

[93] In the 6 months following the announcement of the new conditions, 2,344 schemes were approved, at a total estimated cost of £32,500,500, or over 17 per cent of the total authorized expenditures in the 11 years of the Unemployment Grants Committee's activity. (Ibid., p. 22) Between May 1930 and May 1931 the response of the local authorities to the relaxed conditions, which permitted grants for work on municipal and public buildings, was so great that severe conditions were soon reimposed, and finally the Labour Government announced that no new applications of this type would be considered.

But despite both the testimony of local authorities as to the economic and moral value of these projects and the evidence that, given adequate encouragement, they were willing to undertake them, the central government accepted the recommendation of the Committee on National Expenditure in 1931 that the grants should be substantially reduced and in no case should exceed 25 per cent of the overall cost.[94] At the end of January 1932 the Committee ceased to approve schemes, and with the lapsing in August 1932 of the Development (Loan Guarantees and Grants) Act of 1929, the program of centrally stimulated public works came to an end.

The Extent and Nature of Categorization

Although, as a result of the changes discussed in Chapter III, insurance benefits became available to a constantly increasing percentage of the unemployed, a considerable number of workers were still forced to rely upon the residual poor relief system. For the greater part of the period 1921-31, insurance benefits were, from the recipients' point of view, definitely superior in many respects to the assistance available under the alternative system. Standard benefits were payable without any test of need or obligation to perform test work or other service, and this was also true of "uncovenanted" and "extended" benefits between 1921 and 1928 (except for certain groups of workers to whom a modified needs test was applied), and of "transitional" benefits thereafter. After 1924 in most parts of the country insurance payments compared favorably with those available under the poor law. Justification for a division of the unemployed into two groups, one of which received preferential treatment, could have taken several forms. It might have been argued, in defense of the scope of the insurance system even as expanded:

(a) That, on the analogy of private insurance, the recipients of insurance benefits as contrasted with their uninsured fellow unemployed, had contributed so largely to the financing of the scheme that they were entitled to preferential treatment; or

(b) That the covered group differed so greatly from the group excluded in regard to their industrial quality as to deserve more favorable treatment; or

---

[94] In consequence, 1,330 schemes estimated to cost about £19 millions were withdrawn from consideration by the local authorities.

(c) That it was convenient (even at the risk of giving preferential treatment to the group affected) to provide for the majority of the unemployed by a simple and almost automatically operating relief system.

On the other hand, even from the point of view of the unemployed man, especially if his long-run interests are considered, certain aspects of the insurance benefit might be held to compare unfavorably with the other forms of assistance. For, at least prior to 1924 and in certain areas even in the later years, the money value of benefits compared unfavorably with those available under the alternative general relief system. And, as already pointed out, prolonged unemployment creates needs other than maintenance—specifically, opportunities for work and training. Moreover, for those who have become demoralized and discouraged by continued enforced idleness, some external pressure to take the first steps toward rehabilitation may well be desirable in the long-run interests of the unemployed man himself. Even so, the expansion of the unemployment insurance system so as to make it a more important element in a comprehensive and differentiated relief system could have been explained and defended had it been possible to show:

(d) That the lower benefits were justifiable because they were paid for a period so short that the worker could reasonably be expected to have resources of his own which would supplement the otherwise inadequate benefits; or

(e) That the needs of the group drawing insurance were such that they could be met by the payment of a cash sum, unaccompanied by pressures to undertake training or perform work in return for the assistance given.

Not the least serious of the consequences of expanding the insurance system so widely was the destructive effect of this policy upon the validity of all five of the arguments justifying the scope of the insurance type of benefits by 1931. The precise manner in which the force of each of these arguments was undermined is described below:

(a) The justification for more favorable treatment of the insured worker because he had contributed substantially to the cost of the aid received became ever less tenable. To some extent it was weakened by the growing share of the costs borne by the

Treasury contribution.[95] It was patently invalid in view of the disparity between contributions paid and benefits drawn in individual cases as a result of the relaxation of the contributory requirement and the increases in benefit duration. In the early 1920's benefits could even be claimed by some workers who had paid no contributions at all, as a result of the modifications in the contributory condition introduced by the Act of 1921.

The preferential position of those allowed to benefit from a system which, between 1928 and 1931, gave 74 weeks of standard benefit to the worker who had paid 30 contributions in the preceding 2 years, and which offered transitional benefits (the equivalent of insurance) regardless of need for 96 weeks to the claimant who could show 8 contributions in the last 2 years and for an indefinite period to those who could show 30 contributions at any time, could scarcely be explained in terms of any financial *quid pro quo*. The number of persons drawing unlimited benefits was probably relatively small.[96] But the disproportion between contributions paid and the benefits received by large numbers of the unemployed could not fail to provoke criticism, especially on the part of those who were denied any benefit at all by the application of what became an ever more arbitrary and meaningless contributory rule.[97]

(b) The second defense of the preferential treatment afforded insured workers became equally untenable as the insurance system expanded. It was possible to argue that the original limitations

[95] The percentage of income represented by the government contribution increased from 16.1 in the year ending July 1921 to 33.3 for the years ending March 1930 to date. (*Minutes of Evidence,* p. 149)

[96] Cf. *Appendices to the Minutes of Evidence,* Part V, p. 292. It was also estimated that, up to 1930, more or less continuous unemployment was confined to a very small section of the population, which could not have included more than 100,000 men and 3,000 women. (*Ibid.,* p. 245)

[97] An analysis of a one per cent sample of the insured persons as of July 1930 indicated that, among men insured before July 1921, the largest average number of days of benefit drawn annually (115) during the period of 1,036 benefit days between November 3, 1921 and the end of December 1930 occurred among persons who had paid from 126 to 150 contributions between July 1921 and June 1930, or an average of 15 a year. (*Ibid.,* p. 258) Among the men receiving transitional benefits on February 2, 1931 and who were insured before July 1921, the percentage who had paid no contributions in certain preceding years were as follows: in 1921-22, 11.5; in 1927-28, 23.5; in 1929-30, 39.8. (*Ibid.,* p. 288) For further details of the disproportion between benefits and contributions, see the analysis prepared by the Ministry of Labour for the Royal Commission, *Ibid.,* pp. 241-304.

of the scheme, which called for a minimum number of initial contributions and which adjusted the duration of benefit to the past employment history of the claimant, was picking out for preferential treatment the group of normally employable persons who had shown by their past record that they were seriously intending to gain their livelihood by labor (in contrast to the group of unemployable, casual or work-shy persons who formed the bulk of the able-bodied poor law clients in normal times).[98] But the distinction between the insurance group and the remainder, in terms of employability and willingness to work, became weaker when the ratio rule was virtually suspended, when the contributory qualification was relaxed or practically waived, and when the genuinely-seeking-work clause was abolished.

As pointed out in Chapter III, additional conditions were imposed on claimants to uncovenanted or extended benefits with a view to limiting benefits to persons who were employable but involuntarily unemployed. Unfortunately, however, difficulties in administering these tests in a period of heavy unemployment, and the general pressure to make insurance benefits available to as large a group of the unemployed as possible, practically nullified their effectiveness in separating properly insurable from other unemployed persons.

Much was left to the discretion of administrative authorities in administering the requirements that claimants to expanded insurance benefits should show that they were normally engaged in insurable employment and would normally seek to obtain a livelihood by means of insurable employment; that in normal times insurable employment suited to their capacities would be likely to be available to them; that they had during the 2 years immediately preceding the date of application for benefit been employed in insurable work to such an extent as was reasonable, having regard to the circumstances of the case, in particular to the opportunities for obtaining such employment during the period; or that they were making every effort to obtain employment suited to their

---

[98] Cf. statement of the Principal Assistant Secretary to the Ministry of Labour: ". . . if you want to ensure that the benefit is being paid to the right kind of individual, what is important is the payment of a reasonable number of contributions within a comparatively recent period." (*Minutes of Evidence,* p. 1219) This view of the function of the contributory requirement was also held by the Blanesburgh Committee.

capacities and were willing to accept such employment. No automatic line of demarcation relating to duration of employment was possible and the test cases tended to result in decisions favorable to the applicants unless there was positive evidence that the men had abandoned or refused insurable work, or were very obviously making no efforts to secure it.[99]

The administration of the genuinely-seeking-work clause, applicable to uncovenanted benefit claimants from March 1921 and to all claimants from August 1924 until 1930, presented difficulties for somewhat different reasons.[100] The administrative difficulties arose from the vagueness of the phrase "genuinely seeking work." Its strict application was generally held to be too effective and tended to throw too great a burden of proof on the applicant. The Blanesburgh Committee had stressed the necessity of making clear to claimants what they were required to do in order to satisfy the condition. This suggestion was held to be impracticable and no definition of the condition was embodied in the 1927 Act. The Umpire, in the ruling test case, had held that "the most important fact to be ascertained is the state of the applicant's mind." [101] But this was a peculiarly vague criterion. Because of the administrative difficulties and the unpopularity of the clause, it was, as already noted, repealed in 1930.

The failure of these efforts to distinguish between workers for whom expanded insurance was the appropriate type of benefit

---

[99] Thus in 1928, the Umpire (an independent authority to whom appeals from the courts of referees are finally carried) sustained the claim of a man of 59 who had been employed in insurable employment for 30 years up to 1921 but had not been employed since, even though he believed that the man's chances of obtaining insurable employment in the future were almost negligible, on the ground that the man was persistently seeking this employment. (Decision No. 1526 of 1928) In general "decisions given by the Umpire show that he is reluctant to attempt to lay down hard and fast rules in the case of persons who have been out of employment for a long time but feels it especially important to take all the circumstances into consideration." Registration at an employment exchange was not conclusive proof either for or against the applicant's intention to obtain a livelihood from insurable work. "The Umpire may require proof of personal efforts, over and above registration," but after the repeal of the genuinely-seeking-work clause in 1930, he required less effort on the part of the applicant than was formerly held necessary to satisfy this clause. (*Minutes of Evidence,* pp. 1197, 1224)

[100] For an account of the administration of this clause, see *Ibid.,* pp. 789-94, and *Report of the Committee on Procedure and Evidence for the Determination of Claims for Unemployment Insurance Benefit* (Cmd. 3415, 1929).

[101] Decision No. 1404 of 1926.

8

and those who could suitably be left to the poor law becomes more evident when the industrial qualities of the recipients of the two types of assistance are compared. For the recipients of transitional benefits appeared to be closer in industrial quality to the poor law recipients than to the standard insurance beneficiaries. A study of one-half of one per cent of the persons on the registers of the employment exchanges on February 2, 1931 suggests that, particularly as regards men, there was a marked difference in the industrial quality of those drawing standard and transitional benefits. This fact is the more striking when it is recalled that the numbers drawing standard benefits were swollen by a considerable body of long-period unemployed, since a person who could show 30 contributions in the last 2 years could draw benefits for 74 continuous weeks.[102] Even so, 77.2 per cent of the men receiving standard benefits were classified as having good physique, 20.8 per cent as fair and 2.0 per cent as poor, compared with percentages of 56.6, 34.7 and 8.7 respectively for the men in receipt of transitional benefits. The differences among women were not quite so marked.[103] Classification according to physical defects showed that among the men on standard benefit 85.7 per cent had no physical defects, while the corresponding percentage for recipients of transitional benefits was only 71.5. Among the latter group the proportion with bad eyesight was more than twice as large as that in the group on standard benefit (11.4, compared with 5.5 per cent).[104]

Furthermore, the difference between the groups was equally evident when tests of employability were applied. Judged by the placement standards of the employment exchanges, the recipients of transitional benefits were markedly less eligible than those drawing standard benefits.[105] About 28 per cent of the men on

[102] Of the men in the sample drawing standard benefits on February 2, 1931, 35.9 per cent had drawn benefits for more than 151 days in the year ending January 31, 1931, and 9.6 per cent had done so for more than 251 days. Among women the corresponding percentages were 37.5 and 11.1. (*Appendices to the Minutes of Evidence,* Part V, pp. 294, 295)

[103] 74.2 per cent of those on standard benefit were classified as having "good physique" as compared with 66.4 per cent on transitional benefit. (*Ibid.,* p. 271)

[104] *Ibid.,* p. 272. In the case of women, the relative positions were reversed.

[105] The Ministry of Labour divided a sample group into four categories: (A) suitable on all grounds for submission to a local vacancy, without exceptional features, in the applicant's occupation; (B) fully qualified for submission

standard benefit had served an apprenticeship, compared with only 18.4 per cent of those on transitional benefit.[106]

A detailed analysis of the comparative contribution record of standard and transitional benefit recipients supports the conclusion reached as a result of the personal examination of individual claimants. In the words of the Ministry, "The failure to satisfy the contributions test for standard benefit . . . must be related, at any rate for a proportion of those on transitional benefit, to a lower standard of qualification for employment, and not merely to the decreased opportunities for work in the last two years." [107]

But while there appeared to be a real difference in industrial quality between recipients of standard and transitional benefits, it is doubtful whether the distinction between the latter and those compelled to rely upon the poor law was equally well marked. The Royal Commission made specific inquiry of the local authorities on that point and the consensus of opinion was that little if any distinction existed between the two groups, either in regard to employability or in other respects.[108] The dividing line between those who could benefit from the expanded insurance system, and those who could expect only the less popular poor relief could not, therefore, be explained as corresponding to a real difference in industrial calibre. In fact, the employability of the beneficiaries of the expanded insurance system was more similar to that of the poor law clients than to that of the recipients of standard insurance benefits.

---

by industrial experience, but personal qualifications (age, physical condition, etc.) such as to make engagement doubtful; (C) personal qualifications suitable, but industrial experience such as to make engagement doubtful; and (D) personal qualifications and industrial experience were such as to make engagement doubtful.

The classification of the claimants in regard to these criteria was as follows:

Claims authorized for:	Percentage in group			
	(A)	(B)	(C)	(D)
Standard benefit (men)	81.9	12.3	4.1	1.7
Transitional benefit (men)	51.7	33.2	7.3	7.8
Standard benefit (women)	83.8	11.7	2.6	1.9
Transitional benefit (women)	68.2	20.4	7.0	4.4

Source: Ibid., pp. 272-73.

106 Ibid., p. 279.

107 Ibid., pp. 288-89.

108 Cf. Ibid., Part VII. While this inquiry related to transitional payment applicants, these were, of course, substantially the same group of people who earlier received transitional benefits.

(c) The third justification for the preferential treatment of the persons covered by the insurance system also hardly applied to the situation existing between 1921 and 1928. For, whatever its merits, it would be difficult to defend the arrangement on the grounds of the administrative simplicity of paying uncovenanted and extended insurance benefits.

In order to maintain the fiction that uncovenanted or extended benefits were still in the nature of insurance, their receipt was, as indicated in Chapter III, hedged around by certain limiting conditions, many of which were intended as a substitute for the abrogated insurance contributory requirement. The terms in which these new conditions were couched, and the provision that certain classes of persons, and in particular young single men and women, could receive extended or uncovenanted benefits only if hardship would otherwise be caused, necessitated an investigation of each individual case and usually also a personal appearance of the claimant before a committee. It was no longer possible to follow the more or less automatic and simple procedure which was adequate for determining compliance with the statutory conditions for standard benefits.

Because of the already heavy administrative burdens thrown upon the employment exchange officials by the severe unemployment of the time, the task of deciding these millions of claims was performed until 1928 by the local employment committees,[109] attached to the exchanges, before whom claimants had to appear personally. However, as claimants to extended benefits had also to satisfy some of the conditions applicable to standard benefit claimants, the existing machinery of the exchanges [110] continued to pass upon eligibility as affected by these conditions. All persons obtaining extended benefits had, therefore, to deal with two sets of authorities. Indeed, those recipients for whom the insurance benefits failed to provide maintenance had to come in con-

[109] These committees consisted of a chairman, selected and appointed by the Minister of Labour and three groups of representatives approximately equal in number and also appointed by the Minister. The first two groups were nominated by associations of employers and workers; the third normally consisted of persons representing neither interest.

[110] I.e., the Insurance Officer, subject to certain statutory rights of appeal to the local courts of referees and to the Umpire.

tact with yet a third authority, the supplementing poor law officials.[111]

The administrative work involved in passing individually upon some 25,250,000 claims between 1921 and the end of 1927 was formidable.[112] It was the harder because no formal rules could be applied; the law and the regulations used terms such as "reasonable amount," "would normally seek," "employment suited to his capacities," "making reasonable efforts" and "causing hardship." The employment committees formed sub-committees (rota committees)[113] on which the members sat in rotation, and to which persons not connected with the main committee were coopted. In some areas the pressure of work was so great as to require constant sessions of a number of the rota committees.[114] In 1926 it became necessary for the officers of the exchange to assist in interviewing applicants in certain over-burdened districts and for the committees to act on the officers' reports. The members of the employment committees received no payment for their work other than out-of-pocket expenses, and it is doubtful whether an arrangement of this kind could have been a permanent one, even though during their existence the committees appear to have discharged their onerous tasks with a high degree of conscientious efficiency.

Nor could this arrangement claim the administrative advantage of relieving the central authorities of responsibility for determining the conditions on which residual relief was available. The employment committees acted subject to the general principles embodied in the different acts and in the rules laid down by the Minister. To ensure uniformity of practice and to check upon the conformity of the decisions of the local committees to these rules, their recommendations were subject to test checks at more or less regular intervals by inspectors attached to the Ministry's Divisional Offices. Doubtful cases would be referred back to the committees or to the central office for a ruling. The Ministry was, indeed, finally and very reluctantly compelled, because of the wide

[111] The proportion of cases requiring supplementation, however, steadily diminished. See pp. 107-08.
[112] Ministry of Labour, *Report for the Year 1927*, p. 44.
[113] Consisting of at least two members. As a rule, a woman member was present when women's claims were being considered.
[114] *Report on National Unemployment Insurance to July 1923*, pp. 121-22.

variation in the local standards and the insistent demand of the committees for guidance, to define "hardship" and to draw up a scale of resources, the possession of which should lead to the disallowance of claims from young single men and women and other special groups.[115]

Even after 1928, when the grant of transitional benefits was not discretional provided applicants could satisfy the 8 or 30-contribution rules, it was still necessary to determine whether they also satisfied the two conditions relating to their normal type of employment and the reasonableness of the extent to which they had been employed in insurable work during the preceding 2 years. The adjudicating work was now performed by the courts of referees and it became necessary in 1928 to increase the number of courts from 79 to 141.[116]

(d) The cases in which insurance benefit fell below the amount available from the poor relief system could, during the period 1921-31, scarcely be explained as a consequence of the fact that the former was payable to the short-term unemployed who would possess private resources, while the latter was payable to the long-term unemployed whose resources were exhausted.

Insurance benefits were, as has been shown, paid ultimately almost indefinitely and at uniform rates regardless of the length of unemployment. They were thus either too high for the short-period unemployed or too low for the long-period unemployed. Even when a means test was grafted on to the system for certain groups of applicants for uncovenanted and extended benefits, it was not accompanied by any variation in the benefits paid, corresponding to the degree of need shown. For the employment committees or courts of referees could only grant or withhold the benefit; they could not alter its amount above or below the prevailing rates.

(e) It was also highly doubtful whether the needs of the majority of those who became entitled to benefits by virtue of the

---

[115] *Minutes of Evidence*, pp. 48-49, Questions 193 and 200. The earnings or income of a household from any source were ascertained and divided by the number of persons in the group. If the average income after deduction of rent fell between certain limits, the Minister was prepared to sanction payment of extended benefits. (*Ibid.*, pp. 817-18. Cf. also Ministry of Labour, *Report for the Year 1925*, pp. 70-71.)

[116] Ministry of Labour, *Report for the Year 1928*, pp. 66-67.

1922 Act provided that the Ministry of Labour should pay to the local authority, rather than to the applicant, any benefit allowed for administrative waiting periods in which the applicant had been maintained on relief. In later years the provision was extended to allow repayment to the relief authorities of the amount of relief given to clients who had been erroneously granted less than the full amount of benefit, and in 1931 to allow repayment out of arrears in transitional payments.[119]

But even more important in keeping double payments to a minimum was the fact that the insurance system operated so efficiently that, except for the early years when the changing conditions for benefits during the "special periods" threw an insuperable burden on the local offices and the local employment committees,[120] administrative delays have been relatively few. Payment was normally made on the day it was due. Between June 1922 and December 1931, total repayments to the local relief authorities for relief granted to persons subsequently found to be entitled to benefit amounted to only £1,161,270, or 0.2 per cent of the total amount paid out in standard, uncovenanted, extended and transitional benefits during the same period.[121]

Overlapping Between the Insurance and Relief Systems

It might have been expected from the account of the way in which the insurance system was expanded that there would have been a great deal of overlapping between the insurance and relief systems, taking the form either of frequent transferences between the two, or supplementation of inadequate insurance benefits by relief. Yet such overlapping, except during the early years, was surprisingly small.

A large amount of transference and overlapping between systems is not merely confusing and irritating to the unemployed; it also causes an unnecessary amount of administrative work and thus adds to the cost of unemployment relief. During the years 1921-31, transferences might have been caused by administrative delays, by the operation of the waiting period, by the regulations

---

[119] The most important cases concerned subsequent right to dependents' benefits and restoration of benefit rights as the result of an appeal.
[120] Cf. *Report on National Unemployment Insurance to July 1923*, p. 132.
[121] Ministry of Labour, *Annual Reports*, 1923-24 to 1931.

limiting the duration of benefits, by temporary penalty disqualifications from receipt of insurance benefits, and finally by the necessity of supplementing insurance benefits by relief.

(a) *Overlapping on Account of the Waiting Period*

Administrative delays have been, as indicated above, negligible. The waiting period was at no time long. It fluctuated between 3 and 6 days,[122] although it must be remembered that, even in the absence of disputes or administrative delays, the period of time elapsing between the filing of a claim and the first benefit payment was inevitably often longer than the legal 3 or 6 days.[123] Unfortunately there is no information concerning the extent to which transferences between the insurance and relief systems took place because the unemployed had no resources to maintain themselves during the waiting period. In any case, the relatively insignificant repayments to local authorities for persons waiting longer than the legal minimum period (as pointed out on the preceding page) suggest that transference between the systems on account of the legal waiting period must have been small. The local authorities testifying before the Royal Commission were, however, inclined to argue that a 6-day waiting period was excessive.[124]

(b) *Overlapping Due to Exhaustion of Benefit Rights*

Transferences between the insurance and relief systems for short periods on account of the exhaustion of benefit rights by insured persons have been more common, although on the whole surprisingly unimportant.[125] The operation of the ratio rule and the maximum benefit duration was, as shown in Chapter III, virtually suspended by a series of devices up to 1924, so that for part

[122] Until July 1921, it was 3 days; until 1937, 6 days; and thereafter 3 days.

[123] In Great Britain a benefit week runs from Thursday to Wednesday, inclusive. Payments are made on Fridays. Thus, under the old 6-day waiting period, a worker might register as unemployed on Monday, receive no benefit the first Friday and benefit only for 3 days on the following Friday. (Cf. *Minutes of Evidence,* p. 580)

[124] The National Association of Relieving Officers reported in 1931 that many of their applicants had been living, even when employed, on tradesmen's credit so that they virtually became destitute "within a day or so of becoming unemployed." (*Minutes of Evidence,* p. 755)

[125] No information is available to show how much transference was due to this particular cause, but it cannot have been large in view of the small amount of supplementation due to all causes, as shown in the last section of this chapter.

of the time continuously unemployed persons could draw benefits from the insurance system during the entire period of their unemployment.

From August 1924 to 1928, however, when eligibility was determined on the basis of the number of contributions paid in the preceding 2 years, a situation arose in which workers in one year might be entitled to insurance benefits for a period, then fall back on poor relief, and at the beginning of the second benefit year again become entitled to insurance benefits for a more or less limited period. These transferences of insured persons were considerably reduced by a series of regulations which, however disastrous to the finances of the insurance system, produced an arrangement that was administratively simpler for both relief and insurance officials and also less annoying to the average worker. Until 1928 transferences were kept down by the grant of extended benefits subject to certain conditions. Between 1924 and 1925, when extended benefits were not subject to the Minister's discretion, transferences became even less frequent, as is evident from Table 6 shown later in this chapter. After 1928 they were reduced, first by the abolition of any maximum limit to duration, except that which was implicit in the contributory qualification, and second by the grant of transitional benefits immediately upon exhaustion of insurance rights, provided a worker could show as little as 8 weeks of insurable employment in the past 2 years, or 30 at any time.

The fact that additional weeks of benefit beyond the legal maximum, and, as from 1928, the grant of transitional benefits, followed immediately upon exhaustion of insurance benefit rights is of the utmost importance. From April 1922 to February 1924, however, the additional weeks of benefit granted under the emergency extensions were not payable continuously, but, in order to emphasize their conditional character, were subject to a series of "gaps" of 1 to 5 weeks in which no benefits were payable.

Complaints were made by relief administrators to the Blanesburgh Committee, and by the Scottish Authorities to the Royal Commission, regarding the financial and administrative burdens imposed by these gap periods.[126] These burdens were all the

[126] See *Report of the Unemployment Insurance Committee*, vol. 2, 1927, pp. 96, 110. Precise statistics as to the effects of the gaps on the cost of local relief

greater because large numbers of people reached the gap at about the same time, and remained a responsibility of the relief authorities for too short a time to justify the employment of additional qualified staff.[127] This cause of uneconomical transfer from one system to another was, however, brought to an end by the abolition of the gap system in 1924.[128]

(c) *Overlapping Due to Temporary Disqualifications*

Precise measures of the extent to which temporary disqualification for benefits shifted insured workers on to the poor law are not available. A sample study in 1924 indicated that 6.0 per cent of the disqualified claimants were forced to resort to poor relief. In 1927 the proportion increased to 24.9. These figures, however, represented only 0.3 per cent and 2.2 per cent of the total number of insured unemployed persons in the respective years.[129] In a study of the subsequent history of 2,354 persons with disallowed claims in April 1931, the Ministry of Labour found that only 17 per cent of the sample had obtained relief, a large proportion being married men.[130] These figures, however,

---

are not available for England and Wales, as the results are masked by the co-existence of labor disputes and the absence of detailed breakdowns of the relief expenditures. In Scotland, however, during the first gap period, expenditures on relief to the able-bodied unemployed in industrial parishes rose from £22,449 in the week ending May 20, 1922 to £32,404 in the following week, and to £47,411 in the fourth week of the gap. In April 1923, on the occasion of another gap, weekly expenditures rose from £22,277 to £48,217. (Evidence of the Department of Health for Scotland, *Minutes of Evidence*, pp. 327-28)

[127] On June 6, 1922, 582,175 insured persons were serving a gap period; on July 31, 1922 there were 150,648; on October 9, 1922, there were 51,101; on January 14, 1924 there were 100,973; the following week there were only about 15,000. (*Report on National Unemployment Insurance to July 1923*, pp. 221-23; Ministry of Labour, *Report for the Years 1923 and 1924*, p. 131)

[128] A concession was made as early as July 1922, when the gap was reduced to one week, though it was later increased to 3 weeks. (*Report on National Unemployment Insurance to July 1923*, pp. 65-66)

[129] This conclusion differs from that of Helen L. Witmer in her article, "Some Effects of the English Unemployment Insurance Acts on the Number of Unemployed Relieved under the Poor Law," *Quarterly Journal of Economics*, February 1931, pp. 262-88, which states that "a considerable proportion of the unemployed insured persons looked to the poor law for support because they were denied insurance benefit." It would be more correct to say "a considerable proportion of the unemployed insured persons *who were denied benefit* sought poor law relief," if indeed 24.9 per cent is regarded as a "considerable proportion." This point was questioned in the *Appendices to the Minutes of Evidence*, Part III, p. 111.

[130] *Ibid.*, p. 111. In four-fifths of the cases, the inquiry related to a date at least 6 weeks after the disallowance of benefit. The proportions applying for

do not distinguish between persons temporarily disqualified and those whose disqualification is attributable to failure to meet some of the additional conditions laid down for the receipt of expanded benefits, where disqualification was tantamount to an "out of scope" decision. More than half of the sample studied in 1931 were in the latter category.[131]

The conclusion that relatively little transference between the expanded insurance system and relief was due to temporary disqualification for benefits is further supported by the testimony of the investigators who carried through the Ministry of Labour's study in 1931 regarding the public attitude toward the receipt of poor relief. As a result of interviews with disqualified applicants, the investigators in all except 3 of the 8 industrial areas studied found that there was a marked reluctance on the part of these applicants to apply for relief, even in those districts where the administration was sympathetic and the scale of relief generous.[132]

---

relief varied greatly with sex and marital condition, e.g., single men, 13.1; married men, 52.2; single and widowed women, 3.5; married women, 4.4; juveniles, 1.9.

[131] Disallowance of benefit because the applicant failed to satisfy the special conditions laid down for claimants to expanded benefits have formed a large proportion of all disallowed claims. During 1930 the failure to show that they were not normally insurable, and/or not normally seeking to obtain a livelihood by insurable work, accounted for about 153,000 out of 358,000 disqualified workers. (*Twenty-First Abstract of Labour Statistics,* p. 64)

[132] In view of the many assertions by witnesses to the Royal Commission that the attitude toward receiving poor relief had undergone a complete change in the post-war period, the findings of the investigators deserve record. The authors of the comprehensive *New Survey of London Life and Labour* had also commented upon the fact that large numbers "have come to regard the poor law as one social service among many . . . and appears to them no less honourable than the various health, education and insurance services—something to which they feel themselves equally entitled, and in particular, something to which they may turn when the benefits to be provided by those other services fall short of their needs."

Yet the careful case studies of the investigators for the Royal Commission found this changed attitude only in one area (Sheffield). Indeed, Sir Ronald Davison, who summarized the results of the study, concluded that it bore "ample witness to the very lively dread of falling on the rates [i.e., poor relief] which still prevails in most areas . . . The investigators found . . . many cases in which privation, amounting to destitution, was being endured rather than apply to the Relieving Officer . . . In the minds of the people, there is still a sharp distinction between the other social services, whether contributory or not, which give relief, and the Poor Law." (*Appendices to the Minutes of Evidence,* Part III, p. 112) And again, after commenting on the extent of hardship entailed by the mutual help rendered by other members of the family, he adds, "Undoubtedly it was this vicarious sense of pride or self-respect, which induced many relatives and friends to give support to disallowed persons in their time of need." (p. 113) This reluctance to apply for poor relief appears to have been

The majority preferred to rely on casual jobs, or on private assistance, mainly from other members of the family.[133]

(d) *Overlapping Due to Supplementation of Insurance Benefits by Relief*

Overlapping occasioned by the use of relief to supplement inadequate insurance benefits has also been surprisingly slight.[134] Each local poor law authority could decide for itself whether or not to supplement insurance benefits. Technically, if these were inadequate for maintenance (in Scotland) or for avoiding destitution (in England and Wales), supplementation was the proper duty of the local authority. In practice, however, as there was no uniform standard of maintenance or destitution, the extent of supplementation depended largely on the general social policy and financial position of each local authority, and more specifically on whether its general relief scales, if any, were above or below the unemployment benefit rates.

At first many of the local relief scales ran above unemployment benefits, especially in Scotland.[135] With the rise in benefit rates

---

but slightly affected by the spirit in which public assistance was administered. In four of the areas studied, where the relief scales were high and tests not severe, the percentages applying for relief were not far from the average of 17, while in Liverpool, where the local authority was relatively strict, the percentage on relief was the highest on the list. Changed attitudes toward the poor law appeared to exist only in areas of heavy and prolonged unemployment, where existence on poor relief had become the normal way of life for a large proportion of the working population. The reality of the poor law stigma, despite some "modification in the reluctance of people to have recourse to Public Assistance" in areas of prolonged and heavy unemployment, was also testified to by the Secretary of the Ministry of Health from his personal observation. (*Minutes of Evidence*, p. 315, Questions 2301-4)

[133] The report commented on the small part played by private charity. (*Appendices to the Minutes of Evidence*, p. 113)

[134] Supplementation consists generally of domiciliary (home) relief, in money or kind, granted to persons in receipt of insurance benefits. The statistics of the Ministry of Health include among supplementation cases persons who, while in receipt of benefits, are afforded "medical relief only," although persons in receipt of "medical relief only" are not counted in the domiciliary relief statistics published in the Ministry of Labour *Gazette*. (Letter to author from Ministry of Health, dated June 22, 1938)

[135] In Scotland the scales paid by the principal poor law authorities between 1921 and 1924 provided 22s. 6d. for a man and wife and 3s. 6d. for each dependent child under 16. The corresponding benefit rates in the same period were 20s. and 1s. (*Minutes of Evidence*, p. 328) In England and Wales only 20 of the 220 known family relief scales fell below unemployment benefits. (Ministry of Health, *Annual Report, 1923-24*, p. 91) But, it must be remembered that the relief authorities with published scales in England and Wales were in the minority and were usually the more liberal authorities.

in 1924, this position steadily reversed itself.[136]   From 1924 to 1926 the Scottish authorities were required to supplement benefits only if there were dependent children, and after 1926 they generally ceased to supplement. In England and Wales a similar development occurred.[137]   Supplementation of benefits by relief came to be the exception rather than the rule.

Even in those areas where local relief scales were above benefit rates, supplementation was not automatic. With the exception of some localities, mostly industrial or city areas,[138] supplementation took place only when there were exceptional circumstances.[139]   A very considerable amount of supplementation was attributable to sickness in the family, and a number of authorities appear to have confined their supplementation to medical relief alone.[140]

Between 1924 and 1931, the available figures for Great Britain indicate that the amount of supplementation of insurance benefits

[136] Thus, in Scotland, the comparative rates were as follows:

	Man and wife		Each dependent child	
	Insurance	Relief scale	Insurance	Relief scale
	s. d.	s. d.	s. d.	s. d.
1924-26	23 0	22 6	2 0	3 6
1926-27	23 0	23 or 24 0	2 0	2 0
1927-30	24 0	23 or 24 0	2 0	2 0
Since 1930	26 0	26 0	2 0	2 0

Source: Minutes of Evidence, p. 328.

[137] The number of known relief scales which were below benefit rates had increased to 90 in 1924-25, and to 113 in 1926-27. (Ministry of Health, *Annual Report, 1924-25,* p. 106; *1926-27,* p. 136)

[138] E.g., Birmingham and Manchester. (Cf. Hohman, *op. cit.,* p. 298) In 1932 the Ministry of Health complained that in areas such as Sheffield, Manchester, Derby and Middlesex, relief scales were high and unemployment benefits were supplemented despite the fact that either little work, training or instruction was provided for able-bodied recipients, or else little account was taken of household income. (Ministry of Health, *Annual Report, 1932-33,* pp. 193-94)

[139] The varying practices of the authorities are best seen from their own replies in 1932 to a query put by the Royal Commission on Unemployment Insurance on "the extent to which it has been found necessary to give relief to persons in receipt of unemployment benefit." (*Minutes of Evidence,* pp. 521-32, 560, 582-603; *Appendices to the Minutes of Evidence,* Part I, pp. 5-71. Summaries of some of these replies are given in Hohman, *op. cit.,* p. 297)

[140] A study made in 1931 by the Ministry of Health in 3 selected districts indicated that 50.6 per cent of the cases of supplementation were on account of sickness, and were not therefore directly connected with the fact of unemployment. In the remainder of the cases, supplementation was necessary because of the existence of members of the household not provided for in the benefit scales (15.1 per cent), high rent (2.6 per cent), and miscellaneous causes (5.5 per cent). 26.2 per cent of the cases of supplementation as defined in the inquiry involved "temporary relief pending payment of relief [*sic,* presumably insurance] or wages" and was not therefore supplementation in the sense in which the word is used in this chapter, i.e., concurrent receipt of benefits and relief.

with relief payments, although small to begin with, continued to decrease. On the basis of sample studies of persons claiming benefit on certain dates in 1923, 1924, 1927 and 1931, it appeared that those in receipt of both benefits and relief constituted 8.6, 3.8, 2.1 and 0.6 per cent of all persons with claims to standard or uncovenanted, extended or transitional benefits allowed at the respective dates. These represented 6.9, 3.2, 1.7 and 0.5 per cent of the insured persons registered as unemployed at each date.[141] In England and Wales, the monthly number receiving concurrent relief during the financial year 1928-1929 never reached 10,000.[142] A special return for Great Britain for the week ending February 7, 1931 revealed that 14,155 persons with 47,457 dependents received both kinds of payments *on account of unemployment alone*. This group represented less than 1 per cent of the recipients of standard and transitional benefits in March 1931.[143] It is thus evident that persons receiving concurrent benefits and relief represented a negligibly small and declining proportion of the total number receiving unemployment insurance benefits. Moreover, to the extent that supplementation took place, it was accounted for by a comparatively few localities.[144]

(e) *The Total Amount of Transference and Overlapping*

But, while the extent of transference between the insurance and relief systems attributable to any given factor cannot be shown separately, the fact that the total amount of transference was small and became almost insignificant can be supported statistically. It is clear from Table 6 that, between 1922 and the end of 1931,

[141] Ministry of Labour, *Report on an Investigation into the Personal Circumstances and Industrial History of . . . Claimants to Unemployment Benefit, November 5 to 10, 1923; November 24 to 29, 1924; April 4 to 9, 1927; Appendices to the Minutes of Evidence,* Part V, pp. 264-304.

[142] *Minutes of Evidence,* p. 298.

[143] *Appendices to the Minutes of Evidence,* Part II, p. 102.

[144] In February 1932, of the 145 counties and county boroughs, 18 which contained 37 per cent of the population of England and Wales accounted for 87 per cent of the total number of 24,981 families receiving supplementary relief and for £6,819 of the total of £7,853 granted to these families. (Ministry of Health, *Annual Report, 1931-32,* pp. 193-94) In Scotland in February 1931, 5 authorities out of a total of 55, accounted for 7,780 of the 8,729 persons receiving concurrent relief and insurance and for £418 out of the total of £504 paid to these families. (*Appendices to the Minutes of Evidence,* Part II, p. 98)

only a small proportion of unemployed insured persons in Great Britain were at any given time receiving poor relief. After 1922, apart from the exceptional strike year of 1926, the percentage never rose above 14.7 per cent, and from 1928 it declined rapidly, especially after the abolition of the genuinely-seeking-work clause in March 1930.

The figures in Table 6 include all of the types of overlapping that have been discussed, namely, persons who had exhausted benefit rights, those temporarily disqualified for benefits, persons

TABLE 6. PERCENTAGE OF UNEMPLOYED INSURED
PERSONS IN RECEIPT OF POOR RELIEF IN
GREAT BRITAIN, 1922-1931[a]

Year	March	June	September	December
1922	—[b]	22.1	17.5	15.5
1923	—	14.7	13.7	13.2
1924	—	12.1	8.2	8.3
1925	—	7.8	9.4	12.6
1926	—	25.9	27.7	12.3
1927	—	12.8	11.4	11.2
1928	—	8.2	6.7	7.1
1929	7.7	6.6	6.1	5.5
1930	4.4	1.7	1.6	1.7
1931	1.8	1.7	1.6	2.6

[a] Excluding dependents. Fairly definite data are available for England and Wales. The Scottish statistics prior to 1928 are estimated, as explained in Appendix III; also, because data were not reported in Scotland for June and December before 1928, the figures reported for the preceding May and following January of each year are used. The magnitude of the figures for June and September is due to the fact that the Ministry of Health then included in its count of insured persons in receipt of relief both strikers and employed persons, and these have not been completely eliminated by the procedures described in Appendix III.
[b] Blanks indicate data not available.

Sources: Appendix Tables I, col. 7; IV, col. 6; V, col. 6.

maintained during waiting periods, and persons concurrently in receipt of both benefits and supplementary relief. Moreover, because it has proved impossible to eliminate from the public assistance statistics of England and Wales persons who received relief for reasons other than unemployment (e.g., those employed workers in receipt of medical relief and those relieved on account of labor disputes), the percentages tend to aggravate the extent of overlapping.

The smallness of the percentages after 1928 is the more significant because, in consequence of the method of classifying public

9

assistance recipients, individuals might be counted as insured persons even though they had not been employed in insurable trades for several years.[145]

[145] A man was counted as an insured worker by the public assistance authorities so long as he held card U.I. 40. This was a card issued to unemployed insured workers on first reporting at an employment exchange and was renewed at periodic intervals for as long as the man continued to report.

The Anomalies Regulations, which came into effect shortly before the transitional payments system, aimed to limit the insurance and therefore also the transitional payment claims of certain categories of persons, mainly married women, seasonal and part-time workers, by applying to them additional and more stringent qualifying conditions. But in part the advantage to the finances of the insurance system was purchased at the expense of the local relief authorities who found that some of the disqualified seasonal workers turned to the public assistance system for support.[4]

In consequence, as is evident from Table 7, there was a steady increase in the numbers of persons who received public assistance on account of unemployment. In September 1931 the expanded insurance system had provided benefits to 86.9 per cent of the 2.9 million unemployed, while 69,000 unemployed workers were sup-

TABLE 7. NUMBER OF PERSONS[a] ASSISTED ON ACCOUNT OF UNEMPLOYMENT IN GREAT BRITAIN, 1931-1935

| Date | Estimated number unemployed | Number receiving | | | Per cent of unemployed assisted by | |
		Insurance benefits	Transitional payments	Public assistance	Central government	Local governments
		In thousands				
1931-June	2,720	1,949	427	66	87.4	2.4
Sept.	2,914	2,030	502	69	86.9	2.4
Dec.	2,708	1,345	762	101	77.8	3.7
1932-Mar.	2,715	1,248	864	124	77.8	4.6
June	2,882	1,320	945	130	78.6	4.5
Sept.	2,988	1,345	1,018	140	79.0	4.7
Dec.	2,830	1,200	1,039	168	79.1	5.9
1933-Mar.	2,889	1,190	1,063	180	78.0	6.2
June	2,545	998	996	165	78.3	6.5
Sept.	2,439	912	978	167	77.5	6.8
Dec.	2,313	854	936	192	77.4	8.3
1934-Mar.	2,291	857	905	219	77.0	9.6
June	2,179	871	817	203	77.5	9.3
Sept.	2,170	912	744	188	76.3	8.7
Dec.	2,172	952	728	222	77.3	10.2
1935-Mar.	2,245	991	730	197	76.6	8.8

a Excluding dependents.

Sources: Appendix Tables I, col. 8; II, cols. 2, 3, 7; VI, col. 3.

[4] *Ibid.*, p. 137. Disqualifications of married women did not appreciably add to the burden of the local authorities.

ported by public assistance. By the following December the percentage carried by the insurance and transitional payment systems fell to 77.8 and thereafter fluctuated between 76.3 and 79.1 per cent. Within about 10 months after the beginning of transitional payments, the numbers maintained by public assistance had nearly doubled and they steadily increased despite the decline in unemployment after 1932. By December 1934 the relief authorities were carrying 222,000 workers (and in addition their dependents), or more than at any time since 1922 (excepting only the abnormal general strike year of 1926).

These developments were reflected in the expenditures of the local authorities. Their expenditures for unemployment relief alone almost trebled between 1931 and 1934. (See Table 8.) In addition, their commitments in connection with the work projects under the Unemployment Grants Committee, the road programs of 1920-25 and the Trunk Road and Five Years' programs of 1929-30 involved increased expenditures during these years.[5]

Although the total unemployment relief expenditures of the local authorities were small in relation to the cost of the insurance or transitional payments systems, they became an important item in relation to the normal local budgets. In England and Wales, expenditures on account of unemployment relief alone (excluding administrative costs) during the year ending March 31, 1931 amounted to approximately £1,687,000, or 14.5 per cent of the total of £11,611,000 spent on outdoor relief of all kinds. By the year ending March 1934, they had risen to £5,407,000, or 32.4 per cent of an increased total expenditure of £16,689,000. (See Appendix Table VIII.) In Scotland, the corresponding figures in the same financial years (ending, however, on May 15) were £653,000, or 24.5 per cent of total outdoor and indoor relief costs amounting to £2,665,000, and £2,060,000 or 42.8 per cent

---

[5] While it may be held that in view of the emphasis upon useful projects in work programs the localities were securing a return for their expenditure, it remains true that the projects were instituted as unemployment relief measures, and would almost certainly not have been undertaken in a period of depression without financial stimulus and moral suasion on the part of the central government. Nor does the fact that a considerable proportion of the money for these projects was borrowed obviate the necessity of treating this expenditure as incurred with respect to unemployment, as the future borrowing powers of the localities were thereby curtailed and the repayment of loans was inevitable sooner or later.

of total relief expenditures of £4,815,000. (See Appendix Table IX.) The financial strain on the local tax system can be more clearly appreciated when it is recalled that in 1921 the total expenditure on outdoor relief of all kinds had been only £5,793,000 in England and Wales, and £1,307,000 in Scotland. Thus, although the transitional payments system undoubtedly saved the local authorities from what would otherwise have been an intolerable burden, they were still left to shoulder an unemployment relief bill which caused them serious concern.[6]

Transitional payments as a solution of the financial problems of residual relief had a further disadvantage similar to one already exhibited by the expanded insurance system. For they involved the assumption by the central government of responsibility only for persons who had been insured, and only for so long as these persons could show that they were still normally attached to insurable employments. Therefore transitional payments tended to give relatively more aid to the prosperous than to the depressed areas. For in the latter, characterized as they were by a large proportion of long-term unemployed, it became increasingly difficult for workers to show that they were normally employed in insurable employment and would normally seek to obtain their livelihood by means of insurable industry, and for new entrants to the labor market to secure even the minimum number of paid contributions.

Thus, while in England and Wales as a whole there were only 25.4 persons per thousand on public assistance, in depressed areas, such as the counties of Monmouth and Glamorgan in Wales and Durham in northern England, the corresponding figures were 61.0, 69.4 and 73.4, and in the county boroughs of Merthyr Tydfil (Glamorgan county) and Sheffield, the proportion rose as high as 114.9 and 115.2 respectively.[7] These differences were of course reflected in local taxation.[8] In 1934 the current public assis-

---

[6] They were, however, definitely better off than they were in the fiscal years ending March 1928 and 1929. By March 1934 the number of urban authorities in England and Wales with sanctioned overdrafts had fallen to 18 (as compared with 109 in 1928 and 60 in 1929). The number of authorities levying rates between 16 and 20 shillings in the pound had fallen to 67 (from 180 in 1928) and those with rates in excess of 20 shillings in the pound had fallen to 18 (as compared with 95 in 1928). (Ministry of Health, *Annual Report, 1933-34*, p. 207)

[7] *Report of Investigations into the Industrial Conditions in certain Depressed Areas*, 1934, pp. 90, 167.

[8] Of 67 urban authorities levying total rates in excess of 16 shillings in the pound in 1933-34, 44 were in the depressed areas. Of 18 authorities with rates

tance charges (which included necessary repayments of loans made prior to 1930 to meet deficits largely due to unemployment relief expenditures) represented a rate in the pound of 7s. 9½d., 8s. 5d., and 15s. 7¼d. in Monmouth, Glamorgan and Merthyr Tydfil respectively, while at the same time in certain other areas the corresponding charges amounted to as little as 1s. or even in a few cases 6d.[9]

Recognition of this unequal burden led the national government in the financial years 1934 and 1935 to make special grants in aid of distressed areas. An annual sum of approximately £500,000 was made available to localities in proportion to the heaviness of their outdoor relief burden, on condition that the grant was to be used for the relief of ratepayers and not to facilitate further increases in expenditures.[10]

Effects upon the Insurance System

It is evident from the preceding chapter that the main impetus to the changes introduced in October 1931 was a concern over the mounting debt of the unemployment insurance system. The Act of July 8, 1931 had set the maximum debt limit at £115,000,000, and the Order in Council of October 7, 1931 provided that any further deficits were to be met by non-repayable Treasury grants.

The effects of the institution of transitional payments upon the finances of the insurance system are blurred by three other factors: an increase in contribution rates, a reduction in benefit rates, and the persistence of a heavy volume of unemployment. Contributions were sharply raised in October 1931, so that the total weekly rate for an adult man was 30d. (the worker, employer and government each paying one-third) in place of the previous 22½d. The lowered benefit rates operated from October 8, 1931

in excess of 20 shillings in the pound, 17 were in the Welsh coal mining counties of Carmarthen, Glamorgan and Monmouth. (Ministry of Health, *Annual Report, 1933-34*, p. 207)

[9] *Report of Investigations into the Industrial Conditions in certain Depressed Areas*, p. 167. Cf. also Ministry of Health, *Annual Report, 1932-33*, pp. 161-162, and *1933-34*, pp. 235-36.

[10] The distribution of the grant among localities was agreed upon by the Treasury and representatives of local authorities. If a county or county borough in 1932-33 had incurred relief expenses greater than the sum yielded by levying a 2 shilling rate, it could receive a share in the grant proportionate to this excess. In no case, however, could an authority receive a grant in excess of the sum yielded by a one shilling rate. *Ibid.*, pp. 235-36.

to June 30, 1934 inclusive, after which the rates were restored
to their pre-1931 level by the Unemployment Act of 1934. Unemployment among insured persons remained over 20 per cent
until June 1933, and although conditions steadily improved thereafter, the percentage was still as high as 15.9 by the end of 1934.
These percentages were exceeded only during the early part of
1921, and from September 1930 to September 1931.

It is, therefore, not surprising that for the 18 months after
October 1931 neither the increase in contributions and reduction
in benefit rates nor the limitation of benefit duration to 26 weeks
sufficed to prevent the insurance system from running still
further into debt. Between November 1931 and March 1932 the
weekly excess of expenditure over income averaged £330,200,[11]
and was met by an increase of the debt up to the prescribed maximum of £115,000,000 and in addition a non-repayable Treasury
grant of £444,577. In the following financial year the deficit
(again met by a non-repayable Treasury grant) was only £6,363,-
377, and from June 1933 the system began to show a surplus
of income over expenditure. At the end of December 1933, the
Fund, after retaining a substantial working balance, was able to
repay £4,070,000 of the £115,000,000 the Treasury had advanced. By June 30, 1934 repayments of principal had reduced the
debt to £105,780,000. On December 31, 1934, after a further
repayment of principal amounting to £38,891, the Unemployment
Fund showed a balance of £10,527,185,[12] with the funded debt
standing at £105,741,000.

The full effect of the changes made in 1931 are, however, not
reflected in these financial statistics. They fail to show how great
the expenditure would have been without the limitation to the
duration of benefits in a period of severe unemployment. During 1930 the grant of unlimited insurance benefits to applicants
who could show 30 contributions in the immediately preceding 2
years had resulted in payment of insurance benefits to between
72.3 per cent and 79.1 per cent of all unemployed insured persons.

[11] *Report of the Unemployment Insurance Statutory Committee . . . on the
Financial Condition of the Unemployment Fund on 31st December 1934*, p. 20.
Hereafter referred to as UISC *Financial Report*.
[12] *Ibid.*, pp. 3, 18, 20. For an account of the funding of the debt accumulated
in 1921-31 and its segregation from the current Unemployment Fund, see
Chapter VI.

As a result of the limitations upon the duration of benefit imposed by the Order in Council of October 7, 1931, this proportion fell to a low point of 36.9 during the years 1932-34.[13] It is evident that had the insurance system been required to carry the same proportion of the insured unemployed as previously, instead of ultimately showing a current surplus it would have continued to run heavily into debt despite lower benefits and higher contributions.

Effects upon the National Treasury

Transitional payments as a method of relaxing financial pressure on local authorities differed from the expansion of the insurance system in that their entire cost was financed by general tax revenues. The costs of the insurance system, which fell largely upon employers and workers, were sharply reduced, but they were balanced by increasing expenditures on transitional payments which, in the year ending March 1934, actually exceeded insurance expenditures. Moreover, during 1934 and 1935 special grants were made to the distressed areas. It will be seen from Table 8 that the central government, through the two national systems and these special grants, carried between 91.1 per cent and 97.6 per cent of the direct payments to the unemployed. As transitional payments were financed entirely from general tax revenues, while even the insurance system derived rather more than one-third of its income from government contributions (when payments to cover the deficit are included), it is evident that during the period of transitional payments the greater proportion of the direct unemployment relief costs were paid by the central government.

In addition, new programs involving payments by the central government to the Special Areas Commissioners and the National Council of Social Service were inaugurated. Nor must it be forgotten that under the "derating" scheme of 1929 the central government was annually contributing some £22 millions to the local authorities in England and Wales alone to offset their losses from rates, and another £5 millions as an addition to the block grant.[14]

13 See Appendix Table II, col. 5.
14 See discussion in Chapter IV and particularly footnotes 21 and 22. Under the original settlement, which was subject to periodic revision, the additional money was set at £5 millions a year. The Local Government (General Exchequer Contributions) Act of 1933 fixed the annual amount for the ensuing four years at £5.35 millions.

Not all of this money was used to meet the costs of locally provided unemployment relief, but as at least part of the impetus to the derating scheme was attributable to the effect of the depression on local property values and local relief costs, some part of the grant must be regarded as a contribution from central funds toward these costs. Table 8 shows the distribution of expenditures for unemployment between the central and local governments.

TABLE 8. EXPENDITURES BY THE CENTRAL AND LOCAL GOVERNMENTS ON ACCOUNT OF UNEMPLOYMENT IN GREAT BRITAIN, 1931-1935

Year ending March 31	Central government[a]						Local governments[a]		
	Unemployment insurance	Transitional payments	Unemployment Grants Committee	Road programs	Special grants[b]	Total	Public assistance[c]	Road programs[d]	Total[e]
	In thousand pounds sterling								
1931	73,169	19,247	2,190	5,727	317	100,650	2,315	2,070	4,385
1932	80,310	30,742	2,985	8,309	161	122,507	3,559	2,508	6,067
1933	54,300	50,400	3,500	4,937	15	113,152	5,937	1,886	7,823
1934	40,310	48,442	4,000	2,244	550	95,546	6,882	1,292	8,174
1935	43,909	42,199	4,200	911	555	91,774	8,433	755	9,188

a Excluding costs of administration .
b Expenditures shown in 1931 and 1932 were for work in necessitous areas; in 1933, for National Council of Social Service, which also received £50,000 and £68,000 in each of the next two years (Ministry of Labour, Annual Reports); in 1934, £500,000 were granted to distressed areas; and in 1935, £28,000 were for the Special Areas Commissioners, and £458,500 represented compensatory payments under the "Standstill" Act (see Table 11, Chapter VI).
c The estimates for 1934 and 1935 are less than those shown in Appendix Table X because the central government's grant to distressed areas in 1934 and compensatory payments in 1935 have been deducted to obtain the net cost to local governments.
d Estimated in accordance with the method described in footnote 4, Chapter IV.
e These estimates do not include the local governments' share of expenditures for works begun under the Unemployment Grants Committee. The central government's subsidy varied with the nature of the project (whether revenue producing or not) and included contributions toward repayments of principal only in case of non-revenue-producing projects, the proportion of which is not known.

Sources: Appendix Tables VII, cols. 2, 3, 4, 8; X, col. 2; annual reports of the Road Fund; all other central government expenditures as reported in the annual Civil Appropriation Accounts.

THE APPROPRIATENESS OF THE THREEFOLD PROGRAM

Between November 1931 and January 1935 the economic and social position of unemployed workers depended upon whether they derived support from insurance benefits, public assistance, or transitional payments. In the first case they received a fixed sum which was payable as a right regardless of need, and which, for by far the greater proportion of beneficiaries, appeared to suffice for maintenance without recourse to supplementary aid from public assistance.[15] It will be recalled that those who derived support from public assistance were required to undergo an investigation of needs and resources. As a general rule, assistance was given in the home and in the form of cash. The standard of maintenance, and the extent to which applicants were expected to exhaust their own savings or the income of relatives which was deemed available for support of the client, varied greatly from locality to locality with the political and economic complexion of the district. Recipients could be required to repay public assistance should their circumstances subsequently improve, but this requirement was not generally enforced.[16] As explained in Chapter IV, able-bodied recipients of outdoor relief in England and Wales were supposed to undertake work or to undergo training or instruction, but relatively few of the local authorities possessed adequate facilities. In Scotland the local and public assistance authorities had no power to compel men to work as a condition for the receipt of relief. Yet despite considerable liberalization during the 1920's, the public assistance system was still regarded with acute distaste by the mass of workers who liked to think of themselves as self-respecting.[17] The belief that contact with public assistance was essentially degrading was fostered by the Labour Party and the Trades Union Congress.

From the point of view of the unemployed worker, transitional payments were a strange mixture of insurance and relief. They were available only to persons over 18 who had paid 30 insurance contributions at any time or 8 in the 2 years prior to applying for payments. When first instituted, the majority of the recipients were persons who had previously been drawing transitional benefits. Claimants had to report to the local employment exchange and had to satisfy the same requirements that had formerly applied to them as claimants for transitional or standard insurance benefits, and payments were made through the exchange. The maximum amount of the transitional payment was set at the

[15] See Table 9, page 128.

[16] Even so, between £319,000 and £369,000 annually was repaid or reclaimed from relatives of persons receiving outdoor relief in England and Wales during the years 1931 to 1935. (Ministry of Health, *Local Government Financial Statistics* [England and Wales], Part I)

[17] The evidence collected by the Royal Commission on Unemployment Insurance on this point is summarized in footnote 132, Chapter IV.

Transitional Payments as a Method of
Maintaining the Unemployed

Even if there had been no division of the residual unemployed into two groups, the transitional payments system had obvious shortcomings as a relief system responsible for the maintenance of the majority of the non-insurance recipients. First, it did not meet the objections of those who held that it was undesirable to bring the average unemployed worker in contact with the public assistance system. Second, the payments, being limited to the maximum set by insurance benefits, were not always adequate to meet the needs of the long-term unemployed. Finally, transitional payments, because they were determined by local standards, varied greatly from locality to locality.

The new system met with violent opposition, especially from labor groups, from the start. But it is difficult to disentangle the criticism directed against the imposition of a means test as such from that directed against submission to a means test administered by the ordinary public assistance authorities. It is undeniable, however, that the transitional payments system was marked by some of the characteristics of public assistance. In particular, all applicants and their families had to be investigated by the relieving officer or his subordinates, and frequently also to appear before a local public assistance committee. If it had been desired to perpetuate the view that recourse to public assistance was, if not degrading, at least something to be avoided as long as possible, there were considerations against compelling so many workers to come in contact with the system in order to obtain transitional payments. For it was inevitable that the supposed invidious nature of the contact should have become less obvious when so many previously independent persons were affected by it. And, having once been compelled to take a step hitherto regarded with abhorrence, it was likely that there would be less reluctance to seek public assistance in the future if this should prove advantageous (e.g., in seeking to supplement insurance benefits or transitional payments). On the other hand, if the official view was that public assistance was not in itself degrading (and there had indeed been considerable liberalization of practices and standards since 1920), there was little reason for instituting a separate transitional payments system midway between insurance and relief.

A relief system based upon a means test should presumably provide for the maintenance of those whose resources prove on investigation to be inadequate for the currently accepted minimum standards of living. Yet, however great was the need disclosed, the maximum transitional payment was limited to the amount of the benefit which would otherwise have been payable had the applicant been eligible for insurance. Those for whom this sum failed to provide maintenance were compelled to seek supplementation from the public assistance system, and frequently, because of the differing standards applied to transitional payment and public assistance applicants, to undergo a different type of means test, administered, however, by the same authority as before. This was confusing and irritating to the unemployed and to administrators alike.[24] Had the insurance benefit rates, which by 1931 approached a maintenance standard, prevailed, supplementation would probably have been confined to an insignificantly small group. Benefit rates were, however, reduced in October 1931. As is indicated in Table 9, the transitional payment cases receiving supplementary relief increased during the years in which the system was in operation. It is particularly significant that after 1932 the increase was

TABLE 9. NUMBER OF PERSONS RECEIVING BOTH OUTDOOR
RELIEF AND INSURANCE BENEFITS OR TRANSITIONAL
PAYMENTS IN ENGLAND AND WALES, 1931-1934

Date	Recipients of insurance and relief	Recipients of transitional payments and relief	Total supplemented cases[a]
Feb. 7, 1931	12,221[b]	—	12,221
Feb. 6, 1932	12,250	12,731	24,981
Feb. 4, 1933	11,101	27,782	38,883
Feb. 3, 1934	6,329	30,465	36,794

a The figures cannot be expressed as percentages of total recipients of each type of payment, because the breakdown given by the Ministry of Health relates to one specific day for which the total numbers of recipients are not available. Table 7 shows the total numbers at other dates.
b Includes recipients of insurance and transitional benefits. All figures exclude dependents.

Sources: Appendices to the Minutes of Evidence, p. 76; Ministry of Health, Annual Report, 1932-33, p. 189; 1933-34, p. 232.

24 Intensified by the fact that the areas of the public assistance committees were not, of course, co-extensive with those of the local employment exchanges. In at least one district (Glasgow), the local assistance committee set up special area offices to overcome this difficulty. (Appendices to the Minutes of Evidence, Part VII, p. 436)

confined to transitional payment recipients, i.e., to the group which by definition consisted of those unemployed for a relatively long time, whose resources were presumably approaching exhaustion.

But while there was an undeniable increase in supplementation, its extent even in relation to the total number of transitional payment recipients was still insignificant. That it did not assume greater proportions, despite the encouragement given to transitional payment applicants in some areas "to take advantage of any difference which may exist between the relief scale and the benefit scale," [25] was undoubtedly due in large measure to the fact that many local authorities, especially in Scotland, reduced their relief scales in 1931 to bring them into conformity with the lowered insurance benefit rates.[26]

Perhaps the most outstanding characteristic of the assistance available to the transitional payment applicants was the great diversity of treatment afforded them in different parts of the country. Within the limits prescribed by the regulations, the ministerial circulars and the Act of 1932, the local authorities were free to determine the level of income below which destitution was held to exist, and to define the household resources which might be set against the admitted needs of the family. Despite the impetus given to the publication of relief scales by many public assistance committees as a guide to their subordinate agencies, the tests of destitution and the definitions of available resources varied greatly from one committee to another and even among sub-committees.[27]

Thus there were wide variations in the sum which was held adequate to meet the needs of a man and his dependents.[28] Even more important were the differences which prevailed in the calcu-

[25] Ministry of Health, *Annual Report, 1932-33,* p. 191.
[26] Department of Health for Scotland, *Annual Report, 1931,* p. 144, *1932,* p. 137. By the end of 1931 only 2 Scottish authorities adhered to a scale in excess of benefits.
[27] Occasionally, as in the Tyneside area, local conferences between adjacent public assistance authorities were held with the object of eliminating unjust inequalities, but these seem to have been exceptional and not very effective. (Ministry of Health, *Annual Report, 1931-32,* p. 199)
[28] In cities near Manchester, the allowance for man and wife was 20s. in Manchester, 18s. in Warrington, and 26s. 6d. in Dewsbury, while allowances for dependents and children varied from a flat 2s. in Southport, to the graduated scale in force in Coventry which rose from 5s. for children up to 8, to 12s. for children between 14 and 16 years of age.

lation of resources, possession of which would lead to a reduction or refusal of transitional payments.[29] Above all, there was a wide difference in the extent to which earnings by another member of the family group were counted as income available to a relief applicant and therefore to the claimant for transitional payments.[30]

Even with regard to pensions and other benefits, practice differed. Some authorities (e.g., Dewsbury) ignored disability pensions in calculating the other sources of income available to an applicant; others (e.g., Cardiff) treated each case on its merits, or ignored only the first 7s. 6d. or the first 12s. (as was done respectively in Bury and St. Helens in Lancashire). Similar differences in practice appeared in the treatment of old age or widows' pensions (possessed either by the applicant or members of the family), trade union benefits and workmen's compensation allowances.

In consequence of these great variations in local relief standards and practices, applicants for transitional payments received different treatment in different parts of the country. For example, the percentage of applicants in the first 7 months of 1932 who were granted payment at the full rate varied from 11.2 in Aberdeen to 98.9 in Merthyr Tydfil; the percentage granted at lower rates varied from 0.6 in Merthyr Tydfil to 69.9 in Liverpool, while the percentage of applications refused ranged from 0.5 in Merthyr Tydfil to 37.6 in Halifax. In Great Britain as a whole, the corresponding percentages for the same three categories were 50.8, 30.9 and 18.3.[31]

Even with uniform principles of administration, the percentage of applicants refused payment or granted payments only at reduced rates might have been expected to vary from district to

[29] In Cardiff, Wales, applicants had to exhaust all savings before obtaining relief, while in Middleton (near Manchester) savings up to £500 were allowed and practice ranged between these limits.

[30] In Leicester, everything over 20s. earned by adult sons was held to be available for the upkeep of incomeless parents; in Dewsbury, the corresponding figure was 25s. In Lancashire, 6s. was the maximum in Preston county; in Wigan, the first earning adult was allowed to keep 15s. of his earnings, any surplus being regarded as income available to the family; in Bolton all income of all members was taken into account provided only that all reasonable expenses were subtracted. In Newport, Wales, the earnings of all persons living together (eating from the same table) were set against the determined needs of the applicant.

[31] See *Final Report,* p. 62, for the widely varying practices in other cities.

district with the industrial history, degree of unemployment and availability of work for other members of the family. But the actual variation under the transitional payments system far exceeded any diversity which could be explained on these grounds. Moreover, the areas within which differences of treatment prevailed were too small to permit the attribution of the variations to differences in standards of living or industrial and economic conditions.[32]

In many cases the standards applied differed even among the sub-committees of a local relief authority. In one county council in the Manchester area, a given family would have been awarded from 15s. to 20s. 6d. depending on which of the five sub-committees handled its case. In the Reading district assessments of identical cases by three sub-committees varied from zero to 14s.[33] Frequently persons living in identical circumstances on opposite sides of a street would receive vastly different treatment because their needs and resources were assessed by different local public assistance committees or sub-committees.

It was inevitable that this wide departure from uniformity of treatment should have caused resentment and led to pressure on the central government to prescribe uniform minimum standards. Difference in the treatment of needy persons is, of course, an inevitable consequence of local responsibility. Even before the transitional payments system, the difference in standards of the local authorities had occasioned comment and the central authorities had from time to time endeavored gently to bring the extremes into closer conformity with the average. But when the transitional payments system caused a great increase in the number of persons affected by these local variations, the matter became a subject of national concern. In previous years wide differences in local standards could persist, for payments were financed out of locally collected taxes. Objections could then be met by advice to exert local pressure through the ballot box. But transitional payments were financed out of national taxes levied at uniform

---

[32] Thus, in the area around Leeds, comprised of 8 county boroughs and one county council, a household including the applicant, his wife and 2 sons, earning a total of 52s. weekly and paying rent of 12s., would have been granted nothing in 2 areas, and sums varying from 9s. 4d. to 26s. per week in the others. (Unemployment Assistance Board, *Report,* 1935, p. 152; also pp. 82-289)
[33] *Ibid.,* pp. 169, 219.

rates throughout the country. The Trades Union Congress appears to have been expressing a very generally held view when it asserted to the Royal Commission that:

> "Whatever justification there might be for allowing a local authority to impose tests and make allowances according to its own discretion when dealing with local rates, there is no justification whatever for allowing this procedure in the case of unemployment benefit which is provided by the general tax-payer through the Exchequer." [34]

Provision of Work Opportunity and Training by the Central Government

Throughout the period of the transitional payments system, unemployment among insured workers in Great Britain never fell below 2 millions, and during 1932 and the early part of 1933 it was nearer 3 millions. One consequence of the depression was an increase in both the number and the proportion of workers who had been unemployed a relatively long period of time. In December 1932 there were 461,722 insured workers unemployed for 12 months or over, and another 331,394 unemployed for between 6 and 12 months.[35]

Yet despite the increasing need for positive measures to combat the social and psychological effects of prolonged unemployment, the inhibitive influence of the economy crisis lay heavily over the years of the transitional payments experiment.

[34] *Appendices to the Minutes of Evidence,* Part VII, p. 477. This view was subsequently adopted as a general guiding policy by the Unemployment Assistance Board. See Chapter VIII.
[35] The distribution of insurance and transitional payment claimants in Great Britain by duration of unemployment was as follows:

Period since last registered employment	Jan. 25, 1932 Number	Per cent	Dec. 19, 1932 Number	Per cent	Dec. 18, 1933 Number	Per cent	Dec. 17, 1934 Number [a]	Per cent
Total	2,446,403	100.0	2,415,103	100.0	1,940,900	100.0	1,513,100	100.0
Less than 3 months	1,359,084	55.6	1,310,885	54.3	1,041,300	53.7	794,100	52.5
3 but less than 6 months	394,715	16.1	311,102	12.9	221,800	11.4	181,200	12.0
6 but less than 12 months	355,122	14.5	331,394	13.7	226,100	11.6	171,300	11.3
12 months or over	337,482	13.8	461,722	19.1	451,700	23.3	366,500	24.2

[a] Men only.

Source: Ministry of Labour, *Report for the Year 1932,* p. 10; *1933,* p. 12; *1934,* p. 6.

The already modest public works program was brought to an abrupt conclusion by the lapsing of the legislation under which the Unemployment Grants Committee had functioned. Projects commenced under the plans approved by the Committee were continued after 1932 under the administration of the Minister of Labour, but the numbers employed were small. Between 1932 and 1934, the number of schemes dropped from 265 to 25, and the number of workers employed from 23,975 to 6,779.[36] The relatively ambitious road construction program, instituted in 1929-30, was also severely curtailed. In 1931-32, the peak year of expenditure under this program, probably not more than 17,000 men were directly employed, while in the following years the numbers declined rapidly, to little more than 2,000 during 1934-35.[37]

The transference program, described in detail in Chapter IV, was also of decreasing importance during this period, less because of deliberate economies than because the widespread nature of the depression curtailed employment opportunities in areas which had hitherto absorbed the transferees. By 1933 the numbers transferred from depressed areas to other districts had fallen to 8,000 (as compared to 19,000 during 1931).[38]

Relatively little change was made during this period in the specific transference programs. Minor changes were, however, introduced into the household removal scheme and the arrange-

[36] Ministry of Labour, *Report for the Year 1933*, p. 33; *1934*, p. 28.

[37] The combined Trunk Road and Five Years' Programs of 1929-30 had envisaged expenditures of £48.5 millions, of which the central government's share amounted to £34 millions. In the fall of 1931, by which time projects amounting to £45.1 millions had been approved, commitments were severely curtailed. Local authorities were persuaded to abandon projects not already commenced and to curtail others as soon as technically feasible. The total approved program was in consequence reduced to £23.4 millions, of which the central government's share was to amount to £17.6 millions. By 1934-35 its share had been cut to £16.75 millions. (Ministry of Transport, *Report on the Administration of the Road Fund, 1932-33*, p. 9, *1934-35*, p. 9) The probable numbers employed are calculated on the basis of 2,000 men employed per year for each £1 million spent, as explained in footnote 86, Chapter IV.

[38] The contraction of public works, however, had repercussions on the transference scheme. In 1932 the Ministry of Labour reported that a large part of the transfers in previous years had been to employment on government-aided schemes and that further transfers were impeded by the necessity of giving preference of employment to earlier transferees whose relief jobs were giving out. (*Report for the Year 1932*, p. 23, *1933*, pp. 17, 29) By 1934 the numbers transferred increased to 12,000. (*Ibid., 1934*, p. 24)

ments for the advancement of fares, with a view to making the schemes more attractive.[39]

Training and reconditioning facilities, far from expanding, also suffered directly or indirectly from the economic depression and the urge to cut down expenditures. Because the provision of Government Training Centers continued to be conditioned upon the opportunities of placement on completion of the course, a period of increasing depression automatically involved a restriction of facilities. Several of the centers were indeed closed entirely during 1931, 1932 and 1933. In 1934 the accommodations were increased again in response to the more satisfactory placement experience of 1933, but the centers remained below their full strength. In consequence the proportion of unemployed who were given even the slight technical training afforded by the Government Training Centers was negligible. The number of persons finishing the courses offered dropped from about 7,100 in 1931 to 5,000 in 1934, while the number of unemployed ranged from 2.9 to 2.2 millions.[40]

In 1932 it became evident that continuance of the policy of treating the Transfer Instructional Centers as an adjunct to the transfer program, and restricting entry in accordance with the opportunities for placement on completion of training, would result in their almost complete closure. For the trainees had to a very large extent been placed on public projects financed through the Unemployment Grants Committee, and this program was now being liquidated as part of the general economy drive. It was therefore decided to change the basis of the scheme and to drop the word "transfer" from the name of the centers. Compulsion was abandoned and volunteers were invited to attend reconditioning courses which offered no certainty of placement on completion. This change made it possible to introduce greater variety into the courses and wider latitude with regard to workers to be enrolled, as it was no longer necessary to confine entry to work-

[39] During 1934 the Ministry changed the basis of the grant toward costs of removal and of lodging allowances under the household removal scheme. Grants were also made available to existing employees of a firm which desired to change its location to a new area. The scheme for advancing fares was modified in 1934 to permit grants to persons from depressed areas travelling to interview a prospective employer to whom their qualifications had been submitted by an employment exchange. *Ibid., 1934,* pp. 17, 24.
[40] See Appendix VIII.

qualify an unemployed worker from the right to assistance from the government. On the other hand, it was thought that the requirement would act as a check to unduly generous administration by the local authorities of centrally supplied funds; for, in order to comply with the regulations, more generous treatment of transitional payment applicants would automatically involve more generous treatment of other able-bodied out-relief clients, the cost of whose assistance was met from local tax revenues. Events showed, however, that these hopes were illusory.

The System as a Device to Secure Individual Treatment of Applicants

Despite local administration, there was an increasing tendency to deal with cases schematically and according to formal rules. Although the local authorities, in reply to a specific question, had assured the Royal Commission on Unemployment Insurance that they were equipped to handle an additional relief load, it is doubtful whether they were prepared for so great an increase as was occasioned by the transitional payments system.[50] At first an attempt was made to utilize the existing staff and committees, or at best to dilute them only slightly with new members, in order to secure the advantage of administration by those whose poor law experience best qualified them to undertake it. But soon this "imposed a heavy burden both upon members of the public assistance authorities and upon their staffs." [51]

As new staff were added and sub-committees proliferated to handle the mass of applicants, administration became more routine and less individualized. By 1933 in some areas in Scotland, the authorities rigidly applied the scales regardless of individual differences.[52] At the same time the English Ministry of Health complained of the increasing tendency of committees to make "mechanical decisions on an arithmetic basis without regard to individual circumstances." [53]

[50] Certain officers (e.g., the Public Assistance Officer of Liverpool) had, however, indicated that although premises might be adequate, a considerable augmentation of staff would be necessary and that it might be difficult to recruit enough public spirited citizens to serve on the committees. (*Minutes of Evidence,* p. 547, Questions 2593 and 2597)

[51] Ministry of Health, *Annual Report, 1931-32,* p. 199.

[52] Department of Health for Scotland, *Annual Report, 1932,* p. 140.

[53] Ministry of Health, *Annual Report, 1932-33,* p. 191; see also *Ibid., 1931-32,* p. 199.

The new staff employed to administer the means test to the new group of clients was necessarily recruited hurriedly and was largely untrained. Many of them were unemployed white-collar workers with no previous experience in this type of work. In the years after 1935, when the Unemployment Assistance Board took over a large number of these investigators as part of an understanding with the local authorities, it was found that many of them were unsuited for the type of individualized semi-case work which the Board endeavored to supply and which had always been alleged to be characteristic of local public administration.

The System as a Control on Extravagant Administration of Central Funds

The requirement that the local authorities should apply to transitional payment applicants the same standards (subject to the concessions required or permitted in the ministerial circulars and the Act of 1932) that were applicable to able-bodied clients seeking outdoor relief proved to be a less effective and automatic check upon extravagant local administration of central funds than had been anticipated. The application of the means test to unemployed workers after the twenty-sixth week of unemployment undoubtedly saved money for the taxpayers. In the country as a whole during the period November 1931 to January 1935, only about 50 per cent of the applicants were granted transitional payments at the full rate. Between 14 and 18 per cent were denied payments, while from 31 to 35 per cent were granted payments which averaged 73.3 per cent of the full rate. Nor do these figures indicate the full measure of the savings, for all cases were reconsidered every 8 weeks,[54] and between approximately 3 and 4 per cent of the applicants were refused further payments, while some of the applicants initially securing payments at the full rate were granted reduced payments on renewal. The proportion of women who were denied payments was considerably higher than among the men.[55]

The precise saving to the national Treasury resulting from the transitional payments system can only be a matter of estimate,

[54] Every 4 weeks until May 1932.
[55] Percentages are computed from tables shown in Ministry of Labour, *Report for the Year 1932*, pp. 64-65; *1933*, p. 73; *1934*, p. 65.

since between November 1931 and January 1932 the rates of insurance benefits were lower than those in the immediately preceding years, while the level of unemployment was much higher. It has, however, been estimated by the Ministry of Labour that the total saving to the national government in the years 1932 to 1934 inclusive was approximately £44.5 millions, a sum equal to a little less than one-third of the actual expenditure on transitional payments in this period.[56] Nor were these savings greatly diminished by the costs of applying the means test. The total amount refunded to the local authorities for this purpose during the years 1932-34 was only about £2,016,000.[57]

Yet, considerable as was this economy, there is evidence that in a great many cases transitional payments were made to families who could not be held to be in need when the resources of the family were taken into account. Limitation of payments to persons who are held to be in need calls not only for the determination of a minimum income below which need is said to exist, but also for the definition of those resources which are regarded as available to the applicant to provide this minimum standard. One of the most significant results of the transitional payments experiment was the attention it directed to this dual problem involved in the application of a means test, and in particular to the vital importance of the second component in the test, namely, the determination of "available resources."

Under the transitional payments system, the first standard (the measure of need) was set by the insurance benefits and the prevailing local relief scales. The former set the maximum sum which the family could hope to receive; the latter determined whether all or only part of this sum was necessary to bring the household up to the locally determined minimum subsistence level. Thus, where local standards of maintenance were low, less than the full amount of the transitional payment rate would be granted. But where they were generous, the full maximum would be paid.

[56] The total actual expenditure on transitional payments was £140.2 millions. (*Ibid., 1932*, p. 68; *1933*, p. 74, *1934*, p. 66) The annual savings were approximately double the government's original estimate of £7.5 millions. (*House of Commons Papers*, April 7, 1932)

[57] Ministry of Labour, *Report for the Year 1932*, p. 68; *1933*, p. 74; *1934*, p. 66. The costs of administration during this period, other than the application of the means test, were £8,347,000.

11

Actually, however, the relatively high proportion granted the full rate in some areas, the small proportion of denials of payments, and the fact that the level of reduced grants averaged over 70 per cent of the maximum, were due less to a high standard of maintenance on the part of local authorities than to their generous treatment of resources which were held to be available to the applicant.[58] The practices of the local authorities are known with precision because in 1935, as a result of the "Standstill" arrangement (described later in Chapter VIII), those who, but for the passage of the Unemployment Act of 1934, would have been entitled to transitional payments were permitted to draw either the national allowances of the Unemployment Assistance Board, or the transitional payments they would have received according to the calculations of their public assistance committee, whichever was more favorable. The reports of the Board's officers who had to assess resources on both bases provide a complete account of the practices of the local authorities in handling transitional payment applicants. Their reports show that those authorities (frequently in the more industrialized areas or in those which the Labour Party controlled), which conceived of transitional payments as an expansion of insurance and therefore still a matter of contractual right, were inclined to treat the possession of resources very generously. There was a tendency to take into account the resources of the applicant and his wife only, and to disregard entirely the resources of other members of the household, or to treat only a

---

[58] Cf. pages 129-30. Cf. also the following comments of the officers of the Unemployment Assistance Board in its *Report*, 1935: "The cause . . . is not in scaling allowances for needs, but in the different treatment of resources" (London, p. 90) ; "Anomalies have also arisen by reason of differences in practice in relation to the treatment of earnings of members of the household and of casual earnings of applicants, Army Reserve pay and capital assets" (Manchester, p. 169) ; ". . . household resources were dealt with very lightly for the purpose of transitional payments" (Middlesbrough, p. 182) ; "These disparities are largely due to the varying practices of Local Authorities when taking into account the presence of earning sons and daughters in the household" (Norwich, p. 199) ; "The treatment of resources constitutes the chief difference as between one Local Authority and another" (Glasgow, p. 276). The Minister's Commissioners who took over administration in County Durham also stressed the treatment of available income as the factor making for unduly generous assessments. As a result of stricter application of the "resource" tests, the Commissioners reduced the percentage of grants at the full rate from 92 to 70, and increased the percentage of denials from 1.0 to 6.5. (*Report to the Minister of Labour by Commissioners Appointed to Administer Transitional Payments in the County of Durham* [Cmd. 4339, 1933], pp. 10, 18)

small fraction of these as available to meet the needs of the applicant.[59]

Flagrant cases of waste and irresponsibility, arising from the unauthorized application to transitional payment applicants of standards different from those applicable to ordinary able-bodied relief clients, appear to have been exceptional. It is possible that some local authorities may have been moved by the consideration that refusal of transitional payments to applicants in possession of means might create a further burden on local rates when applicants had exhausted their resources.[60] But in general the failure of the ministerial regulations to act as a more perfect control over extravagance was attributable to other causes, namely, to the magnitude and character of the new group of workers with whom the public assistance authorities had to deal in relation to the number of their other able-bodied clients, and to the social and administrative difficulties attendant upon the application of different tests to two groups whose circumstances and characteristics were very similar.

As a result of these two factors, many authorities were led not to economize in the administration of transitional payments, but to treat their other able-bodied clients more generously. For, whether they interpreted their transitional payments instructions narrowly or liberally, those public assistance authorities which had hitherto administered outdoor relief in a deterrent spirit were in a dilemma. Those who applied these deterrent standards to transitional payment applicants met with objection and resentment from workers who had been accustomed to the more impersonal and non-deterrent insurance benefits. Many authorities came to believe that the strict principles were not

[59] Thus in London, a family of 4, with 2 members earning a weekly total of 75s. 9d., was entitled to a transitional payment of 9s. 6d; in Norwich, an applicant living with father, 2 sisters and a brother, all of whom were working (total weekly income, 173s. 2d.) was granted 10s.; in Nottingham a man with a wife and 3 young and 7 adult children earning a total each week of 273s. was entitled to 23s. 3d.; while in Glasgow an applicant living with 5 brothers and sisters, 4 of whom were earning a total of 143s. 3d. was entitled to 11s. In all cases, no allowance would have been granted had the uniform scales of the Unemployment Assistance Board been applied. It is important to note that these instances were not exceptional, but are examples selected by the Board's officers to illustrate a rather general situation. For other instances, see Unemployment Assistance Board, *Report*, 1935, Chapter VIII.

[60] Cf. memorandum of the Preston (Lancashire) Public Assistance Officer, *Appendices to the Minutes of Evidence*, Part VII, p. 407.

appropriate to their new group of able-bodied clients, many of whom had no previous contact with the public assistance system and the majority of whom differed from the type of work-shy persons for whom the relief regulations had been originally devised.[61] But those authorities which interpreted the original instructions and the rulings of the Ministry of Labour in such a way as to grant the transitional payment applicant more favorable treatment than that afforded the ordinary public assistance client also encountered difficulties. Since the line between the unemployed who could qualify for transitional payments and those who failed to qualify or had never been insured became ever more arbitrary, the inequity of subjecting the two groups to different treatment was evident not only to relief clients but also to the relief administrators.[62]

In many cases the desire of the local authorities to comply with the letter of the regulations, while avoiding what was regarded as unduly harsh treatment of transitional payment applicants, led to more generous treatment of other able-bodied relief clients. This was especially true in Scotland. Already in 1932 the Scottish Department of Health complained that some authorities first decided what standards were appropriate for transitional payment applicants and then adapted the former poor relief practices to the revised standards. In particular, the treatment of households with employed adult members became more liberal.[63] The inevitability of this development was in part recognized by the passage of the Transitional Payments (Determination of Need) Act in November 1932. It permitted the public assistance authorities to grant

[61] As early as October 1931 a number of authorities brought this situation to the attention of the Ministry of Labour. (Ministry of Labour, *Report for the Year 1931,* pp. 89-91)

[62] Cf. Circular 1299 issued by the Ministry of Health in 1932 (*Annual Report, 1932-33,* pp. 191-92).

[63] A number of authorities began to exempt from consideration more than the sum of 7s. 6d. a week which previously had been the common practice. By 1932 "even more striking departures from the old treatment of resources were made." Some authorities ignored up to 25s. or 27s. a week of an employed daughter's earnings. The old overriding maximum of 40s. as the amount of family income above which no relief would be granted was, in many cases, abandoned. During 1932 the standards for determining the existence of need were also made more generous in some areas, especially in the case of adult earning members of a household. (Department of Health for Scotland, *Annual Report, 1931,* p. 144; *1932,* pp. 138-39)

to ordinary applicants for poor relief the same concessions in regard to disability pensions and the possession of house property as were made to transitional payment applicants.

Thus, the transitional payments system led, in the words of the Minister of Health, to "a material departure from existing Poor Law principles." [64] By the middle of 1933, 21 councils and 31 county boroughs in England and Wales were applying in whole or in part the more liberal test of "destitution" permitted by the 1932 Act to all applicants for outdoor relief.[65] The 1932 Act had less influence in Scotland only because "many authorities were already granting applicants for poor relief in receipt of disability pensions or in possession of house property, concessions roughly equal to those permitted by the Act." [66]

The System as an Alternative to Centralized Determination of Relief Scales

Nor did the transitional payments system achieve the third of its administrative objectives. For it soon became evident that the central government could not completely avoid responsibility for determining the standards of relief and the methods of administering the new system. Even the first regulation issued by the Ministry of Labour had contained certain requirements as to the manner in which the means test should be applied. Almost immediately the Minister received requests for guidance as to the treatment of disability pensions and certain types of resources from local authorities who believed that it was undesirable to apply the existing public assistance standards to transitional payment cases. Although the Minister in his reply insisted that standards and methods of treatment were a matter for local determination, he indicated approval of more liberal treatment of transitional payment clients in assessing available resources. Many authorities took the hint. In 1932 this tacit approval became a legal requirement. In the Transitional Payments (Determination of Need) Act, the central government made mandatory the grant of these specific concessions to transitional payment applicants.

---

[64] *Annual Report, 1932-33,* p. 191. Cf. also *Report of the Committee on Local Expenditure (England and Wales),* (Cmd. 4200), 1932, p. 107.
[65] Ministry of Health, *Annual Report, 1932-33,* p. 192.
[66] Department of Health for Scotland, *Annual Report, 1932,* p. 141.

Some degree of central control over the activities of the local public assistance committees was indeed envisaged in the provisions of the order setting up the transitional payments system, for the Minister of Labour was empowered to appoint his own administrators if a local authority refused or failed to discharge with due efficiency the duties imposed upon it. Control over the activities of the local authorities was exercised by the general public assistance inspectors of the Ministry of Health who acted on behalf of the Minister of Labour. Local authorities who were found to be applying unduly generous standards were cautioned, and in many cases this sufficed to eliminate the more flagrant cases. As has already been mentioned, in two instances the Minister of Labour was forced to utilize his powers to supersede local authorities by appointing his own commissioners to administer the means test.[67]

The position of the central government in accepting complete responsibility for financing transitional payments, while attempting by a new administrative device to refrain from accepting an equal responsibility for the amount and terms of the assistance, became ever more untenable. It was forced to assume more control on account of pressure from three directions. From the fiscal point of view, the new administrative device did not afford adequate protection against a too generous expenditure of national funds. Local authorities, faced with the difficult task of administering a relief system which was allied to public assistance and yet technically different from it, pressed the central government for more specific guidance as to the precise nature of the conditions under which this relief was to be available. And finally, the wide differences in treatment of individuals whose relief was financed out of national funds led to public criticism and complaint.

Thus, the nationally set standards for the determination of need and the assessment of resources, which accompanied the establishment of the Unemployment Assistance Board, must be viewed not as a sudden and arbitrary imposition of central control, but rather as an almost inevitable end result, accepted with reluctance

[67] In Rotherham and Durham in 1932. See *Report to the Minister of Labour by Commissioners Appointed to Administer Transitional Payments in the County of Durham* (Cmd. 4339), 1933. See also Ministry of Health, *Annual Report, 1933-34,* pp. 233-34.

ber 1935 by the grant of an additional shilling per week for dependent children, and in March 1938 by an increase of the adult dependents benefit from 9s. to 10s. In the third place, the waiting period was reduced from 6 days to 3 days in March 1937, while in February of that year, sick workers were permitted to claim benefit immediately upon recovery without having to serve the full waiting period.

The Unemployment Act of 1934 maintained the "equal thirds" method of financing the general scheme whereby the costs were shared equally between employers, workers, and the government. The same principle was adopted in the agricultural scheme in 1936, but the contribution rates were much lower.[5] An important change was, however, made by the Act in regard to the funded debt and the reserves of the general scheme. The outstanding debt was separated from the current accounts and was funded at its then figure of £105,780,000, which was to be repaid out of current income at the rate of £5,000,000 annually.[6] Being thus freed of the odium of the past, the insurance system was, as it were, set upon its own feet (except for this fixed annual liability). Each year the newly created Unemployment Insurance Statutory Committee was to report to the Minister of Labour on the financial condition of the Unemployment Fund.[7] The Committee could also make a financial report at other times if it thought fit, and was obligated to do so whenever the Fund appeared likely to become insufficient to discharge its obligations (including the an-

[5] The weekly contribution rate for an adult male in the general scheme was 10 pence until July 1936, when it was reduced to 9 pence. The corresponding rate for the agricultural scheme was 4.5 pence until July 1938, when the rate for most contributors was reduced by 0.5 pence.

[6] This sum included both interest and principal repayments. It was anticipated that these annual payments would liquidate the debt by March 1971. The amending Act of 1938 permitted a proportionate reduction in this annual payment if the funded debt were reduced by repayments of capital sums out of current surpluses.

[7] The Statutory Committee consisted of a chairman and from 4 to 6 other members, at least one of whom was to be a woman, appointed by the Minister of Labour for a period of 5 years. Of the members other than the chairman, 2 were to be appointed after consultation with organizations representative of employers and of workers respectively, and a third after consultation with the Minister of Labour for Northern Ireland. Although the members were in no sense employees of the Ministry or civil servants, their expenses (including salaries or other remuneration), and the costs of the Ministry's officers detailed to serve the Committee, were carried by the Ministry of Labour. Sir William Beveridge was appointed the first chairman of the Committee.

nual debt charge). Whenever the Committee reported that the Fund was likely to be insufficient or more than reasonably sufficient to discharge its liabilities, it was the Committee's duty to recommend amendments which would remove the deficit or dispose of the surplus.[8]

Temporary borrowing was permitted, though severely circumscribed. Sums advanced by the National Debt Commissioners because of inability to meet the annual debt charge were to be repaid within 6 months. Temporary loans by the Treasury from the Consolidated Fund to meet current obligations (other than the debt charge) were repayable before the end of the same financial year. Finally, if the system showed signs of being unable to meet its future obligations, or to provide for repayment of the temporary advances within the stipulated time limits, loans could be obtained from the Treasury out of funds provided by Parliament. But at least one-third of such advances were to be repaid by the end of the subsequent financial year and the remaining two-thirds by the end of the second following financial year.

These limitations on the borrowing powers of the insurance scheme were somewhat relaxed by the amending Act of 1938, which empowered the Statutory Committee to apply part of the reserves in the general account of the current Unemployment Fund toward a reduction of the funded debt. If, having reduced the outstanding debt in this way, the Fund subsequently became unable to meet its liabilities, borrowing to the extent of the capital sum thus paid off was permitted, but the sums advanced had to be repaid by March 1971, the date by which it was anticipated that the whole of the funded debt would be liquidated.

When the separate scheme for agriculture was set up in 1936, the Committee was given similar responsibilities for maintaining

---

[8] Strictly speaking, this was no innovation in principle. Section 15 of the 1920 Act had required that "if it appears to the Treasury at any time that the unemployment fund is in all the circumstances of the case in danger of becoming insolvent, the Minister *shall,* if the Treasury so direct, by order, make such temporary modifications in any of the rates of contributions, or the rates or periods of unemployment benefit, and during such period, as the Minister thinks fit, and as will on the whole, in the opinion of the Treasury be sufficient to secure the solvency of the unemployment fund." But, as the Royal Commission dryly observed, "throughout the period 1920-1932, we know of no occasion on which this procedure was acted upon." (*Final Report,* p. 163)

the solvency of the separate Agricultural Account of the Unemployment Fund.[9]

It is important to observe that neither the 1934 Act nor the Royal Commission, which had originally proposed the creation of the Statutory Committee and outlined its functions in general terms, gave any indication as to the period of time which the Committee was to take into account in evaluating "the financial condition of the Unemployment Fund" and its ability to continue to discharge its obligations. Legally it would have been possible to have financed the insurance system on a year-to-year basis. In fact, however, the Committee adopted a social philosophy and a theory of the functions of unemployment insurance which led them to operate the system on a reserve basis.[10]

THE UNEMPLOYMENT ASSISTANCE SCHEME

The Unemployment Assistance Board, a semi-independent organization appointed by the Crown, was created by Part II of the Unemployment Act of 1934 (also referred to separately as the Unemployment Assistance Act of 1934). It was given a wide mandate to provide for the welfare and general maintenance of persons and their dependent households who were in need because of unemployment. While the Board was ultimately responsible for all persons who were covered by the Widows', Orphans' and Old Age Contributory Pensions Acts, 1925-32, and for juveniles who, but for the industrial circumstances of the time, would have been so covered, it took over its clients in two stages.[11] On January 7, 1935 (the First Appointed Day), it accepted responsibility for all the unemployed who were drawing transitional payments or who, but for the passage of the 1934 Act, would have become entitled to transitional payments. It was originally contemplated that the Second Appointed Day, when the Board was to assume responsibility for other unemployed workers who could not satisfy even the modest contributory conditions of the transi-

[9] Except, of course, that no question of policy arose in regard to the debt charge, since the funded debt was a liability of the general account only.
[10] The financial status of the fund is discussed in more detail later in this chapter.
[11] The dates at which the two groups were to be taken over were to be determined by Parliament and were technically known as the "Appointed Days."

tional payments scheme and for the payment of supplementary allowances to recipients of unemployment insurance, should have been March 1, 1935. But the task of handling and assessing the needs and allowances for nearly 800,000 workers who with their dependents made a total of about $2\frac{1}{2}$ million persons, proved unexpectedly heavy, and was complicated by political difficulties and changes in the regulations to which reference will be made in Chapter VIII. As a result, the Second Appointed Day was postponed and was finally fixed at April 1, 1937.

This national unemployment relief system provided assistance only to insurable persons between the ages of 16 and 65 who were in need and who satisfied certain other conditions, such as being capable of and available for work.[12] The standard of need and the level of maintenance to be provided were, with one exception.[13] not prescribed in the statute, but were to be set by the Board in regulations which required the approval of Parliament.

The decision as to whether an applicant was within the scope of the system, and if so the amount of the allowance payable to him, was made by the officers of the Board, who were responsible to the central government. Certain rights of appeal were, however, permitted the applicant, and cases were heard by the newly created appeals tribunals consisting of a chairman and two other persons, none of whom was a paid employee of the Board. Appeals on questions of scope were referred to the chairman, and could be initiated either by the applicants themselves, or by the local public assistance authority on whom would fall the responsibility of maintaining the applicant if he were declared out of scope.[14] Appeals against the determination of allowances were considered by the full tribunal, but they could be instituted only with the permission of the chairman, who, however, granted it in the majority of cases.[15] Dissatisfied applicants were also encour-

[12] The Board could not provide assistance to persons losing employment on account of direct involvement in labor disputes.

[13] The Act specified certain types of resources possessed by applicants or their dependent households which were to be disregarded in assessing need.

[14] Except that no public assistance authority could appeal from a decision that a particular employment was not insurable under the Old Age Contributory Pensions Acts, or that the unemployment was on account of a labor dispute.

[15] This provision was adopted with a view to cutting down the number of frivolous appeals, or numerous appeals involving a single general principle. The "Standstill" Act (postponing the Second Appointed Day) permitted applicants

aged to discuss their cases with local officers of the Board, who were given considerable discretionary powers. In this respect the unemployment assistance system differed from insurance in that an effort was made to encourage the settlement of as many disputed cases as possible within the Board's own organization.[16]

The allowances were payable indefinitely, so long as a man continued to be unemployed and in need,[17] and did not, by his conduct, place himself outside the scope of the Board's activities. Applicants who had failed, after the imposition of certain specified pressures, to avail themselves of opportunities for employment or training, or who had persistently refused or neglected to maintain themselves or their families, could on the direction of the appeals tribunal be considered as outside the scope of the system.[18] In practice, as will be shown in Chapter VII, relatively little use has been made of this power to exclude persons from the benefits of the scheme.

The Unemployment Assistance Board also has the power to set up training schemes, or to utilize for its clients (with suitable reimbursement) the training programs conducted by the Ministry of Labour. It can also establish work centers of its own or make arrangements with local authorities for certain of its applicants to attend work centers or to become inmates of workhouses maintained by public assistance authorities.

The entire cost of unemployment assistance is directly paid by the central government from the general tax funds.[19] It had

whose allowances were assessed on transitional payments principles to appeal without seeking the chairman's consent.

[16] Officers of the Board explained that this was a deliberate policy, because it was felt desirable to establish close personal relationships between the Board's officers and the individual clients, and to encourage a feeling on the part of the applicants that the system was flexible and reasonable, and that the officers were prepared freely to reconsider all the cases on their merits. Moreover, it was felt that the types of problems involved, namely, those in which it would be necessary for applicants to explain their financial circumstances and personal problems, were not such as could be suitably adjudicated before a formal committee.

[17] Applicants were required to report all changes of circumstances and each case was normally checked every 4 weeks.

[18] Before such a ruling was made, applicants had the right of appearing before the tribunal, and any public assistance authority who, in consequence of the decision, became responsible for the applicant could appeal to the tribunal for a reconsideration of the case.

[19] Technically, until the Second Appointed Day, the costs of allowances were payable from the Unemployment Fund as if they were transitional payments (section 61 (5) of the 1934 Act) ; in other words, they were paid directly by

been contemplated in the Act of 1934 that, after the Second Appointed Day, the local public assistance authorities should contribute annually toward the Board's expenses a proportion of the savings they effected on account of the unemployed workers taken over by the Board at that time.[20] The Second Appointed Day was, however, postponed from March 1, 1935 to April 1, 1937, during which time temporary financial adjustments prevailed. In 1937 a new arrangement was made.[21] Instead of the local relief authorities making an annual payment to the Unemployment Assistance Fund, the Exchequer grant (block grant) payable to them under the Local Government Act of 1929 was correspondingly reduced.

THE INCREASING RESPONSIBILITY OF THE CENTRAL GOVERNMENT

Although the full effect of the changes brought about by the Unemployment Act of 1934 was not felt until after April 1, 1937 (the Second Appointed Day), the increasing importance of the two national schemes became evident immediately. The number of persons obtaining relief from public assistance authorities on account of unemployment steadily declined, as is evident from

the Treasury, but passed through the Unemployment Fund. After the Second Appointed Day, allowances and administrative expenses incurred by other departments (chiefly the Ministry of Labour) were to be payable from the newly created Unemployment Assistance Fund, whose resources were to have been provided mainly by a direct vote of Parliament and, to a much smaller extent, by the local authorities. Administrative expenses were paid by a direct annual grant from Parliament, although until April 1, 1937 that part of the administration which was performed by the Ministry of Labour (representing 56.5 per cent of the total administrative costs in the calendar year 1937) was chargeable against the Unemployment Fund. The salaries of the members of the Board are paid from the Consolidated Fund.

[20] The 1934 Act (section 45) provided for the payment as from the Second Appointed Day of an annual contribution by the local authorities equal to 60 per cent of the estimated expenditures (including cost of administration) of which they would have been relieved in the financial year 1932-33 if the 1934 Act had then been in operation. Expenditures in four test periods (July, September, November and December 1934) were analyzed to determine the "allocated" expenditure (i.e., the expenditure which they would not have incurred if the 1934 Act had been in operation). The allocated expenditure amounted to 28.3 per cent of the total expenditure on outdoor relief in England and Wales during the test periods. This arrangement was to have been in effect from 1934 to 1937, and in 1937 Parliament was to reconsider the matter. (Ministry of Health, *Annual Report, 1935-36*, p. 140)

[21] The Local Government (Financial Provisions) Act of 1937, and the Local Government (Financial Provisions) (Scotland) Act, 1937.

Table 10. After April 1937, when the Unemployment Assistance Board took over its full clientele, there was a sharp drop in the number of persons relieved by the public assistance authorities on account of unemployment. Thereafter between 27,000 and 31,000 persons, or less than one-sixth of the number maintained during the operation of the transitional payments system, re-

TABLE 10. NUMBER OF PERSONS[a] ASSISTED ON ACCOUNT OF UNEMPLOYMENT IN GREAT BRITAIN, 1935-1939

| Date | Estimated number unemployed | Number receiving | | | Per cent of unemployed aided by | | |
| | | | | | Central government | | Local governments[c] |
		Insurance benefits	Unemployment assistance[b]	Public assistance	Insurance	Unemployment assistance	
		In thousands					
1935-Mar.	2,245	991	730	197	44.1	32.5	8.8
June	2,089	912	709	175	43.7	33.9	8.4
Sept.	2,051	867	698	166	42.3	34.0	8.1
Dec.	1,947	822	688	173	42.2	35.3	8.9
1936-Mar.	1,968	844	669	171	42.9	34.0	8.7
June	1,778	750	616	150	42.2	34.6	8.4
Sept.	1,705	690	592	139	40.5	34.7	8.2
Dec.	1,697	744	579	144	43.8	34.1	8.5
1937-Mar.	1,671	732	553	139	43.8	33.1	8.3
June	1,423	583	574	31	41.0	40.3	2.2
Sept.	1,406	592	546	28	42.1	38.8	2.0
Dec.	1,733	896	556	30	51.7	32.1	1.7
1938-Mar.	1,824	995	549	29	54.6	30.1	1.6
June	1,880	1,074	531	27	57.1	28.2	1.4
Sept.	1,881	1,042	532	27	55.4	28.3	1.4
Dec.	1,908	1,076	554	28	56.4	29.0	1.5
1939-Mar.	1,809	977	553	28	54.0	30.1	1.5

[a] Excluding dependents.
[b] Persons receiving assistance in supplementation of insurance benefits are counted only once, as insurance beneficiaries.
[c] Until June 1937 these percentages involve some over-statement as they include an unknown number of supplemented cases. The number of these cases, however, as shown in Tables 6, 9 and 13, is extremely small.

Sources: Appendix Tables I, col. 8; II, cols. 2, 3, 5, 6; VI, col. 3.

ceived public assistance. In March 1939, the national systems aided 84.1 per cent of all the unemployed, while public assistance provided for only 1.5 per cent of them.[22]

The relative importance of the insurance system varied during this period with the course of employment, as might have been ex-

[22] Another 10 or 11 per cent received no assistance at all, presumably because they failed to pass the means tests of the Board or the public assistance authorities, or were temporarily disqualified or serving waiting periods during which they lived upon their own resources.

pected. With the business recession in the winter of 1937, the proportion carried by insurance increased, but the improved employment early in 1939 was reflected first in a decrease in the proportion receiving insurance benefits.

The financial consequences of the increased scope of the two national programs were equally evident, although here too the situation was complicated by the postponement of the Second Appointed Day. The failure of the Board to take over its full clientele automatically reduced the amount of financial assistance which the localities had expected to obtain under the 1934 Act. They gained only by (a) removal of the necessity to supplement transitional payments, and (b) the fact that a few persons previously maintained under the poor law could be transferred to the Board as dependent members of households of applicants who were clients of the Board. But the transfer of both these groups involved insignificant financial savings.[23]

Accordingly the Unemployment Assistance (Temporary Provisions) (No. 2) Act, 1935, authorized the central government to make compensatory payments to the local authorities which were intended to place them in the financial position they might have expected to occupy had the Second Appointed Day not been postponed.[24] The amount of these payments to the local councils represented the difference between the annual savings the councils would have had if the 1934 Act had come into full operation as intended, and the amount they were to have paid to the central government under Section 45 of the 1934 Act. In fact, however, because of the periods selected for the purpose of calculating the loss to the local authorities attributable to the postponement of the Second Appointed Day, they were during this period placed in a better financial position than they would have been in if the full operation of the Act had not been postponed.[25]

[23] In England and Wales only 19,988 persons (with a total of 54,666 dependents), who were receiving poor relief (amounting to £4,703 weekly) in supplementation of transitional payments, were transferred from the poor law authorities, while the savings with respect to persons in group (b) above amounted only to £2,590 weekly. (Ministry of Health, *Annual Report, 1935-36,* p. 141)

[24] This arrangement, originally intended to end in September 1935, was continued until April 1937 by subsequent legislation.

[25] The annual amount of the additional expenditures attributable to the postponement of the Second Appointed Day (calculated at £6,169,892 for England and Wales) was based on the estimated outdoor relief costs in December 1934,

The expenditures of the central and local governments for maintenance of the unemployed are shown in Table 11. Expenditures by the local authorities for the maintenance of the unemployed fell sharply, especially in the years 1936-38 when the compensatory payments to offset the postponement of the Second Appointed Day were being made. Even thereafter, however, the total expenditures of the local authorities were significantly less

TABLE 11. EXPENDITURES BY THE CENTRAL AND LOCAL GOVERNMENTS
ON ACCOUNT OF UNEMPLOYMENT IN GREAT BRITAIN, 1935-1939

Year ending March 31	Central government[a]						Local governments[a]
	Unemployment insurance[b]	Unemployment assistance	Unemployment Grants Committee	Expenditures on the special areas	Compensatory payments to local relief authorities[c]	Total[d]	Net cost of relief on account of unemployment[e]
	In thousand pounds sterling						
1935	43,909	42,199	4,200	28	459	90,795	8,433
1936	42,949	42,423	4,179	690	6,083	96,324	2,730
1937	35,730	37,441	4,066	2,040	5,282	84,559	2,204
1938	37,107	36,689	3,668	4,517	343	82,324	4,806
1939	55,510	35,336	3,511	5,098	—	99,455	5,060

[a] Excluding costs of administration.
[b] Including agricultural fund payments after November 1936.
[c] On account of the postponement of the Second Appointed Day.
[d] In addition, the central government in the period 1935-38 granted a total of £374,800 to the National Council of Social Service, and £2,054,000 to the road programs. Expenditures on the latter could not be shown separately, as in Table 8, because the annual breakdown is not available in later years. These exclusions also account for the difference in the 1935 total on this table and on Table 8.
[e] These net estimates vary from the totals shown in Appendix Table X because of the deduction of the compensatory payments in the years 1935-38, and the addition in the years 1938 and 1939 of the deductions from the block grant which amounted to £2,932,000 annually. In addition to the estimated expenditures shown, the local governments spent an unknown sum toward projects under the Unemployment Grants Committee and the road programs.

Sources: Appendix Tables VII, cols. 2, 3, 4, 8; X, col. 2; and annual Civil Appropriation Accounts (Class V).

than those which had characterized the period of operation of the transitional payments system. Indeed, with the exception of the years 1931 and 1932, the unemployment assistance scheme as fully operated from 1937 caused local expenditures for the relief of unemployment to fall to a lower level than in any year subse-

_____

January and February 1935, a period of very high expenditures. On the other hand, the amount payable under Section 45 of the 1934 Act (calculated at £2,187,074 for England and Wales) was based upon outdoor relief costs in July, September, November and December 1934, a period which included more months in which expenditures were lower. (Ibid., p. 142)

160   INSURANCE AND UNEMPLOYMENT ASSISTANCE

quent to 1922 (see Tables 2 and 8). Furthermore, when allowance is made for the fact that after 1935 the central government greatly increased its expenditures for the Special Areas programs, whereas the expenditures of the localities in connection with the Unemployment Grants Committee are known to have declined, it is evident that by 1939 the central government had assumed the major part of the costs of unemployment relief.

The Financial Status of the Insurance System

Since 1934 the financial position of the insurance system has continually become stronger. The Agricultural Account from the first has shown a surplus.[26] For a complete picture of the status of the General Account, both the current Unemployment Fund and the funded debt must be included, as shown in Table 12.

TABLE 12. The Balance Sheet of the British Unemployment Insurance System, 1934-1938[a]

Year ending December 31	Annual surplus[b]	Cumulative balance	Status of the funded debt[c]	Net financial position[d]
		In thousand pounds		
1934	12,417[e]	10,527	105,741	−95,214
1935	10,923	21,450	105,510	−84,060
1936	17,527	38,977	104,741	−65,764
1937	21,402	60,379[f]	103,122	−42,743
1938	3,575	43,954	81,530	−37,576

a Excluding the Agricultural Account.
b After payment of the debt charge.
c The figures reported by the Statutory Committee refer to September 30; the financial statements of the Fund appearing in the annual reports of the Ministry of Labour, however, show that the status of the funded debt remained unchanged between September 30 and December 31 of each year.
d Obtained by subtracting the cumulative balances from the amount of the funded debt.
e A part of this surplus was used to repay Treasury advances.
f £20,000,000 was applied toward a reduction of the funded debt.

Sources: UISC, Financial Report, December 1935, pp. 3, 34; 1936, pp. 3, 28; 1937, pp. 3, 46; 1938, pp. 2, 25.

It is evident from Table 12 that in each year since the passage of the 1934 Act, the cumulative balance has increased by a substantial amount. By December 1938, the current balance of the

26 Amounting at the end of each year to £647,300 in 1936, £1,177,600 in 1937 and £948,800 in 1938.

Fund stood at £43.9 millions. At the same time the funded debt had been reduced to £81.5 millions, partly as a result of the fixed annual payments required under the 1934 Act as amended in 1938, but mainly because of the repayment of £20 millions from the current fund during 1938.[27] Thus after 1934, not only was the insurance system placed upon a solvent basis, but also it had been able to repay more than one quarter of the debt accumulated in the period between 1921 and 1934.

This achievement is the more remarkable when it is recalled that after 1934 the general insurance system was liberalized in many respects. The Act of that year had restored the benefit rates prevailing prior to the emergency reductions of 1931, and granted additional days of benefit to workers with a record of long continuous employment. Even more important, between 1935 and 1938 the changes in rates of contribution and liberalization of benefits, introduced on the recommendation of the Statutory Committee, had decreased the income of the Unemployment Fund by an estimated annual amount of £6.5 millions, and increased its annual liabilities by an estimated £5.05 millions.[28]

Two aspects of this achievement call for comment. In the first place, the social implications of the funded debt and arrangements for its repayment may be questioned. The debt incurred by the general scheme between 1921 and 1931 was, as has been shown in Chapter IV, almost entirely attributable to the use of the system as the major residual relief carrier. To assess the costs of

[27] As the amending act in 1938 authorized a reduction in the annual debt charge proportionate to the repayment of principal and also permitted additional borrowing by the Unemployment Fund up to the amount thus paid off, the choice facing the Statutory Committee turned upon the relative interest rates paid out on the funded debt and received from the current Unemployment Fund. At the beginning of 1938 the rate paid on the funded debt was nearly 5 per cent, while the Fund was earning only about 2 per cent. By repaying £20 millions of the principal in 1938, the Fund stood to gain about £500,000 a year. (UISC *Financial Report*, 1937, p. 16) It is also true, as the Committee pointed out, that if the probability was high that it would again have to borrow and thus increase the funded debt, it would also have been necessary to speculate on futures in the rate of interest. But the Committee hoped to escape this necessity by recommending repayments "only to the extent that we may reasonably hope not to be forced later to borrow again." (*Ibid.*, p. 14)
[28] In August 1935, the seasonal workers orders were relaxed, thereby increasing the proportion of the unemployed eligible for benefits. In October 1935 allowances for dependent children were increased by 1s.; in March 1937 the waiting period was shortened, and the provision for additional days was made more generous, while in March 1938 the allowance for adult dependents was increased by 1s.

this expenditure against employers and workers during the years 1935 to 1971 can scarcely be defended in economic or social terms. Economically, if repayment was to be spread over a period of years, the logical balancing period would seem to be the much shorter one corresponding to the swings of business activity.[29] Socially, it would have seemed more equitable to have spread the costs of this burden over the entire community, through the more broadly based general tax system instead of concentrating it to the extent of two-thirds on wage and payroll taxpayers, especially when it is recalled that in the later years of the debt repayment period there will be many who were not even alive at the time the debt was incurred.[30] It seems doubtful whether the retrospective enhancement of the reputation of the insurance system during the years 1921-31 can be a sufficient gain to set against the social and economic disadvantages of the method of repayment adopted in 1934.

The second question that is raised by the financial status of the insurance system concerns the principle of reserve financing. There are now essentially two unemployment relief systems, disbursing approximately the same sums annually, one being financed on a reserve, the other on a current cost basis. The logic of the different principles calls for explanation. The decision to finance the insurance system on a reserve basis was, as already stated, made by the Statutory Committee and not by the law. It arose out of the theories held by that Committee as to the basic objectives and functions of the insurance type of payment, and a preference for prior accumulation over borrowing and subsequent repayment.

The Committee stated in its first report that "there can be little doubt as to the importance of avoiding continual changes in the rates of benefit, and to a less extent, in the conditions of

---

[29] The debt is, however, being liquidated more rapidly than originally provided for, by repayments of capital sums out of the current surplus. The discussions of the Statutory Committee in its financial report for 1939 (pp. 7-11) indeed suggest the thought that perhaps the more logical period for financing heavy unemployment expenditures is one that corresponds not to cyclical swings in the economic sense, but to the alternations of war and peace.

[30] Even the Royal Commission, which believed in the principle of repayment, concluded that "it would not be equitable to call upon employers and workers to contribute, separately, at the same rate as the Exchequer toward the repayment of the debt," and suggested that only one-third of the charge for amortizing the debt should be contributed by them. (*Final Report*, p. 346)

benefit and the rates of contribution. To cut down in an ordinary trade depression the protection against unemployment, because the fund is not solvent, is an admission of failure in insurance. To raise the rates of contribution in a depression is only a little less undesirable; it means adding to the burdens of industry just when the chance of early recovery from depression depends on a lightening of the burdens." [31] Since "we must assume that industrial activity will pass through alternations of expansion and contraction . . . an insurance scheme which tries to maintain benefits and contributions at a reasonably steady level will make losses in bad years which must be covered by the surpluses of the good years . . ." And in the second place, the Committee expressed the conviction that the "borrowing powers of the Unemployment Fund should be regarded as a last resort only, for dealing, if necessary, with the final stages of a long depression, whose end can already be foreseen. They are at best a means of retrospective saving; an example of the Unemployment Fund doing what every individual is adjured to avoid." [32]

Acceptance of these two theories led the Statutory Committee to conclude that the "accumulation in advance of a balance sufficient to cover the losses of a normal trade depression is the first condition of saying that the Unemployment Fund is, and is likely to continue to be, sufficient to discharge its liabilities." [33] In subsequent reports the implications of these criteria of a satisfactory social insurance system were made more precise. Specifically, it was necessary for the Committee to determine the period of time over which income and expenditure should be made to balance, and the average amount of unemployment to be budgeted for in this period. It was also necessary, in view of the Committee's insistence upon the prior accumulation of a reserve, to forecast the probable sequence of good and bad years, and to determine the size of the reserve to be accumulated.

---

[31] UISC, *Financial Report*, 1934, pp. 10-11. The Committee expressly pointed out that "the principle is dictated less by financial than by social considerations."

[32] *Ibid. Cf.* also December 1935 report, p. 12. This preference for prior accumulation was, until the amending act of 1938, partly justified by the limitations placed upon the borrowing powers of the Fund. But the discussion of the new powers given by the amending act of 1938 indicated that recourse to borrowing was still regarded by the Committee as an unfortunate expedient to be avoided if possible. (*Ibid.*, 1937, pp. 14-16)

[33] *Ibid.*, 1934, p. 11. Cf. also December 1935 report, p. 5.

In order to determine an appropriate balancing period and the probable course of employment in it, the Statutory Committee sought advice from the Committee on Economic Information of the Economic Advisory Council [34] and adopted an 8-year cycle, beginning with 1936, over which the average rate of unemployment was estimated to be 16.75 per cent.[35] But as any change in benefit rates and contributions, arising out of decisions to distribute surpluses, involved permanent alterations in the relationship between income and expenditure, estimates as to the average amount of unemployment to be expected in 1945 or thereafter were also necessary.[36]

With regard to the size of the reserve to be accumulated, the Statutory Committee expressed in its first report the opinion that it would be unreasonable to expect the system to accumulate a balance sufficient to meet a deficiency of the magnitude incurred in a depression such as that from 1930-33. "But provision for at least half of it appears to be the minimum which should content us," [37] and this minimum sum, calculated at £13,250,000, was provisionally adopted as the standard reserve. In 1936 when the Committee adopted the 8-year cycle as the balancing period and assumed an average rate of unemployment of 16.75, a somewhat different principle was adopted. The standard reserve was to be such "that the fund will never be in debt for more than two years together, since repayment out of income of sums borrowed must be commenced within this period and must be completed within

---

[34] This committee, composed of 9 members and its chairman, Sir Josiah Stamp, was asked to advise the Statutory Committee as to the future prospects of unemployment. The detailed investigation was entrusted to a sub-committee of 4 members under the chairmanship of H. D. Henderson.

[35] The unemployment rate on which the Committee based its discussion in 1934 was 18.1. In 1935 the Committee adopted an average of 17.7 per cent. Thereafter it took into account the estimates prepared for it by the Committee on Economic Information. (*Ibid.*, December 1935, pp. 6-9)

[36] The Committee adopted the practice of using surpluses (over and above the sum required to build up or maintain the "standard reserve") to finance reductions in contributions or increases in benefits during the initial 8-year cycle. But, in accordance with its dislike of too frequent changes in benefits and contributions, it took into consideration the effect that these changes would have upon the balancing point of the Fund in the period after the temporary surplus would have been exhausted. In proposing changes in 1937 and 1938 which would have reduced the balancing point from an unemployment rate of 16.0 per cent to 15.4 and to 15.1 per cent respectively, it was emphasized that the recommendations were justified only because after 1945 it was not unreasonable to assume a mean rate of unemployment as low as 15.1. (*Ibid.*, 1937, p. 12)

[37] *Ibid.*, 1934, p. 13.

the third year." [38] This standard reserve was set at £37.5 millions, being composed of the existing reserve of £21.5 millions,[39] plus the anticipated excess of income over expenditure in the years 1936 and 1937.[40]

The value of these careful attempts to escape from year-to-year methods of financing insurance benefits depends upon the significance attached to the ultimate objective and the probability that it will be attained by these means. As to the objective itself there can be little difference of opinion. Stability of payments to the unemployed and of rates of taxes is clearly desirable in the interests alike of the unemployed and of the taxpayer. The attempt to restrict assurance of this stability to the insured unemployed can be explained by the practical fact that the limited duration of benefits and the restriction of payments to a group with a significant period of past employment make forecasting of the future obligations of the system not entirely a fantastic proposition. Yet even thus protected, the insurance scheme may be subject to unexpectedly high payments since a normal trade cycle is becoming an increasingly rare phenomenon.

Furthermore, the existence of a second national program providing for the maintenance of the unemployed side by side with the insurance system raises doubts as to the extent to which even the presence of a reserve fund would enable the insurance system to escape the vicissitudes of sharp fluctuations in business activity or social policy. For, as is shown in Chapter X, there is now a very close relationship between the two systems. Changes in the levels

---

[38] *Ibid.*, December 1935, pp. 12-13. At the time the Committee believed that this "is most unlikely to be accomplished if in the next two years we are unable to add very substantially to the present reserves of the Unemployment Fund."

[39] The Committee on Economic Information, having advised that the years 1936 and 1937 were likely to be relatively prosperous, and believing that the general level of unemployment in the years after 1944 would be lower than in the period 1936-1943, the Statutory Committee decided to "treat the income of the fund as sufficient for its liabilities, not on the basis of balancing income and expenditure if unemployment averages 16.75 per cent from 1936 to 1943, but on the basis of using up in that period the bulk of our accumulated reserve." (*Ibid.*, December 1935, p. 11)

[40] In fact, the expectations of the Committee were more than realized. In 1936 the actual excess of income exceeded the original estimate of £10.5 millions by £6.8 millions; in 1937 the actual excess was £20.7 millions as compared with an estimated £5.0 millions. (*Ibid.*, 1937, p. 5)

of unemployment allowances are likely to exercise a direct influence upon the benefits offered by the insurance system, while if the insurance system came to be very markedly superior to assistance, there would undoubtedly again be strong political pressure from those representing the interests of workers to increase its scope regardless of the consequences to its finances.

CHAPTER VII

CATEGORIZATION OF THE UNEMPLOYED

UNEMPLOYMENT INSURANCE AND unemployment assistance together carry the categorical treatment of dependency due to unemployment farther than it has hitherto been applied. Previously, under both the expanded insurance and the combined insurance and transitional payments systems the categorical treatment of the unemployed was limited in the following ways: first, with one exception,[1] neither insurance benefits nor transitional payments were paid for an indefinite period. Second, many able-bodied unemployed were excluded from the systems since even the transitional payments aided only those who had at some time worked for a specified period in covered employment. Third, persons for whom the fixed insurance benefits and maximum transitional payments were inadequate for maintenance had to seek supplementary aid from public assistance.

The unemployment assistance plan aimed to remove the unemployed still more completely from dependence upon general public assistance. Payment of unemployment allowances was to continue indefinitely so long as a man did not by his behavior remove himself from the scope of the Unemployment Assistance Board. The Board was made responsible not merely for those who had at some time worked in a trade subject to unemployment insurance, but also for the wider group of persons who were covered by the compulsory old age and survivors insurance plan. Finally, the public assistance authorities were prohibited by the 1934 Act from granting supplementary economic aid to any person for whose maintenance the Board had granted an allowance, and after April 1, 1937 the same prohibition applied to persons drawing insurance benefits who were thereafter to look to the Board for supplementation when necessary, as were persons disqualified for insurance benefits.[2]

---

[1] The worker who could show 30 contributions at any time and satisfy the test of being normally in covered employment could draw transitional benefits or payments indefinitely.

[2] Except for disqualifications on account of labor disputes.

167

Although there are still important groups of employable unemployed outside the scope of the unemployment insurance and assistance systems, it is clear that the principle of categorization of persons dependent on account of unemployment has now been carried very far. After the Second Appointed Day, insurance and assistance together provided maintenance for between 80.9 and 85.4 per cent of the total number of unemployed; [3] and by March 1939 they provided for over 98 per cent of the unemployed receiving assistance from public sources. The categorization is certainly sufficiently complete to raise in an acute form some of the problems presented by the categorical approach. For, even though categorization has been resorted to in Great Britain as the technique for limiting the sphere of responsibility of the socially unpopular public assistance system, it is doubtful whether it can ever be so complete as to embrace all the dependent groups. In so far as some groups remain with the generalized poor relief system, and if there is a considerable difference in the nature of the assistance offered by the various categorical services, special attention must be paid to the principles of eligibility for each type of aid in order that the difference in treatment may be socially acceptable and rationally justifiable. There are also the twin dangers of gaps in coverage and overlapping of functions. On the one hand the desire to evade financial burdens—especially when the division of responsibility is between central and local governments—may involve prolonged and unnecessary jurisdictional disputes regarding the status of individuals. The existence of gaps and anomalous cases is especially probable when the provision of important groups of services is optional with local authorities who, for financial or other reasons, may be unable or unwilling to supply them. On the other hand, the authorities responsible for one type of service may, out of an excess of zeal or desire for enhanced prestige, undertake functions and embrace groups of persons more appropriately provided for by other assistance programs.

The sectional treatment of dependency, especially when it involves the transference of persons from one category to another, calls also for a high degree of administrative cooperation between

[3] See Table 10 in Chapter VI.

the responsible officials, if dual or unnecessary payments are to be avoided and if the applicants are not to be subjected to an unnecessary amount of multiple investigation.

All of these questions are, of course, brought into sharp focus by the creation of the Unemployment Assistance Board. In so far as the fundamental difficulty arises from the fact that the British system of social services still exhibits traces of divergent philosophies regarding the value of the categorical approach or an incomplete application of the categorical policy, a discussion of the basic issues would call for an investigation far wider in scope than that undertaken in this volume. But in so far as the new unemployment assistance system applies the principle of categorization to a very high degree in one field, a study of the British experience since 1934 may be expected to throw some light on certain specific questions raised by this method of treating dependency due to unemployment.

This chapter will, therefore, inquire whether the scope of the combined insurance and assistance systems embraces all those and only those who are unemployed and who experience a common need for alternative income and maintenance of employability. Moreover, since unemployment insurance now represents a category within a category, it is important to inquire whether the line drawn between insurance beneficiaries and assistance recipients is logically defensible. Furthermore, the operation of the administrative arrangements between the different responsible authorities will be examined to discover whether on the one hand there have been awkward and troublesome jurisdictional disputes, and on the other, whether there has been much overlapping of function and duality of administration. Two other questions, namely, whether the demarcation of the unemployed has led to the creation of a privileged group and enhanced the risk of political lobbying, and whether the services provided by the two national unemployment relief systems constitute in fact a justification for further categorization within the employable group, will be discussed in later chapters rather than at this stage because analysis of them cannot be dissociated from other features of the British unemployment relief programs.

The Nature and Extent of Categorization

The scope of the combined unemployment insurance and assistance systems is not completely identical with the employable unemployed group. Certain individuals must still rely on general public assistance because of their failure to satisfy the eligibility conditions in regard to occupation, age, availability and capacity for work, willingness to work and need for assistance. As the scope of unemployment assistance is wider than that of insurance, the following discussion of these limiting conditions will be mainly confined to the former system.

In the first place, unemployment assistance is limited to the occupational group covered by the old age insurance system. This was in keeping with the recommendations of the Royal Commission that the scheme should deal with able-bodied industrial workers who, though anxious to earn their livelihood by employment under a contract of service, cannot find such employment. At the same time it was desired for administrative reasons that the test of qualification should be as objective as possible. But, although the old age insurance acts covered the widest field of all the existing social insurances, limitation of the assistance scheme to the scope of this system means immediately that persons not normally wage earners prior to application are excluded.[4] Thus the former independent worker, or the owner of small property, or the small employer who is forced to seek a livelihood from wage-earning employment and is unsuccessful in his search, is outside the scope of the Unemployment Assistance Board. So also are non-manual wage or salary earners paid at a rate of more than £250 a year.[5]

The effect of the limitation of scope to persons whose normal occupation was employment covered by the old age insurance plan is, however, modified by two factors. First, the Act of 1934 provided a loophole of special significance for young persons by

[4] Voluntary contributors who were allowed to continue under the old age insurance scheme if they had once been in covered employment were excluded on the ground that their contributions were not paid "in respect of their current employment."

[5] Workers engaged in certain types of central or local government work, especially if enjoying pension rights, teachers and employees of railway companies benefiting by superannuation schemes, casual workers, employment in the service of a spouse, and a few miscellaneous groups are also excluded from the right to apply to the Board for assistance if in need, because these employments are not covered by old age insurance.

bringing within scope any person who, while he had not normally "been engaged in any remunerative occupation since attaining the age of sixteen years, might reasonably have expected that his normal occupation would have been such employment as aforesaid but for the industrial circumstances of the district in which he resides." [6] Second, the Board instructed its officers to interpret the provisions in a manner that was relatively generous to the applicant. They were advised to interpret "normal occupation" more widely and flexibly than would be the case in regard to corresponding classes of persons under unemployment insurance.[7]

The officers of the Board were also given certain powers to bring persons within the scope of the Act if it seemed desirable to do so. It was felt that many young persons in particular might prefer to be treated as a dependent member of another applicant's family in order to escape such coercive controls as they might have been liable to if granted an allowance in their own right.[8]

But, while there is reason to believe that the present limitation of scope with reference to normal employment is interpreted very broadly, the question of whether or not an applicant's normal occupation is one subject to old age insurance is still crucial and certain groups are excluded.[9] This failure to include all able-

[6] While the Act specified no age limit, the Board decided that normally this provision should not apply to persons over the age of 25 except in areas suffering continuously from the post-war depression. The wording of section 36 (1)b ii, however, created a curious anomaly. A young worker, who in the absence of covered employment, took work in a non-insurable trade and subsequently became unemployed would be ruled out of scope, whereas another who had never had any work at all, if able to prove that but for the industrial circumstances of the time he would have obtained insurable employment, would be covered by the assistance scheme.

[7] Mere duration of unemployment was not in itself to be conclusive evidence that a man had no longer a covered employment as his normal occupation. Rather, the question was to be decided in the light of factors such as period of unemployment in relation to the industrial circumstances of the area, the past industrial record of the applicant, his recent mode of livelihood, and his age. Cases where the applicant's last employment was at a rate of remuneration above £250 a year were also treated as generously as possible, and given the benefit of all doubt. Thus, a worker whose salary rose for a time above insurable limits and who subsequently became unemployed, would be judged on the basis of his whole work history; he would not be regarded as having lost his normal occupation in covered employment because he was temporarily uninsured at the time he lost employment.

[8] E.g., attendance at training courses, or penalties for habitual failure to seek work.

[9] Cf. *Unemployment Assistance in Liverpool* (Liverpool: University Press, 1938), p. 45: "The general effect of the scope decisions of the Appeals Tribunals is to leave a large proportion of deserving cases in the hands of the Public

bodied employable persons is admitted to be unfortunate even by officials of the Board. It is explained largely by the magnitude of the task given to the new body and by a desire to simplify the administrative problem as far as possible. Moreover, it has been argued that one important justification for the present limited scope is the hope of confining the Board's activity to those persons for whom the requirement to report at a local employment office with a view to placement is not altogether a farce. This argument is strong only with regard to those excluded workers who were previously in the higher income brackets. For the local employment offices cater in the main to the less specialized and less highly paid workers, and are little concerned with the higher paid non-manual workers. But the Unemployment Insurance Statutory Committee did not believe this to be an insuperable objection to recommending the raising of the income level for insurance purposes from £250 to £400 in 1936.[10] Instead they suggested the creation of specialized employment services, and if these were set up, the case for the present limitation of the Board's scope would be weakened. As the system is on a non-contributory basis, no special difficulty arises in regard to the collection of contributions.

There would seem, therefore, to be no good reason why, in time, all able-bodied persons genuinely seeking employment might not be brought under the unemployment assistance scheme, for the arguments that justify special treatment for the group already included apply with equal force to those outside.[11]

In the second place, unemployment assistance covers persons only from the age of 16 to 65. The upper age limit is logical in view of the fact that at this age old age benefits become available to the occupational group for which the Board is responsible.[12] The lower age limit is not so easily explained, as the normal school-

---

Assistance Committee." See also London County Council, *Annual Report, 1937,* Vol. I, p. 29: "The general result . . . has been to leave with the Council . . . a large number of men formerly employed for wages . . . people whose occupation in the past has been normally insurable but who for various reasons have had little employment in recent years."

[10] *Report of the Unemployment Insurance Statutory Committee on Remuneration Limit for Insurance of Non-Manual Workers,* February 7, 1936, p. 17.

[11] The unsuitability of general poor relief for the average normal worker is indeed particularly evident in the case of the worker who has previously earned over £250 a year. In 1940 this anomaly was in large measure removed by the raising of the salary limit for unemployment insurance to £420 a year.

[12] In 1940 the pensionable age for women was lowered to 60.

leaving age is between 14 and 15. It seems probable that the 16-year minimum was selected mainly because the scope of the scheme as a whole is identical with that of the old age and survivors insurance plan and 16 is the age at which contributions to this scheme begin. It is also the age of entry into health insurance and the age at which persons under the unemployment insurance scheme first become entitled to benefits. The selection of this age as the minimum could also be defended practically in view of the relatively small extent of long-continued unemployment among young persons.[13] The maintenance of juveniles between the school-leaving age and the age of 16 would thus normally fall upon their parents unless these were unemployed, in which case dependent's allowances would be paid by the government under the unemployment insurance or assistance programs. And, as the Minister of Labour since 1934 has had and exercised the power to require the attendance at juvenile instruction centers of all unemployed insured juveniles whether drawing benefit or not,[14] the scope of the combined services is—at least on paper—wide enough to provide for the needs of the great majority of the young unemployed for training and work opportunity.[15]

In the third place, certain unemployed persons are excluded on account of failure to prove availability and capacity for work. This limitation, which applies also to insurance claimants, has been interpreted by the Unemployment Assistance Board even more generously than the already wide interpretation adopted by the Umpire, the final appeals authority under the insurance system. According to the Umpire, a claimant must be "actually capable of and available for work of some kind as an employee, that is, capable of and available for doing work of some such kind as

[13] In the 8 months prior to August 1933, the percentage of unemployment among young persons (16-17 years) was 6.8 for boys and 5.8 for girls. In the corresponding period in the following year, the percentages were 5.0 and 4.5 respectively. (Ministry of Labour, *Report for the Year 1934*, p. 42) In subsequent years the market for juvenile labor improved still further, while the greater proportion of those unemployed were out of work for 3 months or less. Of 23,925 juveniles claiming benefits in November 1935, 21,218 had been on the register less than 3 months. In the following year, only 247 out of 26,650 juvenile claimants had been unemployed from 6 to 9 months. All others had been unemployed for less than 6 months. (*Ibid., 1935*, p. 41; *1936*, p. 39)

[14] It will be recalled that young persons are insurable on leaving school, although they are not entitled to benefit until reaching the age of 16.

[15] For the use made of these powers, however, see Chapter IX.

13

is ordinarily done under conditions of employment, and save in special circumstances, capable of doing it in conditions in which employees under contracts of employment ordinarily do work."

It should be noted that it is not necessary that an applicant should be capable of his usual work.[16] Nor could any person be excluded for failing to satisfy the condition because he was attending a training course authorized by the Minister of Labour or created by the Board. Moreover, the Board instructed its staff to take a broader view of the clause than could be taken by the insurance authorities, who were compelled to disqualify benefit claimants for any *day* on which they were unavailable or incapable. The definition was to be, in the words of the Board, "an indication of broad status rather than a condition of daily application." In carrying through this policy after the Second Appointed Day, when the Board took over persons previously maintained wholly by the public assistance authorities, some of the latter even raised doubts as to whether the Board was not interpreting the condition too generously.[17]

Interpretation of incapacity on account of occasional sickness has also been relatively generous to the applicant, at least so far as persons already drawing allowances from the Board were concerned. For these persons, odd days of sickness lasting not more than two weeks were disregarded.[18] Persons not already drawing unemployment assistance allowances, however, would be disqualified under the available-for-work clause. Physical incapacity other than in the form of occasional days of sickness has been broadly

---

[16] E.g., a man accustomed to earn his living at some form of heavy work would not necessarily cease to be qualified if an accident restricted his future field to sedentary or light occupations.

[17] This appears to have been particularly the case with regard to crippled persons and, until the passage of the Blind Persons Act, 1938, to blind persons. (Cf. Unemployment Assistance Board, *Report*, 1938, pp. 15-16, 29 [referred to hereafter as UAB *Report*], and *Unemployment Assistance in Liverpool*, p. 15)

[18] (a) Odd days of sickness (i.e., less than 7 days within a pay week) do not disqualify for assistance. Such odd days of sickness may occur in any number of weeks in the year unless a prolonged record of illness in the past suggests that the frequency of occurrence raises doubts as to whether the sickness is "occasional." (b) One continuous pay week of sickness falling between two weeks of good health, or even between two weeks which included odd days of sickness, will not disqualify for assistance in respect of that week. (c) If a person remains sick for the whole of a second pay week and requires assistance beyond any health benefit to which he was entitled under health insurance, he must apply to the public assistance authority. (*Unemployment Assistance [Periods of Occasional Sickness] Rules, 1937*, No. 263)

the applicant, the essential difference between the two lies in the fact that insurance benefits of a fixed amount are payable for a limited period of time as a right—provided the statutory qualifying conditions are satisfied—and may be spent as the beneficiary wishes, whereas assistance is payable indefinitely, but only on proof of and to the extent of need, and may be withdrawn or payable to another member of the household if misspent. On the other hand, the assistance scheme makes more ample provision than the insurance plan for the needs disclosed. Moreover, the relations between the individual and the administrators in the insurance system are relatively formal, and the opportunities for exercise of discretion by administrators are severely curtailed.[22] The administrators of the assistance scheme, however, have a legal responsibility for the welfare and maintenance of the employability of their clients. And while it is true that the Minister of Labour has the power to make attendance at training courses a condition for the receipt of insurance benefits, and that no such specific power is given to the Unemployment Assistance Board,[23] it is also true that the Minister has exercised this power only in regard to juveniles and, except for a very limited period, not at all in regard to adults. The Unemployment Assistance Board, however, is increasingly applying its sanctions to deal with difficult cases, including cases of refusal to undergo training.

Thus, the further categorization involved in the existence of two special services catering only to the unemployed raises the question whether the scope of each reflects real differences in the industrial qualities and personal needs of the clientele. More specifically, does the insurance system provide for a group for whom fixed payments, only loosely related to individual needs and subject to few pressures to undertake unfamiliar employment

[22] The only important discretionary power left to administrators arises in regard to the safeguards around the definition of suitable work. Subsection (3) of section 28 of the 1935 Act provides that "after the lapse of such an interval from the date on which an insured contributor becomes unemployed as, in the circumstances of the case, is reasonable," workers may be required to accept work other than in their usual occupation.

[23] The Board can, however, apply certain penalties to the so-called "difficult cases" of applicants who have failed to avail themselves of employment or training. The penalties consist of payment of allowances in kind, or payment to some other member of the applicant's household, or payment only on condition that the applicant attend a work center maintained by the Board or a local authority.

and practically none to undergo training or reconditioning, are an appropriate form of assistance? Does the unemployment assistance system embrace within its scope persons who require more elaborate and constructive provision than the insurance system could offer?

There can be no doubt that the majority of the group for whom the Board is responsible consists of persons "less eligible," in labor market terms, than those provided for under the insurance system, and therefore in need of special treatment. Except for the relatively small number of uninsured persons, the only workers with a recent record of employment who became clients of the Board were insured workers who had been disqualified for refusing work or for other reasons. The remainder of the Board's clientele were persons who by definition had been unemployed more than 6 months, i.e., they had exhausted benefit rights in any given year or had not had 30 weeks of work in the past 2 years, or had failed to secure 10 weeks of additional work after exhaustion of benefit rights and thus failed to qualify for benefits in the next succeeding benefit year. They were obviously the long-period unemployed. The majority of persons taken over from the public assistance authorities after April 1937 were also persons with a relatively poor employment record.[24]

On the other hand, the insurance claimants are by definition persons who can show at least 30 weeks of work within the last 2 years preceding application for benefits, or who, having exhausted benefits in one year, have paid at least 10 contributions before claiming benefits in the next year. It is true that since 1934 the provision of extra days of insurance benefits for claimants

---

[24] The relative importance of the different categories as of December each year is indicated in the following table:

Percentage of applicants	1935	1936	1937	1938
With less than 30 contributions in the past 2 years...	76.5	79.4	77.5	70.0
With benefits exhausted in current year, or unable to show 10 contributions since exhaustion of benefits in preceding year	23.5	20.6	16.5	23.0
Not covered by unemployment insurance [a]	—	—	4.1	3.5
Disqualified for benefits [a]	—	—	0.9	1.3
Requesting supplementation of benefits [a]	—	—	1.0	2.3

[a] No cases until after April 1937.

Sources: UAB Report, 1936, p. 55; 1937, pp. 186-87; 1938, p. 59.

with a good record of employment has prevented the insurance system from catering solely to the short-term unemployed.[25] But a comparison of the reported duration of unemployment suffered by the members of the two groups reveals a very real difference in employment experience. A direct comparison is available only for November 14, 1938. It indicates clearly that the insurance system carried mainly the short-term unemployed, while the assistance system was responsible for the bulk of those unemployed for 6 months or longer, and for practically 90 per cent of those unemployed for more than 12 months:

Period of registered unemployment as of November 14, 1938 [a]	Insurance claimants	Assistance applicants
Less than 3 months............	927,854	156,333
3 but less than 6 months.......	110,489	55,201
6 but less than 12 months.......	62,833	88,714
12 months or over............	30,107	248,280

[a] This is the only occasion on which the count taken by the Board and the Ministry of Labour referred to the same day. On three other occasions (May 1935, June 1936, and December 1937), the counts were made on dates between 7 and 14 days apart. If it be assumed that these were nearly enough simultaneous to justify comparison, it can be stated that in these years the insurance system carried between 82.5 and 85.2 per cent of all applicants unemployed less than 3 months; between 52.0 and 61.6 per cent of those unemployed 3 months but less than 6; between 25.0 and 34.8 per cent of those unemployed between 6 and 12 months, and only from 5.8 to 11.0 per cent of those out of work more than 12 months. (Ministry of Labour *Gazette*, June 1935, p. 229; July 1936, p. 260; January 1938, p. 26; UAB *Report*, 1937, p. 70)

Sources: Ministry of Labour *Gazette*, December 1938, p. 484; UAB *Report*, 1938, p. 65.

The differing clienteles of the two systems can also be shown in another way. In November 1938, whereas 82.0 per cent of the insurance claimants had been out of work less than 3 months, and only 2.7 per cent 12 months or more, 45.3 per cent of the assistance applicants had been unemployed for this long period, and only 28.5 per cent of them for less than 3 months.

The persons subject to the Board's jurisdiction are also in special need of measures for the improvement of their condition ". . . with a view to their being in all respects fit for . . . return to regular employment," because such a large proportion of them are older men. In November 1937, 48.0 per cent of the male applicants were over 45; 26.5 per cent were between 55 and 64.[26]

[25] A special return for June 8, 1936 showed that of all benefit recipients, 9.6 per cent had been continuously unemployed for 6 months or more, 4.7 per cent for 9 months or more, and 2.6 per cent for 12 months or more. (UISC, *Financial Report*, 1936, p. 20)

[26] UAB *Report*, 1937, p. 71. The corresponding percentages for selected dates in other years were (for men and women): 1935, 40.7 and 20.7; 1936, 45.7 and 24.3; 1938 (men only), 49.7 and 27.9. (UAB *Report*, 1935, p. 80; 1936, p. 61; 1938, p. 65)

These age distributions contrast sharply with those of insurance claimants, 32.1 per cent of male claimants being over 45, and only 15.1 per cent between 55 and 65. On the other hand, 21.6 per cent of the male insurance claimants were under 25, as compared to 9.3 per cent of the assistance applicants.[27]

By and large, therefore, the line between insurance and assistance separates those who have been unemployed for a relatively long period and those who are in the older age groups from the short-period unemployed and the relatively younger workers. The needs of the two groups can thus be said to differ in two important respects. On the one hand, payment of a fixed sum only loosely related to needs may be appropriate for the short-period unemployed who may be expected to have some small resources. And the risk run by the community in contributing toward payments to workers who in some cases may not be in need is reduced by the limitation on duration. On the other hand, the segregation of the group that is older and suffering from prolonged unemployment makes it possible to apply to them special measures for reconditioning, retraining or for providing permanent occupation outside the normal employment market, which would be inappropriate and uneconomical for the group whose prospects of reabsorption in their normal employment are greater because of their lower age and more recent employment.

From this point of view it may be said that, with one exception, the division of the unemployed into two major categories is ra-

---

[27] Ministry of Labour *Gazette,* January 1938, p. 8. This is the only date on which direct age comparisons are available. Counts made in other years show only the age distribution of insurance and assistance applicants together. A comparison of the combined groups with the recipients of assistance alone reinforces the conclusion that in the clientele of the Board older persons constitute a substantial proportion:

Age groups (men and women)	1935 Insurance and assistance	Assistance alone	1936 Insurance and assistance	Assistance alone
Under 25	21.6	11.4	18.8	9.7
25-34	26.6	26.4	25.2	22.7
35-44	19.3	21.5	20.2	21.9
45-54	17.2	20.0	18.2	21.4
55-64	15.3	20.7	17.7	24.3

Sources: UAB *Report,* 1935, p. 80; 1936, p. 201. Ministry of Labour *Gazette,* July 1935, p. 248; December 1936, p. 442. For 1935 the combined figures relate to a date in May, whereas the assistance figures relate to April.

tionally defensible.[28] The exception arises from the payment of extra days of insurance benefits to a small percentage of workers with a favorable past record of continuous employment, which keeps within the insurance system some workers for whom the type of treatment available under the assistance system would seem to be more appropriate. This anomaly can be explained only by the persistence of the view that insurance is a definitely preferential system of relief from the point of view of the unemployed,[29] despite the very great improvements that have been effected in the alternative or supplementary system since 1920, coupled with a belief that the man who has been in regular employment in the past is in some way more deserving than the man who has had relatively little continuous employment.

The Extent of Jurisdictional Disputes

Responsibility for maintaining the unemployed since 1934 has been divided, although very unequally, between the locally supported public assistance authorities on the one hand, and the centrally financed insurance and assistance authorities on the other. Certain clarifying provisions of the Act of 1934 minimized the possibility of friction between the responsible authorities. As already pointed out, the law provides that public assistance authorities may not supplement unemployment assistance allowances, nor since 1937, insurance benefits. And where the public assistance authorities grant relief to assistance applicants, pending the determination of their status or in an emergency, they are reimbursed out of any allowances subsequently payable.[30] There is, however, some evidence that in certain areas public assistance authorities have, in cases in which recipients of outdoor relief share a home with recipients of assistance, reduced their payments to the

[28] It should be noted that this chapter seeks only to inquire how far the formal division of the unemployed between the insurance and the assistance systems is logically defensible in view of the provision that each system is *legally* able to make. The extent to which the two administrations have utilized their powers to the full, and in particular the extent to which the Board has carried out its mandate to provide for the welfare (other than maintenance) of its clients, will be discussed in Chapter IX.

[29] Cf. UISC *Financial Report,* December 1935, pp. 15-16.

[30] The amount of the reimbursement cannot exceed the amount of the allowance which would have been granted by the Board. Disputes regarding this amount are referred to the appeals tribunals.

former on the ground that the higher unemployment assistance allowances make public assistance payments less necessary.[31]

In general, questions regarding the responsibility of either group of authorities for individual cases have created little friction.[32] Difficulties have most frequently arisen in connection with the determination of the applicant's "normal occupation," for, especially since the Second Appointed Day (April 1, 1937), this has been crucial in determining whether the Board or the local assistance authorities were financially responsible for a given applicant. Until that date all applicants to the Board were persons who had at some time been insured under the unemployment insurance acts, and, with negligible exceptions, all these employments were also covered under old age insurance.[33] Persons who could show 30 unemployment insurance contributions at any time were obviously clients of the Board, unless known facts suggested that insurable employment had been definitely abandoned. But the fewer the contributions paid, the more doubtful it would be whether a person's normal employment was in fact employment within the scope of old age insurance.

During 1935 and 1936 such cases were relatively few. But after April 1937, when the Board assumed responsibility for the

[31] Cf. *Unemployment Assistance in Liverpool*, p. 47. This practice involves, of course, a change in the concept of the "household" previously adopted by public assistance authorities. And, as the Liverpool committee pointed out, the problem would be less serious if the scope of the unemployment assistance system were amended to include all able-bodied unemployed persons and their dependents.

[32] Thus, the eligibility qualifications based on age give rise to relatively few disputes. Disputed cases would arise only where the age given by the applicant fell very close to one or other of the legal limits. But, as the Ministry of Labour had already verified the ages of claimants to insurance benefits who were alleged to be less than 23 or more than 62 years of age, arrangements were made for making these data available to the Board, which thus readily secured information regarding a large majority of its applicants. (In 1938 about 97 per cent of the Board's applicants held unemployment insurance books [UAB *Report*, 1938, p. 59].) Verification of the age of applicants approaching the upper age limit and not previously covered by the insurance system at any time was secured from the departments responsible for the old age insurance system, which had in any case to make the verification for their own purposes. In the case of young applicants, verification through birth certificates was a minor problem.

In fact, disputes regarding decision of scope on the basis of age have been insignificant. In the first four years of the Board's activity, only 39 cases of this kind came before an appeals tribunal, and in 26 of these the Board's decision was upheld. (UAB *Report*, 1935, p. 302; 1936, p. 44; 1937, p. 195; 1938, p. 43)

[33] Section 36 (3) of the 1934 Act provided that questions as to whether any employment was one covered by old age insurance were to be referred to the Minister of Health, whose decision was final.

able-bodied unemployed who had hitherto been provided for by the public assistance authorities, no relatively automatic criterion for determining whether an applicant was a person normally covered by old age insurance (in the wide interpretation given to that condition, described earlier in this chapter) was available. By definition the new group of applicants, numbering some 138,000, had been unable to show 30 weeks of insurable employment under unemployment insurance at any time or 8 weeks in the past 2 years, and each case had to be judged on its merits. Decisions on scope were made in the first instance by the officers of the Board, but appeals could be taken by the applicant or the public assistance authority financially affected to the appeals tribunal, which, however, was composed of members appointed by the Board or by the Ministry of Labour. Thus, superficially at least, the danger was very real that the judgment as to what was to be regarded as a man's "normal" occupation would be made by the party interested in evading financial responsibility. Representatives of the Board have argued that the appeals machinery was an effective safeguard, as the final decision lay in the hands of the chairman who, although appointed by the Ministry of Labour, was a local man selected for his local standing and knowledge, and as a ratepayer could be relied upon not to be unduly sympathetic to attempts by the Board to evade financial responsibility by declaring applicants out of scope. In fact, in the majority of cases, the chairmen have affirmed the Board's rulings on appeals.[34]

After the Second Appointed Day, the question was actively debated whether the Board was refusing in an undue proportion of cases to accept former public assistance cases. During 1937, of 138,442 former public assistance cases, the Board held 90,541 to be within scope.[35] Opinions differed as to the reasons for the rejection of the remaining 48,000. The county public assistance

---

[34] The total number, and the results, of appeals involving the claimant's "normal occupation" were as follows:

	Total	In scope	Out of scope
1935	13	5	8
1936	63	12	51
1937	13,823	3,121	10,702
1938	8,458	1,831	6,627

Sources: UAB Report, 1935, p. 302; 1936, p. 44; 1937, p. 195; 1938, p. 43.

[35] UAB Report, 1937, pp. 28-29.

authorities charged the Board with administering the Act more rigidly than was intended by Parliament.[36] On the other hand, a survey conducted by the County Public Assistance Officers Society in 1937 suggested that, apart from a few individual areas, the decisions of the Board were regarded as reasonable in view of the limitations laid down in the Act. Interviews in 1937 with public assistance officials of some of the larger cities and with other experts confirmed the view that the failure of the Board to take over more public assistance clients was due rather to the wording of the Act than to an administrative policy designed to evade financial responsibility.

No small part of the dissatisfaction expressed by certain local authorities has been attributable to expectations created in 1934 regarding the financial relief they might anticipate. In July of that year, the Ministry of Health issued Circular 1423 regarding the tests of normal occupation for the purpose of determining the contributions which at that time it was expected local authorities would make toward the expenses of the Board. It was then suggested that, generally speaking, the last occupation in which a person was engaged should be regarded as his normal occupation, and that an underlying principle was that a person could not lose his normal occupation merely by unemployment. The officers of the Board, however, in dealing with cases in 1937 generally took the narrower view that, unless an applicant's industrial record showed that he had in recent years had work in an insurable employment for what was considered in all the circumstances a reasonable period, he could not be regarded as satisfying the requirements of the Act. Thus local authorities as a whole had some reason for dissatisfaction in that the determination of the sums payable by them toward the expenses of the Board was based upon the assumption that a larger group of persons would be transferred to the Board than proved to be the case in 1937.[37]

Jurisdictional disputes between the insurance authorities and those responsible for unemployment assistance or public assistance

[36] Letter to the author from the Secretary of the County Councils Association, March 16, 1938.
[37] Some observers have suggested that the disappointment experienced in 1937 may also have been due to the fact that unemployment was less severe in that year, and therefore the numbers transferred were lower than might have been anticipated in 1934.

are even less likely to arise, since the question of eligibility for insurance benefits is largely determined by the objective criterion of the payment of a specified number of contributions. The opportunity for the exercise of discretionary judgments arises only in regard to disallowance of benefits for conduct such as refusal of suitable work or participation in a labor dispute. And here the prestige of the courts of referees and of the Umpire, and the gradual evolution of a large body of case law, reduce the probability that either the Unemployment Assistance Board or the public assistance authorities would challenge decisions in individual cases on the ground that the insurance administrators were influenced by a desire to divest themselves of financial responsibility.

DUAL ORGANIZATION AND OVERLAPPING OF FUNCTIONS

Unemployment Assistance and the Local Assistance and Welfare Authorities

The formal administrative arrangements between the officers of the Board and the local authorities concerned with social services appear in general to have worked smoothly. As already pointed out, the public assistance authorities cannot aid persons whose needs have been taken into account in the determination of an allowance from the Board. As early as 1935, it was arranged that officers of local authorities could ascertain on request the position of any person in relation to the Board and should in turn inform the Board's officers of any relief issued to applicants. In many areas the local officers cooperate informally on common problems, such as the elimination of cases of duplicate relief and assistance, questions of scope, and cases where recipients of public assistance and unemployment allowances are living in the same household.[38]

A measure of cooperation in regard to more general matters of policy is also secured through the advisory committees of the Board whose members include, by definition, persons with experience in public assistance and public health administration, nominated by the local county and county borough councils. Finally, the Board has set up a consultative committee, attended

[38] Cf. London County Council, *Annual Report, 1937*, Vol. I, p. 30.

by representatives of the local public assistance administrators, which discusses questions of procedure arising from the various administrative contacts between the Board and the services provided by local authorities.

Nevertheless, in spite of these administrative arrangements, problems of overlapping and duality of authority inevitably arise because of the instructions given to the Board to assist and promote the welfare of persons in need because of unemployment and their dependent households, coupled with the broad manner in which the Board has admittedly interpreted this mandate.[39] The law limits its activities in only one respect: it may not grant relief arising out of medical needs,[40] and the powers or duties of local authorities in relation thereto and to burials, mental and bodily health and education were expressly preserved. But the line between drugs, which are admittedly outside the Board's responsibility, and special nourishment, the cost of which it is permitted to meet, is not, of course, always easy to draw. Toward the end of 1935, the Board adopted a classification drawn up by an advisory committee created by the Minister of Health in connection with prescriptions under the National Health Insurance Acts.[41]

From the first, however, the Board has granted additional allowances to meet the cost of extra or special food upon a medical certificate, under its general policy of meeting special circumstances. Moreover, the discretionary power to avoid hardship in individual cases by making additional grants to meet exceptional needs and special circumstances has been (as will be shown below) very widely used. Allowances have been increased among other purposes to provide extra clothing for children attending secondary schools, boots for necessitous elementary school children, and traveling expenses of nursing mothers to and from hospitals. But this wide interpretation of provision for the welfare of its clients raises difficult problems in view of the fact that the local authorities

[39] "From the beginning, the Board has regarded as one of its important duties a progressive attempt to bring to bear upon a household in need through unemployment all the help that the social services, both statutory and voluntary, can supply." (UAB *Report,* 1935, p. 16)

[40] This definition includes medical and surgical attendance, nursing, and the supply of medicines and surgical appliances, as well as institutional treatment. Section 38 (4) and 54 (1) of the 1934 Act.

[41] UAB *Report,* 1935, p. 68.

also have powers, and in some cases duties, to provide similar services. In this sense the broad mandate given to the Board may be said to represent a reversal of the general policy which has governed British social service legislation for the last three decades, and especially since the Local Government Act of 1929.[42]

The policy had involved the creation of special administrations for the provision of services to meet special needs common to many sections of the population, whether or not technically destitute. Thus local authorities have powers under the maternal and child welfare and tuberculosis legislation to provide extra nourishment as well as medical treatment, and the provision of milk for mothers and infants under the former service (either free or at a nominal charge) is fairly widespread. Public assistance authorities are responsible for the provision of medical treatment and hospitalization of needy persons. Similarly, local education authorities are empowered in England, and compelled in Scotland, to provide school meals where these are necessary to ensure that children attending elementary schools shall not be unable, owing to lack of food, to profit from the educational service. Here again, there is in England considerable variation in the extent to which the localities have exercised their powers,[43] and in the basis of payment and principles on which the recipients of the service are selected. Local authorities also have powers to provide boots and clothing for school children.

The Board has adopted the general principle that, in so far as the special requirements of its applicants can be satisfied by a public assistance authority in the normal exercise of its powers, they should be dealt with in that manner, but where there is failure to act, the Board accepts responsibility.[44] Yet the Board clearly

---

[42] Cf. *Unemployment Assistance in Liverpool,* p. 39: "If . . . the Board is to satisfy *all* the wants of the unemployed (except medical needs), the conclusion cannot be escaped that something like the old general destitution authority has been brought into existence again, and that the developments of the last three years have amounted to nothing more or less than a 're-integration' of the old Poor Law, so far, at least, as the clients of the Board are concerned." This re-integration was carried one stage further in 1940 by a new responsibility given to the Board to supplement both contributory and non-contributory pensions to aged persons. Significantly also, the name of the Board was simultaneously changed from Unemployment Assistance Board to Assistance Board.

[43] A survey conducted by the Board in 1938 indicated that of the 422,000 school children in applicants' households, 24 per cent received free milk, 5 per cent received free food, and 8 per cent received both. (UAB *Report,* 1938, p. 20)

[44] Cf. *Unemployment Assistance in Liverpool,* p. 7.

faces a dilemma because not all local authorities have availed themselves of their powers, while the criterion of a "necessitous case" varies greatly among local authorities and often differs from that of the Board.[45] The grant of allowances to cover these needs where they are not locally provided for involves a direct contribution from central funds to local services,[46] and is an incentive to local authorities to refrain from exercising functions which they have in the past fulfilled, or which the general policy expressed in the prevailing social legislation (other than the Unemployment Act of 1934) intended they should carry out. On the other hand, failure to grant allowances covering these needs exposes the Board to criticism for failing to provide adequately for the welfare of its clients in areas where the local authority is unwilling or financially unable to exercise its statutory powers, and more generally to the charge that it is attempting to evade financial responsibilities which the Act of 1934 clearly laid upon the central government.

In another direction also, the existence of an organization dealing with a special category and interpreting its duties as widely as the Board has undoubtedly done creates difficulties with other administrators of social services, although not of a type that involves overlapping. For the Board has encouraged its clients to make the fullest possible use of local social services of whose existence they were not previously aware, or of which they had been reluctant to make full use through misunderstanding.[47] On occasion, pressure has been brought to bear on clients to avail themselves of local services. Moreover, it has been a deliberate policy of the Board to direct the attention of local advisory committees to the nature and adequacy of local facilities in the hope of build-

[45] UAB *Report,* 1937, p. 6; cf. also 1935 pp. 45, 70; and Percy Ford, *Incomes, Means Tests and Personal Responsibility* (London: P. S. King and Son, 1939), pp. 14-23.

[46] Cf. *Unemployment Assistance in Liverpool,* p. 12: "Grants [for clothing for children at secondary schools] . . . seem to be a very direct contribution to the education service and barely justifiable on the general grounds of family hardship." "It cannot be gainsaid that the Board makes a considerable contribution to the Public Health Service." (p. 18)

[47] In Liverpool the Board's officers advise every applicant with children of school age, in whose household there is evidence of straitened circumstances, to apply for school meals. (*Ibid.,* p. 11). Quite generally also, the Board has been greatly concerned with the housing problems of its clients and has endeavored to secure better accommodation for them, often by bringing their situation to the attention of the local housing authorities. (Cf. UAB *Report,* 1935, pp. 70-71; 1937, pp. 86-93)

ing up a public opinion that will encourage local authorities to make full use of their enabling powers, or support the Board in its action in meeting the deficiencies.[48]

From the broad social point of view this action must, of course, be regarded as wholly admirable, for it represents merely an attempt to secure the objectives which Parliament presumably had in mind when passing the enabling legislation. But it is apt to create friction between the Board and those local authorities which, as a matter of social policy, have made very restricted use of their powers, and in areas where the financial situation obviously prohibits further local commitments it cannot be expected to produce results.

Strangely enough, the one condition laid down by the law to limit the scope of the Board's activities, namely, the prohibition of provision of medical care, has seriously impeded the Board from adequately carrying out its duty to promote the welfare of persons in need because of unemployment and to reestablish their condition "with a view to their being in all respects fit for entry into or return to regular employment." For, despite the existence of a long-established health insurance system, ill health appears to be a serious barrier to the re-employment or rehabilitation of many of the Board's applicants.[49] Dental and optical defects, to which reference is very frequently made in the reports of officers of the Board, are among the more remediable of these causes of ill health, but are unfortunately not automatically provided for as part of the standard benefits of the health insurance system.[50] And in any

---

[48] Cf. *Ibid.*, 1937, p. 52.

[49] The special inquiry in 1938 into the condition of applicants 30 years of age and under revealed that from 8 to 9 per cent were suffering from mental or physical defects that seriously impaired their employability, and that in a quarter of these the defect was of a dental, optical, or other character that appeared to be remediable. During the same year, 22 per cent of the Board's clients who had applied for entry to training courses were rejected on medical grounds.

In his February 1936 report the English Commissioner for the Special Areas stated that, "The percentage of rejections on medical grounds for the Juvenile Transfer Centres and for the Men's Instructional Centres is alarmingly high." (p. 71) In 1938, the Board reported that, among its older women applicants, "Bad eyes and bad teeth are constant minor defects but heart trouble, rheumatism, and more serious organic complaints are, unfortunately, common." (UAB *Report*, 1938, p. 35) The prevalence of minor optical and dental defects, and a low standard of health and energy among young women applicants were also "a cause for anxiety" to the Board. (*Ibid.*, p. 37)

[50] They are, however, available in the form of additional benefits provided by approved societies which have surpluses.

14

case, some 28 per cent of the Board's applicants have no panel doctor.[51]

The Board has attempted to remedy these conditions by advising applicants to apply to their approved societies (which locally administer health insurance) where facilities are available, and by approaching local public assistance and public health authorities and voluntary organizations. In the case of some of the young applicants for training, it has been possible to use the remedial facilities provided by the Commissioners for the Special Areas at local training centers and in two of the instructional centers. But some local authorities are unwilling or unable to cooperate fully, and the Board has felt increasingly impelled to draw public attention to this serious limitation to its powers to provide for need due to unemployment, even when that phrase is relatively narrowly interpreted.[52]

In one respect, however, overlapping between the national and the local relief systems has been considerably reduced by the post-1934 arrangements. The extent of the shifts of insured persons between the national systems and public assistance has been very considerably reduced, especially since the Second Appointed Day, as is evident from Table 13.

TABLE 13. PERCENTAGE OF UNEMPLOYED INSURED PERSONS
IN RECEIPT OF PUBLIC ASSISTANCE IN GREAT
BRITAIN, 1934-1938[a]

Year	March	June	September	December
1934	6.8	6.3	5.6	7.2
1935	4.9	4.6	4.5	4.8
1936	4.6	4.5	4.3	4.4
1937	4.5	0.4	0.3	0.3
1938	0.3	0.2	0.2	0.3

[a] Excluding dependents.

Sources: Appendix Tables I, col. 7; IV, col. 6; V, col. 6.

These figures, like similar figures in earlier chapters, considerably exaggerate the extent of shifts between systems because the English component includes unemployed persons relieved for reasons other than unemployment (sickness, etc.) [53]

[51] Ibid., 1938, p. 67.
[52] Cf. Ibid., 1938, pp. 4, 25-26.
[53] The more detailed breakdown of the English figures, which has been available since 1937, indicates that for every insured person relieved on account of

The extent to which the categorization of the unemployed leads to multiple investigation of families cannot unfortunately be determined, owing to the lack of relevant data. The principal reason for its existence is undoubtedly the need of dependent families to seek medical assistance from the public assistance authorities. But this in turn is largely due to the fact that the categorical principle has been incompletely applied in another field, for the health insurance system supplies only limited medical services, does not include hospitalization, and provides no treatment at all for the dependents of insured persons. Cases of households in which some members obtain unemployment allowances while others are supported by public assistance appear to be relatively few.[54]

Unemployment Assistance and Unemployment Insurance

Relations between the Board and the Insurance Division of the Ministry of Labour are very close, and cooperation between the two bodies appears in general to be harmonious. Initial applications for assistance are made at the local employment exchanges of the Ministry of Labour, to which applicants must periodically report any changes of circumstances and to satisfy the tests of availability for work and to prove continued unemployment.[55] Moreover, all payments of allowances are made through the local offices, which have also the duty of receiving reports of casual earnings for the week preceding payment and making the necessary adjustments in the weekly payment.[56]

In addition, since a significant proportion of the applicants to the Board are persons who have exhausted insurance benefits, the

---

unemployment there were two relieved for other causes. See Ministry of Health, *Persons in Receipt of Poor Relief (England and Wales)*, published quarterly.

[54] In 1935 and 1937, income from outdoor relief constituted only 3.1 per cent and 3.5 per cent respectively of the total resources other than unemployment assistance possessed by members of the households of Board applicants. (UAB *Report*, 1935, p. 308; 1937, p. 190)

[55] The employment offices report to the Board all cases of voluntary quitting or refusal of suitable work.

[56] In November 1938, an agreement was reached with the Trade Unions Unemployment Insurance Association providing for the payment, in certain cases, of allowances through trade unions which are administering unemployment insurance benefits. The applicant who desires to take advantage of the scheme reports to the exchange to prove continued unemployment, to declare casual earnings, and to report changes of circumstances, but the actual payment is made through the trade union branch secretary or treasurer, who receives each week from the exchange a list of persons to whom payments are due and a check for the total sum payable.

employment exchanges help insurance beneficiaries to complete an assistance application form 10 days before benefits are exhausted, and forward this and the man's insurance record to the local unemployment assistance office. Furthermore, the employment offices furnish the Board's officers information concerning the contribution position, if any, of each new applicant for assistance, as well as particulars of his registration for employment.

These arrangements involve, of course, some additional work for the Ministry of Labour, and for this it is compensated out of the administrative funds voted to the Board. And, while complaints were occasionally made to the author by local office officials concerning the new duties involved in the payment of allowances,[57] there was general satisfaction that the socially unpopular task of carrying out the means test was removed from the employment offices so they could continue unimpaired their relations with their own clients.

From the point of view of the client, however, the cooperative arrangement between the local employment office and the local officer of the Board may be less advantageous in some cases. For, as the offices of the Board are not situated in the same premises as those of the Ministry,[58] the applicant may have to visit two offices if special questions regarding his application for assistance arise or if he is in urgent and immediate need and cannot await a visit from an officer of the Board. Since the territories of the insurance and the assistance systems are not identical, this may involve loss of time and occasionally some confusion. The separation of the local offices of the two systems presumably reflects an underlying desire to emphasize the distinction between the two services and to protect the employment office from association with the means test. Yet it is evident from the above account of the division of administrative work between the two groups that they are already closely associated,[59] and that in the mind of the appli-

[57] Although the local employment offices have long-established procedures for receiving reports of earnings and making necessary deductions from benefit payments, the principles governing the amount to be deducted from allowances were more complicated than those governing deductions from insurance benefits, especially during the "standstill" between the First and Second Appointed Days.

[58] For the policy governing the location of Board offices and the delimitation of their territories, see UAB *Report*, 1935, pp. 24-25.

[59] In addition, many of the unemployment assistance appeals tribunals meet in Ministry of Labour local offices.

cant the distinction between the two must rest rather on the existence of the additional step necessary to secure an allowance, namely, passage of the means test, than on the geographical separation of administrative offices.

Some degree of dual organization is also created by the appeals machinery in that the tribunals of the Board hear appeals against both the amount of the assessment and decisions on scope.[60] Despite the availability of the courts of referees of the insurance system, there was a strong case for creating a separate body to hear complaints regarding the amount of assistance allowances. The courts of referees are selected on a basis which aims to secure persons with knowledge of employment practices and, inasmuch as many of the issues turn on differences of opinion between employers and workers, to reflect both employer and worker viewpoints. But questions involving the proper assessment of resources, and the amounts of allowances involve quite different issues. The conflict is then not between worker and employer, but between the worker and the community as a whole. The adjudicating process does not call so much for a knowledge of industrial conditions and employment practices, as for an acquaintance with local standards of living and needs, and of the economic and social consequences of unduly generous or niggardly allowances.

But, by the same token, there is reason to doubt whether the adjudication of appeals on matters of scope by the chairman of the appeals tribunal, rather than by the courts of referees with their specialized knowledge, is equally justifiable. Most of the disputed scope cases involve determination of the normal occupation of the applicant and his availability for and capability of work and, to a lesser extent, the existence of labor disputes.[61] All these are mat-

---

[60] In fact, 99 per cent of all appeals in 1935 were against the amount of assessment, and even in 1937, when the Second Appointed Day cases were under consideration, they represented 61 per cent of all cases. (*Ibid.*, 1935, p. 302; 1937, p. 194)

[61]

Disputed issues	1935	1936	1937	1938
Normal occupation	13	63	13,823	8,458
Available for work	62	233	1,167	1,255
Capable of work	29	84	1,006	780
Labor disputes	4	100	58	42
Age	4	6	7	22
A combination of issues	11	43	130	212

Sources: UAB *Report*, 1935, p. 302; 1936, p. 44; 1937, p. 195; 1938, p. 43.

ters on which the courts of referees have had long experience, and in regard to which their membership has peculiar competence.

It has been asserted that the courts of referees would be unsuitable bodies to handle the types of cases presented by applicants to the Board because they are necessarily more legalistic in their interpretation of the eligibility conditions, and would take a more narrow view of employability than would be appropriate to the clients of the Board.[62] It must be recalled, however, that the courts of referees under the transitional benefits and transitional payments systems had to handle many cases where the determination of employability and the applicant's normal occupation involved the use of discretion and judgment rather than the formal application of technical rules. And where the eligibility requirements for insurance and assistance differ sharply, as in the treatment of days lost on account of sickness,[63] it is difficult not to believe that guiding principles could have been provided through written instructions. Moreover, under the present arrangements there is a real danger that there may develop an undesirable divergence between the concepts of employability adopted by the Board's officers and by the unemployment insurance administrators. As already pointed out, the Board has been criticized both for adopting a "legalistic" interpretation of the "normal employment" qualification, and for accepting within its fold persons of very dubious employability. In so far as decisions on scope turn upon the question of an applicant's normal occupation and his general standing as an employable person, it might be advantageous to refer them to an authority with special knowledge of the employment market and one likely to apply criteria less open to condemnation for being influenced by financial considerations, or by a desire to give the applicant a particular type of assistance.

Avoidance of overlapping of function is further assured by the concentration of placement work for both insurance and assistance recipients in the hands of the local employment exchanges. Discrimination in placement against assistance clients was seldom alleged, officers of the Board being in general inclined to accept

---

[62] It has been claimed that this would be especially true with regard to workers above the age of 45, and to the treatment of days lost on account of sickness and accident.

[63] See pp. 174-75.

the familiar defense of the employment exchange that assistance clients, who are almost by definition the long-period unemployed, are "less eligible" from the employers' point of view.[64]

Satisfactory division of responsibility has, however, been more difficult to secure in the training programs, and especially with regard to the recruitment of trainees for the instructional centers and their subsequent treatment by the placement authorities. Although the Board has power to set up its own training centers, it decided in its first year to make use of the institutions of the Ministry of Labour, the selection of trainees being undertaken jointly by the officers of the two organizations. But the reconditioning programs have been regarded by the Ministry largely as adjuncts to a geographical transference program, while the development of training centers has been restricted by the opportunities of placing men on completion of training. The Ministry has never seriously attempted to enlist the interest of local communities in the training program. It was, therefore, perhaps inevitable that the Board, as the authority most largely concerned with the welfare of the long-period unemployed, should have been acutely aware of the limitations which these policies imposed on the expansion of training, and especially reconditioning, centers.

During 1936 the Board came to believe that the initial recruitment by the employment offices was failing to bring forth as many trainees as the situation seemed to warrant, and that a more intimate approach, such as could be made on an individual basis by the Board's officers, would bring better results. It was accordingly decided that the Board should take primary responsibility for recruiting from among its own applicants trainees for the instructional centers, and the change was made during 1937. Furthermore, on representations from the Board, the area of recruitment for government training centers, hitherto confined with a few exceptions to the depressed areas, was broadened in July 1936 to include training in the engineering and building trades for men from other areas of heavy unemployment, while by the end of the

---

[64] It is indeed noteworthy that the two senior officials of the Board asserted in 1937 that the setting up of a parallel placement service by the non-insurance system would have been "disastrous." The Social Insurance Officer of the Trades Union Congress also expressed the belief that recipients of assistance do not get, or feel they are getting, any less chance of work than insurance recipients, except for the employer's preference for a recently employed man.

year recruitment for the instructional centers had been extended to cover the whole country.[65]

During the first years of the new arrangement the Board's efforts met with considerable success, and at one time the number of applicants exceeded the places available.[66] The different approaches to the training and reconditioning problem on the part of the two authorities became more marked with the Board's growing realization of the necessity of grappling with the social problem presented by long continued unemployment. Here again, it would seem as if the institutional arrangements for implementing a broad program that embraces both maintenance and job opportunity have not been adequately revised in conformity with the major revisions of policy brought about in 1934. As will be pointed out in Chapter IX, instructional centers are in the main welfare and reconditioning institutions whose utilization should be determined less by considerations of the probability of placement at the end of the course, than by the need of the unemployed for occupation and physical and moral recuperation. As such, it would seem as if they should more logically be under the direction and control of the Board, leaving to the Ministry the more technical and expensive types of training provided by the government training centers, the number of which might with more justification be conditioned by the possibilities of placing ex-trainees.

The possibility of overlapping of functions between the unemployment assistance and insurance systems arises also out of the fact that the former is responsible for the maintenance of persons temporarily disqualified for benefit (except for labor dispute cases) and that, since April 1937, it has had the duty of maintaining needy insurance claimants during the waiting period and of supplementing insurance benefits where these are inadequate to meet the needs of the recipient and his dependent household. It is here that the weaknesses of the dual national unemployment program, to which opponents of this principle have often pointed,

[65] Preference for men from the depressed areas was, however, maintained.

[66] Even in 1937 when, as a result of improved business, the total number of presumptively eligible and suitable men for admittance to instructional centers who were on the unemployment register dropped from 237,885 in December 1936 to 192,962 in December 1937, the number admitted to the instructional centers was 20,588, as compared with 20,872 in 1936. (UAB *Report,* 1937, p. 45) During the summer it was found necessary to relax recruiting efforts owing to the shortage of accommodations. (*Ibid.,* p. 51)

are perhaps most apparent. For, on the one hand, if insurance is to be regarded as a preferential form of aid from which persons may be excluded on account of improper conduct, this penalty may be ineffective if the alternative relief system offers payments that compare favorably with those available under insurance. And, on the other hand, the failure of insurance benefits to cover needs for any substantial number of persons raises the question whether, if the supplementary system has in any case to provide for large numbers, it would not be advantageous to have a single system which would avoid dual administration.

Up to the present it must be conceded that in Great Britain these weaknesses have been more apparent than real. This fortunate result has been due partly to the nature of the benefits provided by the insurance system, and partly because the Unemployment Assistance Board in its treatment of insurance claimants who are disqualified for benefits, or undergoing waiting periods, or receiving benefits inadequate for their needs, has been fully aware of the wider implications of its policy, and in particular of its repercussions upon the prestige of the insurance system. Similar considerations have also weighed with the Unemployment Insurance Statutory Committee in making proposals for changes in insurance benefits.[67]

The extent to which qualified insurance claimants were brought in contact with the assistance system on account of the waiting period requirement has been small, partly because in 1937 the waiting period requirement had been reduced to 3 days. During 1937, of some 30,000 to 40,000 persons serving the waiting period in any week, seldom more than 3,000 applied to the Board for assistance. Nor were all these granted allowances, for the Board was unwilling to encourage improvidence or unwise spending. Hence, except in cases of urgent necessity, allowances were normally granted only to waiting period cases in which the last employment had been of short duration or intermittent, or where wages had been exceptionally low. Where there was reason to

---

[67] The Committee stated that one of the reasons prompting it to increase dependent children's benefits in July 1935 "was the desire of reducing as much as possible any occasion for supplementing benefit to large families, either by unemployment assistance or by public assistance." (UISC *Financial Report*, December 1935, p. 22; also *Ibid.*, 1937, p. 24)

believe that the need of the applicant was due to improvidence, the allowance was frequently granted in kind.[68]

Cases of supplementation of insurance benefits by unemployment assistance were slightly more important statistically, although here too their number was kept low by the fact that insurance benefits had steadily approached the maintenance level and that benefits were also granted to dependents. Nevertheless, despite the fact that the weekly unemployment assistance allowance for a man and wife was 1s. lower than the corresponding insurance benefit for many types of households, the sum payable under assistance exceeded those under insurance in certain types of cases.

In the first place, the dependent children's allowances to recipients of insurance benefits for children below the age of 16 were fixed at the uniform sum of 3s., regardless of the age of the child, whereas the Board's allowances were increased progressively with advancing age (ranging from 3s. for children under 5 years, to 6s. for dependents up to 18 years of age). In the second place, the insurance system provided benefits for only one adult dependent, whereas no such limitation applied to the Board's allowances. In the third place, unlike insurance benefits, allowances could be increased in areas where rents were high. Finally, from 1937 onwards the Board granted additional allowances during winter months.[69] Hence, households with several children above the age of 5, or with more than one adult dependent, or living in high rent areas, were likely to find that the cash income obtainable from the Board would exceed the insurance benefit. Despite these differences, however, up to 1939 less than one per cent of all recipients of insurance (including both the general and the agricultural schemes) drew allowances in supplementation of benefits, while in 1939, the percentage rose only to 1.5.[70]

---

[68] UAB *Report*, 1937, pp. 31-32; 1938, pp. 20-21. During 1938, 186,000 applications for maintenance during waiting periods were received, and over 120,000 granted. (*Ibid.*, p. 60)

[69] In practice, the bulk of the supplementation resulted from the second and third of these facts, a situation which explains why the major part of the supplementation cases occurred in London, a high rent area.

[70] Since the Second Appointed Day, the number of cases of supplementation at any given time have increased from 2,341 (June 21, 1937) to 14,343 (March 13, 1939). (Ministry of Labour *Gazette*, monthly table entitled "Applicants for Insurance Benefits and Unemployment Allowances")

By no means all those who stood to gain by applying to the Board did in fact do so. Dislike of submitting to the means test was apparently sufficiently strong. Indeed, this fact suggests that the major justification for the insurance type of benefits is still valid. Many of the unemployed preferred a less adequate sum payable as a right, to the larger allowance which might have been received, but only after undergoing a test of need with consequent loss of privacy.[71] No doubt also many insurance beneficiaries, being by definition the short-term unemployed, were likely to anticipate speedy reabsorption into employment and to feel therefore it was not worth while to seek supplementation for a short period. Moreover, the Board attempted to keep down the number of claims by refusing to supplement during an initial period of three or four weeks after a substantial period of work, or where the difference between insurance benefit and assistance allowance was not large.[72]

The payment of allowances to persons temporarily disqualified for insurance benefits because of refusal of suitable work, dismissal for misconduct, or voluntary quitting without just cause has presented somewhat greater difficulties. However, the number of cases, although tending to increase from year to year, has never exceeded 0.8 per cent of all beneficiaries (or 7,529 persons in March 1939).[73] Believing that "it would obviously be against public policy to grant an allowance of such an amount or under such conditions as to make the suspension from benefit a matter of indifference to the applicant," [74] the Board has attempted to apply the principle that in general the allowance should be at least 2s. below the benefit rate. This was likely to be almost automatically the case in regard to persons with available resources, or single men living in lodgings. But for other groups the probability that the normal allowance would be equal to or even above the benefit rate was considerable. Where the reduction would not involve undue hardship (the period of disqualification would at most last a few weeks), allowances were to be adjusted so as

[71] For the effects of the assessment of the earnings of working members of the household upon this attitude toward the means test, however, see Chapter IX.

[72] The average supplementary allowance was just over 8s. weekly by the end of 1937, and 7s. 9d. by the end of 1938. (UAB *Report*, 1938, p. 61)

[73] Ministry of Labour *Gazette*.

[74] UAB *Report*, 1938, p. 21.

to produce a result of 2s. less than the insurance benefit rate, although where the benefit rate was 35s. or more a further reduction of 1s. or 1s. 6d. was in order. Finally, in those cases where reductions could not be made without hardship, officers of the Board were directed to pay in kind at least half of the excess of the allowance above rent. Occasionally the allowance is paid to the wife, while in 1938 a few individuals were required to attend a work center.[75]

Unemployment Insurance and Assistance Authorities and the Special Areas Commissioners

The appointment of the two Special Areas Commissioners as semi-independent authorities, with seemingly wide power to promote the economic development and social improvement of these areas, gave rise to new problems of coordination of policy and new possibilities of overlapping of function. In fact, however, the activities of the new bodies were considerably limited by legal decisions and in other ways, so that the problem of proper coordination did not assume serious proportions.

The Minister of Labour assured Parliament that, although independent, "of course the Commissioners will be responsible through me to Parliament for broad policy." Despite this fact, however, the government spokesmen insisted that the independent position of the Commissioners would enable them to carry through experiments on a large scale which would be impossible if they had to "go through the elaborate procedure of Government Departments." [76] It soon appeared that these two policies were incompatible. In fact, the necessity of seeking the Minister's sanction for all main lines of policy made "the Commissioner as much subject to orthodox financial control as any Government Department. Whilst they may not hamper the freedom and initiative of the Commissioner so far as making proposals is concerned, they do result in restricting his powers to carry these proposals into effect." [77]

[75] *Ibid.*, pp. 21, 48.
[76] Statements of the Minister of Labour and the Parliamentary Secretary to the Ministry of Labour in the House of Commons. (*Hansard,* November 14, 1934, p. 2102, and November 15, 1934, p. 2296)
[77] *Report of the Commissioner for the Special Areas (England and Wales),* (Cmd. 4957, 1935), p. 6.

In another way also, coordination of policy was achieved, although at the expense of limiting the activities of the Commissioners. For, with the exception of the small holdings projects discussed in Chapter IX, the latter were forbidden to supplement specific grants made or offered by a government department, nor could they offer to a local authority a grant for any service for which a specific grant was payable by any government department. And the word "payable" was interpreted broadly to mean a grant which a department had power to make, but chose either generally or in a particular instance not to make. Thus not only were the activities of the Commissioners severely restricted, but it became necessary to consult with every department likely to be affected by the Commissioners' proposals. The inevitable delay attendant upon this situation was to some extent mitigated in England and Wales in 1938 by the appointment of an inter-departmental coordinating committee.[78] In the previous year the activities of the two national commissioners had been more closely coordinated by the appointment of a representative of the Scottish Special Areas Commissioner to hold fortnightly consultations with the English body.

Overlapping of function was also to a large extent eliminated by the internal organization of the Special Areas Commissioners' offices. The English body divided its work among four divisions, each headed by an official drawn from the ministry with whose work that section of the Commissioner's activities was most closely allied.[79]

Finally, since the Commissioners were in agreement with the government's general policy of refusing to assist relief schemes designed solely to give employment, the main possibility for overlapping of function arose from their wide powers to provide for the social improvement of the special areas and for training and geographical transference. Friction was avoided so far as the transference work was concerned by a self-effacing attitude on the part of the Special Areas Commissioners who were prepared to recognize the special competence and experience of the Minis-

[78] *Ibid.,* 1937 (Cmd. 5595), p. 8.
[79] Thus, the division responsible for administering aid to local services, housing, and health measures was headed by a senior officer detailed from the Ministry of Health; that concerned with the trading estates and the development of industry was headed by an officer from the Board of Trade.

try of Labour in this field, and confined their activities to assisting financially certain private and voluntary enterprises which afforded training and good prospects of placement and to promoting schemes for settling the unemployed on the land. Conflict over the promotion of physical training courses was avoided by a territorial division of responsibility. The Commissioners financed programs in the special areas, but left their administration to the ministry which gave financial aid only to courses outside the special areas.

Nor has the development of the Commissioners' social welfare program as yet led to any serious overlapping with the functions of the Unemployment Assistance Board. This is partly because the Board's own welfare program is still not fully developed, but any serious expansion of this part of its program would indicate the desirability of transferring the Commissioners' powers to the Board.[80] Against this advantage of administrative simplicity, however, must be set the social disadvantage that would result from the fact that the Board's activities are restricted to measures affecting the unemployed. In areas that have suffered from prolonged depression, the need for welfare services, occupational activities, and social amenities is not confined to the unemployed alone.

CONCLUSION

It must be admitted that many of the problems raised by the attempt to treat the unemployed as a separate group for the purposes of maintenance and ameliorative treatment have arisen in Great Britain in a less acute form than *a priori* reasoning might have suggested. It is true that the separation has not been completely achieved and that there is still a small group of persons seeking wage earning employment who are not covered by the insurance and assistance systems. But jurisdictional disputes as to responsibility for the maintenance of given individuals are relatively rare, and would be still further reduced if coverage of unemployment assistance were extended to embrace all the unem-

---

[80] The original legislation appointing the Commissioners had indeed provided that certain powers should be transferred to the Board on the expiry of the Commissioners' appointment.

ployed and not merely persons covered by the old age and survivors insurance plan.

The further subdivision of the unemployed into insurance claimants and assistance applicants, which is now based largely upon the duration of unemployment, appears to correspond to a very real difference in both the economic characteristics and the economic and social needs of the two groups.[81]

Overlapping between the special unemployment measures and general relief has been greatly reduced, and since the Second Appointed Day the number of insured persons receiving public assistance has fallen to less than one per cent of the insured unemployed, while overlapping on account of supplementation has completely disappeared.

The division of functions and responsibility between the unemployment insurance and assistance systems still gives rise to some unsolved problems. Use of the public employment offices as the common agency for reporting continuity of unemployment, for placement, and for making payments is an obvious convenience. But the geographical separation of these from the area offices of the unemployment assistance system, which administer the means test, while reflecting a desire to preserve the insurance administration from any contamination by the unpopular test and unpleasant associations with a procedure still to some extent reminiscent of the poor law, has certain disadvantages from the point of view of the client. Furthermore, while the use of the appeals tribunals of the assistance system for deciding appeals on determinations of need seems functionally defensible, their use for determining appeals concerning scope, which involve the occupational and employment history of applicants, seems to be an unnecessary failure to make use of the experience of the courts of referees of the insurance system, and to involve dual administrative mechanisms. It would also seem that responsibility for the conduct of the instructional centers should be vested in the Unemployment Assistance Board rather than the Ministry of Labour. Some degree of overlapping between the insurance and assistance systems arises

---

[81] The extent to which use has been made of the powers given to the Unemployment Assistance Board to provide fully for the special needs of its clientele will be discussed in Chapter IX.

because of supplementation of insurance benefits by assistance allowances, and because insurance claimants serving a waiting period or undergoing penalty disallowances for reasons other than the existence of a labor dispute, must seek aid from the Board if in need. But here too the statistical significance of overlapping is extremely small, and appears unlikely to assume serious proportions so long as the Board applies its present policies, and so long as British workers persist in the belief that receipt of a slightly smaller sum if given as a right is preferable to a possibly larger sum obtained by undergoing a means test.

Finally, in view of the mutual interaction of the levels of insurance benefits and assistance allowances, and of the extent to which the policies of the one system affect the other, it is perhaps unfortunate that policy control is vested in two financially independent agencies. But here too the consequences have been less serious than might have been anticipated because of a recognition of this fact on the part of the Unemployment Insurance Statutory Committee and the Unemployment Assistance Board, because of a high degree of consultation and cooperation between the ranking officials of the two agencies, and finally because in fact, if not in theory, the Ministry of Labour is regarded by Parliament as being responsible for both the insurance and the assistance systems.[82]

In any case, discussion of the problems created by the unemployment assistance system must take account of the fact that categorization of dependency is a policy that has been increasingly and deliberately adopted in Great Britain since 1908. The aged, the sick, the blind, the widowed, the orphaned, and the unemployed had all been treated as separate categories by the national government and provided in varying degree with specialized assistance long before the 1934 Act extended the group of unemployed affected by categorical assistance. In the case of the unemployed, the desirability of categorization was explicitly confirmed by the Royal Commission on Unemployment Insurance of 1932, and by many local authorities.[83] Even services provided by the local

[82] Cf. John D. Millett, *The Unemployment Assistance Board.*
[83] The Commission urged the creation of a special local body to administer the residual unemployment relief system. Believing that the group affected "cannot

authorities to meet needs of a less narrowly economic character have been increasingly developed on a categorical basis. A long series of enactments has permitted the local authorities to provide medical treatment, housing, training, additional nourishment and clothing, and these services have normally been administered by more or less independent sub-committees of each local authority. An impetus to further differentiation of services was given by section 5 of the Local Government Act of 1929, which provided that all assistance which could lawfully be provided otherwise than in the form of general public assistance should be provided under the specialized acts as soon as circumstances permitted.[84]

Inevitably this high degree of categorization creates serious problems, many of which, owing to the piecemeal manner in which the new development has come about, are still imperfectly recognized. It is this incomplete application of the categorical prin-

be dealt with satisfactorily by the Public Assistance service as at present organised," the Commission urged that "a part of that service ought to be specially designed for their needs." (*Final Report, p. 279*) A special committee of the local authority, to be entitled the Unemployment Assistance Committee, or a sub-committee of the public assistance committee, was to be set up and its functions were to be performed in association with the Ministry of Labour instead of with the Ministry of Health which exercised general supervision over the local assistance services. The Commission favored the creation of a special committee as being more likely to develop rapidly the appropriate technique and outlook than one which was subject to the same general supervision as other forms of public assistance, and believed that it would be administratively more convenient for the local organization to reflect the central distinction of functions.

This view was echoed by many of the authorities responsible for administering public assistance. Thus, the Association of Municipal Corporations, in testifying before the Commission, urged that the able-bodied unemployed should be taken off public assistance and put in a separate category. (*Minutes of Evidence, p. 540*) The London County Council, after the Second Appointed Day, reported that, "The loss of the more straightforward (and temporarily destitute) cases which have gone over to the Unemployment Assistance Board makes practicable a closer concentration on the social problem cases remaining in the able-bodied category and on the special difficulties of the aged and the infirm." (*Annual Report, 1937, Vol. I, Part II, p. 30*)

[84] The most important of these acts were the Public Health Act, 1875; the Local Government Act, 1888; the Mental Deficiency Act, 1913; the Maternity and Child Welfare Act, 1918; the Blind Persons Act, 1920; the Public Health (Tuberculosis) Act, 1921; and the Educational Act, 1921. By no means all the authorities have as yet followed out this injunction, and it will probably be many years before all of them, and in particular the counties, have reduced general public assistance to a service dealing only with emergency cases and the domiciliary relief of destitution caused by age, sickness, etc., and the institutional needs of the infirm. As a result of the Blind Persons Act, 1938, assistance given to blind persons by local authorities was deemed to be given exclusively under that Act and not under the poor law.

15

ciple, combined with a lack of consistency in the criteria by which eligibility for the different services is determined, that occasions the most serious problems of overlapping of jurisdiction to which the operation of the unemployment assistance system has given rise. If the various locally supplied services were equally available in all areas and not left in large measure to the decision of the localities, if within each area the different eligibility conditions were coordinated, and finally if the central government itself completed the application of the categorical principle in the fields where it is already introduced (and notably in health insurance), then many of the problems to which attention has been drawn in this chapter would be even less significant.

In recent years, and especially since the creation of the Unemployment Assistance Board, there has been a growing recognition of this wider problem. The organization of authorities concerned with public assistance,[85] associations of public assistance and local government officers,[86] and research groups and individ-

---

[85] In 1933, at the Public Assistance Conference organized by the County Councils Association and the Association of Municipal Corporations on behalf of the Public Assistance Authorities, a resolution was adopted calling for a revision and codification of "the various enactments under which maintenance, nursing, medical and surgical treatment and all like personal assistance are afforded to necessitous cases . . . with the object of finally abolishing the Poor Law as such." The Poor Law Amendment Committee of the two Associations, to which the problem was referred, reported that the questions of policy involved extended beyond the mere coordination of relief by local authorities, and that a comprehensive inquiry should properly include also a consideration of the administration of relief by the government and by voluntary agencies. Efforts to induce the government to appoint a Royal Commission proved unavailing, the Ministry of Health expressing the view that this should await further experience in the operation of the unemployment assistance system. In 1937, the Conference devoted a session to the general question of the scope of public assistance, and carried by a large majority a resolution requesting the appointment of a Royal Commission or Departmental Committee to consider the desirability of legislation coordinating all forms of public assistance now administered by local authorities. (See the *Final Report* of the Conference [1937], pp. 72-95.) The corresponding Scottish organization, the Scottish Public Assistance Conference, also devoted considerable time in 1937 to the problems of coordination.

[86] In 1936 and 1937, the County Public Assistance Officers Society made a careful study of the methods of avoiding overlapping between public assistance and other local committees dealing with education, the mentally defective, public health, maternity and child welfare, etc. The paper presented at the various sessions included not merely an analysis of the defects of the existing system, but also examples of the cooperative methods adopted in different localities. The Conference of the National Association of Administrators of Local Government Establishments and the Local Government Clerks Association have also paid increasing attention to the problem.

uals [87] have increasingly pointed out the need for coordination and for the reconsideration of fundamental issues which must precede coordination.

[87] Cf. PEP, *Report on the British Social Services*, June 1937; and Percy Ford, "The Co-ordination of Means Tests," *Public Administration*, October 1937, pp. 385-92, "The Family and the Social Services," *Ibid.*, April 1938, pp. 146-56, and "Means Tests and Responsibility for Needy Relatives," *Sociological Review*, April 1937, pp. 175-89.

Chapter VIII

THE CENTRALIZATION OF UNEMPLOYMENT RELIEF

The post-1934 unemployment relief system in Great Britain is characterized by a high degree of centralization. The unemployment insurance system had indeed been centralized from the first: the novelty of the new situation lay in the introduction of centralization of policy and administration into residual relief, a field traditionally regarded as the peculiar preserve of local authorities. Before analyzing the consequences of this development, a brief summary of the administrative organization of the Unemployment Assistance Board is in order.

The Administrative Organization of the Unemployment Assistance Board

The Unemployment Assistance Board, which is responsible for policy, consists of a chairman, a deputy chairman, and not less than one nor more than four other members, including at least one woman. The members are appointed by the Crown, and receive salaries, but are not civil servants.[1]

The work of the Board is carried out by a centrally appointed staff, the majority of whom have civil service status.[2] The headquarters staff in London is concerned, under the direction of the Board, with the formation of policy and with general administrative control. Day-to-day administration, involving contact with clients, investigation of needs and determination of allowances,

---

[1] The salaries of the Board members are charged to the Consolidated Fund, like those of judges, the Comptroller and Auditor General and a few others whose conduct it is not desirable to review annually when appropriations are being considered. The Board, which took office on July 2, 1934, consisted of 6 members with Lord Rushcliffe (lately Sir Henry Betterton, former Minister of Labour), as chairman.

[2] The entire (relatively small) headquarters staff is on a civil service basis, as are all district and assistant district officers. It was provided from the outset that all area and assistance officers should be permanent civil servants, although in the initial organizing period there were some departures from this rule. The only non-civil service jobs are in the lower grades. (UAB *Report*, 1935, pp. 25-27, 298-301; 1936, pp. 8-9, 149-50)

is carried on from some 240 Area Offices, which are basic offices in the Board's organization.[3] These are supplemented by between 40 and 50 subsidiary offices or "out-stations" which are opened and shut down as need indicates. Furthermore, the Board was permitted to make arrangements with county councils to use certain members of their staffs as agents in areas where it was anticipated that the number of clients would not justify the setting up of a special UAB office. During the first 18 months agency arrangements were made with 35 county councils in England and Wales and 22 county councils and one large burgh in Scotland. By mutual consent these arrangements were not renewed, and by the end of 1936 the Board had its own offices in all except 10 rather remote areas.[4]

The Area Offices are grouped under 27 (originally 28) district offices, each in charge of a District Officer responsible for supervising the work of the Area Offices and the general organization of the Board's work in the district, conducting important negotiations with its local offices, supervising the agency arrangements, ensuring the proper functioning of the appeals machinery and, from the end of 1936 onwards, maintaining contact with local advisory committees. Seven regional officers attached to the headquarters staff have the duty of keeping headquarters acquainted with the practical difficulties experienced in the field and of acting as liaison and information officers between the Board and the district offices.

In fact, however, this high degree of centralization of policy determination and administration is modified by certain other features of the organization of the Board, which have been designed to secure local representation and cooperation. In the first place adjudication of complaints is performed by some 140 local appeals tribunals,[5] each consisting of a chairman and two other members, one being a representative of the workers and the other

---

[3] Certain administrative functions are also carried out by the Ministry of Labour through its employment exchanges, as shown in Chapter VII.

[4] UAB *Report*, 1936, pp. 9-10, 151.

[5] In deciding to set up this number of tribunals, the Board tried to ensure that the district of each tribunal should coincide with one or more of the Board's administrative areas, that the districts should be large enough to provide a substantial volume and variety of appeals but small enough to exhibit some individual local characteristics, and that the load of work should be approximately evenly distributed among the tribunals. (*Ibid.*, 1935, p. 48)

a representative of the Board. The chairmen,[6] who were selected on the basis of their local standing, their knowledge of local conditions and ability to handle appeals procedure, were appointed by the Minister of Labour and not by the Board. Although local opinion was canvassed, political and industrial organizations as such were deliberately not consulted, a fact which was strongly resented by organized labor.[7] The district officers appeared to have played a large part in compiling the list of names sent to the Minister of Labour. The workers' representative was appointed to each sitting by the Board from a large panel of persons representing workers, nominated by the Minister of Labour with the aid of the local employment committees of the Ministry.[8] So far as possible efforts were made to secure representatives of the industrial rather than the political labor movement. The Board's representative was appointed by the Board, but was not a member of its paid staff.[9] The Board aimed to secure the services of "members of the public having good local standing, a reputation of freedom from political bias, and a knowledge of local conditions," [10] and nominations were obtained from responsible persons and from official and non-official bodies.

The appeals tribunals, therefore, consist entirely of local people. Moreover, their decisions are final, there being no superior court of review for coordinating their work comparable to the Umpire in relation to the courts of referees under the insurance system. Members of the tribunals are provided with copies of all the instructions and circulars sent from headquarters to the local

[6] There were also 215 substitute chairmen.
[7] Cf. the Trades Union Congress publication, *Unemployment Assistance Means Test Regulations,* by J. L. Smythe, February 1935.
[8] In 1935 about 7,500 persons were nominated for the country as a whole. It subsequently transpired that, in view of the practice of asking workers' representatives to serve in rotation, the size of the panels was too large to permit individual members to secure adequate experience of the procedure and technique of tribunal work. Accordingly in 1937, on representations from the Board, the numbers were reduced by the Minister. (UAB *Report,* 1935, pp. 49-50; 1937, pp. 57-58)
[9] In 1935, 138 persons were appointed, and another 589 were chosen as substitute representatives from a list of over 5,000 persons. (*Ibid.,* 1935, p. 49)
[10] *Ibid.,* p. 49. In fact, the majority of the representatives had their main contact with social conditions in commercial or professional work, combined in most cases with experience in local government administration or voluntary welfare work.

resources which disqualified an applicant from receipt of an allowance, and the composition of the group whose income might be called upon to help support the applicant and the extent of that support were all left to the Board's determination.

The Provisions of the First Regulations

Two broad problems were faced by the Board in issuing its first regulations which were to give concrete expression to the intent of the Act, namely, whether to lay down specific or general instructions, and whether to adopt standards that would apply to the whole country or to attempt to differentiate by locality. The first issue presented difficulties because, while the regulations had to be approved by Parliament and in providing guidance for local officers had obviously to ensure reasonable uniformity of administration, it was recognized that a service based on need would call for regulations sufficiently elastic to enable individual cases to be dealt with on their merits. A compromise solution was adopted whereby the regulations as drafted set out in specific detail the amount of an allowance in a normal case, and the rules by which resources held to be available for support of the applicant were to be calculated. But provisions were added to permit the exercise of discretion in all cases where there were special or exceptional circumstances.

On the second issue, the Board decided in favor of "meeting equal needs by equal allowances." A single uniform money allowance was to be the standard in all parts of the country, modified only by special allowances to take account of variations in rent. In coming to this momentous decision, the Board was swayed by three considerations. First, investigation showed that, apart from the item of rent, local differences in the cost of living were so small as not to justify different scales and rules for the assessment of need. Second, the Board held that "it would not be generally accepted that a man, wife and children should receive different amounts according to where they lived, if their necessary expenditure was the same." Finally, uniformity in real standards of living appeared to be the necessary corollary of "a service the whole cost of which was borne by the Exchequer." [15]

[15] *Ibid.*, 1935, p. 33.

Thus from the first, the policy of the Board involved the imposition of a uniform national allowance for specified types of persons, and a uniform national standard for the determination of need. Accordingly, the first regulations, issued December 21, 1934, provided for uniform scales of money allowances for households of different types. To ensure a closer approximation to uniform real standards of living, the regulations provided for increases or decreases in the money allowance in cases where rents were relatively high or low.[16] A uniform national standard for the calculation of resources was also laid down.[17]

Prevailing differences in real standards of living among individuals were recognized in the first regulations, other than through the exercise of discretion, only by the provision of a "wage-stop" clause, under which no applicant could receive an allowance which was equal to, or greater than, the amount which would ordinarily be available in the form of earnings if he and the other members of the household whose needs had been taken into account were following their normal occupations.[18] It was estimated that by December 1937, some 6,500 of the current allowances had been reduced on account of the operation of this clause.[19]

[16] The method of adjustment involved the setting of a "basic" rent which was roughly one-fourth of the total allowance. If the actual rent paid was in excess of this basic amount, the allowance could be increased by an amount equal to the excess, or by one-third of the basic rent, whichever was less. If the actual rent paid fell below the basic rent, the allowance was to be reduced by the amount of the difference, although in special circumstances the amount of the reduction could be decreased by a sum not exceeding 1s. 6d. (*Ibid.*, 1935, p. 292)

[17] The regulations provided general rules governing the extent to which capital assets of various types should be taken into account, and their value computed; specified certain types of income possessed by the applicant and the members of his household which were to be disregarded; laid down rules as to the treatment of income from subletting and taking in lodgers, and finally indicated the extent to which income from earnings was to be regarded as available for the support of the applicant and his household. As will be indicated later, a distinction was drawn between the applicant and his immediate family, and other members of the household, the proportion of earnings which the earner could keep for his own use being greater the more remote the degree of relationship to the applicant. (*Ibid.*, pp. 292-93)

[18] This clause was retained in the revised regulations, but was modified by the power to waive its application "where special circumstances or needs of an exceptional character exist."

[19] *Ibid.*, 1937, p. 22.

The Effect of the "Standstill" Act

In fact, however, the uniform national standard was a reality only during the first 6 weeks of the Board's administration and in the period after May 1938. Almost immediately there was an outcry against the new regulations—especially loud from those who had been more favorably treated under the transitional payments scheme, but also from almost the entire labor movement which was officially opposed in principle to any system based upon a means test. The government of the day conceded to this pressure with surprising suddenness, and on February 15, 1935 passed the Unemployment Assistance (Temporary Provisions) Act, introducing the so-called "standstill" arrangement. During its operation—and it was not finally liquidated until May 1938—applicants for unemployment assistance were to be granted either the Board's allowance, or the sum which they would have received had their needs been assessed by the public assistance authorities under the transitional payments system, whichever was the higher. This arrangement, it should be noted, applied not only to those in receipt of transitional payments at the time the Board commenced operations, but also to all subsequent applicants who came to the Board because they had exhausted insurance benefit rights in the current benefit year, or had exhausted benefits in the preceding benefit year and had not subsequently paid 10 contributions which would entitle them, if otherwise qualified, to draw benefits in the current year. Finally, it applied to those who had not paid 30 contributions but had paid 8 in the preceding 2 years or 30 contributions at any time.

Thus the "Standstill" Act perpetuated the very differences in treatment of individuals which it had been hoped would be avoided by the creation of the Unemployment Assistance Board. Its effect was indeed to establish the Board's regulations as minimum standards for the country as a whole. All persons who had resided in areas where the local authority, for reasons of economy or social policy, had provided transitional payments below the standard of the Board's regulations (rather less than half of the Board's clients) were raised to the new level set by the Board.

But the remaining recipients, living in the more prosperous or liberal areas, were allowed to retain their privileged position.[20]

Even after the revised regulations were issued in 1936 [21] which, being somewhat more generous than those previously prevailing, decreased the proportion of applicants for whom assessments under the transitional payments scheme were more advantageous, the minimum standard of the Board was still not uniformly applicable. For, while the right to claim either the Board's allowance or that which would have been payable under the transitional payments scheme was in principle withdrawn,[22] the Board in putting the change into effect profited by its mistakes of January 1935. The inevitably unpopular reductions were carried through gradually, and local advice was sought concerning the timing of the liquidation. For a period of 18 months, the normal assessment of needs, if less than the sum which would have been paid under the "Standstill" Act, could be increased by a reasonable amount, having regard to all the circumstances of the case. During the 18-month period these increased allowances were to be progressively reduced to the standard of the regulations. The local advisory committees were to advise as to the manner and timing of these adjustments in different classes of cases.

At the end of 1936 there were about 170,000 applicants whose allowances, after application of the revised regulations, contained "standstill" additions.[23] During 1937 these additional payments were gradually liquidated in accordance with recommendations

---

[20] The percentages of clients drawing payments under the two sets of regulations were as follows at different times during 1935 and 1936:

Period	Unemployment assistance	Transitional payments
Week ended March 15, 1935	49	51
Week ended May 17, 1935	49	51
Week ended November 15, 1935	48	52
Week ended December 13, 1935	44	56
Week ended June 26, 1936	41	59

Source: Draft Unemployment Assistance Regulations, 1936: Memorandum by the Minister of Labour (Cmd. 5228), p. 12.

[21] Effective November 16, 1936. (UAB Report, 1936, pp. 135-40)

[22] By an order of the Minister of Labour, July 15, 1936, effective November 16, 1936. (Cf. Ministry of Labour, Report for the Year 1936, p. 62)

[23] Of the 620,000 applicants whose allowances were reassessed on application of the new regulations, 230,000 had their needs assessed at amounts in excess of the rates payable under the "standstill," while 210,000 received allowances equal to the "standstill" payment. (UAB Report, 1937, p. 14)

to remind officers with all due emphasis that it rests with them to bring a sense of fairness and reason to bear upon all cases coming before them." "The exercise of discretion to meet the special circumstance of a case remains the most important part of an officer's duty."

Considerable attention was paid to defining the relative spheres of discretionary authority of the district and area officers. The former were in principle given complete discretionary powers not subject to any formal limitations. They were, however, expected to report to the regional officers or to the Board special circumstances affecting large numbers of applicants within their district whose numerical importance might justify a general ruling to avoid overburdening the district officer,[34] or cases which raised difficult questions of principle. Moreover, they were from time to time circularized by the Board as to the general principles which should govern their activities.

Area officers were encouraged to exercise discretion within a more limited range and were instructed to refer to the district officer all cases where, having reached this limit, they believed that hardship to the applicant would result were no further adjustment made.[35]

In practice very great use was made by area and district officers of their discretionary power. In the first year of operation, some 148,000 or over 20 per cent of the cases dealt with at any one time

[34] Thus, in three London areas where rents in general were unduly high, district officers were authorized by the Board to empower their area officers to allow rent up to 2s. 6d. per week above the maximum for which the regulations provided.

[35] The limits were determined by general instructions from the Board. As a rule the criteria were the amount of the extra allowance and the nature of the special circumstances. Thus, area officers could allow up to 10s. for an earning member of a household to meet commitments arising from a court order, but if more was needed the case was to be referred to the district officer. Area officers could make discretionary grants up to 5s. for each item to meet special needs for extra nourishment due to sickness, or the temporary absence of the wife, but should the total of discretionary allowances of this type amount to more than 10s. for one applicant or household, the case was to be referred to the district officer. Similarly, while the area officer was empowered to give discretionary grants up to specified sums to meet certain types of special circumstances, there were others (such as commitments of earning members not arising from a court order, e.g. installment payments, income tax charges, etc., and special expenses of an earning member not arising from the fact of employment) where authority to make a special allowance rested with the district officer, and the area officer had no discretion.

received discretionary additions to the normal allowances provided by the regulations.[36] At the end of the following year discretionary allowances were paid to some 115,000 (or roughly 19 per cent) of the total applicants; at any one time during 1937 there were 150,000 persons (or roughly 25 per cent of all applicants) receiving discretionary allowances.[37]

The extent of the discretionary additions varied from small sums of 2s. to 3s. a week to provide extra milk, eggs, etc., for invalids (usually granted only on production of a doctor's certificate) or considerably larger payments up to 12s. a week for special diets for diabetics, to payment of traveling expenses to visit sick relatives, purchase of clothing where this could not be otherwise secured, and special allowances for the higher maintenance charges of children attending college.[38] Much more restricted use was made of the power to make lump-sum grants (varying from a few shillings to several pounds) to meet exceptional needs (the so-called "pots and pans clause").[39]

During 1937 additional discretionary powers were given to the Board's officers to meet two special situations: the rather general rise in the cost of living which coincided with the onset of winter, and the festive spirit of the Christmas season. In October 1937, the officers were instructed to examine all applications coming up for review and to make discretionary additions to allowances in those in which the rise in prices might create hardship. The increases were normally to be between 2s. and 3s. per week, and priority was to be given to households in which not less than half the total income was represented by an allowance. By the begin-

---

[36] *Ibid.*, 1935, p. 41. The most important types of circumstances justifying these additions were: extra nourishment required on medical grounds, about 38,000 cases; high rents, about 21,000; extra expenses of earners (travelling expenses, tools, etc.), about 43,000; single persons living alone, about 22,000. (*Ibid.*, pp. 41-44)

[37] *Ibid.*, 1936, p. 27, 1937, p. 24.

[38] The reports of the District Officers in Chapter VIII of the UAB *Report*, 1935 (pp. 84-289) contain a very full and fascinating account, with specific case citations, of the wide variety of discretionary allowances. Somewhat less detailed accounts appear in subsequent *Reports* where the district officers' comments have been replaced by those of the regional officers.

[39] In the first four years the number of payments under this clause ranged from 10,000 in 1935 to 23,000 in 1937, and dropped to 20,000 in 1938. In 1937, about half of the payments were less than 20s. in amount, and only 2,500 were for 40s. or more. (UAB *Reports*)

ning of 1938 approximately 263,000 or 43 per cent of all applicants were in receipt of these special additions.[40]

In 1938 the Board decided that it was desirable to embody the principle of additional winter allowances in formal regulations. Accordingly, the Unemployment Assistance (Winter Adjustments) Regulations, August 5, 1938 (Order No. 806), specifically authorized officers to increase allowances "where special needs due to winter conditions exist," and in October the Board defined the winter period as lasting from November 14, 1938 to April 15, 1939.[41]

Late in 1937 the Board was pressed to grant additional allowances at Christmas. While refusing to do this, it permitted some relaxation in the general rules by arranging that the earnings of applicants during the Christmas week should be especially favorably treated in the calculation of resources, and, as in previous years, no account was taken of Christmas presents or charitable payments received at that time.[42] Those fortunate enough to obtain work or gifts were thus placed in a better position during this period than their fellow applicants.

The figures cited by the Board to indicate the extent of discretionary action were fully supported by the testimony of persons interviewed during 1937. There was general agreement that officers made great use of their discretionary powers.[43] Local labor representatives were occasionally inclined to complain that discretionary action was too often exercised in a downward direction, but the more frequent criticism, where any was made, was to the effect that the Board was interpreting its powers too widely. In some quarters the view was even expressed that the Board was using its discretionary powers "to bribe itself into popularity" and regain the prestige lost by its too precipitate action in 1935.[44] Local public assistance administrators were also inclined, as pre-

[40] *Ibid.*, 1937, p. 23.
[41] *Ibid.*, 1938, pp. 18-19, and Appendix I. In November 1938 winter additions were being paid in over 295,000 cases, or more than half of the total number.
[42] *Ibid.*, 1937, p. 25.
[43] Cf. J. D. Millett, *The Unemployment Assistance Board:* "The U.A.B. not only encouraged their local officers to use their judgment, but also made the exercise of discretion possible by defining clearly the objective." (p. 218; see also Chapter VI)
[44] The discussion in Chapter IX of the standard of living provided by the allowances, however, indicates that even with the discretionary grants, the allowances were far from providing an unduly high standard.

viously indicated, to complain in some areas that the Board was using its discretionary powers to invade the spheres of activity of local authorities.

Special Difficulties of the Household as the Unit of Assessment

The adoption of the "household" as the uniform basic unit for the determination of need and the calculation of resources has created peculiar difficulties which might not have arisen in a less highly centralized system. For the composition of the household is determined by many factors in addition to the ties of family feeling. Thus, in some areas, the household will include as members persons only remotely related to the householder who is an applicant to the Board, merely because there is an acute local housing shortage. In other areas the same situation may arise because of long-continued depression which has led to much "doubling up" of needy families. In consequence there is great variation in different parts of the country, because of differences in living habits, with regard to the extent to which persons of varying degrees of relationship may be called upon to contribute to the support of the applicant and his dependent family.[45]

A study carried out by Professor Percy Ford has shown that family groupings differ widely in various parts of the country.[46] Two features of his study of families in receipt of unemployment assistance and of normal families at different periods of time are especially noteworthy: the great variation in the numbers of sons and daughters living in the common household (from 170.8 per 100 families in the Reading assistance cases, to 245.6 per 100 families in Warrington in 1924); and in the number of persons without family responsibility under the poor law who, on the application of a household means test, would be compelled to contribute resources, if any, to the support of the family (varying from 6.5 in southeast London to 48.5 per 100 families in Warrington in 1924).[47]

[45] Not all persons occupying one house or apartment were regarded as members of the household. Two families living together might be treated as two separate households. For other rules adopted by the Board, see Chapter IX, section on the means test and family responsibility.

[46] Percy Ford, "Means Tests and Responsibility for Needy Relatives," *Sociological Review*, April 1937, pp. 175-89; "Family Means and Personal Responsibility," *Economic Journal*, September 1936, pp. 471-79.

[47] Professor Ford points out that the large membership of families in Warrington was a result of the acute housing shortage in that area which was especially

which time information was secured regarding the health and working capacity, the past employment experience, the attitudes to employment, and the home circumstances of the applicants. The reports and recommendations made by the committees indicated that they had taken their responsibilities very seriously. They made available to the Board and to the public not only a detailed analysis of the extent of the problem and the causes of prolonged unemployment among young workers, but also a series of specific recommendations involving matters such as increase in the disciplinary powers of the Board, more effective use of existing powers, the increased use of work centers and of training facilities, and the initiation by the government of a public works policy.[58]

In addition to advising the Board on broad matters of policy and on the methods of adapting the national regulations to the needs of particular localities, sub-committees or individual members of the committees have been increasingly consulted by the officers of the Board regarding the treatment of individual cases presenting unusual problems. The most frequent types of cases have been those involving the application of disciplinary measures to difficult cases (under section 40 of the 1934 Act), the application of the "wage-stop" clause, and those in which the applicant was in need of some service the Board was incapable of supplying but where an individual committee member would be in a position to take up the case himself or to put the applicant in touch with the agency or person best able to give the needed help or advice.

There is indeed considerable evidence to suggest that the activities of the Board and of the advisory committees have, if anything, intensified local interest in the problems of dependency and in the extent of the provision of social services. This has been especially so in regard to three problems which have assumed increasing importance as a result of the considerable but somewhat haphazard development of local social services. The first concerns the extent to which local authorities are making use of their permissive powers, for, as already shown, the zeal with which the Board has in most areas promoted the welfare of its clients and has kept the advisory committees informed of shortcomings in the existing

[58] For details of the committees' findings and recommendations, see *Ibid.*, 1938, pp. 44-52.

local services has focused attention upon the great variety in local amenities in different parts of the country.

The second local problem concerns the lack of coordination between the existing services, particularly in regard to the standards of eligibility and the principles on which payment should be required of those benefiting from them. As already pointed out, careful coordination of policy between the sub-committees administering these services is the exception rather than the rule. The tradition of deterrence, reinforced by the principle of treating each case upon its merits, had served to prevent the adoption of formal principles or scales, even on the part of many of the larger public assistance committees created by the Local Government Act of 1929. The wide publicity given to the Board's scales of allowances and regulations for the assessment of resources and their obvious technical superiority over even many of the existing public assistance scales,[59] have combined to bring home to local administrators the need for the adoption of reasoned standards and for a coordination of the means tests administered by their various sub-committees.

Finally, the action of the Board in encouraging its clients to make use of voluntary welfare organizations as well as other statutory authorities, while it has provoked criticism in some quarters,[60] has also served to direct public attention to the general question of the future function of voluntary groups in view of the great expansion of public social services during the last 30 years. The advisory committees, on which representatives of both governmental and voluntary agencies are represented, are peculiarly well suited to tackle this problem and some of them have already made valuable contributions.[61]

---

[59] This fact was commented on by almost all persons interviewed in 1937 and is confirmed by the research of Professor Percy Ford, who has done more work on this subject than any other investigator.

[60] Representatives of the organized unemployed workers groups have criticized the Board for "forcing workers on to charity" and evading financial responsibilities which it is felt the central government should carry. The Liverpool Advisory Committee found that "there appears to be a tendency for it [the Board] to adopt the policy of relying on them [voluntary bodies] to meet special needs wherever they are prepared to do so," and recommended that "voluntary bodies should refrain, in normal circumstances, from granting assistance of a kind which can be given by the Board." (*Unemployment Assistance in Liverpool*, pp. 42-43)

[61] The Liverpool Committee, in cooperation with the University, initiated an investigation into the manner in which the Board's officers cooperated with local authorities and voluntary bodies, and in 1938 issued the report mentioned above.

Conclusion

The record of the first years of the Unemployment Assistance Board's administration suggests that in the main the more serious dangers accompanying a highly centralized administration have been avoided. Thanks to the emphasis placed upon the exercise of discretion by its officers, and since 1936 to the increasing use made of the services of local advisory committees, the Board has managed to avoid a rigid and inappropriate uniformity of treatment of its clients, and the stifling of local interest and initiative. One indication of this success has been the marked decrease in the hostility to and criticism of the Board that was so widespread in 1934 and 1935.[62] Another is the growing confidence with which the Board began prior to the outbreak of war to tackle certain vital but controversial questions arising out of the comprehensive relief system, and in particular the problem of demoralization caused by prolonged unemployment.

It is more difficult to say whether this achievement will be permanent. Undoubtedly the flexibility of the Board's administration in its first years was attributable in large measure to the imagination and vitalizing energy of its first secretary, Mr. C. W. G. Eady.[63] It is conceivable that, given different leadership, the activities of local officers might have been much more rigidly controlled and circumscribed. Moreover, the continuance of the interest and cooperation of the advisory committees in the problems faced by the Board will largely depend on the attitude of the Board itself toward their functions. If the committees come to be regarded merely as convenient smoke screens, to be consulted only when their opinion is known in advance or their approval is required for some unpopular action, their prestige and their effectiveness in serving as the vital link between the centralized administration and local conditions and viewpoints will necessarily decline. But precedent counts strongly in Great Britain, and it is perhaps not too much to expect that in view of the functions the committees have already performed, a tradition has been estab-

---

[62] For an account of these criticisms, see C. A. Kulp, *Social Insurance Coordination* (Washington: Committee on Social Security of the Social Science Research Council, 1938), pp. 17-20.

[63] Mr. Eady, now Sir Wilfrid, became Deputy Under-Secretary of State in the Home Office in January 1938.

lished which even a reactionary and narrowly bureaucratic Board might find it hard to destroy.

The remaining major objection to the present centralization policy, namely, that it leads to overlapping of machinery in regard to the marginal social services,[64] appears, as has been indicated in the preceding chapter, to result from categorization rather than centralization. It has become an obvious problem since 1934 ·mainly because the 1934 Act carried out the principle of categorization more fully than earlier legislation, because the nationally administered service has interpreted its mandate more broadly, and because the existence of overlapping attracts more attention when it involves overlapping between central and local authorities than when it occurs between various local administrations.

In any case, any judgment concerning the wisdom of the centralization of residual relief administration now existing in Great Britain must take account of the fact that this centralization was adopted only after other methods had been unsuccessfully attempted. Although the Local Government Act of 1929 had greatly widened the areas of the units responsible for public assistance administration, many public assistance officers still hold that the existing units are in some cases too small. Given the existing tax resources of the central and local governments, it was inevitable that the major share of the heavy costs of unemployment relief should be carried by the national government. Indeed, local authorities have to an increasing extent urged that "the state," meaning thereby the national government, should assume entire financial responsibility for the maintenance of the unemployed, and this view has long been echoed by the Labour Party.[65] Dif-

---

[64] Dr. Ursula Hicks (*The Finance of British Government, 1920-1936*, p. 177), in suggesting that the transfer of services en bloc to the central government is one of the more hopeful lines of attack on the problem of local finances, holds there are two major objections to this policy: loss of personal touch in administration, and the expense of setting up elaborate and often overlapping jurisdictions, the latter being the more serious.

[65] The representatives of the County Councils Association so urged before the Royal Commission (*Minutes of Evidence,* p. 631); the representatives of the Association of Municipal Corporations held that workers who had exhausted benefit, those in non-insurable trades, and casual workers "should be provided for at the cost of the state" (p. 525); while the Convention of Royal Burghs in Scotland argued that the unemployed "should be dealt with and be exclusively financed by the state" (p. 583). The majority of the county and county borough representatives on the Committee on Local Expenditure of 1932 also expressed the view that the "responsibility for granting relief to able-bodied persons should be

ferences of opinion among those who adopt this view have centered on the feasibility of combining central financial responsibility with local administration. On the whole, local authorities have argued for local administration, but relatively few specific proposals were advanced for meeting the danger that such a situation would involve irresponsible administration on the part of the localities.[66]

Even the majority of the Royal Commission of 1932, which proposed a locally administered residual relief system "equally available to all able-bodied workers who are involuntarily unemployed," stressed the necessity for a high degree of central control despite the fact that they visualized the central government as contributing not all, but only the major part, of the funds. "Closer central supervision of the arrangements for the assistance of able-bodied unemployed workers is imperative," said the majority. "We attach very great importance, for the general acceptability and success of our proposals, to the exercise by the Ministry of Labour of a full and continuing responsibility for the general terms and conditions of the assistance to be given to the applicants within the scheme." [67]

Admitting that some degree of local variation in treatment was inevitable in a locally administered service, the Commission added that "these variations should be compatible with principles operative over the country as a whole . . . It is equally important in

---

removed altogether from the purview of Local Authorities" and suggested the creation of an independent body to secure "almost complete removal of the whole problem from the sphere of both local and national politics." (*Report* [Cmd. 4200, 1932], p. 114) The representatives of the Trades Union Congress and the Labour Party in their joint statement to the Blanesburgh Committee similarly stated: ". . . the obligation to maintain the unemployed should not rest upon localities. It is unjust that any part of the burden arising from a national problem, which a local authority can do nothing, or practically nothing, to avert, should fall upon local rates. . . . From the point of view of administrative economy and efficiency, the payment of unemployment relief should be in the hands of one authority, namely, that which administers the Unemployment Insurance Scheme." (Unemployment Insurance Committee, *Minutes of Evidence*, 1927, pp. 168, 171)

[66] The representatives of the county councils did, however, suggest that as a safeguard a representative of the local employment committee should be ex-officio a member of the local relief committee, and that central administration should be vested in the Minister of Labour, who was to be assisted by a committee representing the Unemployment Grants Committee, the County Councils Association, the Association of Municipal Corporations, and other government departments concerned. This committee was to act as a coordinating body and as an appeals committee on cases referred by the local authority or the representative of the local employment committee.

[67] *Final Report*, pp. 147, 155.

any scheme of assistance for able-bodied unemployed workers, to guard, as far as possible, against substantial variations in the treatment of able-bodied unemployed workers who are in identical circumstances, but reside in different areas . . . Most of the inequalities in the present system can be removed by a greater degree of central control and direction of local administration." [68]

There was a second reason which impelled the Commission to stress the necessity for greater central control of the standards and objectives of the residual unemployment relief system, namely, the assurance of proper relationships between the scope and nature of the benefits of the insurance and the supplementary assistance schemes.[69] " . . . the provisions in the Insurance Scheme . . . must be considered in close relation to the provisions for workers no longer entitled to benefit. . . . Apart from other considerations, it would lead to serious difficulties if the creation of separate central authorities responsible for insurance and for unemployment assistance produced conflicts of financial interest and of principle." [70]

The Commission made various specific proposals to implement their recommendation that the central government should accept responsibility for the general supervision of the administration and extent of assistance. There was to be no interference with individual cases, but general rules should be laid down for the guidance of local authorities and there should be wide powers to ensure that these were generally adhered to.

The controls exercised by the Minister of Labour were indeed to be very extensive.[71] He was to have power to direct a local authority to adopt a definite scale of relief and definite rules for ascertaining each item of means. " . . . the principles upon which certain items of income are assessed, should, so far as is practicable, be uniform." While some variation in benefit scales

[68] *Ibid.*, pp. 147-48.
[69] "In particular he [the Minister of Labour] should aim at seeing that a proper relation is kept between the relief scales and the rates of benefit provided by the insurance scheme." (*Ibid.*, p. 293)
[70] *Ibid.*, pp. 154-55.
[71] "We intend that the Minister should use his powers to effect conformity to reasonable standards; and we contemplate that he will take steps to improve the standard of payments and administration where such improvement is desirable. But equally he may have to intervene where he believes that the authority errs by excess." (*Ibid.*, p. 153)

might be permissible because of differences in rent levels, cost of food, and transportation and local wage levels, the Minister should assure himself that actual differences did not exceed those justified by these factors. In general, it was expected that greater uniformity would be brought about by consultation and suggestion, but in the last resort "he will have the power actually to impose a scale either on all areas, or on some defined group of areas or on individual authorities." Furthermore, where it appeared that the area of a local authority was unsuitable to the exercise of the functions of the unemployment assistance scheme, while mutual arrangements were to be permitted to facilitate merging and joint administration, the Minister "should have power also to enforce joint administration where he considers it necessary or desirable." Finally, the Minister was to have power "in flagrant cases of maladministration to supersede the Local Authority." [72]

These controls were ultimately to be made effective through financial pressure. Assessments which would otherwise be applicable to an area were to be reduced or adjusted if the local authority were found not to be maintaining standards of good administration.

In view of these specific recommendations, it is clear that the sphere of independence left to local authorities by the proposals of the Royal Commission was much narrower than that generally implied in the phrase "local administration." It is indeed not too much to say that even those who have criticized the creation of the centralized Unemployment Assistance Board have recognized the necessity of increasing central control of the principles of an unemployment relief system which inevitably must be mainly or wholly financed by the central government, and many have admitted that in certain "difficult areas" it might be necessary for the central government to assume direct responsibility for administration. In this perspective, the centralization of unemployment relief administration represented by the unemployment assistance scheme appears to be less a revolutionary break with the past than a selection of one out of two alternatives, both of which involved a high degree of centralization.

[72] Quotations from *Ibid.*, pp. 289, 293, 282, 286, respectively.

17

CHAPTER IX

THE APPROPRIATENESS OF THE PROVISION FOR THE UNEMPLOYED

THE PRECEDING TWO CHAPTERS have examined the organizational structure of the provision for the unemployed in Great Britain in order to discover the extent to which the combination of insurance, unemployment assistance and public assistance has resulted in a well integrated and orderly system. This chapter, on the other hand, will examine the specific nature of the aid provided, and the economic and social problems to which so comprehensive an unemployment program gives rise. Many of these problems are, of course, not peculiar to the realm of unemployment relief. They reflect rather the conflict of two opposing principles in contemporary economic and social life. On the one hand, there is the assumption that the individual is responsible for his own material welfare and that of his family, and the threat of loss of income is relied upon as the ultimate sanction to compel participation in production on the terms dictated by the market. On the other hand, there is a growing acceptance of the view that it is the duty of the government to provide for the maintenance of those who, through forces beyond their own control, are deprived of income. The British unemployment relief system, precisely because the doctrine of government responsibility has here been given its fullest expression, throws into clear relief the nature of the basic problems created by this ideological dichotomy.

In the first place, it will have been observed that the two national programs of unemployment insurance and unemployment assistance represent a compromise between the new and the old views of the proper spheres of individual responsibility and reliance on the government. Unemployment insurance, like all the social insurances, implements the theory that the individual, if satisfying formally prescribed conditions, has a right to specified payments from the government in certain contingencies, regardless of his own resources or those of his immediate family. Unemployment assistance, on the other hand, expresses the view that government aid is available only when the resources of the

238

individual and his family group are insufficient. It is no accident, therefore, that one of the most hotly debated issues in Great Britain since 1934 concerns the justification for the retention of a means test in a comprehensive unemployment relief system, and the extent to which the individual should exhaust his own resources and those of his family or household before receiving aid from the government.

In the second place, the acceptance by the government of ultimate responsibility for maintaining the unemployed—whether by insurance, assistance, or poor relief—raises in an acute form the question of the appropriateness of the standard of living thus afforded. The system is attacked from one side because of its alleged niggardly nature, and from the other because it is asserted that the payments to unemployed persons are so generous that they approach dangerously near the earnings of employed workers and may undermine the incentive to work.

In the third place, with the persistence of mass unemployment and as the provision for maintenance of the unemployed has become more complete and generous, there have been growing doubts whether the functions of the government can be limited to the provision of maintenance and whether the relationship between the dependent individual and the government can continue to be one of claims by the individual unaccompanied by obligations to the government.

Finally, as the numbers of the unemployed and the expenditures on unemployment relief have mounted, the wisdom of a policy so exclusively based on the acceptance of a large volume of unemployment has come to be questioned, and there is an increasing interest in the potentialities of government action looking toward the reduction of unemployment by positive measures to stimulate industry and to prevent the recurrence of severe cyclical fluctuations.

THE MEANS TEST AND FAMILY RESPONSIBILITY

Of all the aspects of the unemployment relief system brought into being by the Act of 1934, none has provoked more bitter criticism and difference of opinion than the requirement that applicants for unemployment assistance should undergo a means test. The Act of 1934 made the household as defined the standard unit for the purpose of measuring need and calculating resources, but it gave no definition of this unit. Persons who were applicants in their own right were clearly excluded from the household of another applicant, and young dependent children and juveniles were equally clearly included. But the task of drawing the line between adults who were members of the household and those whose relation to the group was that of a lodger was extremely difficult.[1] The Unemployment Assistance Board adopted two main principles: first, that persons who were members of the household during childhood should be regarded as members of the household, and second, that those who entered it after reaching the age of employment on terms which made it clear that they were paying a reasonable rate for board and lodging, should be regarded as lodgers, whether related to the applicant or not.

Objection to the household as the unit for assessment of resources has been widespread and vociferous. The Labour Party and organized labor have publicly opposed the imposition of any means test at all, on the grounds that it is merely a continuance of the degrading poor law and is inconsistent with the Labour Party's view that it is the duty of the government to provide the involuntarily unemployed with work or maintenance.[2] This opposition to the general principle of the means test, as applied to the average "thoroughly decent" unemployed person, is not confined to Labour Party members, but is shared by some prominent students of unemployment relief problems, including Sir William Beveridge, because of its discouraging effect upon the desire of the individual to save.

Privately, however, many Labour Party members and trade unionists repudiate this blanket condemnation of the means test

[1] The Royal Commission had frankly abandoned the attempt. Believing that "the facts of family association are so diverse and variable that it is impossible in any statute to restrict the 'family' to which an applicant is assumed to belong, or to define all the considerations that are relevant to a fair assessment of means in every individual case," the Commission somewhat weakly concluded, "account must be taken . . . of the income of the actual household, and of the relationships which may be presumed to exist within it; and the assessment should be adjusted thereto." (*Final Report,* p. 134)

[2] The general point of view of the Party is expressed in paragraphs 82-88 of the Minority Report of the Royal Commission. (*Ibid.,* pp. 415-18) It was reiterated in publications and protest meetings at the time of the imposition of the means test under the transitional payments scheme in 1931, and of the issue of the first regulations of the Board in December 1934.

but sharply criticize the use of the household as the unit for calculating need and resources, and in this stand they were joined by the majority of experts, administrators, and ordinary citizens interviewed by the author in 1937. Indeed, it is not too much to say that the real issue in regard to the conditions of eligibility for the supplementary relief system in Great Britain today is not whether there shall be any test at all, but turns rather on the nature of the test to be applied and the selection of the individuals who are to be subject to it. The problem is a difficult one, and raises fundamental issues.

The arguments of those who support a means test, whether of the household or narrower type, are powerful. The most common argument in favor of a means test of whatever type is the assertion that, in the words of the majority of the Royal Commission of 1930-32, "while the resources available are as limited as they are today, we should think it unfortunate if payments were made to persons who were not in need, at the expense ultimately of those who are most in need." [3]

It is no answer to this argument in favor of the means test to point to the relatively small proportion of applicants denied assistance, as it can always be argued that, but for knowledge of the existence of the test, the number claiming assistance would be greater. A more effective answer is the assertion that the group to which the test is applied, namely, persons who have in the past been wage earners and who have been unemployed for at least 6 months, by definition consists of persons whose resources are likely to be small. If an individual means test is in question, the fact of long unemployment is indeed significant. The analysis of resources possessed by recipients of unemployment allowances, to which reference is made later in this section, suggests that the savings and other resources of the applicants themselves are relatively unimportant. The argument is, however, less effective when the household means test is in question.

---

[3] *Ibid.*, p. 128. This was indeed the most usual argument encountered by the author in numerous interviews in 1937. It is significant, too, that this was the reason most frequently given by Labour Party supporters and trade unionists (including high officials at headquarters) for their criticism of the blanket condemnation by the Labour Party of the means test in principle and for their belief that, as one official put it, "the Party is running its head into a noose on this matter; if it came into power it would never abandon a means test of some kind."

The limitation of the group to whom unemployment assistance is available, namely, unemployed persons normally dependent on income from wages, is, as the Royal Commission had pointed out in 1932, a less effective guarantee than the application of a means test against claims from "temporarily or permanently unoccupied persons who would probably not regard themselves as 'unemployed' if the scheme did not exist." For, on the one hand, the test of "involuntary unemployment" is still imperfect and becomes more so as unemployment spreads and as the offer of work becomes a less frequently available test of willingness to work. Attempts to enforce the "genuinely-seeking-work clause" in the period before 1930 also proved to be administratively troublesome, and to have undesirable social and psychological consequences.[4] And, on the other hand, the effectiveness of the criterion of past employment in certain occupations as a test of dependence on wage income varies with the number of weeks of work required, the period within which past employment must have occurred, and on the tolerance shown in the formulation and administration of the requirements. In all these respects the scope of the unemployment assistance scheme is wide enough to admit many persons whose normal dependence upon income from wages may have been very dubious.[5]

But, while in principle the strength of the argument for a means test as a bulwark against unjustifiable demands upon limited resources must be conceded, the extent of the savings to the community by its application must not be exaggerated. In the first place, the percentage of applicants denied any allowances during the years 1935 to 1938 has been small, varying between 5 and 10 per cent of new or changed determinations in the different months.[6] And, of the Board's applicants in receipt of allowances

---

[4] See Chapter IV, subsection on "Extent and Nature of Categorization."

[5] The rule requiring 30 contributions in 2 years is itself no very strenuous test, particularly when it is recalled that it could be satisfied by 30 days of work in 30 separate weeks. And the qualification to the eligibility clause for unemployment assistance (namely, coverage of persons insured under old-age insurance, or, in some cases, persons who but for the industrial circumstances would have been so insured) is clearly extremely elastic. In fact, many public assistance authorities complained to the author that the Board was "throwing its net too wide" in this connection. See Chapter VII.

[6] Excluding months in which percentages were unusually high or low due to changes in the regulations, the coming into effect of the Second Appointed Day, payment of winter allowances, etc. (UAB annual reports, appendix entitled "Applications for Unemployment Assistance")

dependence upon other members of the household might escape this by removal.[19] The assertion that the household means test was thus leading to the break-up of families was indeed commonly made at the beginning of 1935, and the first report of the Board devoted considerable attention to the problem. The facts indicate that a break-up of homes occurred much less frequently than theoretical considerations would suggest. In only three districts did the problem assume any serious importance.[20] Elsewhere there were either isolated instances, or a total number that was small in relation to the total number of applicants.[21] Furthermore, the reports of the district officers indicate that in the majority of cases the means test was but the last straw added to a situation where there was already considerable personal friction. Somewhat surprisingly, too, cases of removal by applicants were much more numerous than those of removal by earning or resource-possessing members of the household, but they were also more amenable to disciplinary action by the Board.[22]

More serious, though less easily measurable, are two other consequences of the application of the household means test. First, it places a heavy burden on young wage earners. It has already been stated that earnings constituted by far the most important item of resources reported by applicants and their households (70.6 per cent in 1935 and 70.7 per cent in 1937). Indeed, in view of the fact that in these two years another 26.0 per cent and 26.3 per cent were accounted for by other social services (outdoor relief, service pensions, etc.) and social insurance benefits, it will be seen that earnings constituted by far the greater part

---

[19] The inquiry of the Pilgrim Trust into long-period unemployment indicated that sensitivity to dependence on others is particularly acute among the older men. (*Men Without Work*, p. 148) The reports of the officers of the Board covering all types of applicants suggest, however, that statistically the problem is more acute among the young.

[20] UAB *Report*, 1935, pp. 134-36, 181, 235-36.

[21] E.g., in Birmingham less than 25 out of 50,000 applicants (*Ibid.*, p. 111); other areas reported only 2 or 3 cases. The report of the Pilgrim Trust inquiry into the situation of the long-period unemployed confirms this general picture—only 18 homes broken up on account of the household test were discovered, which for the country as a whole suggested a total figure of about 7,500 cases. (*Men Without Work*, p. 148)

[22] As a rule, the Board's officers refused to increase the allowance of applicants who thus left home, or they reduced the allowance below that permitted to single applicants living alone, unless investigation showed that there were other personal reasons or a state of over-crowding which justified removal. Their action was in general upheld by the appeals tribunals.

of *assessable* resources. About 85 per cent of the earnings belonged to household members other than the applicant, and the greatest share of these (50 per cent in 1935, 65 per cent in 1937) was contributed by sons and daughters, while brothers and sisters were the next largest contributors with 16 and 13 per cent in the two years. Spouses of the applicants owned between 4 and 6 per cent of the resources.[23]

In practice therefore the application of a household means test involves placing upon young earners a burden which, in view of the age composition and employment prospects of assistance recipients, is likely to be of long duration. It is a nice question whether important social values are endangered more by permitting the sense of family responsibility to weaken than by extending the area of poverty to the immediate households of those who are unemployed. If it is true, as the investigators for the Pilgrim Trust persuasively argue, that "if we allow standards to be reduced, we are allowing a class to grow up that is unemployable. Poverty is not only a consequence of unemployment but a cause of it," [24] then the social wisdom of reducing many otherwise independent persons to a relatively low standard of living may well be questioned. Moreover, there is considerable evidence that the feeling that a substantial share of additional earnings will be devoted not to improving the earner's economic position but (as the earners see it) to relieving the government of a part of its financial obligations, acts as a real deterrent to initiative in the case of persons who are employed on piece work, or who could hope to secure increases in pay by enhanced efficiency.[25]

And in the second place, the application of the household means test in circumstances where those most affected by it are other earners, brings an even wider group of the population into contact and psychological familiarity with the investigatory procedures associated with the poor laws. If it is hoped to use a means

---

[23] The percentages for other members of the household are shown in UAB *Report*, 1935, p. 308; 1937, p. 190.

[24] *Men Without Work*, p. 133.

[25] This objection was made to the author in many interviews in 1937. Mr. A. D. K. Owen, who was one of the directors of the Pilgrim Trust inquiry, referred to the widespread feeling among earners in families of UAB clients that "any extra effort will be cropped," and was inclined to believe that the deterrent effect upon incentive and initiative was among the most serious consequences of the application of the household means test.

test as a deterrent against too easy reliance upon government support, then it is hardly wise to accustom so many earners to it when they are independent and self-supporting.[26] There is considerable evidence that the British worker would prefer a smaller sum as a right, to a larger amount secured by undergoing what is still widely regarded as a degrading procedure. This consideration is especially important for the present British unemployment relief system, as since April 1937 the Unemployment Assistance Board has had the duty of supplementing insurance benefits where they are inadequate. As already pointed out, for a considerable number of workers (those with large families and living in high rent areas) assistance payments may exceed insurance benefits, and the only deterrent to a large amount of supplementation is the requirement to undergo a means test. If the necessity to supplement insurance benefits is confined to a limited group, there may be reluctance to change status in order to secure a few extra shillings a week.[27] But if while employed and earning, many wage earners have become accustomed to the "means test atmosphere," the temptation to take advantage of supplementation possibilities when unemployed may be more difficult to resist, and should there be any large amount of supplementation, the desirability of retaining a separate insurance system may well be questioned. It was doubtless this possibility that caused a number of thoughtful observers to believe in 1937 that "unemployment assistance may well mean the death knell of insurance."

Advocates of the household means test urge two advantages of this unit of assessment over the alternative of an income declaration relating solely to the means of the applicant.[28] It is claimed that the individual test would seriously curtail the savings

[26] The objection of workers extends not merely to the necessity of reporting earnings and submitting to assessment, but perhaps still more to what they regard as the undesirable publicity given to the existence of poverty and dependence in the household, involved in the verification of reported earnings at the place of employment.

[27] In fact, the Board has adopted the principle of refusing to supplement where the difference between insurance and assistance is very small, or where the applicant had had a substantial period of employment immediately prior to his application for supplementation.

[28] Cf., for example, the suggestion of the minority of the Royal Commission: "If Parliament decided that, after a certain period, a Means Test should be imposed, then in our view it should take the form of a declaration of personal income by the claimant at the [employment] Exchange." (*Final Report,* p. 417)

to the community as a result of the means test. The analysis of resources made by the Board for 1935 and 1937 does indeed support this contention, for in 1935 only 13.7 per cent and in 1937 only 16.0 per cent of all reported resources were owned by the applicants. The addition of the resources possessed by spouses of applicants would have raised these percentages to 20.0 and 21.2 in the respective years.[29]

The second advantage claimed for the household as compared with the individual means test, however, is less impressive in fact than it first appears. For it is argued that the adoption of an individual means test would encourage improper transference of resources to other family members for the purpose of securing eligibility.[30] The 1935 and 1937 analyses of resources possessed by the households of recipients of allowances suggest, however, that the applicants' savings (the sole transferable item of resources) constituted only 0.4 per cent and 0.2 per cent of the total reported resources in the respective years.[31] Moreover, the desire to encourage thrift had led, as already pointed out, to the exemption of a certain proportion of savings from liability to assessment, and to the entire exemption of certain types of savings (e.g., a house owned and occupied by an applicant).

Thus in the last resort the question of the retention of a means test and the choice between the household and some other entity as the unit of assessment involve the weighing of values many of which are unfortunately not easily susceptible of measurement. Any final answer involves estimates of the loss to the community arising from the probable claims which would be made in the absence of a means test. It is bound up with contemporary theories as to the social and economic functions of the family, and the wisdom and effectiveness of attempts to enforce the principle of family responsibility when mutual affection and esteem are inade-

[29] UAB *Report,* 1935, p. 308; 1937, p. 190.
[30] Cf. *Final Report* of the Royal Commission: "It would not be difficult for the individual temporarily to divest himself of means. At least there would be a substantial inducement for him to try to do so; and the cost of the relief scheme would be very heavily increased." (pp. 132-33)
[31] Even the addition of income from subletting and boarders would raise these percentages only to 1.1 and 0.8 respectively, and not all of this income would have been derived from lodgers in houses owned by the applicants. Savings constituted 2.7 per cent and 1.6 per cent of all the resources reported by the applicants themselves, and 2.0 per cent and 0.7 per cent of those reported by their spouses in the two years.

quate inducements. These theories are in turn in process of flux, in view among other considerations of the growing realization that family harmony and cohesion may be adversely affected by the prolonged dependence of adults upon other members of the group.[32]

Nor can the retention or abandonment of the household means test be dissociated from theories as to the nature of the stimuli to enterprise and initiative. If economic activity, such as working and saving, is most responsive to the hope of securing independence and improving one's economic position, there is a danger that enterprise and initiative may be weakened if earning members of the household, and especially the young, feel that their earnings are in large part perpetually mortgaged for the support of the household's unemployed members.

Any final answer also implies a reconsideration of the reasons why individual saving has hitherto been regarded as a peculiar economic virtue. If the philosophy should be accepted that, in view of the normal level of earnings and the frequency of interruptions to earning power, it is the duty of the government to provide a minimum subsistence to all those who are unable to earn because of sickness, unemployment, or old age, then it may be less important than formerly to encourage individual saving to meet these emergencies. The policy of government aid has undoubtedly been in large measure accepted in Great Britain and implemented by the social insurances, although there are still considerable gaps and deficiencies in the provision of security which, even on the theory that individuals should be encouraged to save against loss of income, justify exempting from any means test certain minimum amounts of savings.[33]

The significance attached by the community to the maintenance of the prestige of social insurance benefits as compared to other forms of public assistance is another important factor. Finally, the decision as to the desirability of a means test and the selection

---

[32] Cf. *Men Without Work.*

[33] Thus, the old-age and survivors insurance scheme provides benefits which are inadequate for full maintenance and therefore require supplementation from public or private sources. Similarly, the health insurance benefits fail to provide for dependents, while, as will be shown below, unemployment insurance benefits and assistance provide an extremely low standard of living for those with no other resources.

of the appropriate unit of assessment cannot but be affected by current beliefs regarding the most equitable method of sharing the costs of unemployment. The household or family means test involves the concentration of at least part, and in some cases all, of the costs of maintaining unemployed persons upon those who happen to be living in the household or are members of the family.[34] Yet the general trend of social thinking appears to favor a wider distribution of the costs, and in particular the social insurances have done much to inculcate and to spread the philosophy that the risks of economic life should be pooled over as wide a group as possible.

Faced with these conflicting social values, the British have, perhaps characteristically, adopted a compromise position. They have retained the household means test in principle, but have modified it by exempting important types and amounts of resources from consideration as a concession to the objections of those most adversely affected by it. The most far-reaching of these concessions was made by the amendments of 1941.[35]

THE LEVEL OF ASSISTANCE PROVIDED

The evaluation of standards of living is notoriously difficult, and the question of the adequacy of the standard of living provided by the British unemployment relief system admits of no specific answer. Owing to the gradual increase in benefits, the payments from unemployment insurance had by 1931 come to equal or to exceed the published scales of the local public assistance authorities, which were admittedly intended to provide at least

[34] And, as pointed out in Chapter VIII (pp. 229-32), this distribution of costs is highly arbitrary and varies greatly in different parts of the country, depending on the composition of the household.

[35] The earlier requirement that the resources of all members of the household were to be taken into account in assessing the allowances to be given to an applicant living as a member of a household was substituted by a new rule requiring that the resources of household members other than the applicant, the husband or wife of the applicant and any member of the household dependent on the applicant should not be regarded as the resources of the applicant. Furthermore, a maximum was set to the contribution to be expected from a non-dependent member of the household, and adjustments in the treatment of rent had the effect of further reducing the contribution which such a wage earner would be required to make. For full details of the changes, see *Memorandum by the Assistance Board on the Determination of Needs Bill* (Cmd. 6247, 1941).

bare maintenance. After July 1934 these benefit rates, which had been cut in 1931, were restored. Moreover, it has already been shown that, for persons with no resources and with large families in high rent areas, unemployment assistance allowances were even higher than insurance benefits and after 1937 they could be granted in supplementation of insurance benefits if necessary. Yet even though the unemployment assistance allowances thus provided a standard of living that was in general more generous than that of the prevailing public assistance system,[36] the nature of this minimum standard for persons without resources still remains unknown.

The Unemployment Assistance Board in drawing up its original scale took the position that it "was concerned with such primary needs as those of food, shelter, fuel, clothing and the like," but "did not deem itself to be concerned with scales of assistance so low as to be merely sufficient to support life. Allowances clearly had to be adequate to permit some variety of diet and some command over items which, having formerly been luxuries, are now conventional necessaries." [37]   To reduce these general concepts to specific figures, it studied the scales adopted by local public assistance authorities, the standards adopted in the British Medical Association's "Report on Nutrition," the report of the Ministry of Health Advisory Committee on Nutrition, and the various social surveys which had recently been carried out in London and Merseyside.

In November 1936 the investigators of the Pilgrim Trust endeavored to measure the standard of living of unemployment assistance recipients, and for that purpose adopted as their criterion of poverty the standard devised by Mr. R. F. George [38] which, although higher in some respects than the corresponding poverty standard adopted in some of the other important social surveys, yet appeared more nearly to reflect the standard which

[36] As was shown in Chapter V, the higher payments made to unemployed workers on the basis of public assistance scales were in the majority of cases due to the disregard of certain resources rather than to the adoption of a higher standard of what was needed to maintain an applicant with no resources.

[37] UAB *Report*, 1935, p. 33.

[38] See R. F. George, "New Calculation of the Poverty Line," *Journal of the Royal Statistical Society*, 1937, Part I, pp. 74-95.

the Board had set for itself.[39] This standard includes only expenditures for food, clothing, cleaning materials, light and fuel, and thus makes no provision for replacement of household equipment, insurances, doctors' fees, medicines, or such small luxuries as tobacco, newspapers, and recreation. Yet, as the accompanying summary indicates, 17 per cent of the families visited by the Pilgrim Trust investigators failed to achieve even the low standard of living which Mr. George's budget would provide, while another 27 per cent were within 10 per cent of it in either direction. At the other end of the scale were 37 per cent of the families who were well above the poverty line or even living in moderate comfort.

Standards of living	Number of families	Per cent
Number of families investigated.................	932	100
Families in "deep poverty" (income more than 10% below "poverty line").	159	17
Families in "moderate poverty" (income less than 10% below "poverty line")..	120	13
Families at "subsistence level" (income less than 10% above "poverty line")..	137	14
Families "a little above poverty line" (income 10-25% above "poverty line")........	174	19
Families "well above poverty line" (income 25-75% above "poverty line")........	251	27
Families "in moderate comfort" (income more than 75% above "poverty line").	91	10

Source: Men Without Work, p. 109.

Further analysis of the groups living below the George poverty line suggested that the standard allowances were least adequate in families with three or four children possessing no resources and relying solely upon the allowance.[40] The investigators concluded, however, that unemployment assistance "was providing

[39] Mr. George's standard is based on the British Medical Association's minimum standards for food requirements and on the standards used by various social surveys in regard to clothing, cleaning materials, light, and fuel. The Medical Association's standard for milk was, however, increased by Mr. George slightly, to bring its requirements into line with the more recent recommendations of the Ministry of Health Advisory Committee on Nutrition and the Technical Commission appointed by the Nutrition Committee of the League of Nations health organization. (Cf. *Men Without Work*, p. 105)

[40] Eighty per cent of the cases living "in poverty" were cases wholly dependent on the Board for income, while the relatively large proportion of such cases in Liverpool was attributable to the high proportion of large families in that district. "In these families with children, our impression was that almost invariably there was definite want, either of food or clothing, or more probably of household equipment." (*Ibid.*, p. 105; also pp. 110, 111)

maintenance at a standard which, in view of the circumstances, was a reasonable one for many of those in receipt of it," but that for roughly two persons out of every five among the 55 per cent of the sample who were dependent solely on assistance, the scheme provided "maintenance at a level that cannot be defended except on grounds of maintaining the wage incentive." [41]

This is, of course, the principal dilemma of social provision against loss of income on account of unemployment. For even this relatively low level of governmental provision against insecurity is high enough to have caused concern in recent years regarding the relationship between benefits and assistance payments on the one hand, and wages normally earned when in employment on the other. Inevitably this problem is more acute for the assistance system than for insurance, as the former admittedly bases the amount of an allowance upon the needs of the individual and his dependent household.

The possibility of increasing allowances where rents are relatively high, and the extensive use which the officers of the Board have made of their power to grant discretionary additions, increase the probability that persons with large families in high rent areas may receive more as an assistance allowance than they would have received in wages. Furthermore, the provisions governing eligibility for assistance are sufficiently wide to admit a significant number of persons whose normal income from work (because of irregularity of employment or poor industrial quality) has been relatively low, and are certainly wider in this respect than the provisions governing eligibility for insurance. But even the insurance system is not immune from the danger that benefits may in certain circumstances exceed normal earnings. For benefits, although less precisely adjusted than allowances, still vary with the size of the dependent family.[42]

The Royal Commission had drawn attention to this problem and had concluded that "it is a rule of cardinal importance . . . that the amount of assistance in respect of unemployment, however provided, should be less than the wages of employment. No

[41] *Ibid.*, p. 113.
[42] However, insurance benefits are payable for only one adult dependent, while those for dependent children are uniform and do not increase with the age of the child as do unemployment assistance allowances.

community could afford to relax this rule . . . the inevitable outcome would be a widespread deterioration in workmanship and
in production, from which the unemployed themselves, as well as
the employed, would be the sufferers." But unfortunately its
recommendations ran only in general terms: "The amount of
relief should as a rule fall so definitely below the prevailing level
of wages as to avoid the danger that applicants might consider
themselves to be in a better position when receiving relief than
when earning wages." How this result was to be achieved in a
system based on need, which if possible was to grant allowances
lower than insurance benefits and yet provide "an adequate service
for unemployed industrial workers" and avoid throwing any
large proportion on "a poor law service which was generally
regarded as unsuitable," was not explained.[43]

In 1935 the Unemployment Insurance Statutory Committee,
in deciding to raise the allowances for children by 1s. weekly, had
called attention to the disconcerting fact that, as a result of the
change, an unemployed man with a wife and 5 dependent children
would become entitled to 41s. a week. As the wages of many
unskilled laborers were in the neighborhood of 40s. weekly, the
Committee believed that cases of benefit exceeding wages, "which
now are rare," might become fairly common.[44]

Again, in 1936, the Committee, utilizing the statistical material
which had been prepared by the Ministry of Labour, discussed
the problem at length and decided to use the declared surplus for
increasing the benefits for adult dependents rather than for children, mainly because the former change would increase by less
than 10 per cent the proportion of cases where men were as well
off unemployed as in employment, whereas the latter would increase it by 33.7 per cent.[45]

The Board has also been keenly aware of the dilemma. In its
first report it drew attention to the "difficult problem" of the
relation between assistance and wages, and the danger that too

[43] *Final Report,* pp. 124-25, 148-50.
[44] The general policy of the Committee was governed by the view that
"Unemployment benefit . . . is the direct alternative to wages: insurance against
unemployment is insurance against loss of wages: it is contrary to the fundamental principle of insurance, and the practice of every other form of insurance,
that the indemnity should be allowed to exceed the loss." (UISC *Report,* July
1935 [Cmd. 131], p. 18)
[45] *Ibid.,* p. 61.

close an approximation of the two might diminish both a man's "eagerness to obtain work and his reluctance to relinquish it." [46]

In part, of course, the failure of the Royal Commission of 1932 to make specific suggestions was due to the lack of statistical data which would have indicated whether the provision of an adequate minimum resulted in an excess of relief over wages in a substantial proportion of cases. Thanks to inquiries carried out in recent yea.s by the Statutory Committee and the Board, it is now possible to obtain a more precise idea of the extent of the problem. These inquiries indicate that instances of relief payments in excess of normal wages are confined to a relatively small group of persons, as shown in the summary below:

COMPARISON OF BENEFITS, ASSISTANCE AND WAGES IN GREAT BRITAIN, 1937

	Insurance claimants		Assistance applicants	
	Men	Women	Men	Women
Average payment (incl. dependents' benefits)	24s. 6d.	15s. 2d.	25s. 6d.	13s. 4d.
Median wage rate [a]	55s. 6d.	30s. 0d.	— —	— —
Modal wage [a] interval	— —	— —	40-50s.	20-30s.
Per cent of persons receiving payments:				
Above wages	—[b]	—[b]	0.9	2.2
Equal to wages	0.9	2.4	0.4	1.3
Less than 4s.[c] below wages	1.4	2.8	4.9	10.9
4s.[c] or more below wages	97.7	94.8	93.8	85.6

[a] Full-time weekly wage rate reported by claimants in last employment; wages declared by applicants to be "normal wages." In both cases wages are gross, before social insurance contributions, etc. are deducted.
[b] Included in percentage receiving payments equal to wages.
[c] 3s. for female insurance claimants.

Sources: Results of study made in August 1937, UISC Report, 1937, pp. 20-22, 54; study made in December 1937, UAB Report, 1937, pp. 80-82, 192.

It is evident that the wages reported by both types of recipient of both sexes were considerably above the average payments. Furthermore, among men 97.7 per cent were entitled to insurance benefits that were 4s. or more [47] below their normal full-time earnings, while 93.8 per cent of assistance recipients [48] were in the same position.

[46] UAB Report, 1935, pp. 12, 33-34.
[47] This margin was adopted to allow for the fact that income from wages would normally be subject to deductions for travel, social insurance payments, and other incidental expenses arising from the fact of employment.
[48] Fifty-four per cent of the men obtained allowances that were 20s. or more below their normal weekly wage rate, while another 27.6 per cent drew allowances from 10s. to 19s. 11d. below.

These averages, however, while furnishing support for the view that the amount of relief has *as a rule* been well below the prevailing level of wages, present in some respects too optimistic a picture. Because the rates of reported wages refer to full-time earnings, it is possible that there may be considerable numbers of casual and part-time workers whose actual wages while employed may fall markedly below the weekly full-time wage as reported. Moreover, while the problem may be insignificant for the group as a whole, among certain categories of assisted persons the percentage of cases in which relief payments approximate dangerously near to wages is relatively high.

Both inquiries throw some light on the types of cases in which the margin between unemployment payments and wages is very small or negative. The Board's investigation suggests that the statistically most important group consists of men whose normal wage rates are between 40s. and 49s. 11d. per week, and that in general applicants with allowances very close to previous earnings are mostly men with large families of children.[49]

Among insurance beneficiaries, the statistically most important group (23.7 per cent of all cases where benefit approached wages) were married men with 3 or more children.[50] The problem created by payments which closely approximated or exceeded wage rates is, however, also acute with regard to wage earners in the lowest brackets, a large proportion of whom are young people. Among recipients of allowances, over 52 per cent of the men earning less than 20s. a week received such allowances. Fifty-seven per cent of these were young men between the ages of 16 and 21.[51] Similarly, the study of insurance beneficiaries indicates that among the 9,510 men whose wages did not exceed the benefit plus 4 shillings, 20.2 per cent were juveniles whose normal wages did not exceed 19s. a week, while another 18.1 per cent were men living alone whose normal weekly wages did not exceed 22s.[52]

Thus, although the problem of the close relationship between unemployment payments and wages cannot as yet be said to be acute, for certain sections of the working population it cannot

---

[49] UAB *Report*, 1937, pp. 6, 81.
[50] UISC *Report*, 1937, pp. 55-57. The composition of the family unit can be deduced from the rate of benefit payable.
[51] UAB *Report*, 1937, pp. 81-82.
[52] *Ibid.*, pp. 22, 55.

be disregarded.[53] It is already sufficiently serious to act as a deterrent to increases in insurance benefit rates or assistance allowances.

That part of the problem which is due to the payment of extremely low wage rates to juveniles and young men may perhaps be solved by minimum wage legislation and by measures designed to reduce to a minimum the number of blind-alley occupations into which so many young entrants to industry are attracted.[54] But when the problem arises because of the existence of relatively large families among wage earners whose incomes when working approximated the median wage (as is the case among recipients of unemployment assistance), the situation is less amenable to control.

During recent years various expedients have been suggested. It is noteworthy, however, that the adoption by the insurance system of benefits bearing a proportionate relationship to wages has not been among those seriously suggested as a solution of this particular problem.[55] Those who have most strongly advocated a change of this kind, such as Sir William Beveridge, have been motivated rather by a desire to increase the prestige of the insurance system as compared to assistance, in so far as the highly paid wage earner is concerned. Attaching great importance to the function of insurance as a method of removing as many of the unemployed as possible from contact with the means test, Sir William's proposals (given the wage levels in Great Britain) necessarily imply the relating of benefits to wages only above a

[53] Cf. the Statutory Committee's comment: "Over-insurance occurs in an appreciable number of cases, though the number is small proportionately to the total number of claims." (UISC *Report*, 1937, p. 23)

[54] For an account of these blind-alley employments, see John and Sylvia Jewkes, *Juvenile Labor Market* (London: Victor Gollancz, 1938). A list of some of these occupations will be found in the UISC *Report*, 1937, p. 65. Attention was also drawn to this situation by a number of the Board's advisory committees studying unemployment in 1938. Many of them urged publicity to encourage more responsible methods of employment, greater cooperation between employers and local education authorities, and the provision of technical training during adolescence. (UAB *Report*, 1938, p. 46)

[55] The National Union of Societies for Equal Citizenship was the only body which urged the Royal Commission to recommend that benefits be related to wages, with the object, however, of improving the relative status of women rather than of avoiding any overlapping between benefits and wages. (*Final Report*, p. 216)

minimum level which, for the vast majority of beneficiaries, will be adequate without recourse to some supplementary system.[56]

The imposition of a "wage-stop," or ceiling to the maximum benefit payable, although commanding more support and already embodied in the agricultural insurance system and adopted in principle in unemployment assistance, yet fails to be an adequate solution. For it is not easy to define a limit whose imposition will not run counter to the recognized objectives of the insurance and assistance systems. A limit related to an individual's normal wages has been rejected for the general insurance system on the grounds that the differentiation between individuals would be unjustifiable in a system where the contribution rates are not also related to wages.[57] And in an assistance system designed to act as the major residual relief measure for the needy unemployed, a limit may make it impossible to meet the needs of a considerable proportion of applicants. It was undoubtedly for this reason that the "wage-stop" clause found in the regulations of the Board is qualified by the proviso that this is not to be rigidly applied where there are special circumstances or needs of an exceptional character. The Board indicated that a reduction of between 2s. and 3s. would be appropriate, though this might be increased if the applicant was known not to be availing himself of opportunities for employment. While the decision in individual cases was left to the officers of the Board, they were given certain instructions as to the matters to be taken into consideration in deciding whether hardship would be caused by the application of the clause. Since these instructions in the main lean toward generous treatment of applicants, it is not surprising that during 1937 the "wage-stop" was applied in only 6,500 cases.[58]

[56] In rejecting the proposal to relate benefits to wages, the Commission expressed the opinion that "although it would make the insurance scheme a more effective provision for the highly paid man, it would at the same time (unless contributions were a high proportion of earnings) reduce the benefits payable to the low paid worker whose needs may be no less. *In any event, the rate of dependents' benefit would probably have to remain at a flat rate*" (author's italics). (*Ibid.*, p. 218)

[57] UISC *Report*, July 1935, p. 18.

[58] The Board indicated that the existence of 5 or more children in a family should ordinarily be regarded as constituting "special circumstances," and that officers should hesitate to make an allowance for less than 35s. a week in the case of a man, wife and 4 children living under urban conditions. On the other hand, they were to scrutinize carefully cases where allowances of 45s. would

The alternative type of "wage-stop" clause, such as that found in the agricultural scheme and which was proposed for the general scheme by the Statutory Committee, involves the fixing of a flat uniform sum as the maximum benefit payable in any case. If this maximum were set at a very high level, it would prevent payments in excess of wages only in the relatively small number of cases where these are attributable mainly to unusually large families.[59] Yet, 38.3 per cent of the cases in which normal wages did not exceed the benefit plus 4 shillings, were persons in receipt of 22s. a week or less who would not, therefore, have been affected by the imposition of a "wage-stop" of 41s. But if the maximum were set at a much lower level, the number of cases requiring supplementary aid from some other system would greatly increase.[60]

The root of the difficulty, as the Statutory Committee pointed out in 1938, lies in the fact that there is no relation between wages and needs, and the adoption by the government of a policy of meeting needs in full has drawn attention to the cases in which the discrepancy between needs and earnings is great. There is little evidence in Great Britain of any disposition to argue that because of this discrepancy the attempts of the government to secure a decent minimum for its citizens should be abandoned. Attention has rather been turned to the broad problem of poverty and to devising methods of improving the social effectiveness of the wage system.[61] Indeed, in 1938 the Statutory Committee was

---

be payable if the "wage-stop" clause was overriden since "many families in fact maintain themselves without undue privation on wages of that amount." Moreover, they were to take account of the amount on which the household had lived before applying to the Board.

[59] In fact, the "wage-stop" of 41s. proposed by the Statutory Committee would have prevented benefits from exceeding wages only in cases where there were more than 5 children in the family. No information is available concerning the number of beneficiaries in this category, but the inquiry undertaken in August 1937 indicated that of 389,721 male claimants, only 37,561 had 3 children or more, and of these only 3.9 per cent were earning less than 41s. a week. (UISC Report, 1937, pp. 55-57)

[60] The Statutory Committee recognized this dilemma, and appears to have selected the 41s. limit partly because it believed that at this level supplementation would be so rare as to constitute a relatively small disadvantage as compared to the evil of enabling a man to increase his income by losing employment. (UISC Report, July 1935, p. 18)

[61] Cf. UISC Report, 1937, p. 24. H. F. Hohman (op. cit., pp. 266-67) concludes: "In so far as the dilemma of adequate relief is one aspect of the problem of inadequate wages, it might be met, in part at least, by increasing the 'free'

so impressed by the necessity of raising wages in agriculture in order to attract a more adequate labor supply, that it used this argument in support of a decision to increase benefits even though, in relation to current wages, "insurance under the agricultural scheme is already on a more generous scale than under the general scheme." [62] Minimum wage laws already cover large sections of the working population in both agriculture and industry, and together with a still strong trade union movement, have helped to eliminate the more flagrant cases of unduly low wages. But as the experience of Australia, after years of wage regulation, has shown, and as the now comprehensive unemployment relief system of Great Britain has further underlined, an increase in the general rates of wages to a level sufficient to provide for the needs of the "average" family will fail to meet the needs of those whose membership is larger than the average.[63]

The issue clearly transcends the field of unemployment relief, and it is not surprising that there has been a growing interest in Great Britain in the possibilities of schemes of family endowment such as are already in operation in Australia, New Zealand, and elsewhere.[64] Basically these schemes, which involve the pay-

income available to members of the community in the form of health and educational services, free school meals, opportunities for recreation, and in the important matter of rent, in subsidized housing projects." Cf. also E. W. Bakke (*Insurance or Dole,* p. 223): "Such statements [regarding the dangers of a high standard of living on benefit or relief] seem to me to be ammunition for minimum wage campaigns or revolutionary propaganda rather than adequate reasons for establishing benefit amounts at lower levels." But cf. also Gertrude Williams (*The State and the Standard of Living,* p. 302) who reaches a more pessimistic conclusion: "The choice lies, whatever the social organisation, between the retention of a certain degree of personal freedom and a relatively inadequate subsistence for the unemployed on the one hand, and adequate maintenance and virtual slavery on the other."

[62] UISC *Report,* 1938, p. 15.

[63] It is for this reason that the offer of employment at prevailing wages on public works would fail to be an adequate solution of the difficulties created by the payment of allowances that are in excess of normal earnings. For even if, as has been done in Germany, preference of employment on such projects were given to married men with large families, there would still be cases in which the rate of wages paid would fail to meet the needs of men with a large number of children. Indeed, it may be suggested that the effectiveness of a system of public works, as a solution of this particular difficulty, is greatest with regard to workers whose families are of average size or below.

[64] Cf. W. B. Reddaway, "Family Endowment Reconsidered," *Review of Economic Studies,* February 1938, pp. 128-29; Ursula Hicks, *The Finance of British Government 1920-36,* p. 50; PEP, *Report on the British Social Services,* pp. 166-67; Percy Ford, *Incomes, Means Tests and Personal Responsibility,* p. 74; Constance Braithwaite, *The Voluntary Citizen* (London: Methuen and Co., 1938), p. 15.

ment by the government or from funds contributed by groups of employers of additions to "normal wages" in proportion to the number of children dependent on each wage earner, carry further the application of the categorical principle. The existence of families above normal size, in other words, would be recognized as an independent cause of dependency. Although the adoption of these schemes raises difficult questions of social policy, there is little doubt that it would greatly ease the task of those on whom now rests the responsibility for determining the levels of insurance benefits and assistance payments.

TRAINING, WORK OPPORTUNITY, AND THE MAINTENANCE OF MORALE

In the previous sections of this chapter attention has been concentrated upon measures for the physical maintenance of the unemployed. It has, however, become increasingly evident that other criteria must also be applied to any socially satisfactory and comprehensive unemployment relief system. For, as the Pilgrim Trust has pointed out, "unemployed men are not simply units of employability who can, through the medium of the dole, be put into cold storage, and taken out immediately they are needed. While they are in cold storage things are liable to happen to them." The consequences of prolonged unemployment, involving as they do not merely deterioration of physique and industrial skills but also loss of morale and enterprise, have attracted increasing attention since 1934, and various steps have been taken to broaden the unemployment relief program.

In earlier chapters, the powers of the Ministry of Labour with regard to the transference of workers to areas of greater job opportunity and to the provision of training courses have been described. After 1934 these programs were considerably expanded. Furthermore, under the powers given to the Minister by the Act of 1934 "to defray . . . or contribute towards the cost . . . of training courses, courses of instruction, or courses of occupation, provided in pursuance of arrangements made with the Minister by any public authority or other body," the Ministry of Labour each year disbursed increasing sums to the National Council of Social Service to stimulate the provision of local occupational and recreational centers for the unemployed, and to certain other private organizations.

The Unemployment Assistance Board was also vested with considerable powers to maintain the employability of its clients and to exert pressure on workers unwilling to take advantage of employment or training opportunities. It was authorized, subject to the approval of the Ministry of Labour, to provide and maintain training courses for persons of 18 years of age and over and to make contributions toward the cost of providing or maintaining courses instituted by the Ministry of Labour or by any local authority or any other body. Furthermore, it could make grants in order to permit persons who had undergone training and instruction to secure employment with local authorities for periods up to 3 months, if as a result they would be more fit for entry into or return to regular employment.[65]

In order to encourage workers to undertake training or treatment likely to promote their entry into or return to regular employment, the Board was permitted to pay allowances during attendance at training or instruction courses and to provide for members of the worker's family during the training period. In order to make training available to as wide a group as possible, the Board was also empowered to grant allowances to and finance the training of any worker, whether within the Board's scope or not, who could show that he was unemployed, registered for work at an employment office and over the age of 18. Furthermore, it will be recalled that the Board could apply pressure and even coercion to persons refusing to take advantage of the facilities offered. Workers who had failed to avail themselves of opportunities of suitable employment or training were designated as cases of "special difficulty" and as such were subject to certain penalties. In obstinate cases the Board could grant the allowance only on condition that the applicant should attend at a work center and comply with all the rules in force there while so attending.[66] Finally, the Board could

---

[65] This arrangement was to be subject to the approval of the Treasury and was to provide for the payment of customary rates of wages at the expense of the local authority. The Board, however, was empowered to make contributions to local authorities to offset any additional expenditure arising out of the fact that the work was being utilized as a part of the training course.

[66] Such work centers might either be set up by the Board itself or might be special work centers maintained by a local public assistance authority.

pay allowances conditional on the applicant becoming an inmate of a workhouse maintained by a local authority.[67] If any or all of these developments failed to cause a change of attitude on the part of the unemployed worker, the Board was empowered to take more drastic steps. An officer of the Board could report the case to an appeals tribunal which could direct that the applicant should have no further claims under the unemployment assistance scheme.[68]

The Commissioners for the Special Areas have also wide powers to promote transfer, training, occupational and recreational activity, and settlement on the land of persons in these depressed areas. Since 1937 they have expended funds to attract industries into these areas in order to give local employment. Intensified efforts have been made to encourage whole or part-time employment on the land in other ways. Although, on grounds of economy, the Agricultural Utilization Act of 1931 which enabled the Minister of Agriculture and Fisheries to provide small holdings for unemployed persons was not put into operation, the Minister set up non-official Land Settlement Associations for England in 1934 and for Wales in 1936 to undertake experiments along these lines and secured grants for them from the Development Fund. With financial assistance from the Special Areas Commissioner for England and Wales, a few local authorities were encouraged to develop small holding schemes, and to take advantage of the grants from the central government which were available under the hitherto little utilized Small Holdings Act of 1926.[69]

Finally, as already described, the public assistance authorities have power to apply correctional treatment in the form of test work or institutional assistance to workers who are suspected of being work shy, and since 1930, have been encouraged by the Ministry of Health to make greater use of their powers to set

[67] The Board would refund the cost of maintenance to the local authority in whose workhouse the applicant was maintained and would continue to pay the normal allowance for any dependents in the applicant's household.

[68] This declaration that a man was outside the scope of the Act could be for as long as the tribunal should decide.

[69] Under this Act the Minister of Agriculture and Fisheries could make a grant up to 75 per cent of the estimated annual loss incurred by local councils in carrying out approved schemes. (*Report of the Commissioner for the Special Areas* [*England and Wales*], July 1935, Cmd. 4957, p. 40. Hereinafter cited as *Special Areas Report* [*England and Wales*].)

up training and reconditioning centers to maintain and enhance the employability of their clients.

Provision for work relief and public works has been negligible since 1934. Projects inaugurated under the Unemployment Grants Committee and the road programs were being brought to completion and offered scant possibilities for employment and no new legislative programs were introduced.

On paper the measures for improving prospects of absorption into industry by transference or training, and for maintaining the employability of those who fail to be absorbed in industry appear imposing enough. Yet, as a brief survey of their development will indicate, they still fall far short of meeting some of the more difficult problems created by long-continued mass unemployment. The achievement can most conveniently be evaluated by considering the major types of programs.

Geographical Transference of Labor

Placement work is carried on by some 1,600 local offices of the Ministry of Labour which have developed extensive and convenient clearing arrangements. Moreover, financial assistance to workers in the form of grants or loans for the payment of travelling expenses and for tools has long been available. After 1934 the arrangements facilitating transfer were improved in a number of important respects. In 1934 the employment exchanges were permitted to advance fares to workers from depressed areas travelling to interview a prospective employer to whom their qualifications had been submitted by the exchanges and who had hired them subject to interview. In 1935 this program was enlarged by the provision of supplementary allowances to recipients of insurance benefits or unemployment assistance to meet the cost of lodgings in the new areas, and of special allowances to transferred men who had lost employment in the new district to enable them to stay there while awaiting another job. Workers in the depressed areas who wished to travel to a new district to take up employment, found otherwise than through the employment exchange, were granted free fares instead of fares on loan, a privilege previously reserved for those placed through the exchanges. The exchanges were permitted also to furnish clothing and to meet certain other expenses incidental to transfer.

The household removal scheme, which was begun in a small way in 1928, was extended to provide assistance where younger members of the family (and not merely, as previously, the head of the family) obtained employment in an area offering reasonable prospects of work for the other family members. The juvenile transfer program, which had been facilitated by grants from the Lord Mayor's Fund, was taken over wholly by the Ministry of Labour after July 1934. In addition to paying subsidies to wages sufficient to ensure the young worker a weekly income of 4s. or 5s. after payment of living expenses, the Ministry increased hostel accommodation, paid increasing attention to after care and welfare work, and established centers where boys could undergo short training in a healthy environment to improve their chances of transfer.[70] In 1935 special junior instruction centers were established and arrangements were made with the Y. M. C. A. to send to summer camps juveniles who were about to be transferred.[71]

The additional facilities and financial inducements available after 1934 have very considerably increased the movement away from the depressed areas. On the other hand, apart from the scheme for advancing fares which was not restricted to persons from depressed areas, the numbers affected have been at all times small in relation to the total number of unemployed. Although assisted transference from the depressed areas reached a maximum of 28,000 in 1936,[72] a special inquiry in September 1936

[70] Grants were also made to meet emergencies, such as sickness. After July 1934, the employer was no longer required to make a contribution toward the maintenance grants. In 1935 the Ministry also undertook to supply clothing, a function hitherto performed by the Personal Service League. After-care committees were established in the same year in many areas to secure the cooperation of employers, local committees for juvenile employment, and voluntary welfare workers in assisting the transferees to adjust to their new environment. The Minister also made grants toward the capital expenditures of voluntary organizations providing adequate club accommodation for transferred juveniles.

[71] The centers were operated by the Local Education Committee but financed by a 100 per cent grant from the Ministry of Labour. To encourage boys from the depressed areas to take up agriculture, the Minister gave financial assistance to schemes for training and placing boys in farm work, organized by certain local and private welfare organizations. These, however, did not prove very successful.

[72] This figure does not include persons finding work without governmental aid. In 1937 (the first complete year for which this information is available), in addition to 13,958 adults transferred from the special areas in England and Wales through the governmental or grant-aided schemes, 14,785 persons were

showed that in the English and Welsh special areas alone there were 282,952 registered unemployed; and that whereas in the preceding nine months unemployment in these areas had decreased by only 10.9 per cent, it had decreased by 13.1 per cent in Great Britain as a whole.[73] Moreover, between 1934 and 1936 the percentage of the men wholly unemployed in the special areas who had been out of work for a year or more remained high (51 to 53 per cent) as compared with the average percentage in Great Britain, which fell from 30 to 16 per cent,[74] and although by 1937 the number of the unemployed in many of the depressed areas had fallen in comparison with 1929, the percentage of unemployment among insured workers had increased.[75]

In the second place, it will have been clear from the preceding account of the various measures that the majority of them have been available only to persons from the depressed areas.[76] While it is true that continuous unemployment is very largely concentrated in these districts,[77] there are still large numbers of long-period unemployed in areas not officially regarded as "depressed" who are necessarily excluded from the advantages of these special measures.

Experience has shown, too, that even as a solution of the problem of the depressed areas, transference has serious limitations. Local authorities in more prosperous areas, whose cooperation was necessarily sought in the provision of housing and other social amenities for the transferees, have frequently been reluctant to encourage the arrival of new, potentially dependent persons.

known to have obtained work in other areas through their own efforts. (*Special Areas Report* [*England and Wales*], 1937, p. 192.) For more detailed analyses of the nature of transference, see *Minutes of Evidence* of the Royal Commission on the Geographical Distribution of the Industrial Population, 1938, pp. 322-31. The net results of all the transference programs are shown in Appendix VIII.

[73] *Special Areas Report* (*England and Wales*), November 1936, Cmd. 5303, p. 21.

[74] *Ibid.*, 1936, p. 24.

[75] S. R. Dennison, "State Control of Industrial Location," *The Manchester School*, Vol. 2, 1937, pp. 147-48.

[76] The areas regarded as "depressed" for this purpose are much more numerous than the areas scheduled under the special areas legislation. For the geographical location of "depressed" areas, see *Minutes of Evidence*, Royal Commission on the Geographical Distribution of the Industrial Population, pp. 322-25.

[77] In July 1935 the percentage of claimants unemployed for 3 years or more was 26 in the English special areas and 7.5 in Great Britain as a whole. In July 1938 the corresponding percentages were 22.5 and 6.4. (*Special Areas Report* [*England and Wales*], 1938, p. 20)

Older workers with families were not only unwilling to move because of social ties and an unfailing optimism that the revival of local industry was imminent, but they are in any case poor transference material because of the preference of industry for younger workers. Moreover, the depressed areas were the sites of coal mining and the heavy industries and geographical transference has normally involved also occupational change for which the older men are ill adapted. For these reasons the transference program has been largely concentrated upon the younger workers. But while there is some evidence that in the special areas transference has largely succeeded in removing the younger workers who are not so demoralized as to be in need of reconditioning or stronger measures,[78] the transference of these workers has in turn met difficulties, and the social wisdom of this policy has been increasingly questioned. A further obstacle has been the unwillingness of parents to allow their children to take work involving residence in another part of the country, and juvenile workers in particular have been prone to return home because of homesickness.[79] Although the after-care work organized by the Ministry of Labour in recent years has diminished these obstacles to transfer, they are still of importance. In 1937 the Ministry itself conceded that the peak of juvenile transference had been reached.[80]

More serious from a long-run point of view is the social problem created by a successful transference policy concentrated upon the younger workers. For it drains away from the depressed areas the more enterprising and energetic members of the community, and tends to leave a population composed almost exclusively of olders workers suffering more or less continuous unemployment.[81] It tends also to create a disproportionately large

[78] Cf. Men Without Work, p. 221.

[79] The Ministry of Labour reported that of nearly 150,000 men and 40,000 women transferred from the depressed areas between 1928 and the first half of 1937, some 49,500 men and 5,600 women are known to have returned to these areas. (Royal Commission on the Geographical Distribution of the Industrial Population, Minutes of Evidence, pp. 256-57) Between October 1934 and September 1937, of 19,569 boys transferred by the Ministry, 7,591 returned home. The corresponding figures for girls were 16,688 and 7,981. (Ibid., p. 331) With the improvement of business in 1937, there was an increase in the proportion of transferees returning to the special areas. (Special Areas Report [England and Wales], 1937, pp. 30, 44)

[80] Ministry of Labour, Report for the Year 1937, p. 42.

[81] The investigators of the Pilgrim Trust pointed out that after transference and any probable revival of industry "there will remain something essentially

19

public assistance problem.[82] The effect of this selective process upon the vitality of social institutions and upon the chances of attracting new industries to the depressed areas is already evident in such districts as South Wales.[83] For these reasons many of those who have long advocated the policy of transference are increasingly recognizing that additional measures are urgently needed.[84]

Vocational Training for the Unemployed

There was relatively little change in the governmental measures for providing vocational training in the period after 1934. The previous arrangements comprising government training courses, domestic and individual vocational training for women, and occasional technical courses for juveniles were continued. An increase in the number of government training centers for men in 1936 was offset in 1937 by the decision to reserve 4 centers and 200 places at a fifth for soldiers and airmen during the last 6 months of their period of military service. There was, however, a considerable increase in the numbers completing the courses each year, although the proportion which terminated prematurely also increased, as shown in Appendix Table XII.

Nevertheless, the number of enrollees remained small in relation to the number of unemployed. The provision of the courses continued to be dominated by the probabilities of placement on completion of training, but this can hardly account for the relative

abnormal and unhealthy about the situation. For it remains true that while in the Midlands and South about 3 per cent of all older unemployed workers are long unemployed, in Wales the proportion is nearly seven times as great." (*Men Without Work*, p. 214) In the special areas "unemployment is coming to be regarded as something normal, and there is the real danger that an unemployed class will be created." (*Ibid.*, p. 213)

[82] The Commissioner for the English Special Areas attributed the heavy cost of public assistance in the special areas (over 80 per cent of which was on account of relief for the aged and sick poor) to this change in the age composition of the population in these areas. (*Report*, Nov. 1936, pp. 70-71)

[83] See R. K. Owen, "The Social Consequences of Industrial Transference," and Michael Daly, "A Reply," *Sociological Review*, July 1938, pp. 236-61; also the rejoinder by Mr. Owen, *Ibid.*, October 1938, pp. 414-20.

[84] Thus the English Special Areas Commissioner, who had from the first regarded transference as one of the essential measures for dealing with the unemployed in these areas, reported in November 1936 that while "transference is making a big contribution to the reduction of unemployment in the Special Areas, especially among young persons. . . . I do not regard it as sufficient by itself to solve the problem of the areas." (*Report*, 1936, p. 25. Cf. also *Ibid.*, 1937, p. 44)

insignificance of the program because the centers never at any time were filled to capacity. Much more important is the fact that, since the program was regarded as an aid to transference, recruitment for the courses was almost exclusively confined to the special areas and other districts characterized by severe and prolonged unemployment. In the spring of 1937, however, the courses in building and engineering were opened to applicants from all parts of the country, while in June 1938, the list of recruiting areas was widened and in October courses in draftsmanship were open to all applicants regardless of residence.

This policy has not merely limited the vocational training opportunities of persons in other parts of the country,[85] but has also concentrated recruitment on an increasingly unresponsive field. For, as a result of the transference measures, the residual young unemployed in the special areas have tended to be persons among whom the demoralizing consequences of prolonged unemployment were already evident, and who could scarcely be expected either to volunteer for training which led almost invariably to employment, or to profit from training if accepted.[86]

Recognition of this fact led the Ministry of Labour in 1936 to open a preparatory center in South Wales, where preliminary training could be given to young men whose suitability for the more technical courses was in doubt. This center appears to have been very successful.[87]

It is possible also that the types of training offered failed to make any great appeal to the unemployed. Relatively few changes in the curriculum (except the abandonment of certain courses in trades for which demand appeared to have declined) were made during these years, and much of the training was for occupations in which trade unionism was well entrenched and likely to oppose

[85] The UAB urged that in the future greater attention should be paid to the vocational training of the long-unemployed wherever resident. (UAB *Report*, 1938, p. 25)

[86] The English Commissioner for the Special Areas referred in 1936 to the large numbers of young men under 25 who "either rejected the proposal of training at the interview, or failed to attend after acceptance." (*Report*, November 1936, p. 124)

[87] During 1936, 1,231 men were admitted, of whom 677 passed on to government training centers. In 1937, 865 men were recruited for the government training centers. (Ministry of Labour, *Report for the Year 1936*, p. 29; *1937*, p. 28) The center was closed in 1938, but another was contemplated at Liverpool.

both recruitment and recognition of the trainees as qualified workers. New courses in draftsmanship and in telephone installation introduced in 1937 were, however, very popular.[88]

In addition to these vocational training schemes, both the Ministry of Labour and the Unemployment Assistance Board made arrangements with certain organizations to provide vocational training for unemployed men, but the numbers of men affected have been small.[89]

The courses for women were characterized by even less variety and imagination. Apart from the insignificant individual vocational training scheme, domestic service continued to be the only type of vocational training available.[90] In 1937 the Unemployment Assistance Board drew attention to the need for courses for women normally engaged in factory work and in 1938 special training for female factory workers was provided on one of the "trading estates" established by the English Special Areas Commissioner, while the Ministry of Labour supplied funds for a vocational course for female silk weavers, organized by a local authority in the West Cumberland special area. Domestic training failed to attract many workers, and during the later years attendance at the centers was maintained largely by extending the facilities to juveniles.[91]

Vocational training for unemployed juveniles was practically non-existent, for the junior instruction centers continued on their previous non-vocational basis. Apart from the training in domestic service available to girls between the ages of 15 and 21, which reached between 2,200 and 2,900 girls annually, no serious efforts were made during this period to provide technical training for juveniles. For some years arrangements had been made with

[88] Ibid., pp. 28 ff. For list of the trades in which training was offered in 1937, see Ibid., p. 104.

[89] The Ministry of Labour gave assistance to a few voluntary organizations providing training for unemployed men from the depressed areas in domestic employment and for employment as barmen. In 1936 and 1937 the numbers undergoing such training were 1,376 and 1,088 respectively. (Ibid., 1936, p. 30; 1937, pp. 30-31) The Unemployment Assistance Board also arranged for a small number of its clients (227 in 1937) to take courses at the British Legion School of Taxi Driving. (UAB Report, 1935, p. 62; 1937, pp. 41-42)

[90] Even the one center which specialized after 1937 in training secondary school girls concentrated on cooking and housekeeping courses to fit trainees for positions in institutions, hospitals, etc.

[91] The number of adult women completing the courses fell from 2,429 in 1932 to 904 in 1937. (Ministry of Labour, Report for the Year 1932, p. 38, 1937, p. 32)

the Y. M. C. A. and the Boy Scouts Association to provide boys with training for employment on the land, in the merchant marine service and in domestic service in institutions, but the numbers affected have been small and in the main have been confined to boys from the depressed areas. Apart from the training for the mercantile courses, the type of training available appeared to have little appeal to juveniles.[92] There were, however, signs that the absence of these facilities was beginning to attract attention.[93]

Occupational and Recreational Activity

After 1934 more attention was paid to the instructional centers. The area of recruitment, already widened during 1935, was, at the suggestion of the Unemployment Assistance Board, extended to the entire country in 1937 although preference was still given to applicants from the special areas. In the same year, the Board was given primary responsibility for recruitment among its own applicants in the hope that a more individual approach would bring better results. The summer camps which had been initiated in 1934 were continued, and in 1937 additional centers were opened. In 1936 and 1937, local training centers were created in some of the special areas to enable men who disliked leaving home to accustom themselves to training conditions in a familiar environment, and to supply dental and other treatment for men hitherto rejected on account of remedial medical defects.[94] Changes were also made in the curriculum, physical training being provided at all residential centers and more attention being paid to workshop and other courses for men unfit for pick-and-shovel work, and to recreational activities.

The total numbers affected in 1937, however, remained small in relation to the volume of long-period unemployment. Moreover, wastage in the form of dismissal or voluntary withdrawal increased. There was, too, a decline in the proportion subsequently placed in employment,[95] a fact which further tended to discourage recruitment.

[92] *Ibid., 1937*, pp. 43-44; *1938*, pp. 43-44.
[93] Cf. *Special Areas Report (England and Wales)*, 1937, p. 5; John and Sylvia Jewkes, *op. cit.*
[94] By the end of 1938 there was accommodation for 750 men at the local training centers. For the results of this experiment, see Ministry of Labour, *Report for the Year 1938*, pp. 106-07.
[95] However, a follow-up study made by the Unemployment Assistance Board in 1938, indicated that in addition to 2,855 men who were placed on completing

The success of the voluntary physical training courses which had been inaugurated in the special areas in 1932 led the Ministry of Labour to expand the number of its demonstration centers after 1935 in other areas of heavy unemployment. In the depressed areas the Special Areas Commissioner took over the financing of the classes, but their operation was controlled by the Ministry. During 1937 some 20,490 persons attended, but as the sessions were relatively short (the maximum attendance was limited to 12 weeks, with sessions on alternate days), a truer picture of the relative importance of these centers is presented by the numbers enrolled at the end of each year (6,654 in 1936 and 7,923 in 1937).[96]

Inadequate as it was, however, the provision of occupational and recreational activity for men was superior to that for women. Although both the Ministry of Labour and the Unemployment Assistance Board on numerous occasions expressed concern over the hopelessness and deterioration of older unemployed women with negligible chances of reabsorption in private industry, little was done beyond the establishment of a center in London where training was given in cookery, needlework and handicrafts, and occasional short courses run in cooperation with private organizations which aimed at most to give "mental and moral encouragement."

The courses for juveniles which were definitely non-vocational were expanded during this period largely as a result of the changes introduced by the Unemployment Act of 1934. For the first time a statutory obligation was imposed on local higher education authorities to submit proposals for courses to the Minister of Labour. A grant of 75 per cent of the net expenditure was made from central funds, while grants up to 100 per cent of the costs were available in areas with heavy unemployment or unduly high local tax rates. The Minister was given power to require the attendance, not only of juvenile benefit claimants, but also of any young person between the school-leaving age and 18 who was capable of and available for work but who had no work or only

the course, another 2,906 had found employment of varying duration. Nevertheless, the Board concluded that men who had accepted training did not find work to a greater extent than those who refused. (UAB *Report,* 1938, pp. 26-27)

[96] Ministry of Labour, *Report for the Year 1936,* p. 31; *1937,* p. 31.

part-time or intermittent work, and thereafter non-benefit recipients constituted a large proportion of those enrolled.[97]

Although the National Advisory Councils for Juvenile Employment in both England and Wales and in Scotland had "confirmed [their] opinion of the general adequacy of the objective and framework of the original scheme," [98] steps were taken by the Ministry of Labour and the education authorities to improve the service. Arrangements were made with the inspectors of the central education authorities to inspect the schools, conferences of superintendents were held, and there were attempts to secure a more balanced curriculum. Many local education authorities in England and Wales took advantage of the power given to them in 1937 to provide medical and dental facilities, and these powers were extended to the Scottish authorities in 1938. With the assistance of the Commissioner for the Special Areas and the National Council of Social Service, holiday camps were established in 1937. The Unemployment Insurance Act of 1938 empowered education authorities to provide meals for juveniles attending authorized courses and to provide free milk and biscuits for all juveniles in attendance.[99] But many of the earlier problems remained. The fluctuations in numbers and the irregularity of attendance operated against the provision of orderly and educationally valuable courses, and in some areas the numbers were too few to justify the formation of special classes, while in others, difficulties were experienced in obtaining suitable premises.[100] Thus, although there was a marked increase in attendance after 1934 (see Appendix Table XII), the problem of unemployed youth was still largely unsolved.

For the small group of the unemployed who were maintained by the local public assistance authorities, opportunities for training and reconditioning were equally meager. With the exception of a few progressive authorities, such as the London County Council,

[97] For a description of the objective of the courses, see *Ibid., 1934*, p. 48.
[98] *Ibid.*, p. 50.
[99] By the end of 1938, however, only 28 authorities had approved schemes for meals and 4 for free milk and biscuits. (Ministry of Labour, *Report for the Year 1938*, p. 46)
[100] See *Ibid., 1935*, p. 50; *1936*, p. 47; *1937*, p. 46.

there appears to have been little response to the efforts of the central authorities to stimulate the establishment of courses.[101]

Increasing efforts have been made in recent years to offset the social consequences of unemployment by the stimulation of voluntary recreational and occupational centers for the unemployed. These efforts have been of various types, ranging from the provision of club rooms that afforded little more than shelter and warmth to unemployed groups to organized courses in physical training and craftsmanship, and in some cases even developing into well organized community centers serving unemployed and employed alike. The National Council of Social Service, which had been promoting the formation of clubs and recreational centers, was recognized by the government as the logical coordinating agency for these activities and, as already stated, was assisted by grants from the Ministry of Labour and the Commissioner for the Special Areas.[102] These grants, together with private contributions, were used to supply organizers, train personnel, and to pay organizing expenses and part of the costs of equipping and securing suitable premises. By the end of 1937 it was estimated that there were 1,550 of these centers with a total membership of 150,000 at any one time.

In the English and Welsh special areas further grants were made to unemployed groups who desired assistance in carrying out local improvements initiated by themselves. The men gave their labor, and the Special Areas Commissioner provided tools, materials and working clothes, and usually a daily meal. By December 1938, 134 of these schemes employing some 4,000 volunteers had been thus assisted.[103]

The vitality of many of these occupational and recreational clubs and centers cannot be denied, and their expansion consti-

---

[101] In 1935 the Department of Health for Scotland reported that the authorities were not using their new powers except in isolated cases. (Department of Health for Scotland, *Annual Report, 1935,* p. 147) The reports of the English Ministry of Health between 1936 and 1939, in contrast to those of earlier years, make no mention of any training or reconditioning activities.

[102] In addition to direct governmental aid, the Unemployment Assistance Board gave discretionary allowances to applicants who were being trained as leaders for these clubs. (UAB *Report,* 1936, p. 51; 1938, p. 40)

[103] *Special Areas Report (England and Wales),* 1938, pp. 54-55. The total sum granted amounted to £58,800. In Scotland it proved difficult to secure voluntary labor for local schemes.

tutes one of the most interesting social developments of recent years. But their importance as a contribution to the problem of prolonged and heavy unemployment must not be over-estimated. The sponsors of the club movement are the first to admit that there was "no intention to solve the economic problem of unemployment. . . . Neither was it suggested that the occupational clubs were in any sense of the word, a substitute for normal wage-earning employment." [104] These clubs have undoubtedly, at least for a period, relieved the drabness of the lives of the unemployed and for some groups and individuals have formed a center of interest that even surpassed that of normal employed life. But, as the careful study by the Pilgrim Trust makes clear, the club movement is at best a "makeshift" response to the needs of the unemployed and "the clubs that already have what might be called a permanent survival value are only a relatively small number." [105]

Quite apart from the doubtful wisdom of building a group organization confined to the unemployed, thus further segregating them from the normally occupied population, the clubs have faced difficulties in attracting a balanced membership and have at all times been precariously financed. Moreover, if the clubs are to develop as a permanent institution, more professional and trained leadership and staffing are called for.[106] And where the clubs have expanded to include employed men also and have taken on the character of community centers, while the danger of segregation of the unemployed is reduced, the extent to which they meet the peculiar problem of the unemployed is correspondingly lessened. "For what is needed, if anything effective is to be done for the middle-aged and younger men, is something more alive and active. The provision of rest and recreation carries with it the risk of pauperization. . . . What is needed . . . is something that will prove to an unemployed man that he can work, and that he is a useful member of society." [107]

[104] R. Clements, "The Administration of Voluntary Social Service," *Public Administration*, October 1939, p. 362.
[105] *Men Without Work*, p. 386; see also Part V.
[106] *Ibid.*, pp. 379-87.
[107] *Ibid.*, pp. 382, 384.

The Promotion of Settlement on the Land

There is general agreement on the part of administrators, experts, and spokesmen for political parties, that no major solution of the unemployment problem can be expected from attempts to settle the unemployed on the land.[108] The lack of land suitable for small holdings, the general economic structure of the country, the long industrial background of the group who form the major proportion of the long-period unemployed and the expense involved—all conspire against the success of this kind of an undertaking. Nevertheless, since 1934 there have been increasing efforts to develop small holdings, group holdings, and the cultivation of garden plot allotments, partly in the hope of creating self-sustaining employment for a limited number of older men, and partly in order to provide healthy occupation and some improvement in the standard of living of persons who are expected to be dependent on the government for their main support for a more or less indefinite period.

Of these programs the most ambitious was the small holdings scheme which was developed by the Land Settlement Association with financial assistance from the English Commissioner for the Special Areas, and by certain local authorities with similar aid and with additional assistance from the Ministry of Agriculture and Fisheries. The program was conceived as a method of assisting suitable men of and above middle age, whose prospects of reabsorption into private industry were remote, to achieve a modest independence by life on the land as small holders in relatively prosperous areas where their children could hope to secure local employment without great difficulty. The scheme involved the setting up of a number of groups, each supplied with a central

---

[108] Cf. C. S. Orwin and W. F. Darke, *Back to the Land* (London: P. S. King and Sons, 1935). The authors conclude that the transfer of large numbers to agriculture would depress existing agricultural standards of living, contract the market of existing growers, and add little to the demand for manufactured goods. Similarly, an inquiry organized by Viscount Astor and Mr. Seebohm Rowntree and others led the investigators to conclude reluctantly that the possibilities of large-scale settlement were much less than some of them had believed. Similar conclusions were reached by Mr. A. W. Menzies-Kitchin, of the Cambridge School of Agriculture, in a survey conducted for the Carnegie Trustees. Even the Labour Party has claimed only that land settlement schemes "may play a small but useful part in providing work and increasing home food supplies." (*Labour and the Distressed Areas: A Program of Immediate Action*, published by the Labour Party, January 1937, p. 12)

farm and warden, and consisting of up to 40 small holdings varying in size from 3 to 10 acres. After a year's training, during which time they continued to draw unemployment assistance allowances together with certain supplementary allowances, the men were transferred to their holdings, where they were provided with working capital and operated their holdings under the general supervision of the warden.[109] The settlers were required to pay a fair rent for the house and land and to repay part of the initial working capital. In Wales the land settlement scheme was a form of cooperative farming. The men were paid a minimum weekly wage, and the risks were carried by the group as a whole.

By the end of 1938, the small holdings scheme had scarcely achieved even the modest hopes placed upon it. Some 1,500 families (including trainees and tenants in occupation) had been transferred since the inception of the scheme, but about one-third of these families had abandoned their holdings. Moreover, as the Unemployment Assistance Board pointed out in expressing its concern that the scheme was not proving more effective in absorbing the middle-aged married applicants for whom it was devised, the numbers settled must be considered in relation to the total number of eligible unemployed men in the special areas (those between 35 and 60 numbered more than 60,000 in 1938). And until the end of 1938 the scheme was almost entirely confined to unemployed workers from the special areas, particularly in the north of England. Few schemes were developed in Scotland.[110]

The reasons for this limited success are not hard to find. The programs are expensive,[111] and the selection of appropriate lands

[109] For an account of the projects undertaken by the two Land Settlement Associations and by the county councils of Durham and Glamorgan, see *Special Areas Report (England and Wales)*, 1935, pp. 39-46; February 1936, pp. 47-61; November 1936, pp. 95-112, 196-98; 1937, pp. 137-42. See also the *Annual Reports* of the Land Settlement Association.

[110] UAB *Report*, 1938, pp. 31-33.

[111] It had originally been estimated that the cost would average about £800 per settler. By 1936, however, it was seen that the cost would be around £1,200 in the schemes initiated by the Land Settlement Association (of which £700 represented expenditures for the purchase of land, construction of buildings, provision of utilities, etc., £200 the proportionate share of the expenses of the central farm and the costs of training, £260 working capital, and the remainder for contingencies). The schemes of the Welsh Land Settlement Society were expected to average £1,000 per settler, while the more modest schemes organized by the Durham County Council averaged £650 without taking account of the costs of working capital. (*Special Areas Report [England and Wales]*, November 1936, pp. 103-04, 110)

and the erection of dwellings necessarily take time. But the high percentage of wastage among a group selected with extreme care and already given some preliminary training suggests that the basic difficulty lay in the fact that, as the Unemployment Assistance Board pointed out, "life as an independent small-holder has only a limited appeal to the long-unemployed who are, almost without exception, men with a history of wage-paid industrial employment." [112] The scheme, in other words, was lacking in appeal precisely to the group for whom it was especially devised.

The small holdings scheme aimed at ultimate self-sufficiency and independence. Two other programs, the group holdings and the allotments schemes, also provided the unemployed with an opportunity to work on the land, but assumed that the operators would never be wholly dependent upon the yield of their holdings.[113] In both cases, the Unemployment Assistance Board agreed to continue payment of allowances so long as the worker was unemployed, and to disregard, in calculating resources, the value of all produce consumed by the group-holder and his household. Furthermore, the Board undertook to disregard any profits obtained during the first year of operation, and in subsequent years to deduct any expenses incurred from the profits, and to take the latter into account only where they were substantial.

The group holdings schemes aimed to provide middle-aged and married workers with small pieces of land, varying in size from one-fourth to one-half acre and as close as possible to their homes,

[112] UAB *Report*, 1938, p. 31. *Cf.* also *Men Without Work*, p. 217: "Unemployment has come upon them [the middle-aged and older workers] when it is far more difficult to think in terms other than those of the ordinary work they are accustomed to." The Commissioner for the Special Areas attributed the disappointing results of the scheme in West Cumberland to the fact that "the average Cumbrian would prefer to be engaged as an agricultural settler on a wage paid basis to being called upon to face the risks attendant upon endeavour to earn a living out of the Small Holding." (*Special Areas Report,* [*England and Wales*], 1937, p. 50)

[113] The cottage homestead program, which was carried into effect during 1938, appears to have been an adjunct to the transference schemes rather than a land settlement program, although it involved settling workers in cottages with about half an acre of land. Its main object was to encourage the transference of children of unemployed men from the depressed areas to areas of good employment without breaking up the family, and was based on the assumption that these new entrants to the labor market would readily be absorbed, while the parent, who might be too old to secure new full-time work, could yet find a healthy occupation in tending his holding. By the end of 1938 the initial experimental 250 families had been transferred. (UAB *Report*, 1938, p. 34)

on which they could grow vegetables for home use and keep poultry and pigs. These holdings were grouped in units of 10 or more. Each worker was provided with seed and fertilizers, chickens, materials for erecting poultry houses, and other miscellaneous equipment. In many cases technical advice and assistance were supplied by the expert agricultural staffs of the local county councils. The cultivation of the plot was expected to absorb only leisure time, leaving the worker free for part or full-time employment, but for unemployed men it was thought to be sufficiently large to provide healthy and remunerative outdoor occupation, assist in the maintenance of employability, and to afford training for the operation of full-time holdings.[114] By the end of 1938 there were 5,663 group holdings in England and Wales, 3,311 of which were in the special areas.

These schemes are, of course, much less costly than the full-time settlements. The capital expenditure per man was from £10 to £20, between 20 and 25 per cent of which was repayable in the second and third years. But since the operations can never be self-sustaining, and the yield from the holdings serves to increase the operators' standard of living rather than to decrease the government's expenditure for unemployment relief, the total cost of the schemes is high and the fact that they have not made more progress can hardly be a matter for surprise. Furthermore, the securing of suitable land at a reasonable price in the vicinity of workers' dwellings has presented serious difficulties.[115]

The least ambitious of the schemes which involved bringing the unemployed in contact with the land were the efforts made to stimulate the provision of allotments or large gardens, usually about 1/16 of an acre, whose yield should provide sufficient market produce for the needs of an average-sized family but leave no surplus for sale. For many years local authorities and allotment societies had facilitated the cultivation of garden plots, and the movement reached a peak during and immediately after the 1914-18 war. Efforts to revive the scheme with a view to providing occupation for the unemployed were made by the Society

[114] For a fuller description of these schemes, see *Special Areas Report (England and Wales)*, 1935, pp. 46-48; February 1936, pp. 61-64; November 1936, pp. 112-16; 1937, pp. 101-04.
[115] *Ibid.*, February 1936, p. 64; 1938, p. 51.

of Friends, and in 1935 the English Commissioner for the Special Areas offered financial assistance to local authorities in securing suitable land. The initial response was slow, and by 1938 only 4,264 allotments were thus assisted, while in the country as a whole the movement showed a declining tendency.[116]

Two other relatively unimportant experiments in land settlement deserve at least brief mention. In 1934 the Society of Friends inaugurated a subsistence production plan at Upholland, Lancashire, with the object of assisting older unemployed men to produce goods for their own use on a collective basis. To encourage this scheme the Unemployment Assistance Board agreed to disregard the value of any produce obtained during the first year in assessing the resources of members of the group who were applicants for allowances. In 1936 and 1937, when the membership of the project included some 200 applicants, the Board, in recognition of the value of the training provided by the scheme to the long-unemployed, granted £3,000 towards expenses.[117] In 1938, however, the Society of Friends was compelled to discontinue the scheme for financial reasons. A somewhat similar plan, operating in Monmouth, received assistance from the Commissioner for the Special Areas, but grants were discontinued in 1938 as a result of an investigation indicating that the plan could not be conducted on a self-supporting basis.[118]

The last of the special measures for settling the unemployed on the land was initiated in 1929 and aimed to settle on forest holdings married ex-miners from depressed areas. By 1934 the number of families settled had increased from an initial 30 to 69. Thereafter the numbers declined and although the plan was revised in 1937, the numbers attracted were small.[119]

[116] The total number of allotments in the English special areas which were assisted by the Central Allotment Committee fell from 57,000 in 1934 to 46,000 in 1938. For an account of the allotment schemes, see *Special Areas Report* (*England and Wales*), February 1936, pp. 64-65; November 1936, pp. 116-18; 1937, pp. 104-07, 1938, p. 55. See also *Special Areas Report* (*Scotland*), 1938 (Cmd. 5905).

[117] A fuller account of this project will be found in *Men Without Work*, pp. 354-70.

[118] *Special Areas Report* (*England and Wales*), 1938, p. 57.

[119] Only 15 families were settled during 1937. Recruitment was thereafter limited to the special areas. In addition to reasonable costs of removal, the families were given a grant of £5 and a further grant of £10 on an installment basis for the development of the holding. (Ministry of Labour, *Report for the Year 1937*, p. 19)

Public Works

No change in the general attitude towards the desirability of instituting public works was discernible after 1935. Small payments continued to be made for the completion of projects commenced under the Unemployment Grants Committee. But by the end of 1937 only 2 schemes, employing 303 men, were in operation.[120] The grants under the road programs also created only a negligible volume of employment.[121]

Even after the appointment of the Commissioners for the Special Areas, the restrictive attitude towards public works remained. The Act did not include the provision of employment among the duties of the Commissioners, and grants to assist certain of the more familiar types of public works were effectively prevented by the clause which forbade the Commissioners to supplement (with certain minor exceptions) specific grants made or offered by a government department.[122] Their powers to grant financial aid to local authorities and non-profit corporations for services for which they were not already receiving a government grant [123] were in some respects more restricted than those of the Unemployment Grants Committee, and less likely to achieve results because the areas dealt with were by definition depressed and largely incapable of contributing their share of the new expenditure. The Commissioners' powers to create employment in other districts for persons from the special areas were also materially restricted by pledges given by the government during the passage of the Bill. In fact, however, the Commissioners appeared to have shared the prevailing official view that there was "no justification for spending money without resultant economic value, merely to provide employment.[124]

---

[120] *Ibid.,* p. 23.

[121] Between 1935 and 1938, the central government spent only £1,143,000 on the road programs. *Annual Reports of the Road Fund.*

[122] The Commissioner for England and Wales pointed out that this clause prevented him from giving any financial assistance toward the construction of roads, bridges, tunnels, canals or quays, or to any educational service. (*Special Areas Report,* 1935, p. 7)

[123] This restriction was slightly modified by the amending act of 1937, which permitted grants toward the repair or improvement of streets in areas certified by the Minister of Transport as being wholly or mainly required for purposes other than through traffic.

[124] *Ibid.,* p. 23. The English Commissioner reported that he was "pleased to find in dealing with representatives of local authorities in the special areas

Hence, the few grants that were made were limited to projects which were likely to effect permanent improvement of an economic or social nature and which the authorities could afford to maintain when completed.[125] With this emphasis, it is not surprising that despite the formal offer to grant assistance toward the capital costs of hospitals and similar institutions, and for housing projects, the number of projects carried through was small. Although by the end of 1938 grants for hospitals, sewage disposal and other health improvements amounting to £6.1 millions in England and Wales and £1.9 millions in Scotland had been approved, the reports of the Commissioners contain continuing complaints of the delay in commencing work and of the leisurely fashion in which the local authorities took advantage of the grants available.[126] Grants for housing projects were also made by the English Commissioner through a special organization, the North Eastern Housing Association Ltd. By December 1938 commitments amounting to £1,162,000 had been made for these projects.[127]

POSITIVE MEASURES TO REVIVE INDUSTRY

With the exception of the appointment of the Special Areas Commissioners in 1934, there was no significant change in the passive attitude of the British government toward unemployment up to the end of the period covered by this study. This attitude

that most of them have no wish to undertake relief schemes which do not yield justifiable value in addition to providing work." (*Ibid.*, p. 6) In 1938 the Scottish Commissioner, in reporting on his public works schemes, proudly asserted that not one had been approved to "relieve unemployment or which could have been carried out without a grant." (*Special Areas Report* [*Scotland*], 1938, p. 18)

[125] *Special Areas Report* (*England and Wales*), 1935, pp. 23, 27. It was expressly stated that the provision of employment to counteract the depressing effect of long-continued unemployment "has not been treated as a controlling factor in determining the merits of any scheme, but has been subordinated to the obtaining of value for work." (p. 23)

[126] *Special Areas Report* (*England and Wales*), 1938, pp. 58-59, 92; *Ibid.* (*Scotland*), 1937, p. 108. The Scottish Commissioner estimated in 1938 that it would be three years before the commitments entered into were fulfilled. (*Ibid.*, 1938, p. 18)

[127] *Ibid.* (*England and Wales*), 1938, p. 92. In Durham and Tyneside some 8,045 houses had been completed, the total cost amounting to £3.5 millions. In West Cumberland progress was slower, only 30 of 445 houses planned for having been completed. (*Ibid.*, pp. 67-68) No housing association was formed in Scotland until November 1937. By the end of 1938 plans were under consideration for the construction of about 5,000 grant-aided houses. The total commitment in 1938 amounted to £700,000. (*Ibid.* [*Scotland*], 1938, pp. 28, 74)

extended also to all proposals for using fiscal and monetary policy as a weapon to promote economic revival. Thus it might have been expected that even though there was little interest in public works as a device for offsetting the consequences to the individual of prolonged unemployment, they might nevertheless have been favored as a technique for implementing a controlled expansionist policy. But the prevalence of the "Treasury view" regarding the limitations of expanded public works effectively inhibited any such venture.[128]

Fiscal and monetary policy continued to be dominated by deflationary theories. "Conditions clearly called for some relaxation of deflation the moment confidence was restored. . . . It appears that exactly the opposite policy was followed. Income and capital taxation was maintained at crisis rates after the crisis had passed, and was only partially relaxed after 1934." [129] The effects of the economy wave which followed the events of 1931 were indeed less evident between 1934 and 1938, and local investment expenditure in particular began to revive after 1934.[130] But, as Dr. Hicks points out, "while such an extension of public investment may well be very desirable on long-run grounds, it would surely have been more appropriate in 1932-33 than in 1935-36." [131]

Positive action by the government for the revival of industry was thus limited to the measures taken in regard to the special areas.[132] The initial powers given to the Commissioners hardly

[128] For a careful analysis of the extent to which an expanded public works policy might have been expected to succeed, see Ursula Hicks, *The Finance of British Government*, pp. 218-30. Although critical of the Treasury view, she concludes that, "Expenditure policy can only hope to cover part of the field in any case. The difficulties of carrying it out successfully in this country appear to be formidable." (p. 230) In regard to types of projects most likely to command sufficient popular and business support to overcome psychological, administrative, and financial obstacles, she comments on "the somewhat melancholy fact of the immense economic superiority of a rearmament campaign over other forms of public works available in Great Britain." (p. 225)

[129] *Ibid.*, pp. 374-75. See also Chapter XVIII.

[130] Local public issues on the stock exchange totalled £8 millions in 1931, £36 millions in 1934, £51.1 millions in 1935, and £79.5 millions in 1936. (*Ibid.*, p. 375)

[131] *Ibid.*, p. 375.

[132] The discussions between the Minister of Labour and representatives of certain industries in 1936, which were published under the title of "Absorption of the Unemployed into Industry" (Cmd. 5317, 1936), although referring to the desire of the government "to omit no step which might assist in the relief of unemployment," were concerned mainly with the possibility of increasing absorption by the reduction of overtime and the desirability of governmental action to avoid "bottle-necks" and blind-alley employments.

20

warranted high expectations. They were specifically barred from carrying on any undertaking for the purpose of gain or from providing financial assistance to any such undertaking.[133] In consequence of these limitations, in England and Wales by the end of 1935 only £688,700 out of a total commitment of £3,443,000 took the form of assistance to industry.

The Commissioner for England and Wales drew attention to the crippling effect of these limitations on his powers, and largely owing to his influence two acts made possible direct financial assistance to industry. In May 1936 the Special Areas Reconstruction (Agreement) Act authorized the Treasury to set up the Special Areas Reconstruction Association, Ltd. This body could loan capital to firms establishing or developing business in the special areas which were unable to raise capital through ordinary business channels.[134] At the end of the same year Lord Nuffield set up the Nuffield Trust with a capital of £2 million to aid in reconstructing industry in the special areas and to bring in new industries. The Special Areas (Amendment) Act of 1937 was, at least in principle, even more important. In order to induce businessmen to establish factories in the special areas, the Commissioners were empowered to lease factories to organizations carried on for profit, and to give direct financial assistance over a period of not more than 5 years toward rent, income tax or rates.[135] The Commissioners could also contribute toward the cost of drainage schemes, although the land might be occupied for the purposes of gain. Finally, the amending act authorized the Treasury to make loans to companies set up to provide factories for new industrial undertakings in certified areas, and to make loans to the businesses occupying the factories.[136]

[133] Except that grants could be made if the project were carried on primarily with the object of providing means of livelihood for the persons engaged on it, in order to make them independent of unemployment assistance or poor relief.

[134] The Association was financed mainly by banks and financial houses, but the government contributed toward management expenses and guaranteed the Association against losses up to 25 per cent of the total loans made, subject to a maximum of £1 million. Not more than £10,000 could be lent to any firm and the period of the loan could not exceed 5 years.

[135] The Finance Act 1937, authorized the Treasury to remit in whole or in part the National Defense Contributions under similar conditions.

[136] The certified areas included the special areas and other areas certified by the Ministry of Labour to be districts characterized by prolonged and severe unemployment, dependent largely on one or more depressed industries, and in which revival of employment was improbable without financial assistance.

In consequence of these enlarged powers, by the end of September 1938 grants to industry became an increasingly important feature in the special areas program. But the net result of the many-sided activities of the Commissioners was disappointingly small. By September 1938 only some £8,500,000 out of total commitments of £16,770,000 had been actually spent in England and Wales. The effect of grants to local development councils and of efforts to revive interest in recreation centers (which in the first years constituted the main lines of activity) was difficult to assess. More was hoped from the establishment of "trading estates" which were expected to prove attractive to industrialists. Yet by the end of 1938 the English Commissioner reported new employment totaling only about 2,200 at the two estates.[137] Contributions under the 1937 Act toward rates, taxes and rents were made to only 60 firms in England and Wales and 29 in Scotland, while by September 1937, 43 undertakings in England and Wales had been assisted by the Nuffield Trust. The English Commissioner reported serious difficulty (especially in South Wales) in attracting the interest of business men, and concluded by 1936 that the policy of "persuasion" of industrialists had failed.[138] The lack of success of the various measures is perhaps best indicated by the statistics of factory growth, in regard to which the English Commissioner commented, "these dismal figures speak for themselves."[139]

The Commissioners did indeed win from the government an agreement that, in letting government contracts and in locating

[137] *Special Areas Report* (*England and Wales*), 1938, pp. 39-40. The estates were financed by loans from the Special Areas Fund secured by a debenture on their assets. But they were not expected to pay interest on loans in the first years. By 1938 the capital expenditure involved had amounted to £2.6 millions. (Royal Commission on the Geographical Distribution of the Industrial Population, *Minutes of Evidence,* p. 264)

[138] *Special Areas Report* (*England and Wales*), 1935, pp. 14-15; November 1936, p. 37. A circular addressed to 5,829 English firms in 1935 asking whether they had recently established or contemplated establishing branches in the special areas, and if not why not, elicited only 1,763 replies, 1,313 of these answering every question negatively. (*Ibid.*, February 1936, p. 5)

	1934	1935	1936	1937
[139] New factories in England and Wales	478	488	551	541
Those in the special areas	7	2	8	17
Expanded factories in England and Wales	144	182	201	237
Those in the special areas	2	6	3	5

Sources: Special Areas Report, February 1936, p. 3, November 1936, p. 59, 1937, p. 32, 1938, p. 22.

factories required for the defense program, preference should be given to the special areas "all else being equal." The House of Commons also passed a resolution in 1936 regarding the desirability of encouraging manufacturers contemplating settlement in England to locate in the special areas.[140] But these actions, although attaining some success, did not lead to the creation of net new employment and can at best be regarded as measures to control location in favor of the special areas.[141] Whatever increase of employment has taken place in these areas is largely attributable to the general revival of industry, and in particular to the increasing armaments expenditures which have been of special benefit to these districts characterized as they are by heavy industries.

The reasons for the failure of the Special Areas Commissioners to contribute more effectively both to the revival of industry as a whole and to its location in the special areas are not far to seek. The geographical scope of the program was in any case very limited. Only three districts in England and Wales and one in Scotland were scheduled as special areas,[142] and little use has been made of the Ministry of Labour's powers under the 1937 amending act to certify non-special areas for the purposes of financial assistance. Many districts, even among those long recognized administratively by the Ministry of Labour as depressed areas, were not included. Thus the contribution which the Commissioners could

---

[140] Ministry of Labour, *Report for the Year 1937*, p. 25. In fact, no direct pressure was applied except to foreigners. (Royal Commission on the Distribution of the Industrial Population, *Minutes of Evidence*, p. 270)

[141] By the end of 1937, 8 government factories and 5 agency factories had been or were to be erected in the special areas, while 4 others were under construction in adjacent areas. A number of factories required by the defense program were set up in areas of heavy unemployment other than the special areas. A preference for the special areas is also required to be given by the London Passenger Transport Agreement Act (1935) and the Railways (Agreement) Act, 1935. For an account of the operation of these measures, see *Ibid.*, pp. 266-73.

[142] The areas scheduled were (1) the County of Glamorgan (excluding Swansea, Neath, Bany and Cardiff), the mining areas of Monmouthshire (excluding Newport), the borough of Pembroke; (2) the Tyneside and the remainder of County Durham except for industrial Teisside; (3) West Cumberland and the rural district of Alston; (4) the middle industrial belt of Scotland, excluding Glasgow. The authors of *Readjustment in Lancashire* (Manchester University Press, 1936), a survey conducted by the Economics Research Section of the University of Manchester, make a strong case for including at least the coal, chemical, and weaving districts of Lancashire among the special areas. No areas in Yorkshire were scheduled, despite the depressed condition of cities such as Sheffield and Rotherham.

make was small. At most, they could influence location rather than the general expansion of industry.

Moreover, the areas as defined were often too limited to permit the Commissioners to undertake radical measures. Thus in South Wales, despite the economic unity of the region and the dependence of the north-south mining valleys on improved communications and export facilities, the boundaries of the scheduled special areas excluded Cardiff and other coastal cities. In Scotland the scheduled industrial area excluded the city of Glasgow, which was the natural center of the district.

These limitations are the more significant in that both South Wales and Cumberland, and to a lesser extent Durham also, are relatively remote. Development of the first two areas, which because of their mountainous character have great possibilities as amusement centers in addition to their industrial potentialities, calls for large-scale improvements in means of communication not only within the areas but even more importantly in those giving access to them. Such measures not only involve great capital expenditures and the cooperation of many authorities outside the special areas, but also face opposition from vested industrial and transportation interests. And these impediments have so far been more powerful than any desire to give effective assistance to the special areas.[143] Reference has already been made to the limitations on the powers of the Commissioners, especially prior to 1937. But their hands were also tied by the fact that in the main their powers to act were conditional upon the cooperation and approval of other government departments. Nor within the special areas could they override the powers of the numerous local authorities who still exhibited an unwillingness to forget local jealousies in the interest of the area as a whole.

Finally, the Commissioners faced a conflict between desirable short and long-run policies. Belief that the plight of the special

[143] The most outstanding case is the failure to pass a bill for the construction of a bridge over the Severn (which would have vastly improved the competitive position of South Wales and its accessibility to tourists) due to the opposition of the railways, certain coal mining interests and the apathy of a number of local authorities. (Cf. *Special Areas Report* [*England and Wales*], November 1936, pp. 53-55) For the influences which impeded similar improvements in communications in the other two areas, see *Ibid.*, pp. 55-59; and *Ibid.*, 1937, pp. 86-87.

areas was due to dependence on single industries, whose prospects of ultimate revival were at most limited, suggested a dual policy: liquidation in the form of transfer of labor to other areas, in which the Commissioners could assist only by contributions to workers willing to move and not by measures to stimulate industry in more promising locations outside the area; and the introduction of new industries which would make for greater diversification. But this policy, desirable in itself as a long-range measure, did little for the long-period unemployed. The new industries demanded young workers, and a large proportion of women,[144] whereas the unemployed were mainly older men accustomed to work at relatively high wages in the heavy industries. Thus, although there was some increase in net employment, there was relatively little decline in net unemployment.

CONCLUSION

It is difficult to resist the conclusion that, in contrast to the considerable degree of success with which the British have handled the problem of maintaining the unemployed, their approach to the more difficult social and psychological problems created by the fact of long-continued unemployment has been very limited and often half-hearted. As has been shown by the preceding account, public works have been insignificant and the more important measures of transference, training, land settlement, and the provision of occupational activity have affected but a relatively small portion of the unemployed. Moreover, to a very large extent the measures have been concentrated on the unemployed in the special areas, and where they have not been expressly so limited, preference has usually been given to these workers. Yet although the unemployed in these areas bulk large in the group among whom the demoralizing effects of continuous idleness are most evident, they comprise by no means all of the long-period unemployed.[145]

[144] In 1938 the English Commissioner reported that the new industries in the special areas employed a higher proportion of women than did industry on the average in Great Britain. (*Ibid.*, 1938, p. 32)

[145] Even in 1934, 15.3 per cent of the men unemployed 12 months or more were in the supposedly prosperous areas of London, the South East, the South West, and the Midlands. (Ministry of Labour, *Report for the Year 1934*, p. 6) The Pilgrim Trust investigators pointed out that "almost a third of the long-unemployed in this country over the age of 55 live in the prosperous areas of the South and Midlands." (*Men Without Work*, p. 213)

The number of long-unemployed persons cannot be stated with any definiteness because of the method of measuring duration of unemployment which results in an over-optimistic figure.[146] Even so these measures show that between 1935 and 1938 the number of unemployment assistance applicants, who comprise the majority of the long unemployed,[147] with a period of registered unemployment of 12 months or more fluctuated between 248,280 and 345,147.[148] A special inquiry undertaken by the Board in October 1938 into the extent of employment obtained by its applicants during the 3 preceding years revealed a more gloomy picture: 34 per cent had had no employment during the entire 3 years, 36 per cent had been without work for at least $2\frac{1}{2}$ years out of the three, another 15 per cent had worked between 6 months and a year, while 12 per cent had secured employment for one year but less than two.[149] Since, as already pointed out, the vast majority of applicants to the Board are persons who cannot show a relatively short recent period of employment, it is evident that by the end of 1938 the number of the long-period unemployed (meaning those who require something more positive than a mere cash payment) was closer to 500,000 than to the 248,000 shown by the method of count adopted by the Ministry.

Those concerned with the personal and social consequences of unemployment have increasingly urged that continuous unemployment creates a social situation of which the community must take account, and that a program which confines itself to the provision of maintenance fails to solve one of the most serious of contemporary problems.[150] The inadequacy of the existing measures to provide for the needs of two groups, namely, young workers

[146] The method of measuring unemployment as adopted by the Ministry of Labour disregarded employment which lasted not more than 3 days. But as little as 4 days of continuous work could remove a man from the group with the longest period of unemployment and place him among the short-term unemployed.

[147] See Chapter VII, pp. 178-79.

[148] UAB *Report*, 1937, p. 70; 1938, p. 65.

[149] *Ibid.*, 1938, pp. 65-66. These groups accounted for 499,630 out of 518,770 applicants.

[150] Cf. H. F. Hohman, *op. cit.*, pp. 269-86; R. C. Davison, *The Unemployed*, pp. 201-57, and *British Unemployment Policy since 1930* (London: Longmans, Green and Co., 1938); E. W. Bakke, *Insurance or Dole*, pp. 199-206; W. H. Beveridge, *Unemployment*, Chapter XVIII; Royal Commission on Unemployment Insurance, *Final Report*, Chapter IX.

under 30 and the older unemployed men,[151] among whom the demoralization of idleness is especially evident, has become increasingly clear from recent investigations. The analysis of unemployment among men under 30 (constituting approximately one-fifth of all male applicants in 1938) made by the advisory committees of the Unemployment Assistance Board has been a sharp challenge to complacency, for it showed not only that prolonged unemployment was serious among this apparently eligible group, but also that the evil consequences of enforced idleness were already evident. About 20 per cent had had no employment in the 3 years prior to 1938, 39 per cent had had less than 6 months of work, 18 per cent had worked between 6 and 12 months, 17 per cent between 1 and 2 years, and 6 per cent between 2 and 3 years.[152]

Furthermore, the interviews of the committees indicated that from 25 to 30 per cent of the young men were either content with their position or had resigned themselves to it.[153] The investigators of the Pilgrim Trust also drew attention to the number of young men who have, because of long-continued unemployment, lost all feelings of independence,[154] and in 1936 the English Commissioner for the Special Areas complained that "there is too large a number of young men in the Special Areas who are content to live in idleness as State pensioners and are unwilling to make any effort to find work . . . they are in fact demoralised by the seeming inevitableness of unemployment." [155] In 1938 the Commis-

[151] Except in the special areas, the problem among juveniles is less one of offsetting the consequences of continuous unemployment than of the improvement of the educational and placement institutions to avoid the creation of a large number of unemployed young adult workers who have been permitted to enter blind-alley occupations, or jobs paying low wages, and who on reaching maturity are laid off, with no marketable experience and a poor educational background. (See John Jewkes and Alan Winterbottom, *Juvenile Unemployment* [London: George Allen and Unwin, 1933]; John and Sylvia Jewkes, *op. cit.*) In the special areas, however, the English Commissioner reported that "probably the most serious human problem . . . is that presented by unemployment among young men between 18 and 21. . . . Many of these young persons have done practically no work; they have been brought up in a house where the father has been continuously out of work, and they have little or no conception that a man's ordinary occupation should be such as will provide the means of subsistence for himself and for his family." (*Special Areas Report* [*England and Wales*], February 1936, pp. 68-69)

[152] UAB *Report*, 1938, p. 45.

[153] *Ibid.*, pp. 48-49.

[154] *Men Without Work*, pp. 220-29.

[155] *Special Areas Report* (*England and Wales*), November 1936, p. 128. The percentages of young men unemployed 12 months or longer in the special

sioner reiterated his view that neither the measures available under the Special Areas Act, nor the training and transference facilities of the Ministry of Labour were wholly adequate to bring young men in the special areas within the range of useful occupation and opportunities of available employment.[156]

The extent of demoralization due to continued idleness among the younger men is further indicated by the response of this group to opportunities for training and reconditioning. The reports of the officers of the Unemployment Assistance Board concerning their experience in attempting to recruit volunteers for these courses painted a picture of a generation of young men who had become so resigned to continued idleness that they resented any attempts by officials to interfere with the way of life to which they had become accustomed.[157] The prospect of establishing new relationships and submission to the discipline of work, even though accompanied by a change of environment and more adequate food and clothing, made no appeal.

Equally serious in social terms, although perhaps calling for different remedies, is the problem presented by the long-period unemployed in the older age brackets who, it will be recalled, constitute a large proportion of the clientele of the Board.[158] Few of the measures discussed in this chapter touch this group. Retraining and transference are measures that for obvious reasons hold out little hope for them, and these programs have often been specifically limited to the younger men. Both subsistence production schemes and garden allotments seem to appeal to the middle-aged rather than to the older man.[159]

---

areas were, of course, especially high, ranging from 12 to 35 per cent of those aged 18-20, and from 38 to 57 per cent of those between 21 and 24 years of age. (p. 123)

[156] *Ibid.,* 1938, p. 9.

[157] See especially the reports of the local officers in UAB *Report,* 1936, pp. 85, 102, 109, 119. The regional officers referred almost unanimously in 1938 to the "unsatisfactory attitude" of the applicants toward training proposals and to the large numbers who refused training without any good reason. Cf. *Ibid.,* 1938, pp. 82, 97, 121, 147, 172.

[158] "In the Special Areas something between half and two-thirds of the older men have come to accept unemployment and might find it difficult to return to work if work were available, while in the prosperous areas the proportion is very much smaller, probably something under one-third." (*Men Without Work,* p. 214)

[159] *Ibid.,* pp. 215-16. Cf. also *Special Areas Report* (*Scotland*), 1938, p. 47.

Yet despite widespread recognition of the need for special measures for the older unemployed, no effective action has been taken. There was even a tendency on the part of persons interviewed by the author in 1937 to argue that, especially in the special areas, these men must be regarded as a "lost generation" for whom nothing could be done. There would seem to be much point to the suggestion of the Pilgrim Trust investigators that if a permanent or rotating public works program could not be provided for this group, it would be more logical to recognize them as permanent pensioners and to pay them a fixed allowance without the requirement of continuous submission to investigation and means tests.[160]

In part the failure of British programs to tackle the problem of social and personal demoralization caused by long-continued unemployment is attributable to the difficult nature of the problem itself. Attendance at occupational or reconditioning centers is obviously only a temporary alleviation unless it is followed by immediate reabsorption into employment. Expansion of technical training courses calls for a higher degree of planning and a more technical economic forecasting service than has yet been contemplated by the government. It would be unrealistic to disregard the criticism that would be directed at a government service which trained thousands of men for skilled jobs which, because of new inventions or market shifts or business depression, failed to materialize. It would, however, seem that certain long-time trends in demand for specific types of skilled workers might be forecast with a fair degree of accuracy, and that a government interested in avoiding the occurrence of bottle-necks might come to regard a public works program for ex-trainees as one device for maintaining the skills thus acquired and for making training more attractive.[161]

When idleness has persisted so long that demoralization is already evident, more difficult problems arise. For reliance can no longer be placed on the offer of inducements; the individual must

[160] Their studies indicated that men aged 50-64 could hold their jobs after reemployment just as well as men in the 35-49 age group and better than those in the 21-34 age group. The problem was not one of unemployability in other words, but of lack of opportunity to work. (*Men Without Work*, pp. 217-19)

[161] Some of the advisory committees which investigated the problem of the younger unemployed urged the desirability of making arrangements with local authorities to provide 3 months' employment for men who had completed training. (UAB *Report*, 1938, p. 51)

be compelled to participate in certain programs, since if left to himself he will take no action.[162] The British have been peculiarly reluctant to apply even the coercive measures provided for in existing legislation. Compulsion to attend training or occupational courses has not been resorted to in recent years. Fears of authoritarian controls have intensified the opposition of organized labor to any action by the government which savored of compulsion. The Unemployment Assistance Board has also been chary of applying its disciplinary powers, in part no doubt because of a timidity born of its unfortunate experience of popular disapproval at the time of the "standstill" crisis. Each report has made clear the Board's concern about the consequences of long-continued unemployment. Yet despite the fact that it is specifically given the duty of promoting the welfare of persons in need of work "and in particular, the making of provision for the improvement and reestablishment of the condition of such persons with a view to their being in all respects fit for entry into or return to regular employment," it has so far refrained from performing what in some respects is its major justification for existence as a separate administrative body. It has also little used its power to declare workers out of scope as a punitive measure, or to require attendance at work centers as a condition for receiving assistance.[163] Its action in 1938 in requesting the local advisory committees to study intensively the problems of workers under 30 years of age suggested an increased willingness to grapple with the situation, but the report made in that year indicated that in many respects the Board was unwilling to go as far as many of its committees recommended.[164]

[162] "There is a residue of men who have settled down to life on allowances, and are in need of the discipline of work and a normal and ordered life if they are to be shaken out of their apathy." (*Ibid.*, p. 27)

[163] During the first years of the Board's existence no use was made of the power to require attendance at a work center. Even by 1938 the number of cases was small (75) owing to the lack of facilities, while in only another 164 cases was receipt of allowance made conditional on entry into a work house. (*Ibid.*, pp. 22-23, 48)

[164] The committees stressed the need for more discipline and control, urged that payment should be made conditional on acceptance of training, that more use be made of the Board's power to make arrangements with local authorities for employment of its clients for a 3-month period, and finally, several committees recommended the Board to urge a program of public works. The Board did not endorse this suggestion but instead asked that its clients be given preference in employment on government contracts. (*Ibid.*, pp. 49-52)

But while technical and political difficulties of this kind may have prevented more thorough exploitation of the possibilities of training and a fuller use of coercive controls, they do not account for the unwillingness to develop a more adequate work relief or public works program. To assert that there has been a tendency to evaluate the desirability of these programs in terms of financial and economic considerations, to the disregard of human and social values, is merely to restate the problem. Undoubtedly consideration of cost has loomed larger in Great Britain than in some other countries, because the type of work program envisaged has been a public works program rather than a work relief program. The strong popular aversion to the work test and its association with poor law practices would have precluded the adoption of the compromises of a cheaper work relief program with its absence of standard conditions of wage rates and hours of employment. Thus, the alternative was a costly public works program or none at all. Nor can political factors be disregarded. The Conservative Party, the most powerful political group throughout the greater part of the period from 1935 to 1938, was unlikely to favor measures which might have involved increased taxes and some encroachment of governmental activity into the traditional spheres of private enterprise. But even the Labour Party, although adopting the slogan "work or maintenance," has shown a disposition to concentrate upon the latter objective, and has failed to dramatize the potentialities of an adequate work program.

CHAPTER X

UNEMPLOYMENT RELIEF AND POLITICS

THE RISK THAT UNEMPLOYMENT RELIEF policy will become an issue in national politics has undoubtedly been enhanced by the increasing categorization and centralization of unemployment relief that have characterized British policy since 1934. This danger has indeed been frequently commented upon in Great Britain. In 1929 and 1930 when the transfer of the public assistance functions of the boards of guardians to the counties and county boroughs was under discussion, many of the more thoughtful spokesmen for these larger authorities disliked the change because they feared it would make public assistance an issue in local elections. The Royal Commission of 1932 was sharply critical of the situation during the 1920's: "Each successive Government has made changes in the [unemployment insurance] scheme, which have been determined less by the need for the careful balancing of income and expenditure than by a desire to attract, or do as little as possible to repel, electoral support." [1] And representatives of both employer and worker organizations, as well as experts appearing before the Commission, urged the necessity of safeguarding unemployment insurance from the effect of political interference.

At the time of the creation of the Unemployment Assistance Board, considerable attention was paid to the possibility of keeping questions of unemployment relief out of politics and two devices were adopted with this objective in view.[2] In the first place the Board, which was responsible for administration and policy, was set up as a semi-autonomous body appointed by the Crown, and although loosely linked to the Ministry of Labour, it was in large

---

[1] *Final Report*, p. 164.
[2] See *Parliamentary Debates* in November 1933. The government claimed that the object of the creation of the Board was to free the Minister "from responsibility for individual decisions while maintaining the right of Parliament to approve the general policy to be followed and the general standards of assistance," and in the debates government supporters defended the proposals as an attempt to place unemployment assistance outside political influence. (Cf. Millett, *op. cit.*, pp. 34-45)

measure independent of it. Its requests for funds [3] were indeed transmitted to Parliament by the Minister and the maximum amount of its administrative expenses were determined by him with Treasury consent. Moreover, its rules were subject to confirmation by the Minister, and its draft regulations governing the determination of needs and the assessment of resources were to be submitted to him. But in presenting the regulations to Parliament for approval, the Minister could make variations and amendments only if he informed the Board of his intention, and received from it a report which was to be laid before Parliament together with a statement of his reasons for the variations or amendments. Yet, at least in theory, the Board was independent of the Minister, who on various occasions referred to it as "this independent body" and denied responsibility for its action when questioned in Parliament. The Minister of Labour was thus in the strange position of acting as a spokesman for the Board before Parliament, but was apparently not responsible for its specific actions.[4]

In the second place, while the regulations of the Board had to be laid before Parliament for approval, the legislature could only approve or disapprove of them as a whole. No parts could be amended,[5] a limitation on the powers of Parliament which was described by one member as an "offense against constitutional practice." [6]

This attempt to set up the Board as a body theoretically independent of the Ministry of Labour and to a large extent outside parliamentary control was not a happy one. The relationship of the Board to the Ministry, particularly in regard to the initiation of changes in policy, the extent to which its proposals were immediately to be brought before Parliament, and the nature of the line differentiating broad matters of policy from purely admin-

[3] The amount of the funds payable into the Unemployment Assistance Fund was to be such "as the Minister after consultation with the Board may, with the consent of the Treasury, determine to be necessary." (Section 47(b) of the *Unemployment Act* of 1934)

[4] The Board had to make an annual report to the Minister, who was to present it to Parliament. But it was apparently intended that Parliament should not discuss specific items of the Board's policy or the treatment of individual cases except when appropriations or the annual reports were under consideration.

[5] This rule was so rigidly interpreted that on one occasion the Speaker ruled that the house could not even change a comma. (*Parliamentary Debates,* December 17, 1934, p. 923)

[6] *Ibid.,* November 27, 1934, col. 725.

istrative actions, were all highly ambiguous. The attempt to limit the freedom of Parliament to criticize and control the actions of the Board represented a departure from accepted constitutional theories and parliamentary practice. Events were indeed to prove that the attempt to create an independent or semi-independent status for the Board could not insulate it against political pressure if its actions offended a sufficiently large number of people in constituencies of different political complexions. Three weeks after its first regulations went into effect, its supplementary appropriations were under discussion and called forth a bitter attack on its policy which resulted in the passage of the "Standstill" Act.[7] It became evident that Parliament could not and did not desire to evade control of social policies affecting a large and vocal section of the population and that it would not allow the government of the day to disown responsibility for the Board's policies. The only consequence of the alleged independence of the Board and the ambiguity of its relationship to the Minister of Labour was to deprive it of a ministerial spokesman in Parliament and before the public who would energetically defend its actions because he carried a clear responsibility for them.[8]

It is indeed highly doubtful whether any single measure for dealing with loss of income due to unemployment can be removed from the political arena, unless it affects only an insignificant proportion of the unemployed. Proponents of social insurance have frequently urged, as an advantage of this method of providing security, that it permits an orderly and rational determination of the benefits payable and of the conditions of eligibility, which can be embodied in a permanent scheme and thus removed from immediate political controversy. This hope was certainly not realized by the British unemployment insurance system. During the 1920's, as described in Chapter III, the scheme was at all times susceptible to political influence. The expansion and contraction of the system,

---

[7] The circumstances surrounding the creation of the Board and the gradual abandonment of the fiction of independence have been analyzed by J. D. Millett in his book, *The Unemployment Assistance Board*.

[8] Cf. W. Ivor Jennings, *Cabinet Government* (New York: Macmillan, 1936), p. 82: "The chief result of 'taking unemployment assistance out of politics' is that the Board has no means of defending itself against attacks." Mr. Millett (*op. cit.*, p. 272) suggests that the simulation of independence made the Board even more cautious than a responsible minister need have been, for they were distrustful of their own resources for defense.

and the changes in levels of benefits and conditions of eligibility very largely reflected the political complexion of Parliament. The British experience in the post-war years also indicates that prevailing views as to the proper type of provision for those at any time excluded from insurance react upon the insurance system itself. For, in the absence of any second line of defense which commanded the support of politically effective groups, there was a tendency to expand the insurance system to provide also for these excluded persons.

The Unemployment Act of 1934 adopted a new device to which much publicity has been given and which, it was hoped, would in large measure succeed in removing from immediate political pressures questions affecting the insurance system. Following the recommendation of the Royal Commission, the Unemployment Insurance Statutory Committee, a non-political body, was set up to give advice and assistance to the Minister of Labour and to perform certain specified duties. These duties involved very considerable powers to suggest modifications of, and changes in, the insurance system. It could exercise these powers in four ways.

In the first place, as already indicated, when the Committee considered that the Unemployment Fund was likely to continue to be insufficient or more than reasonably sufficient to discharge its liabilities, it had the duty of making recommendations involving changes in contributions (other than the government contribution) or in benefit rights of all or of special classes of insured contributors. After 1936 it was given the same duties and powers with regard to the agricultural account. Public notice was to be given of its intention to make these recommendations, and any representations made were to be taken into account. Within two months after the receipt of the Committee's report the Minister of Labour was to lay it before Parliament, and, if amendments were proposed, it was his duty after consultation with the Treasury to embody them in a draft order, which upon approval by both houses would become effective. If, however, the Minister disagreed with the Committee, he was empowered to suggest other amendments which would have been within the Committee's powers to suggest,[9] but

---

[9] A list of the many provisions of the Act to which amendments could be recommended by the Committee is given in Part II of the Third Schedule to the Unemployment Act of 1934.

which would have the same effect on the finances of the insurance scheme. In this case, however, the Minister was to lay before Parliament a statement of his reasons for failing to embody the Committee's recommendations in his draft order.

In the second place, before making any regulations (except those relating to instruction and training) or any orders under the anomalies regulations, the Minister was required to submit a draft to the Committee.[10] In considering the regulations, the Committee was to give public notice of its intention and to take account of objections and proposed changes made in writing by persons affected or their representatives. On receipt of the Committee's report, it was the duty of the Minister to draft an order to be laid before Parliament for approval, either with or without any amendments suggested by the Committee. But if he failed to give effect to any of the Committee's recommendations, he had also to submit a statement giving his reasons.

In the third place, the Minister was empowered to refer to the Committee for consideration and advice any questions relating to the operation of, or the advisability of amending, the unemployment insurance acts. Finally, the Act of 1934 laid upon the Committee the specific duty of making proposals for extending unemployment insurance to agricultural workers, after hearing the views of workers, employers, and any government departments affected.[11]

At first sight it would appear as if the hopes of those who believed that the creation of the Statutory Committee would remove unemployment insurance questions from the political arena had been fully realized. The Committee has handled a number of important problems of policy affecting all aspects of the insurance system. It has made recommendations concerning the extension of insurance to agricultural workers. Between 1935 and 1938 it examined and reported on 29 sets of draft regulations, which

[10] For the purposes of this section, the word "regulations" is used broadly and includes all orders and special orders (other than those relating to special and supplementary schemes and to anomalies provisions) made by the Minister. In urgent cases the Minister could issue provisional regulations, which, however, could not continue in force for more than 3 months after receipt of the Committee's report.

[11] A similar special charge was laid upon the Committee by the Unemployment Insurance (Agriculture) Act of 1936, clause 14 of which directed the Minister to refer to the Committee the question of the desirability and practicability of including employment as a private gardener among insurable employments.

21

involved questions such as the extension or contraction of the list of insurable employments,[12] refunds of contributions for agricultural workers hired on long-period contracts, and a number of minor administrative matters.[13] It has similarly considered and reported on draft anomaly orders affecting seasonal workers. The Minister has freely exercised his power to refer questions of policy to the Committee for advice; among the more important matters were the advisability of raising the salary limit for non-manual workers, the general treatment of the so-called "inconsiderable" employments, the insurable position of share fishermen and private gardeners, chauffeurs, and government dockyard workers retired on pension, and the payment of benefits and contributions for holidays and suspensions.

In the exercise of its duty to propose changes in contributions or benefits whenever the Unemployment Fund appeared likely to be insufficient or more than reasonably sufficient to meet its liabilities, the Committee has made recommendations for changes in contributions, in benefit rates for adult dependents and for children, for a reduction in the waiting period, and for the grant of additional days of benefit.

Finally, in the course of its reports, the Committee has drawn attention to certain problems of interest to the insurance scheme which appeared to call for parliamentary action or further investigation.

Organizations and representatives of individuals and groups affected by all proposed changes have fully exercised their right to appear before the Committee to make suggestions or to raise objections, and the legal obligation of the Committee to take these into consideration has compelled it to make public its reasons for failure to adopt any of the suggestions. In consequence, the Committee's reports have provided a very full analysis of both the

[12] The more important of these regulations have concerned the insurable position of persons working a very few hours per week, those employed in the mercantile marine or by local government authorities, pit-head bath attendants, persons working for both covered and uncovered employers, those engaged partly in agriculture and partly in industry, persons employed in domestic service for non-profit-making organizations, and outdoor domestic servants in private employment.

[13] E.g., modifications in methods of collecting contributions, benefit payment procedures, membership of courts of referees, procedures to be adopted when submitting questions of insurability to the Minister, certification of inspectors, and the treatment of days of sickness during the waiting period.

nature of the unemployment risk and of the social, economic, administrative, and financial considerations involved in evaluating various possible changes.[14] Their reports on the financial condition of the Unemployment Fund, to which great authority is attached, have been given wide publicity and have undoubtedly contributed much to an understanding of the issues involved, and have carried considerable weight with Parliament. The modifications in draft regulations proposed by the Committee have usually been embodied by the Minister in the final orders submitted to Parliament for approval, and on at least one occasion a draft regulation was withdrawn on the Committee's advice. Amendments proposed by it in regard to matters submitted by the Minister have in general been embodied in legislative proposals in substantially the form suggested, the only important exception being the failure to implement immediately the Committee's proposal to raise, for the purpose of coverage, the salary limit for non-manual workers from £250 to £400 a year. Their recommendations for changes in benefits or contributions arising out of their annual survey of the finances of the scheme have, with one minor exception, been accepted by Parliament.[15]

As a result of suggestions made by the Committee, the National Debt Commissioners in 1935 modified the policy previously governing the investment of the Unemployment Fund.[16] In 1938 an amending act enlarged the Committee's powers to repay part of the funded debt, and modified the previous provisions governing the annual fixed debt charge on the Fund, thus correcting a situation to which the Committee had drawn attention in its earlier reports. Again, various statistical inquiries were undertaken by the Ministry of Labour regarding problems to which public attention had been called by the Committee.[17]

---

[14] See especially the *Reports on the Financial Condition of the Unemployment Fund,* 1935 and 1937; the *Report on Remuneration Limit for Insurance of Non-Manual Workers,* 1936; the *Report on Draft Unemployment Insurance (Inconsiderable Employments) (Persons under Sixteen) Regulations,* 1935.

[15] In October 1935, Parliament adopted the Committee's recommendation that benefits for dependent children should be increased by 1s., but rejected the accompanying proposal, to which the Committee had attached some importance, that the maximum benefit payable in any case should be 41s.

[16] For details of the change, see UISC *Financial Report,* December 1935, pp. 3-4.

[17] The most important of these was a study of the relationship between benefit rates and normal wages. The results were published by the Committee as Appendix C in its financial report for 1937.

Finally, as will be clear from the discussion of the finances of the insurance system (in Chapter VI), it was in fact the Committee which made the important decision as to whether the insurance scheme should be financed on a pay-as-you-go or on a reserve basis.[18]

Yet, outstanding as have been the achievements of the Committee, its importance as a device for permanently safeguarding the insurance scheme against political pressures must not be exaggerated. Though its advice has generally been followed, its recommendations on some important issues have been rejected or ignored by Parliament. Thus, in addition to ignoring the proposals to raise the salary limit for non-manual workers and to impose at 41s. "wage-stop" to benefits, Parliament rejected the contribution and benefit schedules proposed for the agricultural insurance scheme because, and significantly, it was felt desirable to provide higher benefits than those proposed by the Committee.[19]

There are indeed other facts which suggest that the main reasons for the Committee's undoubted success and prestige since 1934 may be personal and environmental, and therefore not necessarily permanent. Before analyzing these influences, however, it is desirable to dispose of one explanation occasionally advanced to account for the success of the Committee, namely, that its task has been an easy one since its guiding principle as laid down in the law has been the maintenance of solvency. At most this explanation could account for its success in carrying out its duties as a custodian of the funds. But even here, a study of the reports of the Committee indicates that the maintenance of solvency in itself was not a narrow financial question but one that raised far-reaching social and economic issues. It is true that at an early date the Committee declared its intention to confine itself so far as possible to purely financial matters.[20] Yet even the financial powers of the

18 It is important to note that the Committee's findings as to the existence or non-existence of a surplus, and as to the financial significance of their recommendations, are binding on the Minister of Labour and every other authority except Parliament. (*Ibid.*, July 1935, p. 13)

19 For a comparison of the Committee's proposals and the rates finally adopted, see *Ibid.*, 1937, p. 42. As has already been stated, the Committee's recommendation to raise the annual salary limit for non-manual workers was adopted in 1940, but the limit was set at £420 rather than £400.

20 "Still less do we mean that, in making our financial report under Section 59, we are precluded from considering the merits of various proposals for improving the working of the Insurance Scheme. In making recommendations

Committee to use part of any surplus for repayment of the funded
debt involved much more than a mere financial transaction, requiring as it did a balancing of the claims of present as against future
generations of contributors.[21] And as soon as the Committee came
to discuss the disposal of a declared surplus, it was obvious that
no guidance was provided by the criterion of maintenance of
solvency. The choice between alternative proposals involved fundamental issues of social policy, such as the determination of "what
proportion of the total unemployment, and what types of unemployment, should be covered by insurance benefit, and what should
be dealt with in other ways," or the choice between financing
unemployment relief by social insurance taxes or by general tax
revenues.[22] Similarly, proposals to raise benefit rates involved
judgments as to the proper relationships between wages and benefits, and the long-run soundness of a relief system which made
direct provision for families in a society operating under a wage
system which made no such provision. Hence, the injunction to
maintain solvency offered little or no guidance to the Committee
in making some of its most controversial recommendations. Indeed on one occasion the Committee refrained from proposing
a change in benefit rates on the ground that the decision should be
made "only after full consideration by Parliament, as an act of

---

either for the allocation of a surplus or for the meeting of a deficiency, we are
bound to discuss questions of principle affecting the working of the scheme.
But our first approach must be financial: that of considering the best use to
make of any given sum of money and not that of passing annually in review
the working of the insurance scheme in all its details." (*Ibid.,* July 1935, p. 15)

[21] Until the amending Act of 1938, such repayment could not be reflected in
any reduction of the fixed annual payment of £5 millions which the Fund was
compelled to make toward the debt. Hence a decision to devote the surplus to
repayment meant only that the debt would be paid off earlier than 1971. Thus
"the only effect would be to relieve the three contributory parties of a charge
of £5 millions in each year from 1964 to 1971, when a large proportion of the
present generation of insured persons will no longer be in industry. This use
of the surplus would not only make it impossible for a large proportion of
the present contributors to get the advantage of the surplus in better benefits.
It would expose them to risk of losing some of the benefits which they now
enjoy. If, through an unfavorable turn of events, we found later that the Unemployment Fund was deficient, and that contributions must be raised or
benefits must be lowered in order to correct the deficiency, we should be compelled to deprive those whose contributions had gone to build up the surplus
of something that they now enjoy. The surplus would have been paid away
irretrievably. . . . We find it hard to believe that we should be doing justice
to the present contributors to the Fund, already burdened with liability for the
past debt, by hastening by a few years the final extinction of the debt." (*Ibid.,*
1936, pp. 15-16) See, however, the 1940 report which proposes extinction by
1941.

[22] *Ibid.,* December 1935, p. 16

deliberate social policy, and not simply because a decline of unemployment has produced a surplus in the Unemployment Fund." [23] Throughout the Committee's reports there is explicit recognition that their recommendations involved matters of social policy rather than purely financial considerations.[24] Thus, the explanation of the success and prestige of the Committee must be sought elsewhere than in the fact that its task was the formal and easy one of maintaining solvency.

The Committee has undoubtedly been fortunate in its personnel, and especially in its chairman, Sir William Beveridge, who appears to have been the guiding influence. His reputation in the field of unemployment insurance has lent great weight to the Committee's recommendations.

In the second place, the task of the Committee has been greatly facilitated by the fortunate fact that in its first years it was considering the problem of disposal of a surplus rather than methods of meeting a deficit. It is difficult not to believe that, had the economic situation been one that involved curtailment of benefits or increases in contribution rates, their recommendations on these controversial issues would have aroused bitter differences of opinion, which would only have been resolved in the political arena.[25]

Even more important is the fact that the Committee, although selected on a non-political basis, has adopted a consistent philosophy regarding the functions of unemployment insurance and one which accords with the prevailing political sentiment. That philosophy involves the views that unemployment insurance, by

[23] *Ibid.*, p. 21. In 1938 it refrained from using any part of the agricultural account's surplus for providing benefits for juveniles under 16, on the ground that their treatment under the law "was a deliberate decision of policy by Parliament; this should not be changed without a full consideration of the educational and other issues involved." (*Ibid.*, 1938, p. 16)

[24] In recommending a maximum weekly benefit amount of 41s., the Committee drew attention to the fact that the limit should not be regarded as affecting directly the financial condition of the Fund. (*Ibid.*, July 1935, p. 19) See also the December 1935 Report, pp. 16-17, 27.

[25] The reports of the Committee show a clear recognition of this situation. Thus, the Committee referred to "the extreme difficulty of lowering benefits again, once they had been raised" as a reason for rejecting proposals to use the 1935 surplus to raise benefits (*Ibid.*, Dec. 1935, p. 20) ; and on various occasions indicated a preference for "flexible" liberalizations, meaning thereby those whose subsequent withdrawal, should financial circumstances so dictate, would give rise to least opposition.

relieving workers of the necessity of submitting to a means test, is definitely a desirable and preferential form of relief which should be made available to as wide a group as is consistent with economic and financial limitations,[26] and that frequent and short-run changes in either benefits or contributions are undesirable for employers and workers alike.

Undoubtedly also the existence of the unemployment assistance system has from one point of view served to facilitate the operations of the Statutory Committee. There can be little doubt that decisions by the Statutory Committee to exclude certain types of persons from insurance or, more generally, to maintain the solvency of the insurance system, have been facilitated because of the fact that there now exists an alternative to insurance that is politically more acceptable than the old pre-1920 poor law. Pressure to extend the insurance system, regardless of the financial and economic consequences, is much less than it was in the 1920's.

On the other hand, the existence of an important secondary unemployment relief system, which is undoubtedly sensitive to the prevailing currents of opinion, constitutes a potential danger to the insurance system and adds to the difficulties of the Statutory Committee. For any serious liberalization of assistance places an indirect pressure on the Committee to increase the benefits of the supposedly preferred insurance system in order to maintain its prestige.[27]

Thus despite the safeguards introduced by the Act of 1934, it seems probable that the combination of categorical treatment of the unemployed and a highly centralized administration which

[26] See, for example, the discussion on pp. 14-18 of the December 1935 report of the Committee; on pp. 19-20 of the 1937 report; and especially the Committee's attitude to the low proportion of agricultural workers ranking for insurance benefits, p. 12 of the 1938 report.

[27] The Committee was well aware of this difficulty, and in its 1939 report (p. 12), in discussing the desirability of adjusting benefit rates to changes in the cost of living, the Committee emphasized the desirability "of securing that the problems of wages, unemployment benefits and unemployment assistance are dealt with on similar or at least on related principles. . . . Once it has become clear that the Unemployment Fund has a surplus for distribution these considerations [of changes in the cost of living and rates of unemployment assistance] are not irrelevant to the decision of what is the best use of such a surplus." See also *ibid.*, Dec. 1935, pp. 22-23, 28. Cf. the Royal Commission: "Psychologically it would be difficult to maintain for long an insurance scheme unless its benefits were actually greater than the amounts normally payable on a relief basis." (*Final Report*, p. 149)

now characterizes the British unemployment relief system, has increased the likelihood that unemployment relief will "enter into politics," and that the unemployed may become a politically effective group. The unemployment assistance scheme will in its general policies undoubtedly continue to reflect the views of the predominant political groups as to the treatment that is appropriate for unemployed people. And although the Statutory Committee may in some measure protect the insurance scheme from politically dictated changes, its chances of continuing to do so will be considerably affected by the prevailing economic situation and by the policies of the politically susceptible Assistance Board.

This ultimate sensitivity to political control was indeed openly welcomed by organized labor at the time of the passage of the 1934 Act.[28] But also those who believe in economic as well as political democracy may properly question the desirability, and not merely the feasibility, of attempts to remove from politics questions which in recent years have involved very substantial expenditures and have vitally concerned the lives of between 1.3 and 2.3 million workers and their families.[29]

In any case there are two kinds of political influence in the sphere of unemployment relief. It may be exercised in regard to the nature of the policies to be applied to broad groups of persons, or in regard to the treatment of given individuals. The alternative of locally administered general public assistance was not immune from political influences in the second sense. It is at least questionable whether a system in which the treatment afforded individuals is influenced by their personal political affiliations is not as socially harmful as one in which the general principles governing the treatment of all the unemployed are determined by the views of the majority party. The choice, in other words, may be between two imperfect alternatives.

Perhaps all that can be hoped for is a system in which political influence and affiliations do not affect the treatment received by

---

[28] Cf. the statement of the Trades Union Congress in a leaflet attacking the means test: "But if we cannot at present abolish the means test, it is an advantage that the rules governing it are centralized, because in that way its operation can be watched better throughout the country and measures can be taken to expose what is going on." (J. L. Smythe, *Unemployment Assistance Means Test Regulations,* February 1935)

[29] Cf. also Millett, *op. cit.,* Chapter VII and p. 251.

individual claimants, but in which there is a frank recognition of the political character of decisions regarding the general principles governing the treatment of unemployed persons as a group. From this point of view the British unemployment relief system since 1934 must be judged to have achieved a large measure of success. The vast majority of the unemployed are now provided for by two systems in which, thanks to the integrity and non-political character of the civil service, politics play no part in the treatment accorded different individuals. And the general principles are in the last resort determined by Parliament. The only ultimate safeguard against irresponsible action by that body is, of course, the influence of an informed public opinion; and the Unemployment Insurance Statutory Committee, and to a lesser extent the Assistance Board in its annual reports, are contributing to a wider understanding of the implications of available alternatives.

PART V

BRITISH UNEMPLOYMENT PROGRAMS AND POLICIES

CHAPTER XI

REVIEW OF BRITISH EXPERIENCE

NONE OF THE THREE MAJOR METHODS by which Great Britain has attempted to provide for unemployed workers not benefiting from a strictly limited insurance system has proved completely successful. It would indeed be optimistic and naive to assume that there is any completely satisfactory solution of the hydra-headed problem of unemployment relief. Nevertheless, the most recent British experiment, unemployment assistance, represents undeniable progress when the problem of providing for the unemployed is regarded as a whole.

Certainly the experiment of expanding the insurance system was unsatisfactory in many ways. Even as a device for relieving the finances of hard-pressed local relief authorities, it was far from ideal. It tended to give the least assistance in relation to their needs to those areas where unemployment was heaviest and most continuous, for in these areas the proportion of workers who could satisfy even the modest contributory requirements of the expanded insurance system continuously decreased. And the contributory requirement could not be altogether abandoned so long as the system was still dignified by the name of insurance. Furthermore, the desire to preserve what are usually conceived to be the peculiar values of a necessarily limited insurance system made it essential to rationalize each liberalization as an emergency measure, and to attempt the increasingly difficult task of differentiating between those persons who were entitled to "normal" benefits and those who were admitted to them as a consequence of the emergency.

This situation reacted adversely on the finances of the local relief authorities in two ways. On the one hand, the persistent adherence to the assumption that the situation was abnormal discouraged any long-range planning and led to last-minute decisions to expand the conveniently available insurance system for strictly limited periods of time—which, however, always proved to be too short.

311

312   UNEMPLOYMENT PROGRAMS AND POLICIES

This uncertainty as to future policy inhibited the building up of adequate staffs or the development of constructive programs on the part of local relief authorities, as they could always gamble on the prospect of yet further expansions of the insurance system. And, on the other hand, the imposition of gaps interrupting the continuous receipt of insurance benefits, and additional conditions to be satisfied by the beneficiaries of the expanded insurance system, left the local authorities with a significant relief burden. This burden was the more onerous and difficult to plan for because it was often temporary and always unpredictable, determined as it was by the decisions—which necessarily involved the exercise of judgment and discretion—made by central administrative authorities over whom they had no control.

Expanded insurance was also destructive of the integrity and prestige of the insurance system when regarded as an isolated institution. The fact that the use of the insurance system as the major residual relief measure involved an increase in insurance benefits was not necessarily a disadvantage inasmuch as this increase could have been, and indeed to some extent was, offset by increases in contributions. Much more serious, because more costly, was the continual extension of the duration of benefits and the relaxing of the eligibility requirements, the cost of which was charged to the insurance fund until 1930 and led to the accumulation of a heavy debt. The expansion of insurance benefits to ever more marginal groups cut the ground from under every theory which might have justified the prevailing scope of the system. And if the line between those who drew the insurance type of benefit and those who were maintained on the residual relief system could not be defended on "strict insurance" principles, it was equally inexplicable in terms of the industrial qualifications and character of the different groups or of the peculiar appropriateness of the type of treatment afforded each group in relation to its needs.

Nor could this absence of logical categorization of the unemployed, inherent in the combined plan of expanded insurance plus a residual poor relief system, claim the advantages of administrative simplicity. For, as already explained, the discretional element in determining claims to expanded insurance benefits, inherent in the application of qualifying criteria which could no longer be written in specific numerical terms, involved individual consideration of literally millions of claims to eligibility.

The succeeding three-fold system (insurance, transitional payments, and public assistance) may be held to represent some improvement over the earlier arrangements. The restoration of limited benefit duration not only removed a heavy financial obligation from the insurance system and permitted it again to attain technical solvency, but also was a first step toward a more logical grouping of the unemployed. Admittedly the guarantee to the unemployed of specified payments unaccompanied by the necessity of submitting to a means test, undertaking training or unaccustomed employment or performing test work, involved an economic and social risk to the community in the form of direct financial cost, postponed economic and occupational readjustment, and possible demoralization of workers. But the 26-week normal maximum benefit duration set a limit to the extent of the risk that is incurred.

Yet, although the line between those entitled to "unconditional" benefits and those excluded was now more rationally defensible, the three-fold system which operated between 1931 and 1935 created new and equally indefensible distinctions within the group excluded from insurance. Those who were granted transitional payments and those who were left to the poor law did not constitute two separate groups essentially different in their industrial experience or quality or in the duration of their unemployment. Nor, from the point of view of the nature of the assistance provided, was there a sufficient difference between public assistance and transitional payments to justify the continuance of the dual residual relief system. Indeed, as has been shown, there was a steady tendency for the treatment of the able-bodied public assistance clients to be influenced by and approximate to that afforded under the transitional payments system. Both systems were equally unsatisfactory from the worker's point of view in that both involved the application of a means test and contact with public assistance authorities. Indeed, since the maximum transitional payment could not exceed prevailing insurance benefits, workers with large family responsibilities and no other resources were compelled to seek supplementary public assistance. And, with the exception of a small number of local authorities, neither residual system provided the reconditioning, training, or work opportunity needed by their clientele which consisted almost by definition of the long-period unemployed.

As a method of relieving the financial burdens of local assistance authorities, the transitional payments system exhibited the same weaknesses as expanded insurance. The longer the depression continued, the greater became the proportion of the unemployed who failed to satisfy the nominal contributory requirements for transitional payments, and the larger the number maintained by the local authorities, an increase which was greatest in the most depressed and therefore financially weakest areas.

Even as a device for relieving the central government of the necessity of exercising control over administrative policy while continuing to provide 100 per cent of the funds, the transitional payments system failed to achieve its objective. For it demonstrated that local freedom to interpret need and define assessable resources was incompatible with the protection of the financial interests of the central government, in view of the existence of a number of local authorities whose belief in the desirability of applying a means test to the unemployed was at best half-hearted. Furthermore, the experience with transitional payments revealed the untenability of widely different treatment of applicants in a system wholly financed by central government funds.

In comparison with these two earlier experiments during 1920-31 and 1931-35, the present insurance and assistance system represents real progress. Considering first the nature of the provision made for the unemployed, it is evident that the unemployment assistance scheme goes far toward eliminating the preceding dual and unjustifiable residual relief system, although it still fails to do so completely. For, owing to the limitation of scope of the assistance scheme to that of the old-age insurance system, a relatively small number of potential wage earners are still denied unemployment assistance and must rely on public assistance.

With this exception, however, all the unemployed are provided for under either insurance or assistance and it now becomes possible, especially since the central government is the single fiscal and administrative authority for both groups, to adjust the nature of the aid available so that it is appropriate to the needs of each group.

Insurance benefits are now, with two exceptions, payable only to those who have been unemployed a relatively short period of time and who can show a significant period of past employment. The exceptions arise from the facts that insurance still fails to cover all persons who are in wage earning employment and thus benefits are denied to some short-period unemployed, and that the payment of additional days of insurance benefits to persons with a long, past record of continuous employment leads to the inclusion among insurance beneficiaries of persons for whom, because of the length of their unemployment, insurance benefits would seem to be an inappropriate type of assistance.[1]

So far, the major division between the two groups is logically defensible, although it is still an open question whether the period of 26 weeks is the proper point at which payment of unconditional benefits ceases to be an appropriate form of assistance and a negligible risk to the community. It is also clear that much still needs to be done to improve the other-than-maintenance services, such as training or work, provided for the long-term unemployed. And it is also questionable whether the continued attempt to make insurance "preferable" to assistance by providing higher cash benefits is justifiable. For it becomes increasingly evident that, to both the worker and society at large, the essential difference between insurance and other types of aid to the unemployed lies not in the amount of the benefits but in the conditions under which they are available. The right to draw a specified sum that at least approximates the maintenance minimum, without the necessity of undergoing a means test or accepting unfamiliar jobs or submitting to other coercive controls, is the vital element in insurance to which the worker attaches value.[2] And these characteristics of insurance are of vital interest to the community at large, for herein lies the financial and economic risk of the institution. The problem is how to assure that this form of aid is available to all and only those types of workers for whom it is appropriate. The retention of the belief that insurance benefits must also be higher in amount than assistance, and that insurance

---

[1] Except in so far as it could be argued that the fact of continuous employment in the past made them less liable to be demoralized by drawing "unconditional" benefits for a lengthy period.

[2] Cf. Bakke, *Insurance or Dole*, pp. 188-96, 229-30.

benefits should be paid for a lengthy period to those who have been steadily employed in the past, can be explained only in terms of a failure to recognize that, with the vast improvement that has taken place in the treatment of the residual unemployed, the necessity for a separate, independently financed insurance system may have disappeared.

To avoid misunderstanding, it should be emphasized that this conclusion does not mean that the "insurance" type of benefit should be abandoned. On the contrary, British experience has shown that the worker attaches tremendous value to the right to draw a specified benefit (which he designates by the word insurance) for at least the first few months of his unemployment. British experience also indicates that, provided certain safeguards are adopted, this right can be conceded without undue financial cost or economic risk to the community at large. The question now at issue is whether the desirability of granting this right to the unemployed is not so firmly established and generally recognized in Great Britain as to make it unnecessary to identify it with an independent and separately financed unemployment insurance system.

From many points of view, unemployment insurance in Great Britain has already served its historical function. It was the ideal instrument for effecting a significant break in the deterrent treatment of insecure workers, because its apparent analogy with private insurance made the change acceptable to a society which was dominated by business ethics and which stressed individual economic responsibility. This reversal of policy was the more acceptable in that originally the numbers benefiting from the change were relatively few and so selected that it could plausibly be argued that they were unlikely to be corrupted by more generous treatment. The close connection between benefits paid and contributions collected appeared also to be a guarantee against uneconomically high payments. But within less than 30 years it has become obvious that such a limited system could not continue to exist side by side with other institutions without influencing them and being influenced in turn. In fact, unemployment insurance has served as the entering wedge for a radical change in the provision made for all the unemployed.

Unemployment insurance may indeed be a self-destroying institution, if the British experience be any guide. Created to make more acceptable provision for a limited group of unemployed persons, its integrity could be maintained only if the treatment of those excluded was so improved as to relieve the pressure for undesirable expansions of the insurance system. But once so improved, the case for the maintenance of an independent, and particularly a separately financed, insurance system is greatly weakened.

Its retention, in the face of the vast improvement in social provision for the unemployed which has taken place in Great Britain, leads to a desire to provide higher cash benefits (either by increasing flat rates or by relating benefits to wages) because of the belief that, as the worker has contributed to this service and not to assistance, he should receive more. Still more importantly, the identification of specified benefits, obtainable under certain conditions, with a specific method of financing renders unnecessarily difficult the task of making these benefits available to the extent that social and economic considerations might dictate. For, as the Unemployment Insurance Statutory Committee pointed out, these considerations may suggest a wider use of the insurance type of benefit. Yet, since insurance is still financed by equal contributions from employers, workers and the public, increased use of the insurance type of benefit results in placing an increasing share of the costs of the entire unemployment relief program on workers and employers. And this may be a socially and economically undesirable result. But it is equally possible that economic conditions might indicate the unwisdom of extending the scope or duration of insurance benefits as widely as the yield of wage and payroll taxes would permit.

The dilemma presented by the fact that social and economic considerations may suggest on the one hand a wide extension of the insurance type of benefit, and on the other a restricted use of the taxes from which these benefits are financed, cannot be solved so long as the belief is retained that wage and payroll taxes must provide the exclusive or at least the major share of the funds for this particular type of aid for the able-bodied unemployed. A solution can be hoped for only if the two aspects of the unem-

22

ployment relief problem—decisions as to the types of benefits to be made available and the scope of each, and decisions as to how the total costs are to be distributed—are separated.[3]

It may be objected that such an approach, involving different types of treatment for different groups of unemployed but a basic unification of the financing of all types of aid, would lead to the loss of some of the peculiar values which were the objective of unemployment insurance, and the dangers must not be under-estimated. In historical perspective it can now be seen that, from the point of view of the unemployed, insurance had the advantage that it appeared the only method of guaranteeing him a form of security preferable to the alternative of poor relief. It was a method of committing the community to a more generous social policy, and the earmarking of certain taxes—especially the compulsory collection of a contribution from the worker—appeared to be a way of implementing this guarantee. The apparent contractual element in the institution seemed an assurance against reactionary changes by subsequent governments. In fact, however, benefit rights have on occasion (notably in 1931) been curtailed. From the point of view of the members of the community who do not directly obtain benefits, the institution of insurance appeared to be a bulwark against mounting costs and unduly generous benefits, but here too its effectiveness has been less than had been originally anticipated. A system which is largely financed by earmarked taxes from the worker is likely to be susceptible to pressure from organized labor to offer preferential treatment to those who have contributed. The experience of the Statutory Committee has already indicated that the benefit rates of a separate insurance system, which claims to be preferential, cannot but be influenced by the benefit policies of the major alternative relief system, which does not pretend to be bound by limitations such as the concept of solvency and is frankly reflective of the political mood of the time.

Thus the experience of Great Britain suggests that the institution of social insurance is no final safeguard against these risks. Both the levels of benefit and, perhaps even more importantly, the conditions under which they are available, have been changed with

---

[3] In principle, of course, separation takes place as soon as any part of the insurance benefit is paid for by a contribution from the general tax funds.

changes in government, and in economic conditions, and in social philosophies.

From the financial point of view, the combination of insurance and unemployment assistance also represents real progress. As a method of relieving local authorities from the ruinous costs of unemployment relief, the combined insurance and assistance measures are more satisfactory than the earlier devices. On the one hand, the central government has clearly accepted responsibility for maintenance of the group normally employed in occupations subject to old-age and survivors insurance who fail to qualify for or have exhausted insurance benefits. And once accepted, a man is not thrown back on the local authorities merely because of the length of his unemployment. Moreover, the assumption by the assistance system of responsibility for supplementing inadequate insurance benefits and for paying adequate unemployment allowances which the public assistance authorities may not supplement, prevents the central government from indulging in economies by cutting insurance benefits or assistance allowances at the local ratepayer's expense.

From another angle the financial picture presented by the combined insurance and assistance measures is less amenable to a common-sense interpretation. For there are now two financially independent systems, one deriving its funds from equal contributions from employers, workers, and the general taxpayer, and the other financed wholly by the taxpayer. The financial planning period of the insurance system is an 8-year cycle, over which it aims to remain solvent, but no more than solvent. In recent years it has accumulated reserves which are expected to avoid the necessity of running into debt for more than two consecutive years and have permitted repayment of a significant proportion of the debt accumulated prior to 1931. This technical solvency and long-period planning of the insurance system, which since the 1934 changes has provided aid to between 37.4 per cent and 57.1 per cent of the total number unemployed, have, however, been possible only because the general taxpayer has supplied on a year-to-year basis 100 per cent of the funds for unemployment assistance, which in the same period has provided for between 28.2 and 40.3 per cent of the unemployed.

Whether or not this situation represents financial progress over that prevailing in the two earlier experiments depends in large measure upon the importance attached to "insurance" as a separate institution. Undoubtedly its prestige is greater when the cost of maintaining the residual unemployed (i.e. those not strictly meeting the original insurance eligibility qualifications) is charged against the central government as a separate item, rather than against the insurance fund as a mounting deficit. If, however, for the reasons already given, the case for the maintenance of a separately financed insurance system in Great Britain has become greatly weakened, the necessity to maintain its prestige also disappears. The abandonment of the concept of a separately financed insurance system would have facilitated the removal of another anomaly, namely, the assessment against wage and payroll taxpayers up to 1971 of contributions to be used for repaying a debt incurred in the years 1921 to 1931.

This conclusion involves no condemnation of the attempt to build up reserves, or to pay off deficits from subsequent surplus yields of taxes collected at uniform rates. On the contrary, experience has shown that wage and payroll taxes, provided their rates are not too frequently changed or excessively burdensome, are convenient fiscal devices, and that the earmarking of taxes for specific expenditures is not without value. It is also increasingly evident that the attempt to balance income and expenditure over an annual period is particularly unsatisfactory when the expenditure item is susceptible of such wide fluctuations from year to year. The considerations urged by the Unemployment Insurance Statutory Committee in favor of long-period planning for the insurance system, namely, that in periods of depression it is socially undesirable to reduce benefit rates and economically unwise to increase tax rates, are, however, equally applicable with regard to the residual relief system.

Finally, the combined insurance and assistance program has proved to be a more convenient administrative device than had at first been anticipated. It is true that the attempt to vest responsibility for the policies and administration of the residual unemployment relief system in an independent body has proved abortive and unfortunate. But here, too, the British gift for compromise and for abandoning theories when they prove inconvenient in

practice has triumphed. For almost all practical purposes the Unemployment Assistance Board is subject to parliamentary control.
But retention of the fiction of formal independence places it at a
serious disadvantage, as it lacks its own spokesman and its actions
must be defended in Parliament by a Minister who may occasionally disclaim responsibility because of the technical independence
of the Board. This disadvantage is not counterbalanced by the
admittedly increased influence and power of making itself heard
by other government agencies—especially the Treasury—which
the Board obtains by virtue of its separation from the Ministry
of Labour. This fact, coupled with the close relationships between
insurance and assistance, suggests the advisability of placing the
administration of both services as coordinate units under the
authority of a single Minister. This suggestion would presuppose
the maintenance of the Unemployment Insurance Statutory Committee in its present semi-independent status, but would involve
giving to that body the same broad powers with regard to the
assistance scheme that it now exercises with regard to unemployment insurance.

Certainly the day-to-day administration of the current British
program operates with surprising smoothness, and the extent to
which officials trained rigidly to observe the limits of legal authority
have adjusted themselves to a service calling for a wide exercise
of discretion, has agreeably surprised even those who were initially
most critical of this experiment in centralization.[4]

Despite prophesies of disaster, centralization of unemployment
relief administration has operated with a high degree of adaptability to local and individual needs. The gibe frequently directed
against the Assistance Board—that it is nothing more than public
assistance administered by the central government and as such
achieves no more than could have been secured by devoting equal

----

[4] Professor John Hilton, who has always stressed the importance of treating
"each unemployed person as a separate and distinctive case needing special
aid," and who in 1934 "deplored it [the Unemployment Assistance Board] in
itself and no less for the arguments on which it was based," was by 1937
asserting that "no social service on so large a scale had ever been created
in this country within so short a time—or so admirably and efficiently created.
. . . I will take the U.A.B., not for the taint it inherits, but for the public
service it is, and for the instrument of social betterment it may yet become."
("The Public Services in Relation to the Problem of Unemployment," *Public
Administration,* January 1937, pp. 3-9).

care and funds to a reform of local assistance—is unjustified because it overlooks the extent of the reform needed and the fact that one of the major obstacles to reform is the small size of the typical local administrative unit.[5] Even since the reorganization following the Local Government Act of 1929, many of the local administrative units are too small to provide an adequate service in view of the magnitude of the unemployment load. Many of the services now seen to be essential to a socially satisfactory unemployment program, especially those looking toward increasing occupational and geographical mobility, cannot be performed by numerous subordinate governmental units. It is no mere accident that the admittedly most progressive local public assistance authority, the London County Council, is also the largest and the innovator of a new administrative technique which involves central formulation of uniform scales of relief and the transference of increasing responsibility and discretion to paid officials (the adjudicating officers) who work under the general and somewhat remote supervision of a partly elected and partly coopted committee.

At the now predominantly important central level, division of function between the officials of the Board and the insurance administrators is in the main clear cut and makes for speedy and efficient operation. Consultation and close contact between individual officials of the two services overcome many of the difficulties against which the law does not and could not always provide. Exceptions to this rule, such as the performance by appeals tribunals of functions more appropriate to courts of referees and the divided responsibility for recruitment and operation of reconditioning centers, could be removed by minor reorganization. The inconvenience to clients and administrators of the geographical separation of the local offices of the two services is a consequence of that same desire to maintain the insurance system as a distinctive institution and of a failure to realize wherein lies the essential difference between the two, to which reference has already been made. It is, moreover, doubtful whether the stimulus to a more zealous

---

[5] It is noteworthy, for example, that the authors of the *Report on the British Social Services* (London: Political and Economic Planning, 1937) who attach great importance to the alleged vast improvements in local public assistance, appear to base their generalizations very largely upon the only body specifically cited by them, namely, the London County Council which, as they admit, being the largest, is hardly a typical authority. (pp. 152-53, 156)

regard for the welfare of the unemployed, which comes from the appointment of the Special Areas Commissioners, is adequate compensation for the existence of these separate and semi-independent bodies. Here too, however, an eventual merging of the common functions would appear relatively easy to accomplish.

On the other hand, the increasingly wide interpretation placed upon the mandate of the Board to provide for the welfare of its clients creates a need for trained and specialized social workers which has not yet been satisfied, and the training and calibre of the Board's investigating officers who make the vital personal contacts with clients leave much to be desired.[6] This situation is, as already explained, in part a historical accident which the Board is endeavoring to overcome, but the development of a staff adequately trained for the new type of service cannot be hoped for until there is more general recognition that this service demands better trained and therefore more highly paid staff.

ACHIEVEMENTS AND FAILURES, 1920-1938

Technical analysis of the operation of individual programs tends always to obscure the larger picture. A proper evaluation of the British handling of the problem of unemployment relief demands, therefore, that this detailed analysis be supplemented by a survey of the broader achievements and weaknesses. Foremost among the achievements is the basic stability of the British program. Neither wild-cat schemes involving irresponsible financial methods and fantastically disproportionate treatment of the unemployed or sections of the unemployed in relation to other groups, nor extreme reversals of policy from generous provision to an almost complete absence of aid have characterized the British treatment of the unemployment relief problem. Regardless of the specific programs in operation, Great Britain has provided continuous maintenance for her unemployed. Crises and emergencies have affected levels

---

[6] This absence of professional training is not, however, characteristic only of the centrally administered social services. Despite the recent increasing professionalization of the employees of public assistance staffs, it still remains true that the public assistance work is the stepchild of the local social services and is remunerated accordingly, while the methods of recruitment and training of local officials in general were criticized by the Departmental Committee on the Recruitment and Training of Local Government Officers.

of benefits, methods of financing and the relative responsibilities of the central and local governments, but they have never been permitted to endanger the basic economic security of the unemployed man. And while the general level of maintenance despite a marked improvement cannot be regarded as unduly high, it has, for the statistically important mass of unskilled workers, compared very favorably with wages, and in certain cases even exceeded them.

Equally impressive are the orderly procedures and high degree of freedom from political or personal bias toward the individual which have in general characterized the administration of the various measures. This is especially evident with regard to the programs administered by the central government. The professional integrity of the civil service, which has often been remarked upon, has left its imprint in this field also.[7] The observer of the operation of the various programs effective since 1920 cannot but be struck by the extent to which the administrators of the different services have been conscious of a common objective—the provision of income to the unemployed. Officials of public assistance, unemployment insurance and unemployment assistance with very few exceptions appear to have cooperated harmoniously and closely in their local areas, and to have in the main subordinated mechanical administrative convenience to considerations affecting the welfare of the unemployed.

Among the achievements of the British system, the success with which private citizens have been led to cooperate with the administration on a voluntary basis, or on payment of purely nominal honoraria, deserves special emphasis. At every point the British unemployment programs are buttressed by groups of cooperating citizens.[8] Sometimes, as with the courts of referees of the insurance system and the unemployment assistance appeals tribunals, these groups are given specific quasi-judicial functions and render decisions, some of which are binding even on the central

[7] Cf. Kulp, *op. cit.*, pp. 17, 56-58.
[8] This use of cooperating citizens is not peculiar to the unemployment relief system. For a list of advisory committees attached to other departments, and a favorable evaluation of their effectiveness, see John A. Perkins, "Permanent Advisory Committees to the British Government Departments," *American Political Science Review,* February 1940, pp. 85-96. Cf. also Millett, *op. cit.*, pp. 277-82.

department responsible to Parliament.[9] Sometimes, as in the case of the local advisory committees of the Assistance Board, they are set up to advise local administrators in regard to the application of general rules in their own area or to the treatment to be applied to special classes of individuals. Sometimes, as with the local employment committees attached to the employment exchanges, they serve as a general consultative body and provide an informed and interested group from which members of special committees may be recruited. More recently the Unemployment Insurance Statutory Committee, essentially a non-official body, has been given final authority to determine the financial condition of the insurance fund, which, as was shown in Chapter VI, has involved far-reaching powers to determine the scope and function of the unemployment insurance system. The Committee has also very considerable advisory powers on vitally important problems.

Nor does this enumeration exhaust the list of non-official, unpaid bodies which are brought into contact with the various unemployment programs. Among others which play or have played an important role are the rota committees, which passed on claims during the period of expanded insurance, the juvenile advisory committees, the English and Scottish National Advisory Councils for Juvenile Employment, the National Land Settlement Associations, and the various committees and commissions that have investigated different phases of the operation of the unemployment relief programs.

This enlistment of the services of private citizens at every stage of the policy forming and administrative activities is of the utmost value. It adds greatly to the technical efficiency of the service. Questions regarding the prevailing wages for specific types of employment, trade union requirements and customary conditions of work, the prospects of employment in specific types of occupation, can all be more speedily and effectively answered when administrators can count upon the continuous assistance of a body of local employers' and workers' representatives to whom these questions can be referred. Similarly, problems which arise in a service based upon need, such as the nature of local standards of

[9] In the insurance system, appeals go from the courts of referees to the Umpire, who is a direct employee of the Crown enjoying practically judicial status and whose rulings are binding even on the Minister.

living or the levels of local rents, can be handled more easily if local knowledge and advice are available. The rigors of centralization can thus be tempered.

The presence on adjudicating bodies of laymen, especially those representing the interests of employers and workers, contributes toward the efficiency of the service also in that it tends to keep legal formalities to a minimum,[10] encourages discussion of disputed points in language familiar to the worker, and furnishes the private individual some guarantee against bureaucratic tyranny. A decision in which his peers have participated is more likely to be accepted as fair by the applicant, although it would be unreasonable to expect complete satisfaction with the appeals machinery on the part of applicants since to the worker any group with power to pass on his rights and possessing more complete knowledge of the technicalities involved must appear to be a hostile body.[11]

At the worst, this continuous contact with and shared responsibility for the administration of an important social service may act merely as a shelter for the administrator. He can call upon outside witnesses to support the action he has taken and secure at least formal exoneration. But, because Great Britain has been in general unusually successful in securing the services of competent, conscientious and frequently outstanding citizens, and because this type of public service is accorded respect and authority, these "lay administrators" can and do also influence policy.

Finally, from the wider point of view, the participation of the lay public is important, for it disseminates a better knowledge and understanding of the issues and the problems faced by administrators and thereby helps to create that informed public opinion which in the last resort can be the only safeguard against political irresponsibility.

In another direction also this continuous provision for the maintenance of the unemployed is noteworthy: it has been achieved concurrently with a growing concern on the part of the national government for the financial condition of local authorities. The realization that central assumption of the major share of the cost

[10] It is significant that lawyers as such may not appear before courts of referees or appeals tribunals.

[11] For an illuminating account of the workers' attitude toward the courts of referees, see Bakke, *The Unemployed Man,* pp. 100-11.

of unemployment relief was an inevitable consequence of the relative fiscal resources of central and local governments was indeed slow. And there was even more resistance to recognition of the fact that some measure of central control must accompany central financial responsibility. Ultimately both issues have been faced and policy has been adjusted accordingly. The present high degree of centralization of financing, policy formation and routine administration, whatever its disadvantages, represents a more realistic approach to hard facts than does the policy of those who, disregarding the implications of central participation in financing, urge that the administration of relief should be turned over to the localities.

The success with which the British have dealt with the problems involved in operating an increasingly categorical unemployment relief program must also be ranked among the achievements of the years since 1920. Admittedly there are serious disadvantages inherent in the categorical approach. But while a non-categorical service, offering a socially acceptable level of maintenance and appropriate preventive measures to all incomeless persons regardless of the cause of their dependency, would undoubtedly be preferable to the amalgam of relief institutions that characterizes most industrial countries in the twentieth century, there are serious administrative and financial obstacles in the way of its achievement. The very magnitude of the problem of developing adequate social provision against all forms of insecurity suggests that progress could hardly have been made on all points simultaneously. The increased expenditures due to the larger volume of dependency, and the high cost per case resulting from more adequate provision, and the adoption of positive and preventive measures, have created a fiscal problem beyond the competence of local authorities. If central aid, necessarily involving some central control, thus becomes inevitable, concentration on certain categories of dependency might well seem to be the lesser of two evils. For at least it sets limits to the extent of central interference in local autonomy. Local authorities would still be free to act independently with regard to those outside the categories provided for by the central authority. Furthermore, there are important differences among dependent persons in regard to their needs and the services which would be appropriate. Even in a unified service certain forms of categorization would inevitably develop because of the technical nature of the services to be performed and the segregation of the groups needing them.

But at this stage it is meaningless to discuss whether Great Britain could have developed her broad social service program other than by the route of categorization. The important fact is that she did adopt it in her treatment of the unemployed and has operated a categorical service so as to avoid many of the more obvious disadvantages. This has been possible largely because both among policy forming authorities and administrative officials there has been a high degree of cooperation, a sense of common function, and a widespread belief that considerations of common sense and fair play to the unemployed should prevail over legal and administrative niceties. On the other hand, some of the disadvantages of categorization will remain so long as there is an incomplete development of other categorical services, in particular the health program [12] and those other services whose supply depends upon the social policy and fiscal abilities of a multitude of local authorities.

On the negative side, the greatest shortcoming of the British unemployment relief programs is undoubtedly the almost exclusive concentration on maintenance and the neglect of more positive policies. Despite the considerable development of training, transference and occupational measures that characterized the period from 1934 to 1938, the lives of the great majority of the long-period unemployed were scarcely affected. Public works instituted for the purpose of providing employment were avoided as a deliberate policy, and the extent of employment in the special areas on local amenities and projects economically justifiable was negligible. Nor can the efforts to stimulate private employment be regarded as anything more than half-hearted concessions to a growing public concern over the persistence of continuous unemployment. The areas selected for special assistance were few in number, and their boundaries were not such as to make possible an effective long-range policy. The powers of the Special Areas Commissioners are still severely limited, and more ambitious schemes involving im-

[12] Cf. PEP, *Report on the British Social Services,* pp. 168-69.

provement of the competitive position of these areas have failed to overcome the opposition of private interests. Even the long overdue appointment of a Royal Commission to inquire into the general question of localization of industry cannot, in view of the membership of that body, be regarded as evidence of a serious intention on the part of the government to grapple with a problem that necessarily involves some limitation on the traditional freedom of private entrepreneurs. Despite the almost unanimous warnings of all students and investigators, British unemployment policy still concentrates too exclusively upon the provision of maintenance.[13]

THE NATURE OF THE BASIC PROBLEMS

It does not, of course, follow that unemployment relief measures, formally similar to those in Great Britain, would operate with equal success elsewhere. Quite apart from the relative economic homogeneity (in terms of price and wage levels) and the small geographical area of Great Britain, there are certain imponderables which render precarious any such forecast. Some of these, such as the nature of the civil service, a widespread acceptance of the responsibility of the government for the economic security of the individual, a preference for common-sense practice over the niceties of theoretical principles, and a tradition of public service among the general public, have already been referred to in the preceding pages. But there are others equally important. The British worker appears bitterly to resent the means test and to value a payment given as a matter of right so highly that he will even accept a possibly lower payment in return for this concession. This psychological attitude facilitates the maintenance of relationships between the benefit schedules of insurance and assistance which might be untenable elsewhere. The strong opposition of the British worker to what he regards as official interference with his private life tends also to keep individual case work to a minimum, and helps to account for the fact that so comprehensive a relief system has in the main been carried through without the development of a large body of professional social workers, as is to be found, for example, in Germany or the United States. The power of Parliament freely

[13] See Chapter IX, footnote 150.

to amend legislation and thus to correct interpretations of legislation at variance with its original intent, and the peculiarities of the parliamentary system with the opportunities it affords for criticism, coupled with the existence of a relatively strong and certainly vocal political and economic labor movement, have also been of the first importance.[14]

Yet, although specific forecasts are pointless, a study of the manner in which another country has grappled with a now almost universal problem is not altogether without value. For at least some light is shed upon the nature of the underlying problems. Governmental policy toward the unemployed, however it develops in the future, will, if British experience be any guide, have to adjust itself to certain basic facts. Perhaps the most important of these is a changed view of the mutual responsibilities of the individual and the government, and of the social and economic functions of the family. The poor law, which had until recent years served as the unique instrument for discharging governmental obligations to the needy individual, had a straightforward answer to these questions. It had expressed the view that the responsibility of government for the economic welfare of the individual was limited. The family was assumed to be the basic economic unit, and if natural affection was an inadequate stimulus, coercion could be employed to compel the family to support its needy members. Economic dependence, where it was not due to youth, old age, or sickness, was an indication at worst of unsocial conduct, at best of a grave defect of character. Assistance was, therefore, to be given in the main under deterrent conditions and on a very low standard.

The system worked because the assumptions on which it was based were not too violently at variance with the economic facts and social habits of the time. But the late nineteenth and early twentieth centuries changed the economic and social world in which this system had to operate. Increasing productivity widened the gap between the standard of living enjoyed by the active participant in production and the recipient of government support. The growth of a more sensitive social conscience, and the emergence of politically powerful labor parties have rendered this wide gap

[14] Cf. Millett, *op. cit.*

ever less tolerable, and with the broadening of the franchise politicians could no longer afford to neglect the views of an important group of voters.

This changing view of what constituted acceptable treatment of dependent persons might still have failed to influence legislation and administrative practice, or at most might have involved more favorable treatment of selected groups only, had it not been for the practically continuous depression which characterized the British economy during the period covered by this study. This depression, bringing with it unemployment heavy in terms both of the proportion of the population affected and of the duration of unemployment per worker, has vitally affected the problem of government provision for the unemployed. It hastened the general recognition of the inappropriateness of the principles on which governmental assistance had previously been based, because more people were affected by the relief system. Moreover, the existence of unemployment as a mass phenomenon sharply challenged the view that unemployment was largely within a man's own control. Economic dependence was no longer characteristic of the unfortunate or unworthy few, and in consequence "unemployment" has become almost synonymous with "involuntary unemployment." At the same time the consequences of prolonged idleness became so obvious that the government was compelled to expand its program beyond the mere provision of maintenance.

Similar developments have conspired to weaken the economic unity and social cohesion of the family. Family employment (except in agriculture, itself a steadily less significant source of livelihood) has become rare. Changing techniques of production and currents of world trade have called for a high degree of mobility of labor, which by breaking up the family in a geographical sense has also weakened the ties of mutual intra-family obligation. This mobility has been specifically fostered by the government itself. Measures to encourage geographical transference have, as indicated previously, assumed increasing importance, and the government has often even enforced a certain degree of geographical and occupational mobility as a condition for receipt of government assistance. Through its educational policy too, it has weakened the sense of obligation and close family feeling. On the one hand, it has made a breach in the theory of family responsibility by the very fact that it relieves parents of the costs of education. On the other, by providing subsidized higher education, vocational and technical training, it has encouraged young people to improve their economic situation and establish wider contacts, all of which tend to weaken family ties, at least between parents and children and among brothers and sisters.[15]

The institution of social insurance has indeed reinforced these tendencies which operate against the continuance of the family as the basic mutually interdependent economic unit. By providing specific cash sums to individuals regardless of resources possessed by themselves or their relatives, this institution has made a vital concession to the view that in some circumstances the individual should expect aid from governmental institutions before exhausting the resources of his family.

But, while the economic and social environment of the twentieth century has brought an awareness of the unsuitability and unacceptability of the old theory as to the relative economic responsibilities and obligations of the individual and the family on the one hand, and the government on the other, no satisfactory philosophy has yet replaced it. The problem is two-fold. It is necessary to redefine the limits of private mutual responsibility and to determine what obligations the government may demand from the individual in return for such assistance as it is required to provide. Developments in Great Britain point to a continuous narrowing of the mutual responsibilities of the family, and a reduction in the extent to which an individual is expected to exhaust his own resources before seeking government aid. But the new philosophy has been very unevenly applied, even within the field of unemployment relief. The resulting coexistence of different social services, each adopting its own criteria for determining the limits of family responsibility, creates administrative difficulties and anomalous situations, as well as confusion in the public mind. These difficulties will not be resolved by any mere alteration in mechanisms or administrative techniques. The need is for the evolution of a new social philosophy concerning the economic function of the family, and this is no easy task for, as already pointed out, it must not merely reflect the actual strength of family feeling but also take into account the prevailing stimuli to enterprise and initiative.

[15] Cf. Gertrude Williams, *The State and the Standard of Living,* pp. 321-25; Percy Ford, *Incomes, Means Tests and Personal Responsibility,* pp. 1-13.

In Great Britain the pendulum has swung far towards investing the government with vast responsibilities for the economic welfare of the individual, unaccompanied by a parallel development of the economic demands which the government may make upon the worker and of preventive as opposed to salvage policies, but there is already a growing awareness of the fact that this development is too one-sided to endure.[16] In the interests of the individual and of the government alike, social policy in the future must evolve in a more positive direction to redress the balance. Here also, however, the evolution of a new definition of the mutual economic responsibilities of the supported individual and of the government, and its implementation in legislation and administrative practice will be no easy task. Both will make great demands upon the worker and the government.

For the policy of prevention, for which Sidney and Beatrice Webb so persuasively argued thirty years ago,[17] is now seen to involve much more than the mere extension of social insurance systems to provide cash income that obviates the necessity for contact with a degrading poor law. On the part of the worker it involves that most difficult sacrifice, a change of attitude toward the demands which the government may make upon him.[18] The requirement to change his occupation, to remove from hopelessly depressed areas, to undergo training which will maintain and improve his employability, must be recognized not as coercive and repressive tyranny but as the inevitable concomitant of the wider responsibility which the government has assumed for his economic welfare.

On the other hand, this increased governmental responsibility will and must, if it is to be accompanied by adequate safeguards, immeasurably widen the sphere of government action. Attempts to encourage mobility of labor involve not merely the supply of information concerning job opportunities throughout the country, but also the offer of financial inducements to offset the financial

[16] Cf. PEP, op. cit.: "The first consideration of social service policy should, we believe, be the progressive reduction in size of the public assistance and unemployment assistance class, by concerted measures to prevent people from being forced down into, or kept in, that class." (p. 170)

[17] Cf. Minority Report of the Royal Commission on the Poor Laws and Relief of Distress (Cmd. 4499, 1909), pp. 721-1238.

[18] Cf. Hohman, op. cit., p. 356.

23

costs of movement, and of training facilities to equip workers with essential skills. Stimulation of geographical mobility raises also the question whether the government should not intervene to prevent undesirable concentrations of industry or the development of areas dependent solely upon single industries.[19] The maintenance of morale and working efficiency may necessitate the operation of large public works programs and constructive measures intended to increase private employment, which may call for a change in prevailing concepts as to the proper spheres of governmental and private economic activity. Any increase in the pressure on individuals to accept unaccustomed jobs, or in the extreme case the use of the threat to withhold assistance as a technique for enforcing downward adjustments of the general wage level, will call for a considerable expansion of the administrative organization and an increased degree of administrative discretion. Above all, it will require the application of a higher degree of exact and technical economic analysis to provide a sound basis for these drastic policies than governments have yet been willing to contemplate, or, indeed, than the science of economics has yet made available.

Against this background the other facts which will condition the development of governmental policy in regard to the unemployed appear relatively unimportant. Yet taken alone they are sufficiently challenging and deserve at least brief mention. Perhaps the most obvious is the inevitability of central government participation in the financing of the various measures. This necessity follows from the sheer magnitude of the expenditures occasioned by contemporary unemployment in relation to the resources of subordinate political units. But in whatever form provided— whether as a subsidy to the insurance system to make possible extended benefits, or as a grant to local relief authorities, or as a separate relief system differing from insurance with respect to the benefits provided and the conditions governing their receipt—it is to be expected that the authority providing the major share of the funds should seek to exercise some control over the nature of the service, if only in view of its interest in the magnitude of the resulting bill.

[19] For an analysis of some of the wider implications of a policy of controlled location, see S. R. Dennison, "State Control of Industrial Location," *The Manchester School*, No. 2, 1937; R. C. Tress, "Unemployment and the Diversification of Industry," *Ibid.*, No. 2, 1938.

This financial pressure toward the assumption by the central government of increasing responsibility—at least for the conditions under which assistance is available, if not necessarily for the day-to-day administrative routine—is reinforced whenever the government undertakes positive and constructive measures. Many of these, such as the stimulants to mobility, technical and vocational training, and the development of public works programs, cannot economically or satisfactorily be provided by the small local authorities which have been the traditional relief administrative units.[20] Only experience can show whether or not the combined effect of these trends, fortified by the desirability of integrating all parts of the employment and unemployment programs, will lead in other countries, as in Great Britain, to a high degree of centralization of policy making and administration. The fact remains that the issue today can no longer be stated in terms of the simple antithesis of central versus local administration.

A study of the evolution of British policy toward the unemployed suggests another, and to some observers disconcerting, conclusion, namely, the impossibility in a democracy of divorcing problems of unemployment relief from politics. The nature of the assistance to be given to a large segment of the population and the allocation of the costs of an item which bulks so large in the national budget inevitably and properly become matters of broad public policy. In the face of this situation, the increasing centralization which has characterized British experience in the last twenty years has at most hastened an inevitable development. Indeed, one may hazard the guess that even if other factors had not led to a high degree of centralization of day-to-day administration, there might well have been a trend toward centralization of policy as a consequence of the increasingly political implications of the dual problem of unemployment relief.

The problem facing contemporary industrial democracies is thus no longer how to remove the question of unemployment relief from politics, but rather at the policy-forming level how to combine adequate responsiveness to changing political views with that minimum stability of policy which is essential for effective administra-

---

[20] Cf. the conclusion of the Royal Commission on Local Government in the Tyneside Area that, over a wide range of social services, even the largest units of present-day local government are too small. (*Report,* [Cmd. 5402, 1937], p. 73)

tion. On the day-to-day administrative level, the problem is how to devise adequate democratic controls to assure that the intentions of the majority are not being flouted by administrative acts, without at the same time permitting the treatment received by individuals to be affected by their political affiliations.

Lastly, the study of British unemployment relief policy suggests that social policies and programs cannot operate in watertight compartments. The attempt to limit preferential treatment to a specific group, which characterized the scope of the initial British unemployment insurance act, failed precisely because it represented an attack on one front only and neglected to cope with the needs of those who were excluded from or could no longer claim insurance, in regard to whom a revision of policy was long overdue. The consequence of the sharp difference of treatment afforded those who were covered by and those who were excluded from unemployment insurance gave rise to an unstable situation in which there was irresistible pressure on successive governments to extend the benefits of the preferential system to those excluded.[21] As a result, both the insurance and the residual systems underwent modifications.

In the last resort, of course, what is true of the different programs for dealing with the unemployed is true also of the relationship between unemployment relief policy as a whole and other social services. So long as the treatment of dependent persons fails to reflect prevailing social standards, liberalization of the provision for so numerically important and economically significant a group as the unemployed tends to stimulate liberalization in other fields also. For a community which has accepted the idea of the basic minimum as fully as has Great Britain, the discovery that the sum of money necessary to assure this standard to an unemployed man may be in excess of that earned by many workers in full employment acts not solely as an argument to reduce unemployment assistance, but becomes also a challenge to remove the social inadequacies of the wage system.

---

[21] As was prophesied by Sidney and Beatrice Webb as long ago as 1909, "For the government to provide means of rescue or provision for this or that section, and not for the other sections, is practically certain to lead to the provision being swamped . . . by those for whom it was not intended, but for whom no alternative provision is made." (Minority Report of the Poor Law Commission, op. cit., Part II, p. 1176)

APPENDICES

Appendix I. Measures of Unemployment in Great Britain

The statistics of unemployment in Great Britain are based on the registration of unemployed persons at the employment exchanges and there have been no periodic estimates of unemployment apart from these registrations. Two basic official unemployment series have been constructed from the registration data: (1) the number of insured persons recorded as unemployed on one day in each month, or the series relating to *Books Lodged* [1] (column 7, Table I); and (2) the number of persons on the registers of the employment exchanges, or the *Live Register* (column 6, Table I).

All unemployed insured persons, when reporting to the exchange to make a claim for benefits, are required as part of the procedure to "lodge" their books. Thus this series of statistics includes persons who are currently receiving benefits, as well as those whose claims are under consideration. It also includes unemployed insured persons who have made no claim or have been disqualified for benefits, but who continue their registration for employment. In addition, the number of books lodged includes the *Two Months' File,* which consists of the books of insured persons who are no longer reporting to an exchange but are not known to be employed, ill, deceased, or no longer resident in the country. Two months after an individual has ceased to report, his book is removed to the *Dead File* and he is no longer counted among the unemployed.[2]

While these series are comprehensive and useful in the administration of the insurance system, they have definite limitations as a measure of unemployment for the purposes of this study. First, they exclude the uninsured unemployed. Second, prior to September 1934 they exclude unemployed persons 14 and 15 years of age because they were not covered by insurance,[3] and until May 1936 agricultural workers are excluded for the same reason.

---

[1] The "unemployment book" is a two-page card held for the worker by his employer, who affixes an unemployment stamp to the book as each week's contribution. In July of each year the currency of each book expires and it is delivered to the employment exchange to be exchanged for a new one.

[2] "Even after the period of two months has expired, books are retained in the Two Months' File if it is definitely known that the person is still out of work and desiring employment, but such definite knowledge is rare and it may be taken that in general the Two Months' File covers no more than two months." (Ministry of Labour, *Memorandum on the Influence of Legislative and Administrative Changes on the Official Unemployment Statistics* [Cmd. 2601, 1926], p. 3. See also *Memorandum on Certain Points Concerning the Statistics of Unemployment and of Poor Law Relief* [Cmd. 2984, 1927], pp. 3-4, in which the Ministry of Labour concludes that the measure of unemployment would not be seriously affected by disregarding the *Dead File* but including the *Two Months' File.*)

[3] Since they have been counted, their numbers have fluctuated from 6,700 (Sept. 1934) to 27,556 (Jan. 1935) persons on the register, plus between 1,100 and 10,600 in the *Two Months' File.*

These deficiencies are corrected to a certain extent by the series known as the *Live Register,* which consists of all registered unemployed persons and thus includes unemployed uninsured persons in so far as they register at an exchange.[4] The persons counted, however, are those unemployed on the day of the count, so that persons employed on a short-time basis on other days and persons temporarily out of work are also included in the figures.

The *Live Register* still leaves out of account the uninsured who fail to register for work. Moreover, it is less comprehensive in regard to insured persons than the *Books Lodged* series because it does not include the *Two Months' File,* nor the unemployed persons covered by the special schemes for banking and insurance. The latter exclusion is relatively unimportant,[5] but the former is more serious. While some authorities hold that the inclusion of the *Two Months' File* may lead to some over-statement of the numbers unemployed,[6] the study by the Ministry of Labour in 1925 indicated that its exclusion would tend unduly to understate unemployment, especially when administrative or legislative changes are in progress.[7] Unfortunately, however, information concerning the *Two Months' File* and the special schemes for banking and insurance is available only since 1924 and 1926 respectively. Prior to these years the Ministry did not publish the number of books in the *Two Months' File,* although a file distinct from the unemployment books representing "live claims" was maintained.[8]

Thus it is obvious that neither the *Live Register* nor the *Books Lodged* by itself shows the total number of unemployed. In Table I the estimate of the number of unemployed presented in column 8 and used throughout this study represents the most comprehensive index of unemployment that can be compiled from available sources. Essentially what has been done is to add to the *Books Lodged* the number

---

[4] The uninsured registered group would include the able-bodied persons required by poor law authorities, or after 1934 by the UAB, to register as a condition for receiving assistance. An analysis by the Ministry of Labour in 1925 showed that the uninsured persons on the register were "mainly domestic servants, agricultural workers and juveniles under 16." (*Memorandum on the Influence of Legislative and Administrative Changes on the Official Unemployment Statistics,* p. 2)

[5] Between 1931 and 1937 the numbers of unemployed covered by these schemes varied between 2,300 and 5,300.

[6] Thus Sir William Beveridge states in "An Analysis of Unemployment," *Economica,* November 1936, p. 368: "It seems likely . . . that the Two Months' File is an excessive allowance for persons unemployed and available for work but not caring to register. This file automatically carries for two months every married woman disallowed as being really not in the industrial field who does not think it worth while to register for work; women and girls form nearly half of the . . . file, though they are only one-sixth of all the unemployed on the register."

[7] *Memorandum on the Influence of Legislative and Administrative Changes on the Official Unemployment Statistics,* p. 6. Changes tending to make benefits easier to get have resulted in the registration of unemployed insured persons who had hitherto not done so, while restrictive changes have led to the withdrawal of some registrations or to failure to register initially. When unemployed insured persons cease to register, the effect is at once reflected in the more sensitive *Live Register* where they cease to be counted immediately, although they continue for a period of two months to be counted among *Books Lodged.* The *Live Register* will thus respond more rapidly to legislative or administrative changes, but may understate the actual volume of unemployment.

[8] Cf. John Hilton, "Statistics of Unemployment Derived from the Working of the Unemployment Insurance Acts," *Journal of the Royal Statistical Society,* March 1923, pp. 154-93.

of uninsured persons on the register (or, alternatively, to add to the *Live Register* the *Two Months' File* and the special schemes).

In addition to these specific inclusions and exclusions, three other qualifications must be borne in mind in using Table I as a measure of unemployment. First, although the most comprehensive figure available, it still does not include unemployed persons who do not register at employment exchanges. Very probably, however, their numbers are extremely small, especially in recent years. All claimants for insurance benefits, transitional payments or unemployment assistance allowances have been compelled to register in order to receive benefits. Moreover, it has become a general practice for the poor law or public assistance authorities to require their able-bodied applicants to register as a condition for receipt of relief. However, the increase in registrations following the administrative changes in 1928 and 1929 and the legislative changes in 1928, 1930 and 1934, which favored the claimants, and the decrease following the restrictive changes introduced in 1928 and 1931, are evidence that not all the unemployed had registered. Second, until January 1932, column 8 includes a relatively insignificant number of employed persons (3,000 on Jan. 25, 1932).

Third, all the unemployment figures prior to 1937 tend to overstate by a small but significant amount the volume of unemployment because of the procedure used for counting the unemployed. Up to September 1937, the persons counted as unemployed on a given Monday ("the day of the week on which the count is invariably taken" [9]) included persons who, unknown to the exchange with which they were registered, had secured employment since last reporting at the office. As the exchanges generally required reporting on two or three days a week, including Monday, it can be seen that those persons who secured employment on the day of the count or even the preceding Saturday or Friday, could be reckoned among the unemployed on Monday.[10] The corrective procedure now in use consists essentially in marking especially the cases of uncertainty and in ascertaining during the week following the day of the count whether the day of the count was in fact a day of unemployment. The publication of the unemployment totals is then deferred a week until the persons who worked on the day of the count are deducted. The new method reduced the number of insured unemployed on September 13, 1937 by 43,687 or 3.3 per cent in comparison with the old method of counting, and the rate of unemployment among insured persons was reduced from 10.1 to 9.7.[11]

[9] Ministry of Labour *Gazette*, October 1937, p. 379.
[10] An individual was considered continuously registered if he had reported to the exchange within the last three consecutive days (including Monday). Sundays are never taken into account. (*Ibid.*, p. 379.)
[11] In addition, the new method reduced the applicants for unemployment benefits under the general scheme by 6.2 per cent, and under the agricultural scheme by 5.3 per cent. Applicants for unemployment assistance allowances were reduced 1 per cent. (*Ibid.*, p. 379.) Cf. also *Ibid.*, December 1937, pp. 470, 471)

The preceding discussion of the facts to be borne in mind when using the figures presented in Table I is summarized briefly below:

Column (1): Figures refer to one day in each month.

Column (2): Includes claims admitted or under consideration for insurance benefits (uncovenanted, extended, transitional and standard) and transitional payments and unemployment assistance allowances, together with insured persons not entitled to benefits or allowances. Includes persons 16 years and over through 1927, persons 16-64 through June 1934, and from September 1934 those 14-64. Beginning with July 1936 unemployed persons covered by the agricultural scheme are included in this and all other columns, as well as certain classes of domestics from September 1938. Data not available for this column prior to 1924. Figures shown are equal to column 6 minus column 5.

Column (3): Not available prior to 1924.

Column (4): Not available prior to 1926. Prior to September 1936, figures refer to insured unemployed; thereafter, to claimants for benefits.

Column (5): Not available prior to 1924. Includes able-bodied persons required to register by poor law authorities, and after 1934 by the UAB, as well as any persons under 16 (prior to September 1934), and agricultural workers or other non-insured persons who may have registered for employment. From September 1936, includes a small number of insured persons under the special schemes for banking and insurance.

Column (6): Sum of columns 2 and 5.

Column (7): Sum of columns 2, 3 and 4.

Column (8): Sum of columns 5 and 7 (or, alternatively, 3, 4 and 6); except in 1921-23 when, because the *Two Months' File* and data for the special schemes were not available, the higher number of column 6 or 7 has been used. As a result, unemployment may be understated in these years, although juveniles under 16 and agricultural workers (until covered by insurance) would be included.

Sources: col. 6 (1921-25), *18th Abstract of Labour Statistics,* pp. 90-91; col. 7 (1921-25), *21st Abstract,* pp. 46-48; cols. 2, 3, 5 (1924-25), *Memorandum on the Influence of Legislative and Administrative Changes on the Official Unemployment Statistics* (Cmd. 2601, 1926), p. 5; cols. 2-7 (1926-39), *Gazette,* table entitled "Unemployment Insurance Statistics: Great Britain" to June 1928 and thereafter "Composition of Unemployment Statistics: Great Britain;" col. 9 (1921-33), *21st Abstract,* pp. 46-48, (1934-Dec. 1936), *22nd Abstract,* p. 58, (Dec. 1936-June 1937), computed from *Gazette,* and thereafter *Gazette,* Nov. 1938, p. 424, Dec. 1939, p. 409.

TABLE II. NUMBER AND PER CENT OF THE UNEMPLOYED AIDED UNDER
THE INSURANCE AND SUPPLEMENTARY NATIONAL SYSTEMS
IN GREAT BRITAIN, 1922-1939

Date	Number of claims admitted			Per cent of unemployed aided			Per cent of insured unemployed with insurance claims admitted
	Insurance system	Supplementary systems	Total	Insurance system	Supplementary systems	Total	
(1)	(2)	(3)	(4)	(5)	(6)	(7)	(8)
	In thousands						
1922-June 6	421	269	690	28.0	17.9	45.9	28.0
July 31	338	690	1,029	23.4	47.8	71.3	23.4
Oct. 9	290	756	1,046	20.9	54.4	75.3	20.9
Nov. 20	954	153	1,107	66.7	10.7	77.4	66.7
1923-Apr. 30	800	261	1,061	63.0	20.6	83.6	63.0
1924-Dec.	544	491	1,035	43.1	38.9	82.0	44.7
1925-Mar.	—	—	1,093	—	—	83.8	—
June	520	472	992	37.5	34.0	71.5	38.8
Sept.	—	—	1,205	—	—	85.2	—
Dec.	—	—	971	—	—	79.8	—
1926-Mar.	—	—	877	—	—	75.5	—
June	—	—	1,475	—	—	84.6	—
Sept.	—	—	1,356	—	—	81.8	—
Dec.	—	—	1,141	—	—	79.7	—
1927-Mar.	505	384	889	41.7	31.7	73.4	44.0
June	—	—	825	—	—	75.6	—
Sept.	—	—	876	—	—	75.3	—
Dec.	—	—	943	—	—	77.9	—
1928-Mar.	—	—	868	—	—	75.2	—
June	—	—	1,057	—	—	82.3	—
Sept.	—	—	1,118	—	—	80.8	—
Dec.	973	119	1,092	71.8	8.8	80.6	75.4
1929-Mar.	—	—	952	—	—	77.1	—
June	—	—	951	—	—	79.7	—
Sept.	810	130	940	65.1	10.4	75.5	69.5
Dec.	—	—	1,126	—	—	81.8	—
1930-Mar.	—	—	1,534	—	—	89.7	—
June	1,384	323	1,706	72.3	16.9	89.2	74.8
Sept.	1,537	342	1,879	69.8	15.5	85.3	72.6
Dec.	1,973	383	2,356	79.1	15.4	94.5	81.8
1931-Mar.	1,937	401	2,338	72.3	15.0	87.3	74.9
June	1,949	427	2,377	71.7	15.7	87.4	74.0
Sept.	2,030	502	2,532	69.7	17.2	86.9	72.4
Dec.	1,345	762	2,107	49.7	28.1	77.8	51.7
1932-Mar.	1,248	864	2,112	46.0	31.8	77.8	48.1
June	1,320	945	2,265	45.8	32.8	78.6	47.7
Sept.	1,345	1,018	2,362	45.0	34.1	79.0	47.2
Dec.	1,200	1,039	2,239	42.4	36.7	79.1	44.4
1933-Mar.	1,190	1,063	2,252	41.2	36.8	78.0	43.4
June	998	996	1,994	39.2	38.9	78.3	41.1
Sept.	912	978	1,890	37.4	40.1	77.5	39.5
Dec.	854	936	1,790	36.9	40.5	77.4	38.9
1934-Mar.	857	905	1,763	37.4	39.5	77.0	39.7
June	871	817	1,688	40.0	37.5	77.5	42.2
Sept.	912	744	1,656	42.0	34.3	76.3	45.0
Dec.	952	728	1,680	43.8	33.5	77.3	46.5
1935-Mar.	991	730	1,721	44.1	32.5	76.7	47.1
June	912	709	1,621	43.7	33.9	77.6	46.4
Sept.	867	698	1,565	42.3	34.0	76.3	45.3
Dec.	822	688	1,510	42.2	35.3	77.6	45.1
1936-Mar.	844	669	1,513	42.9	34.0	76.9	45.9
June	750	616	1,366	42.2	34.6	76.8	45.0
Sept.	690	592	1,282	40.5	34.7	75.2	43.6
Dec.	744	579	1,323	43.8	34.1	77.9	46.6
1937-Mar.	732	553	1,285	43.8	33.1	76.9	47.0
June	583	574	1,157	41.0	40.3	81.3	43.8
Sept.	592	546	1,138	42.1	38.8	80.9	45.3
Dec.	896	556	1,452	51.7	32.1	83.8	54.3
1938-Mar.	995	549	1,544	54.6	30.1	84.7	57.4
June	1,074	531	1,605	57.1	28.2	85.4	59.9
Sept.	1,042	532	1,574	55.4	28.3	83.7	58.5
Dec.	1,076	554	1,630	56.4	29.0	85.4	59.0
1939-Mar.	977	553	1,530	54.0	30.1	84.1	56.7

NOTE: Explanatory notes and sources for each column will be found on pp. 345-46.

APPENDIX III. ESTIMATED NUMBER OF PERSONS RECEIVING
POOR RELIEF OR PUBLIC ASSISTANCE ON ACCOUNT
OF UNEMPLOYMENT IN GREAT BRITAIN

In order to compare the relative importance of the insurance and residual relief systems in Great Britain as a whole during the period 1921-1939, it is necessary to make various adjustments in the poor relief statistics (1) because of the differences in the classifications used in the several series available, and (2) because the statistics for Scotland and for England and Wales are reported separately, include somewhat different information and refer to different months in the year.

Both England and Scotland distinguish between outdoor (domiciliary) relief and indoor (institutional) relief. In England up to 1920, outdoor relief to the able-bodied was negligible.[20] With the growth of unemployment after 1920, it became impossible to provide institutional care for all able-bodied needy persons and recourse was had to the provision of the Relief Regulation Order of 1911 which permitted the payment of outdoor relief if a special report on each case was made to the Minister of Health and he did not express disapproval. Undoubtedly a small number of employable persons continued to receive indoor relief on account of unemployment, but, except in cases of sickness, these would be mainly the habitually workshy or those for whom deterrent, if not punitive, treatment was considered necessary. Since 1920, therefore, the figures relating to poor relief or public assistance given to able-bodied persons in England and Wales have usually been derived from data concerning recipients of outdoor relief alone. Although the exclusion of institutional cases may involve some under-statement, the error cannot be large.[21]

Statistics for Scotland are more precise. Until 1921, no relief could be granted to able-bodied persons.[22] Beginning in that year, however, the Scottish parish councils were authorized under emergency legislation to grant relief to the "destitute able-bodied unemployed and their families."[23] Since May 1922, published Scottish statistics have distinguished among both indoor and outdoor relief recipients

[20] *Minutes of Evidence*, p. 272.
[21] After 1920, in spite of a heavy increase in unemployment (see Table I, col. 8), the number of persons receiving indoor relief remained fairly steady, ranging from 186,000 in 1920 to 226,000 in 1927 and 1928, and by 1931 it had dropped to 212,000. On the other hand, the number of outdoor relief recipients rose from 306,000 in 1920 to over a million in the years 1922-24, and again between 1926 and 1928. (Averages as of January 1 each year and include dependents. *Minutes of Evidence*, p. 278; *Twenty-Second Abstract of Labour Statistics*, p. 194)
[22] The statistics were compiled under the main heads of sane poor in receipt of indoor or outdoor relief. (Scottish Board of Health, *Annual Report*, 1922, p. 176) The Scottish Board of Health became the Department of Health for Scotland on January 1, 1929.
[23] *Ibid.*, p. 117.

348

those who received aid on account of unemployment, and in the figures shown for Scotland in later tables the unemployed recipients of both types of aid are counted. The inclusion of unemployed recipients of indoor relief makes little difference in the totals, however, because they represented less than one per cent of the unemployed outdoor relief recipients in every year between 1922 and 1931, except 1930 when the proportion was 1.1 per cent.[24]

For Great Britain as a whole, reliable figures showing the number of persons receiving relief solely on account of unemployment can be obtained only with great difficulty, both because of the different statistical classifications adopted by England and Wales and Scotland and because during the period covered by this study the classifications themselves were changed in each country. Not only is it necessary to separate from all able-bodied persons those relieved on account of unemployment, but in the English statistics dependent members of the families of these recipients must be excluded if a figure comparable to that estimated in Appendix II for insurance beneficiaries is to be obtained.

Analysis of Statistics for England and Wales

Segregation of Persons Relieved on Account of Unemployment

Only since June 1937 is it possible to find published figures that give for England and Wales the exact number of persons receiving public assistance on account of unemployment. Before this date adjustments in the available statistics are necessary.

The estimates for England and Wales in Table IV, p. 356, are derived from available reports by several different procedures, each adapted to the peculiar difficulties presented at different periods of time.

Between 1922 and 1926, use is made of two basic statistical series which have been published continuously by the Ministry of Health since March 1922. One gives the number of persons (including dependents) in receipt of outdoor relief, distinguishing (a) persons ordinarily engaged in some regular occupation from (b) all other persons.[25] The other series classifies group (a) into (c) persons (including dependents) insured under the unemployment insurance acts and (d) all other persons ordinarily engaged in some regular occupation.[26] For the purpose of obtaining an estimate of those relieved on account of unemployment, only group (a) and its subdivisions (c) and (d) are of interest. The totals reported for group (a) are shown in column 5, Table III, those of group (c) in column 2 of the same table, and those of group (d) in column 4 (see p. 351).

---

[24] *Ibid.,* 1931, p. 178.

[25] The figures are averages of the numbers for each Saturday in March, June, September and December. Persons receiving medical relief only are excluded; also the insane, and casuals. (1922-26, *Twentieth Abstract of Labour Statistics*, p. 191; 1927-36, *Twenty-Second Abstract*, p. 198)

[26] 1922-26, *Twentieth Abstract*, p. 192; 1927-36, *Twenty-Second Abstract*, p. 199.

24

Group (a), and therefore (c) and (d) also, include some persons who should not be counted as persons relieved on account of unemployment. While the figures undoubtedly relate mainly to unemployed persons, they include an unknown number of employed persons.[27] Furthermore, the direct reason for the grant of relief even to unemployed persons was not always unemployment. Other factors such as sickness or emergencies accounted for a certain, although probably small, proportion of the cases.[28] In addition the group includes persons whose families were in need because of an industrial dispute,[29] and also others in receipt of aid who may not have been wage earners in the strict sense of the term, but persons working or previously working on their own account.

A comparison of the numbers of persons reported in group (a) with the numbers reported in another return published by the Ministry of Health reveals discrepancies which can be used to exclude from the figures reported for groups (c) and (d) those persons relieved in the years 1922-26 for reasons other than unemployment. For January 1 of each year since 1922, the Ministry has reported the number of persons in receipt of outdoor relief on account of unemployment.[30] The comparison of the two returns is presented below:

Date	Relieved persons ordinarily engaged in some regular occupation [a]	Persons relieved on account of unemployment [b]	
		Number	Per cent
	In thousands		
January 1, 1923.......	752	722	96.0
January 1, 1924.......	591	525	88.8
January 1, 1925.......	385	326	84.7
January 1, 1926.......	563	487	86.5
January 1, 1927.......	858	632	73.7

[a] These figures (except 1923) are obtained by averaging the data reported on each Saturday in January and the preceding December, and are, of course, only approximate for January 1 of each year. The figure for 1923 is the average reported for December 1922 in the *Twentieth Abstract of Labour Statistics*, p. 192. Dependents are included. (Ministry of Health, *Statements Showing the Number of Persons in Receipt of Poor Law Relief in England and Wales, in the quarter ending* . . . March 1924 to March 1927.)
[b] Including dependents. (Ministry of Health, *Persons in Receipt of Poor Relief* [*England and Wales*], 1938, p. 25)

[27] It was pointed out by the Secretary of the Ministry of Health that "a person in work, whose sick child was being attended by the District Medical Officer, would be included." (*Minutes of Evidence*, p. 279)
[28] When the classification was first made, the Ministry of Health advised that the analysis "be accepted with caution, since it is impossible to be certain that the classifications have been interpreted in an absolutely identical sense by all officers making returns. It is, for example, uncertain how far the figure for unemployed insured persons receiving outdoor relief includes or excludes persons who were relieved for causes, such as sickness, other than want of employment." (Ministry of Health, *Annual Report*, 1922-23, p. 77)
[29] Note, for example, the great increase in the numbers in column 5 of Table III during the engineering and shipbuilding strikes in 1922 and the general and mining strikes in 1926.
[30] The categories of persons relieved on account of unemployment were: men; women (wives living with husbands, wives of men in institutions, widows, wives living apart from their husbands, and single women); and children (those living with fathers, children of men in institutions, children of widows and of wives living apart from their husbands, children of single women, and other children). Those afforded outdoor relief other than on account of unemployment included persons relieved on account of sickness, accident, bodily or mental infirmity, ill health of a dependent, and wives of men receiving indoor relief. (Cf. *Persons in Receipt of Poor Relief* [*England and Wales*], 1939, pp. 16-17)

TABLE III. ANALYSIS OF THE NUMBER OF PERSONS (INCLUDING DEPENDENTS)
ORDINARILY ENGAGED IN SOME REGULAR OCCUPATION WHO RECEIVED
OUTDOOR RELIEF IN ENGLAND AND WALES, 1922-1939

Date	Unemployed persons insured under the unemployment insurance acts	Uninsured unemployed persons registered at employment exchanges	All other persons ordinarily engaged in some regular occupation	Total
(1)	(2)	(3)	(4)	(5)
		In thousands		
1922-Mar.	794	—	65	859
June	1,090	—	63	1,153
Sept.	757	—	52	809
Dec.	695	—	57	752
1923-Mar.	636	—	67	703
June	576	—	50	626
Sept.	551	—	47	598
Dec.	522	—	50	572
1924-Mar.	506	—	50	556
June	422	—	42	464
Sept.	328	—	38	366
Dec.	333	—	39	372
1925-Mar.	346	—	40	386
June	355	—	36	391
Sept.	438	—	36	474
Dec.	510	—	43	553
1926-Mar.	501	—	40	541
June	1,642	—	39	1,681
Sept.	1,665	—	36	1,701
Dec.	490	43	535	1,068
1927-Mar.	407	41	97	546
June	361	34	89	485
Sept.	345	32	89	466
Dec.	369	34	95	499
1928-Mar.	351	35	96	481
June	287	29	95	411
Sept.	252	31	93	376
Dec.	260	37	99	396
1929-Mar.	265	39	123	427
June	209	36	110	354
Sept.	194	35	104	333
Dec.	198	42	113	352
1930-Mar.	200	34	121	355
June	94	18	120	233
Sept.	94	21	114	229
Dec.	115	29	121	265
1931-Mar.	128	38	151	317
June	117	35	132	285
Sept.	117	39	126	282
Dec.	179	57	138	374
1932-Mar.	224	71	161	456
June	230	78	151	459
Sept.	246	80	154	480
Dec.	290	99	170	560
1933-Mar.	304	106	192	602
June	263	97	161	521
Sept.	254	101	165	520
Dec.	302	116	177	595
1934-Mar.	314	128	189	631
June	272	114	181	567
Sept.	226	122	179	526
Dec.	305	136	189	631
1935-Mar.	216	151	198	565
June	184	135	192	511
Sept.	173	127	186	487
Dec.	184	137	199	520
1936-Mar.	171	142	206	518
June	147	118	188	452
Sept.	131	111	184	426
Dec.	142	113	189	444
1937-Mar.	137	109	203	450
June	35	46	166	247
Sept.	30	43	160	233
Dec.	33	46	169	247
1938-Mar.	33	46	175	253
June	30	42	167	240
Sept.	29	41	158	229
Dec.	32	42	164	238
1939-Mar.	32	41	177	250

NOTE: Explanatory notes and sources will be found on pp. 349-53 of this Appendix.

The percentages in the last column, p. 350, have been applied to the figures shown in columns 2 and 4 of Table III for the years 1922-26 to obtain the lower numbers found in columns 2 and 4 of Table IV, with the following modifications: (1) The percentage shown for January 1, 1923 has, in the absence of more specific information, been applied to the figures reported for March-September 1922.[31] (2) Taking into account the seasonal movement of unemployment and the great probability that during the winter months persons relieved on account of unemployment would constitute a particularly high proportion of relieved persons ordinarily engaged in some regular occupation, it has seemed undesirable to apply to the entire year the proportion existing in January.[32] Therefore, figures for the months from December 1922 through September 1924, and again from December 1925 through March 1926, have been reduced by percentages five points less than those shown above for January 1, 1923, 1924 and 1926.[33] (3) Because the increase in the numbers of insured unemployed persons in receipt of outdoor relief in 1925 (col. 2, Table III) was attributable mainly to a growth in the total number of unemployed insured persons, the percentage shown for January 1, 1925 has been applied without reduction to the figures reported for December 1924 through September 1925. (4) As an aftermath of the general strike in 1926, the numbers of relieved persons in June and September of that year consisted very largely of unemployed insured persons. Therefore, the 1926 percentage has been applied without reduction to the figures reported for these months.

After October 1926, a closer approximation of the desired estimate is possible as the Ministry of Health, in consultation with the Ministry of Labour, revised the basis on which the outdoor relief returns from local authorities were classified. Recipients of poor relief (and their dependents) were henceforth divided into four classes:

Class I. Persons insured under the unemployment insurance acts *who are unemployed* and holding card U.I. 40 issued by an employment exchange. (This card was a receipt given the worker when he lodged his unemployment book with the exchange on becoming unemployed and making a claim for benefit.)

Class II. Persons not insured under the unemployment insurance acts *who are unemployed* and holding a registration card E.D. 24 issued by an employment exchange.

[31] Because of the restrictions on insurance benefits current at the time and the existence of gaps in uncovenanted benefits in June 1922, the proportion of persons relieved under the poor law on account of unemployment was likely to have been particularly high.

[32] Three special returns by the Ministry of Health relating to the able-bodied persons receiving unemployment relief in June of 1927, 1928 and 1929 (*Unemployed Persons in Receipt of Domiciliary Relief in England and Wales*, Cmd. 3006, 1927; Cmd. 3218, 1928; Cmd. 3433, 1929), and another return for March 31, 1930 (*Persons in Receipt of Poor Relief in England and Wales*, 1933), permit a comparison with the January figure in these years. These returns showed a considerable variation during the year, the mid-year percentages being lower than those for January 1.

[33] As the January 1 percentage in any year appears to be more representative of the situation in the preceding December than of that in December of the same year, the January 1924 percentage, for example, is applied to the figures for December 1923 and for March, June and September 1924.

Class III. All other persons ordinarily engaged in some regular occupation.

Class IV. All other persons in receipt of outdoor relief.

The last of these classes is clearly of no interest for this study. The figures reported for the remaining three classes, however, are shown from December 1926 through March 1939 in columns 2, 3, and 4 of Table III.

Classes I and II are now limited to unemployed persons, but it is still not known whether all of these persons were relieved *on account of unemployment* as distinct from other reasons. As stated on page 350, other factors, such as sickness or emergencies, may have caused a certain, though probably small, proportion of them to seek relief. An inquiry instituted by the Ministry of Health in 1934 revealed that in four "test periods"—July, September, November and December—the expenditure on account of unemployment alone amounted to 90.7 per cent of the total for Class I recipients, and 98.2 per cent for Class II recipients.[34] In the preceding years, especially after 1931 in view of the reductions in the benefit rates and more stringent eligibility requirements of the insurance system, it is probable that the percentage was even larger. The over-statement of the relief load attributable to unemployment would not, therefore, be very great if from December 1926 through March 1937 the whole of Classes I and II were assumed to be unemployed persons relieved on account of unemployment. Thus, between these dates the reported figures shown in columns 2 and 3 of Table III have been entered without change in columns 2 and 3 of the final estimate shown in Table IV on page 356.

Greater difficulties are, however, presented in estimating the number of persons reported in Class III who were wage earners and were relieved on account of unemployment. After October 1926, cases of employed persons, whether insured or uninsured, who were actually or "constructively" [35] in receipt of relief were counted only in Class III.[36] Among other changes, this involved the transfer of strikers from Class I to Class III.[37] But it is not known how many of the

[34] Ministry of Health, *Annual Report*, 1935-36, p. 140. No other data on unemployment relief expenditures for the different classes were compiled by the Ministry. The more detailed statistics published by the Ministry after April 1, 1937, which differentiate unemployment from other causes of relief extended to normally employed persons, are unfortunately not helpful in the present instance. For the period covered is subsequent to the Second Appointed Day, when the general relief authorities could give only medical relief and emergency aid to persons falling within the scope of the unemployment insurance and unemployment assistance schemes (i.e., to all of Class I and most of Class II).

[35] Whenever relief was granted to any member of a family, the head of the family was considered "constructively" in receipt of relief and included in the statistics under the statutory provision that relief to the dependent was relief to the head. (*Memorandum on Certain Points Concerning the Statistics of Unemployment and Poor Law Relief* [Cmd. 2984, 1927] p. 2) Officially, under the Relief Regulation Order of 1930, relief could not legally be given to an able-bodied person while in employment, except on account of sickness or accident or to defray burial expenses. But the relief authorities were allowed to relieve destitution in cases of sudden and urgent necessity, and it was probable that some of them placed a generous interpretation on this phrase. (*Minutes of Evidence*, p. 318)

[36] *Minutes of Evidence*, p. 279.

[37] Letter from the Ministry of Health to the author. This accounts in part for the drop in Class I between September and December 1926 (see Table III, column 2), and the increase in Class III over the same period (see column 4).

persons reported in this class were normally wage earners not registered at an employment exchange but were receiving relief on account of unemployment.

In all probability, however, the number of unemployed wage earners in Class III was small. To begin with, the majority of the poor relief authorities made registration at an exchange a condition for the receipt of relief by able-bodied persons.[38] Hence most of the persons normally engaged in some regular occupation would, if not insured, appear in Class II. Furthermore, it is known that during the week ending February 7, 1931, of 46,340 heads of families relieved on account of unemployment only 3,964 or 8.6 per cent were in Class III. At that time Class III consisted mainly of elderly persons and independent workers such as hawkers, peddlers, canvassers and newsvendors, together with a relatively small number of agricultural laborers living at a distance from employment exchanges.[39] Again, in 1934 it was found that in the four test periods previously mentioned, expenditures on account of unemployment alone amounted to only 6.1 per cent of the total expenditure for Class III.[40] Neither of these measures, however, affords a safe basis for deflating the figures from 1927 to 1937. For it is doubtful whether the small proportion of those relieved on account of unemployment who fell in Class III in February 1931 was characteristic of all the years between 1927 and 1937. The same difficulty applies to data based on the year 1934, which moreover relate to expenditures rather than to persons. Both sets of figures, however, support the conclusion that the proportion of persons in Class III drawing relief on account of unemployment was very small.

The determination of the proportion of the persons reported in Class III who were wage earners relieved on account of unemployment is aided by an examination of the more exact Scottish statistics. For almost every month since October 1928, the Scottish reports distinguish able-bodied unemployed persons (and their dependents) from others included in Class III.[41] The proportions of able-bodied unemployed in this class have been applied to the English figures in column 4, Table III for the corresponding months to obtain the deflated figures shown in column 4 of Table IV, with two exceptions. First, since the Scottish monthly figures are not available prior to October 1928, the average percentage prevailing in Scotland between November 1928 and December 1930 (8 per cent) is applied to the English figures for the period between March 1927 and June 1929. It is obvious that this will give only an approximate figure.[42]

---

[38] *Minutes of Evidence*, p. 274.
[39] *Appendices to the Minutes of Evidence*, Part II, p. 76.
[40] Ministry of Health, *Annual Report*, 1935-36, p. 140.
[41] Ministry of Labour *Gazette*, table entitled "Poor Relief in Great Britain." The persons included in Class III in the English and Scottish reports are comparable, although this term is not used in Scotland.
[42] It may indeed be an over-statement inasmuch as the inquiry of February 7, 1931 indicated that *expenditures* for relief to the unemployed in Class III were higher in England than in Scotland (8.6 per cent of the total, as against 6.6 per cent). The prevailing Scottish percentage is derived from *Minutes of Evidence*, p. 330.

Second, since it is known that the figure for December 1926 was swollen by the inclusion of a large number of strikers, the average percentage prevailing in Scotland cannot be applied to this month. Accordingly, it has seemed safer to reduce the total for this month shown in column 5, Table III, by the January 1, 1927 deflator on p. 350. The result appears in column 5, Table IV. The number of persons shown in column 4, Table IV for this month is obtained by subtracting the sum of columns 2 and 3 from the total number deflated as explained above.

Finally, beginning with June 1937, it is possible to use the figures published by the Ministry of Health in its quarterly statements of *Persons in Receipt of Poor Relief (England and Wales)* which show the number of persons receiving public assistance on account of unemployment. These statements also appear in current issues of the Ministry of Labour *Gazette*.

Segregation of Wage Earners and Their Dependents

The totals in column 5 of Table IV of persons in receipt of relief on account of unemployment are still not comparable with the numbers of insurance beneficiaries shown in Table II, because dependents are included. Beginning in October 1926 the Ministry of Health has distinguished in its reports between wage earners in Class I and their dependents, and since June 1931 a similar breakdown has been carried through for Class II. But to date no segregation is available for Class III.

Only rough methods of segregating dependents from main recipients can be used for the period prior to 1926. It is known that in the period 1922-25 the proportions of men, women and children in the total number of persons ordinarily engaged in some regular occupation and in receipt of outdoor relief remained practically constant, with men constituting 25 per cent of the total, women about 24 per cent and children between 51 and 52 per cent.[43] The Ministry of Health has indeed suggested that, at least so far as Class I is concerned, the number of insured persons, as distinct from dependents, might be approximated by dividing by four the total of relieved insured persons including dependents.[44] This may result in some under-statement because there would always be a certain number of women drawing insurance benefits in their own right or insured women who might be heads of families. Moreover, the more detailed breakdown for later years suggests that in all classes the average size of the family was less than four. It was 2.6 to 2.7 for Class II, 3.5 for Class III, and for Class I varied from 3.5 when the number relieved was around 450,000 to 3.9 when the total was around

---

[43] Ministry of Health, *Annual Report*, 1924-25, p. 103.
[44] *Ibid.*, 1925-26, p. 108.

TABLE IV. ESTIMATED NUMBER OF PERSONS RECEIVING RELIEF ON ACCOUNT OF UNEMPLOYMENT IN ENGLAND AND WALES, 1922-1939

Date	Wage earners and their dependents				Wage earners alone			
	Unemployed insured persons (Class I)	Uninsured unemployed persons (Class II)	All other ordinarily occupied persons (Class III)	Total	Unemployed insured persons (Class I)	Uninsured unemployed persons (Class II)	All other ordinarily occupied persons (Class III)	Total
(1)	(2)	(3)	(4)	(5)	(6)	(7)	(8)	(9)
	In thousands							
1922-Mar.	762	—	62	825	218	—	18	236
June	1,046	—	60	1,107	299	—	17	316
Sept.	727	—	50	777	208	—	14	222
Dec.	632	—	52	684	181	—	15	196
1923-Mar.	579	—	61	640	165	—	17	182
June	524	—	46	570	150	—	13	163
Sept.	501	—	43	544	143	—	12	155
Dec.	437	—	42	479	125	—	12	137
1924-Mar.	424	—	42	466	121	—	12	133
June	354	—	35	389	101	—	10	111
Sept.	275	—	32	307	79	—	9	88
Dec.	282	—	33	315	81	—	9	90
1925-Mar.	293	—	34	327	84	—	10	93
June	301	—	30	331	86	—	9	95
Sept.	371	—	30	401	106	—	9	115
Dec.	416	—	35	451	119	—	10	129
1926-Mar.	408	—	33	441	117	—	9	126
June	1,420	—	34	1,454	406	—	10	416
Sept.	1,440	—	31	1,471	411	—	9	420
Dec.	490	43	254	787	139	16	70	225
1927-Mar.	407	41	8	456	118	15	2	136
June	361	34	7	403	105	13	2	119
Sept.	345	32	7	384	100	12	2	113
Dec.	369	34	8	412	104	13	2	119
1928-Mar.	351	35	8	393	98	13	2	113
June	287	29	8	323	78	11	2	91
Sept.	252	31	7	291	69	11	2	83
Dec.	260	37	8	306	71	14	2	87
1929-Mar.	265	39	10	314	71	14	3	87
June	209	36	9	254	56	13	3	72
Sept.	194	35	8	237	53	13	2	68
Dec.	198	42	9	249	54	16	3	72
1930-Mar.	200	34	8	242	54	13	2	69
June	94	18	6	118	25	7	2	33
Sept.	94	21	7	122	25	8	2	35
Dec.	115	29	10	154	31	11	3	44
1931-Mar.	128	38	14	180	34	14	4	52
June	117	35	14	166	32	13	4	49
Sept.	117	39	14	170	32	15	4	51
Dec.	179	57	18	253	50	21	5	76
1932-Mar.	224	71	21	317	64	26	6	96
June	230	78	18	326	66	28	5	100
Sept.	246	80	16	341	72	30	5	106
Dec.	290	99	22	412	85	37	6	129
1933-Mar.	304	106	23	434	90	40	7	137
June	263	97	19	379	79	38	5	122
Sept.	254	101	20	375	78	39	6	123
Dec.	302	116	26	444	92	44	8	144
1934-Mar.	314	128	27	469	96	49	8	153
June	272	114	23	408	84	44	7	134
Sept.	226	122	19	367	72	48	5	125
Dec.	305	136	23	465	94	54	7	155
1935-Mar.	216	151	26	393	71	60	8	138
June	184	135	21	341	60	54	6	120
Sept.	173	127	17	318	57	51	5	113
Dec.	184	137	21	342	60	55	6	121
1936-Mar.	171	142	21	334	57	57	6	120
June	147	118	16	281	49	48	5	102
Sept.	131	111	14	256	44	46	4	94
Dec.	142	113	15	270	47	47	4	98
1937-Mar.	137	109	14	260	46	46	4	96
June	12	41	4	57	4	18	1	23
Sept.	9	38	4	51	3	16	1	20
Dec.	11	41	5	57	4	17	1	22
1938-Mar.	10	40	4	55	4	17	1	22
June	9	38	4	51	3	16	1	20
Sept.	9	36	4	49	3	16	1	20
Dec.	10	38	4	52	4	16	1	21
1939-Mar.	9	36	4	49	4	16	1	21

NOTE: Explanatory notes and sources will be found on pp. 352-57 of this Appendix.

100,000.[45] It therefore seems reasonable to apply a deflator of 3.5. From 1922 through 1925 the figures in columns 6 and 8 of Table IV are those in columns 2 and 4 divided by 3.5.

The separation of dependents from main recipients in Class II from December 1926 through March 1931 (after which date precise information is available) can be relatively easily accomplished. According to a letter from the Ministry of Health to the author, the average size of the family in this class during the period for which separate particulars are available was practically stable at 2.7, but fell to 2.6 when the total number relieved rose above 100,000. Since in this period the numbers in the class were well below the 100,000 limit, column 3 of Table IV has been divided by 2.7 to give the figures for these years shown in column 7 of the same table.

The segregation of dependents from main recipients in Class III can be effected by utilizing the results of a special investigation of the Ministry of Health in 1932. This showed that the average size of the family in this class was 3.5 (including the head of the family). The Ministry stated in a letter to the author that "normally there would be little variation in the average size of the family in these classes from year to year and the average ought to be regarded as fairly applicable over a series of years."

Column 8 of Table IV therefore represents column 4 divided by 3.5. It is possible that some error may be involved in applying to the unemployed wage earners in this class a deflator applicable to the group as a whole, but the error cannot be great for the deflator approximates closely the independently discovered deflators applied to Classes I and II.

ANALYSIS OF THE SCOTTISH STATISTICS

Since 1922 the Scottish statistics have reported for three days in each year (January 15, May 15, September 15) the number of destitute able-bodied unemployed receiving relief on account of unemployment.[46] Obviously neither employed persons nor unemployed persons relieved for reasons other than unemployment are included, so that the difficult problem of excluding them from the reported figures— so troublesome with regard to the English statistics—does not arise here. A further advantage of the Scottish method of reporting is that dependents are shown separately from the main wage earners. And, beginning in 1926, persons receiving relief as a result of strikes have been specifically excluded.

Until October 1928 only the totals of wage earners (with and without their dependents) relieved on account of unemployment were

---

[45] The decline in the average size of Class I families with the increase in the number relieved reflects the fact that, when the total number relieved is small, the cases calling for supplementation (i.e., where insurance benefits are likely to be inadequate because of the needs of large families) tend to be a larger proportion of the total.

[46] The May 15th figures through 1928, furthermore, show separately the numbers receiving outdoor and indoor relief on account of unemployment.

TABLE V. NUMBER OF PERSONS RECEIVING RELIEF ON ACCOUNT OF
UNEMPLOYMENT IN SCOTLAND, 1922-1939

Date	Wage earners and their dependents				Wage earners alone			
	Unemployed insured persons (Class I)	Uninsured unemployed persons (Class II)	All other ordinarily occupied persons (Class III)	Total	Unemployed insured persons (Class I)	Uninsured unemployed persons (Class II)	All other ordinarily occupied persons (Class III)	Total
(1)	(2)	(3)	(4)	(5)	(6)	(7)	(8)	(9)
	In thousands							
1922-Jan.	—	—	—	100	25	—	4	29
May	—	—	—	137	34	—	6	40
Sept.	—	—	—	144	36	—	9	45
1923-Jan.	—	—	—	148	37	—	7	44
May	—	—	—	141	35	—	7	42
Sept.	—	—	—	142	35	—	7	42
1924-Jan.	—	—	—	128	32	—	5	37
May	—	—	—	102	25	—	5	30
Sept.	—	—	—	78	19	—	3	22
1925-Jan.	—	—	—	81	20	—	3	23
May	—	—	—	76	19	—	3	22
Sept.	—	—	—	88	22	—	3	25
1926-Jan.	—	—	—	115	29	—	4	33
May	—	—	—	119	30	—	6	36
Sept.	—	—	—	116	29	—	8	37
1927-Jan.	—	—	—	119	30	—	10	40
May	—	—	—	111	28	—	9	37
Sept.	—	—	—	100	25	—	8	33
1928-Jan.	—	—	—	105	26	—	9	35
May	—	—	—	92	23	—	6	29
Sept.	65	9	3	78	19	4	1	25
Dec.	70	8	3	80	20	4	1	25
1929-Mar.	68	9	3	80	19	4	1	25
June	63	7	3	73	18	3	1	23
Sept.	61	7	3	71	18	3	1	22
Dec.	61	8	3	72	18	3	1	22
1930-Mar.	60	6	3	69	18	3	1	22
June	25	4	2	31	7	2	1	10
Sept.	28	4	2	34	8	2	1	11
Dec.	37	6	3	46	11	3	1	15
1931-Mar.	40	8	4	51	12	4	2	17
June	38	7	4	50	12	3	2	17
Sept.	42	7	4	54	13	4	2	18
Dec.	58	9	5	72	18	4	2	24
1932-Mar.	63	10	7	80	20	5	3	28
June	64	11	6	81	21	6	2	30
Sept.	74	13	5	92	25	7	2	33
Dec.	84	15	7	107	28	8	3	39
1933-Mar.	93	18	8	119	31	9	3	44
June	86	19	7	112	30	10	3	43
Sept.	89	19	7	116	31	10	3	44
Dec.	97	22	10	129	34	11	4	49
1934-Mar.	148	23	11	182	50	11	4	66
June	154	43	9	207	47	18	4	69
Sept.	129	43	8	181	42	18	3	63
Dec.	139	47	10	197	43	20	4	67
1935-Mar.	97	49	12	158	33	21	5	59
June	83	46	9	138	30	20	4	54
Sept.	77	45	8	131	29	20	3	52
Dec.	71	45	10	125	28	20	3	51
1936-Mar.	69	46	9	124	27	20	4	51
June	66	42	8	116	26	19	3	47
Sept.	63	40	7	109	24	18	3	45
Dec.	63	40	7	110	24	18	3	45
1937-Mar.	61	39	7	106	24	17	3	43
June	2	10	3	15	1	5	1	7
Sept.	2	10	3	15	1	5	1	7
Dec.	2	10	3	16	1	5	1	7
1938-Mar.	2	10	4	16	1	5	2	7
June	2	9	4	15	1	4	1	7
Sept.	2	9	3	14	1	4	1	7
Dec.	2	9	3	15	1	5	2	7
1939-Mar.	2	9	4	16	1	5	2	7

NOTE: Explanatory notes and sources will be found on pp. 357, 359.

reported, and these are shown in Table V (columns 5 and 9) for the period between January 1922 and May 1928.[47] No attempt is made to distribute the totals in column 5 among the groups designated in the headings of columns 2, 3 and 4 (corresponding to Classes I, II and III in the English reports) because available methods of accomplishing this breakdown appear unsatisfactory. However, following a suggestion of the Department of Health for Scotland, the number of insured wage earners (excluding dependents) shown in column 6 has been estimated on the basis of the proportion they formed of wage earners plus dependents (column 5) in 1928 and 1929 (the first years in which such information became available), i.e., roughly one-fourth. Column 8 is obtained by subtracting the estimated figures in column 6 from the reported totals in column 9.

From October 1928 to date, figures have been published in the Ministry of Labour *Gazette* which show as of the 15th of each month the numbers relieved on account of unemployment in the following categories: the insured unemployed registered at an employment exchange (column 2) ; the uninsured unemployed so registered (column 3) ; and all other unemployed persons in receipt of relief due to unemployment (column 4). For each of these groups dependents are shown separately.[48]

Combined Statistics for England, Wales and Scotland

The combined estimates of the number of persons in receipt of relief on account of unemployment, derived from available sources by the procedures described in the foregoing pages, are presented in Table VI on page 360.

It should be remembered, however, that the figures for England and Wales and for Scotland are not precisely comparable. First, the Scottish figures are exact, whereas those for England are approximations. Second, the English statistics probably involve some overstatement, due mainly to the impossibility of completely eliminating strikers. In Scotland, strikers and their dependents (numbering 137,699 in September 1926) are excluded from the reported figures. Third, the English figures are averages of the numbers receiving relief on each Saturday in the months shown, while the Scottish figures are the numbers receiving relief on the 15th of each month shown.

Finally, the two sets of figures are not entirely comparable for specific dates. Prior to 1928 the Scottish figures are available for

---

[47] Department of Health for Scotland, *Annual Report*, 1929, p. 203.
[48] The September 1928 figures are the figures reported for October 15th. Another series of Scottish statistics, beginning September 1929 and published in the *Twenty-Second Abstract of Labour Statistics*, p. 201, parallels the English table in the same publication. Persons ordinarily engaged in some regular occupation in receipt of relief are segregated into the three groups corresponding to the English classification. As in the English statistics, however, dependents are shown separately only for Classes I and II. Class III includes some persons relieved for reasons other than unemployment. Their numbers can be determined by comparing them with the figures published in the *Gazette*, but it is impossible to segregate dependents in this category. Cf. also *Minutes of Evidence*, p. 330.

January, May and September only in each year, whereas the English are available for March, June, September and December. While the Scottish figures for September can with relatively little error be added to English figures for September, it was necessary in compiling Table VI to add the Scottish figures for January 15 to the English figures for the preceding December, and those for May 15 to the English figures for June. No measures of relief on account of unemployment in Great Britain as a whole can, however, be presented for March each year, prior to 1929.

TABLE VI. ESTIMATED NUMBER OF PERSONS RECEIVING RELIEF ON ACCOUNT OF UNEMPLOYMENT IN GREAT BRITAIN, 1922-1939

Date	Number of persons (including dependents)	Number of persons (excluding dependents)	Date	Number of persons (including dependents)	Number of persons (excluding dependents)
(1)	(2)	(3)	(1)	(2)	(3)
	In thousands			*In thousands*	
1922-June	1,244	356	1931-Sept.	223	69
Sept.	920	267	Dec.	326	101
Dec.	833	239	1932-Mar.	397	124
1923-June	710	205	June	407	130
Sept.	686	197	Sept.	433	140
Dec.	607	174	Dec.	518	168
1924-June	491	141	1933-Mar.	553	180
Sept.	384	110	June	491	165
Dec.	396	113	Sept.	491	167
1925-June	407	117	Dec.	573	192
Sept.	490	140	1934-Mar.	651	219
Dec.	566	162	June	615	203
1926-June	1,573	452	Sept.	547	188
Sept.	1,587	457	Dec.	662	222
Dec.	906	264	1935-Mar.	552	197
1927-June	514	157	June	479	175
Sept.	484	147	Sept.	449	166
Dec.	517	154	Dec.	467	173
1928-June	415	120	1936-Mar.	457	171
Sept.	369	107	June	397	150
Dec.	386	112	Sept.	366	139
1929-Mar.	395	113	Dec.	381	144
June	326	95	1937-Mar.	366	139
Sept.	308	90	June	73	31
Dec.	320	94	Sept.	67	28
1930-Mar.	311	92	Dec.	72	30
June	150	43	1938-Mar.	71	29
Sept.	156	46	June	66	27
Dec.	199	59	Sept.	63	27
1931-Mar.	231	69	Dec.	67	28
June	216	66	1939-Mar.	65	28

APPENDIX IV

TABLE VII. EXPENDITURES OF THE INSURANCE AND SUPPLEMENTARY NATIONAL SYSTEMS IN GREAT BRITAIN, 1921-1939

Fiscal year	Insurance system						Supplementary system		
	Benefits	Travelling expenses of covered workers	Approved courses of instruction	Administration	Other payments	Total	Payments to the unemployed	Administration	Total
(1)	(2)	(3)	(4)	(5)	(6)	(7)	(8)	(9)	(10)

In thousand pounds sterling

(1)	(2)	(3)	(4)	(5)	(6)	(7)	(8)	(9)	(10)
1921	34,126	1	—	1,099	197	35,422	—	—	—
1922	52,910	2	—	4,838	2,022	59,773	—	—	—
1923	41,943	1	—	4,451	5,234	51,630	—	—	—
1924	36,019	2	—	4,086	10,251	50,358	—	—	—
1925	44,616	2	—	4,595	5,197	54,411	—	—	—
1926	43,704	3	—	4,890	2,815	51,411	—	—	—
1927	38,704	4	—	3,513	642	42,863	—	—	—
1928	36,484	3	—	4,914	5,197	46,598	—	—	—
1929	46,766	8	24	5,072	2,573	54,443	—	—	—
1930	42,274	12	25	5,168	6,764	54,242	3,690	295	3,985
1931	73,042	7	120	5,250	2,596	81,015	19,247	1,070	20,316
1932	80,169	8	133	5,364	4,784	90,458	30,742	1,633	32,375
1933	54,171	5	123	4,213	5,510	64,023	50,400	3,386	53,786
1934	40,193	6	111	3,756	13,671	57,737	48,442	3,740	52,182
1935	43,805	8	96	4,144	6,031	54,084	42,199	4,010	46,209
1936	42,715	11	223	4,609	5,112	52,670	42,423	4,289	46,711
1937	35,332	16	382	4,944	5,101	45,774	37,441	4,402	41,843
1938	36,692	14	401	5,128	25,109	67,343	36,689	4,708	41,397
1939	55,094	15	401	6,267	7,110	68,887	35,336	4,299	39,635

Column (1): Fiscal year ended July 1921-26; thereafter March 31. Data for 1927 (except in col. 3 which covers 12 months) are for 9 months. Data for 1937-39 include agricultural insurance.

Column (2): Standard insurance and expanded insurance benefits.

Column (6): Including repayments of Treasury advances and interest and amortization payments on debt (£20,000,000 in 1938); small payments for banking and insurance schemes; adjustments with Eire and Northern Ireland; refunds to workers at age 60 under the 1920 Act and compensatory payments at age 50 under the 1924 (No. 2) Act; since 1937, rebates for "long hirings" under the agricultural insurance system.

Column (7): Expenditures for the insurance system are those reported in *Unemployment Fund Accounts* for the government's fiscal year. Insurance expenditures on a calendar year basis from 1934 onwards may be found in the *Financial Reports* of the UISC.

Column (8): 1930-37, including transitional benefits, transitional payments, and unemployment assistance allowances reported in *Unemployment Fund Accounts*. 1938 and 1939, unemployment assistance payments on a fiscal year basis are reported in *Civil Appropriation Accounts;* figures include costs of training centers and 1938 special coronation payments.

Column (9): 1930-34, administrative expenses of the Ministry of Labour, reported in *Unemployment Fund Accounts*. 1935-37, including expenses of Ministry of Labour, reported in *Unemployment Fund Accounts,* and those of the UAB, found in *Civil Appropriation Accounts*. 1938 and 1939, administrative charges of the Ministry of Labour appear among UAB payments on a fiscal year basis in *Civil Appropriation Accounts*. Beginning with its annual report for 1936, the UAB has reported its expenditures on a calendar year basis.

APPENDIX V. THE COST OF POOR RELIEF OR PUBLIC ASSISTANCE FOR THE UNEMPLOYED IN GREAT BRITAIN

Expenditures for the unemployed in Great Britain as a whole must be ascertained separately for England and Wales and for Scotland as were the numbers of persons relieved on account of unemployment, described in Appendix III. Like the expenditures for the insurance and supplementary national systems shown in Appendix IV, they relate to both the unemployed and their dependents.

ANALYSIS OF STATISTICS FOR ENGLAND AND WALES

The Ministry of Health did not publish separate returns of the expenditures on outdoor poor relief to the able-bodied before April 1922. An official estimate of £500,000 was, however, made for the year 1921, and for 1922 the reported expenditure was £8,000,000, both sums excluding administrative charges. No breakdown of these sums is available for these years.[49]

Expenditures on Account of Unemployment

Expenditures for each of the three classes of unemployed persons referred to in Appendix III have been reported separately by the Ministry of Health only since the year 1934-35. Prior to that year the Ministry merely segregated the expenditures for Class I from the total for Classes I, II and III. Until 1928, the expenditures for Classes II and III appear together in column 4, Table VIII, p. 365. Since October 1926, simultaneously with the adoption of the new classification described in Appendix III, figures relating to the average weekly expenditures by quarters and for each of the three classes are available from other sources.[50]

As indicated in Appendix III, expenditures on account of unemployment will not be greatly overstated if the whole of the amounts spent for the Class I and II unemployed are counted. But for Class III the analysis carried through by the Ministry of Health in 1934 showed that only 6 per cent of the expenditures were on account of unemployment relief. In view of the changing conditions under which both insurance and relief were available during the period 1927 to 1929, however, it is unsafe to apply to all the years a percentage prevailing in 1934. A somewhat safer method would be to follow the same procedure used in Appendix III to segregate the unemployed persons and to allocate expenditures within this class on the basis of

[49] *Unemployment* (Cmd. 2082, 1924), p. 11.
[50] Until September 1930, in *Minutes of Evidence*, p. 275. Similar figures for subsequent years were supplied to the author by the Ministry of Health and are on file at the offices of the Committee on Social Security.

TABLE X. ESTIMATED COST OF RELIEF ON
ACCOUNT OF UNEMPLOYMENT IN
GREAT BRITAIN, 1923-1939

Year ending March 31	Unemployment relief in money and kind	Cost of administration	Total cost of relief to the unemployed
(1)	(2)	(3)	(4)
	In thousand pounds		
1923	11,062	1,081	12,143
1924	7,557	800	8,357
1925	4,853	593	5,446
1926	6,350	657	7,007
1927	12,611	1,040	13,651
1928	7,219	831	8,050
1929	5,213	661	5,874
1930	4,318	467	4,785
1931	2,315	300	2,615
1932	3,559	416	3,975
1933	5,937	577	6,514
1934	7,382	695	8,077
1935	8,891	769	9,660
1936	8,813	757	9,570
1937	7,486	325	7,811
1938	2,217	260	2,477
1939	2,128	—	—

APPENDIX VI. BENEFIT RATES UNDER THE INSURANCE SYSTEM

Since 1911, many changes have been made in the rates of benefit for different classes of workers. These changes were not always made by formal acts of Parliament, but, especially since 1931, also through Orders in Council, or, since 1934, through orders issued by the Minister of Labour on recommendation of the Unemployment Insurance Statutory Committee subject to the approval of Parliament. The dates on which these changes became effective are not always easy to ascertain. It has, therefore, been thought convenient to indicate the rates prevailing at any given time. This information is supplied in Table XI.

TABLE XI. BENEFIT RATES PREVAILING UNDER THE UNEMPLOYMENT INSURANCE ACTS, 1913-1939

Period[a]	Men (s. d.)	Women (s. d.)	Young Men (Age 20 / 19 / 18)	Young Women (Age 20 / 19 / 18)	Boys	Girls	Adult dependent (s.)	Each dependent child (s.)
GENERAL SYSTEM	*Age 18 and over*				*Age 16-17*	*Age 16-17*		
Jan. 8, 1913–Dec. 24, 1919	7 0	7 0	—	—	3 6	3 6	—	—
Dec. 25, 1919–Nov. 7, 1920	11 0	11 0	—	—	5 6	5 6	—	—
Nov. 8, 1920–Mar. 2, 1921	15 0	12 0	—	—	7 6	6 0	—	—
Mar. 3, 1921–June 29, 1921	20 0	16 0	—	—	10 0	8 0	—	—
June 30, 1921–Nov. 9, 1921	15 0	12 0	—	—	7 6	6 0	—	—
Nov. 10, 1921–Aug. 13, 1924	15 0	12 0	—	—	7 6	6 0	5	1
Aug. 14, 1924–Apr. 18, 1928	18 0	15 0	—	—	7 6	6 0	5	2
	Age 21-64		*Age 20 / Age 19 / Age 18*	*Age 20 / Age 19 / Age 18*				
Apr. 19, 1928–July 4, 1928[b]	17 0	15 0	17 0 / 17 0 / 17 0	15 0 / 15 0 / 15 0	6 0	5 0	7	2
July 5, 1928–Mar. 12, 1930	17 0	15 0	14 0 / 14 0 / 14 0	12 0 / 10 0 / 8 0	6 0	5 0	7	2
					Age 17 / Age 16	*Age 17 / Age 16*		
Mar. 13, 1930–Oct. 7, 1931	17 0	15 0	14 0 / 14 0 / 14 0	12 0 / 12 0 / 12 0	9 0 / 6 0	7 6 / 5 0	9	2
Oct. 8, 1931–June 30, 1934	15 3	13 6	12 6 / 12 6 / 12 6	10 9 / 10 9 / 10 0	8 0 / 5 0	6 9 / 4 6	8	2
July 1, 1934–Oct. 30, 1935	17 0	15 0	14 0 / 14 0 / 14 0	12 0 / 12 0 / 12 0	9 0 / 6 0	7 6 / 5 0	9	2
Oct. 31, 1935–Mar. 30, 1938	17 0	15 0	14 0 / 14 0 / 14 0	12 0 / 12 0 / 12 0	9 0 / 6 0	7 6 / 5 0	9	3
Since Mar. 31, 1938[c]	17 0	15 0	14 0 / 14 0 / 14 0	12 0 / 12 0 / 12 0	9 0 / 6 0	7 6 / 5 0	10	3
AGRICULTURAL SYSTEM								
Oct. 29, 1936–Mar. 30, 1938	14 0	12 6	10 0 / 10 0 / 10 0	9 6 / 9 6 / 9 6	6 0 / 4 0	5 0 / 3 6	7	3
Mar. 31, 1938–Mar. 29, 1939	14 0	12 6	12 0 / 12 0 / 12 0	9 6 / 9 6 / 9 6	6 0 / 4 0	5 0 / 3 6	7	3
Since Mar. 30, 1939[c]	15 0	13 0	13 0 / 13 0 / 13 0	10 0 / 10 0 / 10 0	7 6 / 5 0	6 0 / 4 0	9	3

[a] The periods are those during which the rates indicated were in operation.

[b] The Unemployment Insurance Act, 1927, which became effective on April 19, 1928, for the first time distinguished young men and women from boys and girls. The special rates for young men and women, however, came into effect on July 5, 1928, and prior to that date they continued to receive benefit at the same rate as adults.

[c] From April 11, 1940, benefits under the general scheme for the first two dependent children were increased by 1s.; effective August 1, 1940 benefits were increased 3s. for men and women and 2s. for young men and women. In the agricultural system, an increase of 3s. for men and young men and women was adopted.

APPENDIX VII. THE NET ADDITIONAL COSTS OF EXPANDING THE INSURANCE SYSTEM

FINANCIAL EFFECTS OF THE CHANGES IN THE CONTRIBUTORY REQUIREMENT AND THE DURATION OF BENEFITS

During the period of uncovenanted benefits (March 3, 1921 to July 31, 1924) the effect of relaxing the contributory requirement and extending the maximum benefit duration was to some extent offset by the increase in contribution rates provided by the Unemployment Insurance (No. 2) Act of 1921. It has indeed been asserted by officials of the Ministry of Labour that because of the increased contributions uncovenanted benefits were not the cause of the debt of the Unemployment Fund, since by August 1924 the debt had fallen to about £4 millions "and would very soon have disappeared." [54] But to look only at the state of the debt is to disregard the fact that in the absence of uncovenanted benefits the Fund might have shown a surplus. An examination of the finances of the scheme during the period supports this latter probability.

Of the total of £128,304,000 paid out both in covenanted and uncovenanted benefits (including dependents' allowances) between November 8, 1920 and June 30, 1923, the amount paid as uncovenanted benefits might "safely be put at more than one-half of the total."[55] Thus the cost of this type of benefit was approximately £64,152,000 until July 1923. The annual additional sum attributable to the higher rates of contributions after July 4, 1921,[56] may be estimated at £36,029,000 for the two-year period.[57] Hence some £28,123,000 of the cost of uncovenanted benefits during this period was not provided for out of increased contributions.

From July 1923 to August 1924, for the final period during which uncovenanted benefits were paid, the total benefit disbursement was approximately £40,000,000.[58] Assuming that at least half of this sum continued to represent the cost of uncovenanted benefits, it would appear that the presumed £18,000,000 annual increment attributable to the contribution increase of July 1921 did, for this final period and this period only, roughly meet the cost of these benefits.

[54] Testimony of the Accountant General to the Ministry of Labour before the Royal Commission in 1931. (*Minutes of Evidence*, p. 194)

[55] Ministry of Labour, *Report on National Unemployment Insurance to July 1923*, pp. 11-12.

[56] Excluding the increase in November 1921 which was imposed to finance the new dependents' benefits.

[57] Estimated by multiplying the estimated numbers of 7,083,700 male and 2,727,946 female contributors by the respective total contribution increase of $8\frac{3}{8}$d. and $8\frac{1}{12}$d. per week. This is probably an over-estimate since a certain proportion of the contributors were boys and girls who were charged half the adult rates. The total contribution income (including the government's share) during the period amounted to £90,832,800. (*Ibid.*, p. 90)

[58] A. H. Reede, *The Actuarial Aspect of Unemployment Insurance: British Experience* (Pennsylvania State College Studies, Vol. I, No. 1, 1936), p. 17.

It is, unfortunately, not possible to estimate the expenditure attributable to relaxations of the conditions under which covenanted benefits could be drawn during the period 1921 to August 1924.[59]

In August 1924 the contributory requirement was altered so as to require 30 contributions in 2 years before ordinary benefits could be obtained, but at the same time it was provided that the Minister of Labour could waive this requirement when he saw fit, and that extended benefits could be made available to persons who had exhausted their ordinary benefits or did not have sufficient contributions to qualify. The cost of the waiver was estimated by the Government Actuary at £10,000,000 a year on the basis of a Live Register of 1,000,000.[60] Since the average Live Register in the 45 months from July 1924 through March 1928 was about 1,250,000,[61] it would appear that the total cost of the waiver up to April 1928 was about £38,437,000.[62]

From April 1928 transitional benefits were payable to applicants who failed to meet the normal contributory requirement, while persons who could show 30 contributions in the past 2 years could claim standard benefit up to 74 weeks. No estimate of the cost of transitional benefits prior to April 1929 can be made as the necessary statistics concerning numbers of claimants are lacking. But from April 1929 to April 1930, it is known that the Treasury paid about half the cost of transitional benefits (including administrative expenses) and that the Treasury payment for that year amounted to £3,985,000.[63] Thereafter transitional benefits ceased to be chargeable against the Unemployment Fund.

Only a rough estimate of the costs of paying insurance benefits beyond 156 days can be made. In June 1931, the Royal Commission estimated that the annual cost of benefits paid in excess of 156 days was roughly £9,100,000.[64] Allowing for the changing volume of unemployment, the cost of unlimited benefits at this rate would be approximately £22,000,000 during the period April 1928 to September 1931.

---

[59] According to an investigation conducted in 1923, 67.3 per cent of a sample of 10,000 (out of about 1,200,000) benefit claimants had drawn more benefits than they would have been entitled to if the 1-to-6 rule had not been relaxed; what proportion of these drew covenanted benefits, however, is not known. (Ministry of Labour, *Report on an Investigation into the Personal Circumstances and Industrial History of 10,000 Claimants to Unemployment Benefits, Nov. 5 to 10, 1923*, p. 43)

[60] Ministry of Labour, *Unemployment Insurance (No. 2) Bill, 1924: Report by the Government Actuary on the Financial Provisions of the Bill*, April 4, 1924 (Cmd. 2109, 1924), p. 6. See also *Unemployment Insurance Bill, 1925: Report by the Government Actuary on the Financial Provisions of the Bill*, July 2, 1925 (Cmd. 2451, 1925), p. 3.

[61] *Minutes of Evidence*, pp. 159-60. With a Live Register of 1,250,000, an annual cost of £10,250,000 has been assumed.

[62] This estimate is probably conservative. During the period July 1924 through March 1928, total expenditures for benefit payments were almost £163,400,000 (*Twenty-Second Abstract of Labour Statistics*, pp. 68-9). The sample investigations of 1924 and 1927 showed respectively that 47.4 per cent and 43.2 per cent of authorized benefit claimants were drawing extended benefits. (Ministry of Labour, *Report on an Investigation into the Personal Circumstances and Industrial History of . . . Claimants to Unemployment Benefit, Nov. 24 to 29, 1924* (1925), pp. 78-79; *April 4 to 9, 1927* (1928), p. 28)

[63] *Minutes of Evidence*, p. 147.

[64] This assumed a Live Register of 2,500,000 (*First Report*, p. 47), whereas the average register was 1.28 millions in 1928-29, 1.28 millions in 1929-30, 2.25 millions in 1930-31 and 2.71 millions in 1931-32.

FINANCIAL EFFECTS OF THE RELAXATIONS OF 1930

From 1930 onwards the number of persons to whom the Unemployment Fund was liable to pay benefits was increased as a result of the changed criterion of involuntary unemployment (and in particular the abolition of the genuinely-seeking-work clause). The financial effect of this change cannot be exactly measured, but on the basis of the evidence of the Accountant General to the Ministry of Labour before the 1932 Royal Commission, it may be estimated that in the 18-month period between March 1930 and the fall of 1931, the cost to the Fund was approximately £5 million.[65]

FINANCIAL EFFECTS OF THE CHANGES IN BENEFIT SCHEDULES AND CONTRIBUTION RATES

The increase in benefits for three months in the spring of 1921 was accompanied by no change in contributions, but this was rectified in July 1921, when the benefits were reduced to their old level and contributions were raised. Contribution rates were again raised at the end of 1921 to finance the new benefits provided for dependents, but the relation between income and expenditure was once more disturbed in August 1924 by an increase in the rate of ordinary benefit, and in January 1926 (under the 1925 Act) by the reduction of the contributions by workers and employers in order to offset in part the additional tax on them necessitated by the new old-age insurance scheme. The difference was to have been provided by an increased contribution from the Treasury, but pressure for public economy led to the passage of an act in April 1926 which, instead, reduced the Treasury contribution. In 1928, although the single adult benefit rates were reduced by one shilling, the adult dependent's allowance was increased by two shillings, while contributions for juveniles between the ages of 18 and 20 were reduced. There was a slight rise in the Treasury contribution from April 1929, which was soon more than offset by the increase in adult dependents' and juveniles' benefits in March 1930.[66]

Unfortunately, no exact figures for the cost of these changes over the whole period are available, but it has been estimated by the Accountant General to the Ministry of Labour that the net cost of the changes in contributions and benefits caused by the Acts of 1925 and 1926 was £15,370,000 up to June 1, 1929, and that the increased

---

[65] The Accountant General estimated that the 1930 relaxations involved an annual increase in benefit payments of £8.75 millions on the assumption of a Live Register of 2.3 millions. (*Minutes of Evidence*, p. 147) Actually, however, the average registration was 2.25 millions in 1930-31 and 2.7 millions in 1931-32, giving for the 18-month period ending October 1931, a total cost of £13.72 millions (£8.56 millions in 1930-31 and £5.16 millions in the half year 1931-32). By no means all of this £13.72 millions would have been chargeable on the Unemployment Fund, however, for the greater part of these additional claimants, especially during 1931, would have been recipients of transitional benefits and hence financed by the Treasury. Thus, if it is assumed that the Fund bore one-third of the cost, or a little under £5,000,000, the financial effect of this particular change will, if anything, be over-estimated.

[66] Royal Commission on Unemployment Insurance, *First Report*, p. 23.

rates of benefit of 1930 added an annual sum of £4,250,000 (on the assumption of a Live Register of 2,300,000).[67] From April 1930 to September 1931, therefore, with an average Live Register of 2,339,-000, the 1930 increase of benefits accounted for £6,483,000 of the total deficit. Thus, merely from 1925 onwards, these increases in benefits, unaccompanied by appropriate increases in contributions, added some £21,853,000 (i.e., £15.37 million between 1925 and June 1929, plus £6.483 million from April 1930 to September 1931) to the deficit by the end of 1931. In so far as these increases in benefit rates were rendered imperative by the attempt to use the insurance system to provide for long-period unemployment, it can be said that this share of the debt was directly attributable to the policy of expanding the insurance system.

Estimated Total Costs of Extensions of Insurance

The total amount by which these various extensions of the insurance system increased expenditure chargeable against the Unemployment Fund is set out in Table 5, Chapter IV. At first sight the total cost of £119,398,000 appears excessive, especially in view of the fact that by December 1931 the net debt of the Fund amounted to only £110,320,000. But, as pointed out above, this merely indicates that, had the insurance system been confined to the payment of covenanted or standard benefits, it would have shown a surplus in the period 1920 to 1931. After 1933, when stricter insurance conditions were again in effect, a surplus did indeed materialize. By December 31, 1937 the funded debt had been reduced from £115,000,000 to £103,-122,000 by payments out of current income,[68] while the now separate general account of the Unemployment Fund showed a balance of £60,379,006.[69] Finally, in making the individual estimates, the most conservative assumptions were made, while because of the absence of data the cost of some of the expanded insurance benefits (e.g., transitional benefits from 1928 to 1929) are not included in the total figure. It does not seem likely, therefore, that the estimated total cost of expanding the insurance system, namely £119,398,000, is excessive.

---

[67] These estimates take no account of the effect of the increase in benefits, brought about by the Act of 1930, or the cost of transitional benefits. (*Minutes of Evidence,* p. 147)

[68] A borrowing limit of £115,000,000 was set by the (No. 2) Act of 1931. By the Order in Council of October 7, 1931, the Treasury was to meet any deficit once this borrowing limit was reached. This occurred early in 1932 and the Treasury made good deficits of £444,577 and £6,363,377 in the financial years ending March 31, 1932 and March 31, 1933 respectively. Until June 30, 1934 any surplus in the Unemployment Fund was to be used for repayment of the debt. Under the 1934 Act the accumulated debt was funded and the insurance system was obligated to pay the Debt Commissioners £5 million annually, a sum that included both interest and sinking fund.

[69] UISC, *Financial Report* 1937, p. 46. It is true that from October 1931 higher rates of contribution prevailed, but these were again reduced in July 1936 on recommendation of the Statutory Committee, as a method of reducing the surplus. On the other hand, the benefit rates prevailing in 1931, which were reduced in October of that year, were restored in July 1934 and an increase of one shilling weekly was given to children in October 1935. The waiting period was reduced to three days in 1937. Moreover, after 1934 extra days of benefit beyond the usual 156 were given to persons with a long record of steady employment. Finally, during four of the five years in which this surplus was accumulated, unemployment was exceptionally heavy.

APPENDIX VIII. TABLE XII. TRAINING AND INSTRUCTION PROGRAMS OF THE NATIONAL GOVERNMENT

Items	1929	1930	1931	1932	1933	1934	1935	1936	1937	1938
Government Training Centers (Training Courses for Men)										
Centers at end of year	11	10	9	9	8	9	9	11	14	16
Places	3,300	3,770	3,650	3,280	3,190	3,560	4,245	6,255	5,003	8,739
Persons admitted during year	6,560	8,608	7,979	5,236	5,254	6,970	10,168	14,250	16,092	11,579
Persons completing course	4,768	6,204	7,170	4,843	4,432	5,087	7,205	10,693	10,761	9,175
Persons entering employment	4,429	5,160	5,290	3,440	3,728	4,819	7,059	10,398	10,424	8,315
Premature terminations	792	1,611	1,709	1,047	844	1,134	1,663	3,083	3,939	3,550
Training Courses for Women[a]										
Centers at end of year	39	38	37	33	32	32	37	39	37	38
Persons completing course	3,800	3,906	5,640	5,133	4,682	4,078	4,050	3,286	3,407	3,775
Persons entering employment	3,435	3,963	4,437	4,178	3,940	3,403	3,313	3,275	2,789	1,926
Premature terminations	489	480	564	653	566	498	523	517	454	540
Individual vocational training grants	0	216	165	21	72	79	99	169	156	222
Instructional Centers										
Centers at end of year[b]	5	10	6	11	12	15	17	15	24	25
Places[b]	1,200	1,880	1,100	2,200	2,420	3,300	3,995	4,420	4,535	4,535
Persons admitted during year[c]	3,518	9,886	7,652	6,654	10,545	16,248	18,077	20,872	20,588	23,772
Persons entering employment	1,608	6,530	5,667	2,815	1,406	2,475	3,105	3,896	3,053	2,415
Persons transferred to other programs	117	188	67	50	165	127	14	416	421	622
Premature terminations	1,029	2,487	1,724	736	855	1,280	2,609	3,959	5,285	7,571
Persons completing course, not placed	29	597	392	1,748	8,064	12,205	12,214	13,013	11,486	13,607
Junior Instruction Centers										
Centers at end of year	87	114	163	140	121	111	188	187[d]	156	157
Classes at end of year				30	17	13	17	22[d]	31	37
Persons attending during year	60,750	88,300	143,900	136,700	101,600	113,500	169,000	191,000	20,013[e]	23,732[e]
Highest daily average attendance	7,997	16,381	22,914	21,077	20,781	19,075	30,248	37,726	27,449	29,039
Evening classes:										
Persons attending during year		2,186	—	12,400	8,800	5,500	9,000	7,200		
Highest monthly average		820	3,754	4,834	3,432	2,436	3,409	2,914		

[a] Adults and juveniles.   [b] Not including summer camps.   * Including summer camps.   [c] Including summer camps.   [d] January 1937.   [e] Overall average daily attendance.

Sources: Compiled from annual reports of the Ministry of L bour, 1929-1938.

INDEX

375

effect of relief on work incentive, 255-59; health of, 189-90; juveniles, 80, 173, 230-31, 339n; long-term, xvi, 40-50, 58-59, 65, 73-77, 80-83, 90, 94n, 98-99, 114, 117, 126, 132-38, 178, 180, 194-96, 230-31, 263, 271, 277, 290; number of, 52-53, 75, 115, 157, 343; numbers assisted, 52-53, 58n, 115, 157, 244n, 347, 360; numbers unassisted, 157n; older men, 247n, 293-94; older women, 274; political pressure of, 308; rehabilitation of, 74, 132-38, 155, 188-90, 230-31, 263-84, 291-96, 315-16, 328-29, 373; responsibility of government for, xiii, 117, 234-37, 238-39, 251; responsibility toward government, 330-33; segregation of, 277; short-term, xvi, 64, 65, 98, 125, 178-79, 180, 195-96, 315; suitability of provisions for, 172n, 239, 246, 253, 254-55, 323-24, 329-36; young adults, 292-93, 295; see also Industrial quality; Insured workers; Training programs
Unemployed Workmen Act (1905), 3
Unemployment: basic problems, xiii, 329-36; depressed areas, 56-57, 58n, 64, 268; distribution of, 56-57; duration of, 73n, 132, 179, 291n, 292n; effect of public works on, 86-89; estimation of, 339-42; expenditures on account of, 55-56, 70, 120, 121, 159, 361, 367; extent of, 52-53, 114n, 115, 119, 157, 164, 184n, 343; local advisory committees' study of, 229-30, 292, 295; measures to reduce, 230-31, 239, 284-90; opposing principles for relief of, 238-39; per cent among insured workers, 35, 56n, 268, 343; social consequences of, xiii, xiv, 73-74, 263, 291-96; special areas, 16, 290, 292-93; test of involuntary character of, 41, 43n, 92-93, 242; see also Unemployed
Unemployment Act (1934), 5, 45n, 119, 142, 149-51, 153, 156, 158, 161, 167, 182n, 214, 243, 372n
Unemployment assistance: and PA, 159, 167, 181-82, 185-86, 188, 319; and UI, xviii, xix, 176-81, 196-200, 248-49, 319; conditions for receipt of, 92-93, 154, 170-76, 242n; cost of, 121, 159, 244, 361; coverage, 10-11, 153-54, 167, 170-71, 182-84, 242; disqualifications, 10, 154n, 155, 167, 170-76; duration, 10, 155, 167; evaluation of, 170-76, 311, 314-23; ex-

clusions, 11, 168, 170-76; financing of, 11, 155-56, 162; First Appointed Day, 153, 155n; liquidation of "standstill," 217-19, 228-29; medical assistance, 186-90; penalties, 175, 177, 231, 264-65; political pressures, 297-99, 308-09; recipients, 115, 157, 253-55, 257-59, 347; Second Appointed Day, 153, 154, 156-58, 182-84, 190, 198n; training programs, 155, 174, 176, 195-96, 264-65, 272; see also Administration; Age; Appeals; Household; Local authorities; Means test; Resources of applicants; Standstill Act
Unemployment assistance allowances: average weekly amount, 257; compared to PA, 232, 252-53, to TP, 229n, to UI, 177, 198-200, 249, 252-53, 315-16, to wages, 216, 230n, 255-59; cost of, 121, 159, 244, 361; dependents, 198, 255; discretionary allowances, 198-200, 215, 216, 220-25, 259, 260, 276; effect of Standstill Act, 217-19; high rent areas, 198, 200, 215, 216, 220-21, 223n, 229n, 255; land settlers, 279, 280; large families, 259, 260; maximum, 216, 231, 260; payment procedures, 191; standard of living, 154, 219, 225n, 251n, 252-54; supplementary, xvii, 11, 154, 167, 185, 197-200; uniform national standard, 10, 215-17, 228-29, 232
Unemployment assistance applicants: age distribution of, 179-80; compared with UI claimants, 177-80; contribution record of, 126n; effect of means test on number of, 199; employment record of, 179, 291-92; health of, 189-90; industrial quality of, 177-79, 189-90; normal occupations of, 182-83; percentage denied, 242; percentage insured, 182n; previous wages of, 257; procedure for applying, 191-93; receiving additional allowances, 218-19, 223-25; receiving less than TP, 229
Unemployment Assistance Board: appeals from decisions of, 211, 212n, 154-55; appointment of, 146, 153, 297-98; clientele of, 178-81; criticisms of, 187n, 188, 194, 225-26, 232-34, 237; discretionary powers of, 154-55, 171, 186, 214-15, 221-26; independent status of, 297-99; mandate of, 10, 11, 146-47, 153, 155, 175, 186-91, 202; name changed,